THE REPUBLICAN ROMAN ARMY:
A SOURCEBOOK

The Republican Roman Army assembles a wide range of source material and introduces the latest scholarship on the evolution of the Roman army and the Roman experience of war. The author has carefully selected and translated key texts, many of them not previously available in English, and provided them with comprehensive commentaries and essays.

This wide-ranging survey of documents recreates the social and historical framework in which ancient Roman warfare took place – from the archaic and Servian period through to the Late Republic. The topics addressed extend beyond the conventional questions of army mechanics such as strategy and tactics, and explore questions such as the army's influence on Roman society and its economy.

Complete with notes, index and bibliography, *The Republican Roman Army* provides students of ancient and military history with an unprecedented survey of relevant materials.

Michael M. Sage received his Ph.D. from the University of Toronto in 1973 and has been a member of the faculty of Classics at the University of Cincinnati since 1975.

THE REPUBLICAN ROMAN ARMY

A Sourcebook

Michael M. Sage

Routledge
Taylor & Francis Group

NEW YORK AND LONDON

First published 2008
by Routledge
270 Madison Ave, New York, NY 10016

Simultaneously published in the UK
by Routledge
2 Park Square, Milton Park, Abingdon, Oxon OX14 4RN

*Routledge is an imprint of the Taylor & Francis Group,
an informa business*

© 2008 Michael M. Sage

Typeset in Times New Roman by
Swales & Willis Ltd, Exeter, Devon
Printed and bound in Great Britain by Antony Rowe Ltd,
Chippenham, Wiltshire

British Library Cataloguing in Publication Data
A catalogue record for this book is available from the British Library

Library of Congress Cataloging in Publication Data
A catalog record for this book has been requested

ISBN 10: 0–415–17879–7 (hbk)
ISBN 10: 0–415–17880–0 (pbk)
ISBN 10: 0–203–92661–7 (ebk)

ISBN 13: 978–0–415–17879–2 (hbk)
ISBN 13: 978–0–415–17880–8 (pbk)
ISBN 13: 978–0–203–92661–1 (ebk)

CONTENTS

CONTENTS

ABBREVIATIONS

AC	*Antiquité Classique*
BAR	British Archaeological Reports
CAH	*Cambridge Ancient History*
ClAnt	*Classical Antiquity*
CQ	*Classical Quarterly*
JHS	*Journal of Hellenic Studies*
JRS	*Journal of Roman Studies*
PBSR	*Papers of the British School at Rome*
TAPhA	*Transactions and Proceedings of the American Philological Association*

INTRODUCTION

The last three decades have seen a renewed interest in both Greek and Roman military history. The focus of recent studies has shifted from the traditional areas of tactics, strategy and battle analysis to a greater emphasis on the relationships of armies to the societies that produced them and to recreating the experience of battle in the ancient world.

In Republican military studies the traditional areas have long received attention, owing to the well-recognized connection between changes in the Roman army and the political fortunes of the Republic, but they have recently been approached from a far wider perspective than had earlier been the case and new methods of analysis have been brought to bear.

The second line of analysis owes it origins to the epoch-making study by John Keegan, *The Face of Battle* (New York, 1978), which attempted to recreate the experience of battle over the course of five hundred years. The detailed descriptions of the battles of the Second Punic War and of some of the battles that marked Rome's expansion into the eastern Mediterranean as well as Caesar's accounts of his Gallic campaign and the Civil War provide material for such a reconstruction that has no parallel in earlier or later Roman history.

This sourcebook is an attempt to bring together relevant ancient testimony on various aspects of the Roman army and its relation to Roman society to the end of the Republic. Commentary has been added to place these passages in context and to provide some of the insights offered by recent scholarship on these problems.

The sources

Any attempt to trace the history of the Roman army during the Republic faces formidable problems. This is especially true of the written sources that are fundamental to tracing the evolution of Roman tactics and strategy. The major historical sources for the earliest period, Livy and Dionysius of Halicarnassus, both writing towards the end of the first century, anachronistically project the army of the third and second centuries back into the Regal period and the first centuries of the Republic. This may in part be due to the fact that the birth of historical writing at

1

Rome took place about 200, precisely in the period. Although historical writing focused on politics and military affairs, it tended to avoid technical details of army organization and structure. There are occasional exceptions to this indifference but they mostly concern modifications to weapons associated with major political and military figures such as the changes in the javelin or *pilum* ascribed to Marius and Caesar. However, they seem to be the product of interest less in these details than in the figures themselves. It is significant that none of the major changes in army organization have found their way into the historical record. Although both Livy's and Dionysius' histories contain valuable digressions such as their accounts of the Servian army (see pp. 19ff.) they make no attempt to integrate them into their narratives. The one exception to this is the account of the Roman army by the mid-second-century Greek historian Polybius. Unlike Livy and Dionysius he had personal experience of warfare and an interest in its technical side as reflected in his comparison of Roman tactical formations with the Greek infantry phalanx. Polybius' main aim was to explain the success of Rome's army to a Greek audience and in doing so he gave the most detailed account of the Roman army of the mid-second century that we possess. It is fundamental to any description of the Roman army of this period.

The most significant contribution to understanding the evolution of tactics and organization is provided by the antiquarian tradition which arose in the second century. The most important author is M. Terentius Varro, who wrote in the middle of the first century. Unfortunately, much of this work has been lost and survives only in fragments quoted in later authors. Antiquarian writers were unconstrained by the rules of historical writing that discouraged the use of technical terms and allowed only limited treatment of institutional development. These were, in fact, the very questions that preoccupied antiquarian writers. It is likely that an antiquarian writer is the source of the digressions in Cicero, Livy and Dionysius on the Servian army. The fragmentary nature of the extant material and its often narrow focus prevent the antiquarian tradition from offering a coherent account of army development, but it is vital to the construction of such an account.

Military manuals offer little help in reconstructing Roman military history. The earliest known work by Cato the Elder (*c.* 160) is available only in fragments. It does show some interest in the history of the Roman army and in practical military matters such as military organization and various battle formations. The extant military manuals are all of imperial date and fall into two classes: collections of stratagems or manuals of advice for commanders. They occasionally preserve anecdotes useful for historical purposes but for the most part they are of little use. There are some exceptions such as the second-century AD works, such as the manual on tactics by Arrian and his account of his expedition against the Alans while governor of Cappadocia in 135 or the manual by Pseudo-Hyginus on the layout of the Roman camp, that do deal with technical matters but their subject is the army of the Empire. There is a noticeable change in military manuals in the late Empire where the focus of these works shifts to the practical aspects of warfare. Of particular use is the work of Vegetius, who does employ sources dating from the

Republic, in particular Cato's manual. However, it is often difficult to separate genuine Republican material in his work from later developments.

Material remains can be useful in elucidating certain aspects of Roman warfare. Pictorial representations of equipment and of combat are especially helpful for periods for which we have little or no written information. Weapons finds can both confirm written descriptions and aid the understanding of the use of such equipment in battle. Of special importance in understanding second-century Roman camps has been a series of five second-century Roman camps near the site of Numantia in north central Spain.

Inscriptions are less helpful for the Republican period than Empire. They are relatively few in number and are confined to the elite. Of more importance are the *Fasti*, especially the list of consuls and of those commanders who celebrated a triumph. The consular list seems to be accurate as far back as the mid-fourth century, but even for earlier periods it forms the basis for any chronological reconstruction of the period. There are serious problems with reliability of the list of triumphators prior to the third century and there are some serious gaps in the list as we have it, but it does serve as a check on accounts found in the written sources.

The reliability of accounts of campaigns and battles prior to the third century has always been a problem. The earliest campaigns for which the sources provide some sense of the overall strategy involved are the campaigns against the Samnites and Gauls after 300. This is also the period when at least the general course of individual battles, such as Sentinum in 295, can be reconstructed with some accuracy. In general, serious problems remain even for later battles. The two greatest difficulties are the problem of matching the topography of the battle site with the description given in the sources, for example the various locations suggested by modern scholars for the battle of Cannae in 216, and the reliability of troop and casualty numbers.

Despite these difficulties a coherent account of the development of Rome's military forces can be traced. The information is uneven, with the earliest period giving rise to the most serious problems. Many of these difficulties are the result of the tradition's lack of interest in technical matters. It is telling that the sources are silent on the causes of and the individuals involved in major tactical changes that occurred during the Republic.

1

ROME'S EARLIEST ARMIES: THE
ARCHAIC AND SERVIAN PERIOD

Political and social institutions

By the beginning of the sixth century Rome had become one of the largest cities in Italy and the western Mediterranean. Despite the heterogeneous origins of its population it had a common culture and a typical political structure. In the Forum, the *Lapis Niger* or black stone dating from the second quarter of the sixth century and the earliest extant official document shows that Latin was the official language and that the writing and the carving of inscriptions were already a part of Roman practice. Appearing on that inscription is the Latin word for "king." It is also found on a fragment of pottery found under the Regia of a somewhat earlier date. These finds support the Romans' view that their earliest form of government was a monarchy. The traditional chronology that developed listed seven kings from the first Romulus to the last Tarquinius Superbus and assigned 254 years to the kings. The number of kings and the duration of their reigns have an artificial look to them. Except for the founder, Romulus, the names of these kings and certain of their actions may have some historical foundation, but the veracity of these accounts is anything but assured. Nevertheless, certain of their acts seem to have a historical foundation.

Although kings are common in early Italy, it is an unusual feature of Roman kingship that it was not hereditary, but elective. The most basic attribute of the king was his *imperium*. It denoted the ability to exercise supreme command, especially in wartime. After the expulsion of the kings it denoted the sum total of particular magistrates' powers, both civil and military. At its base this power had a strong religious element, for *imperium* was joined with *auspicium*, the right to consult the will of the gods with regard to an activity. This link is also manifest in the need for *imperium* to be conferred by religious act, which signified that the holder was acceptable to the gods. Closely tied to the king and the transmission of kingship were the composition and nature of the regal Senate. It seems clear that the regal Senate was in origin a council of advisors to the king. It seems likely that parallel to other such councils the members of the Senate were chosen by the kings themselves.

Citizens who are labeled as patrician raise a particular problem. During part of the fifth and the fourth century patricians monopolized political and religious office in the state. However, it is clear from the non-patrician names appearing in the list of early consuls that they did not hold a monopoly in the earliest days of the Republic or probably during the monarchy. Patrician status may have its origin in the standing and power of the heads of leading families. Over time because of their power and influence they came to monopolize certain prerequisites especially of a religious nature which in turn gave them access to political office.

Of direct importance for the study of Roman military history has been the idea that the patricians formed the original Roman cavalry. But at Rome cavalry service was later based upon wealth and not any other form of status, and that the state unlike Greek city-states supplied horses would seem to indicate that the early Roman cavalry, though it probably did include patricians, was not exclusively a patrician body.

The structure of the archaic army

The infantry

1 VARRO, *ON THE LATIN LANGUAGE* 5.89.1

The ancient tradition universally linked the earliest structure of the Roman army to an original tribal system whose creation was attributed to the first king, Romulus. In the Republican period the names of these tribes which are of uncertain origin are found as the names of a special group of cavalry centuries known as the *sex suffragia*. There is also a striking prevalence of multiples of three in later Roman military formations that makes clear how central this division is to Roman military organization and supports the authenticity of a three tribal system. The size of the army is not incompatible with what appears to be the population of regal Rome.

> [They are called] soldiers [*milites*] because at first the legion was composed of 3,000 men, the individual tribes of the Titenses, Ramnes and Luceres each contributing 1,000 soldiers.

2 PLUTARCH, *ROMULUS* 13.1

Plutarch, writing at the end of the first century AD, exemplifies the tendency of ancient Greek and Roman authors to ascribe the origins of institutions to specific dates and to view them as the work of a particular historical figure. In the Republic and Empire the term "legion" referred to the basic military unit of the Roman army, but it also could be used of the army as a whole. Plutarch's reference to selection as the origin of the term is explained by the fact that in Latin the verb meaning "to select" is *legere*.

> After Romulus had founded the city, he divided up those capable of bearing arms into military units. Each unit consisted of 3,000 infantry and 300 cavalry. The unit is called a legion because the men selected were chosen for their warlike character from the entire population.

The cavalry

Information on the early Roman cavalry is more detailed than that concerning the infantry. The cavalry usually plays a decisive role in accounts of early battles. This must surely have been the result of the perennial association of the horse in combat with the elite that is visible in the Mediterranean area and elsewhere. That association was fostered not only by the advantages that the horse conferred in battle, but also by the wealth necessary to raise and support it.

The date when true cavalry, that is cavalry fighting from horseback, originated is a contentious issue. Some scholars have argued that true cavalry only appeared at Rome during the Samnite wars of the last half of the fourth century. They view the pictorial representations of riders that we have as representing mounted infantry. In part, this is the result of a peculiar feature of our historical narratives of early battles. In most of them at some point in the battle the cavalry dismount to engage the enemy. The true cavalry probably appeared around 600 at Rome in Etruria as the result of Greek influence. It was at this time that the Greeks also began using true cavalry. Significantly, the western Greek states, which were in most immediate contact with the Italic peoples, were especially strong in mounted formations.

The origin of the Roman cavalry

3 LIVY, 1.13.8

Livy's account of the creation of the cavalry formations represents one of the two traditions. It is at least in part the same as that given by Varro (**1**). However, Livy's account does not make clear whether these names refer to the cavalry centuries alone or to the three tribes. He mentions the creation of the *curiae* (geographical groupings of clans, thirty of which made up the earliest assembly at Rome) but not the tribal system. This must have been an inadvertent omission, as he never mentions the creation of the army by Romulus. He seems to have placed the passage at this point because of the etymology of the Titenses, which is linked to the wars against the Sabine king of the town of Cures, Titus Tatius. The names seem to have been of Etruscan derivation. This can best be explained by assuming that the tribal system was created around 600, when men with strong Etruscan affinities occupied the kingship. This would fit with the view mentioned above that true cavalry appeared about the beginning of the seventh century under Greek influence.

At the same time [when the wars against the Sabines were concluded], [Romulus] enrolled three centuries of horse. One was named Ramnenses after Romulus, the second was called Titienses after Titus Tatius and the last was known as the Luceres. However, the origin and name of the last is uncertain.

Dionysius presents the other major ancient tradition on the creation of the cavalry. In this version the cavalry is the result of the formation of a royal guard. It may be that this story arose from speculation on the origin of the *tribunus celerum* (literally "fast" or "speedy"), who in historical times was an officer associated with the mounted portion of the ceremonies that marked the beginning and end of the campaigning season. It seems likely that these tribunes once had a military function, perhaps controlling the cavalry, who might well have been at first named *celeres*, the speedy ones. The centurions mentioned by Dionysius as commanding units of one hundred men seem to be an artificial creation based upon the etymology of the name. Cavalry units of one hundred seem far too large. Valerius Antias was a historian of the first century BC.

> After Romulus had established the Senate from one hundred men, he saw that he had need of a formation as a guard for his own person and for service in pressing matters. He chose three hundred men from the most distinguished families who were the most physically fit. The *curiae* selected them as they had done the senators; each *curia* chose ten men and Romulus constantly kept them around his person. They were called *celeres*, a name given them according to the majority of writers because of their speed in carrying out their tasks. However, Valerius Antias claims that they were so called because that was the name of their commander. This leader (Celer) was an extremely distinguished man, who had three centurions under him. In the city they followed Romulus about and executed his orders, and on campaign they were in the vanguard and the king's companions in arms. They fought on horseback in suitable terrain and on foot where the ground was rough and unfit for cavalry.

Varro's etymology of *turma* is incorrect. The real derivation of the word is unknown. Each unit of thirty men was presumably under the command of a *tribunus celerum* and three decuriones of lesser rank each commanding a troop of ten horsemen. There is a good chance that this pattern of command does in fact stretch back to the kings. The *turma* remained the standard unit of legionary cavalry through the imperial period. There were originally three military tribunes assigned to the infantry of the legion and these would parallel the three tribunes of the cavalry. Later the *tribunus celerum* disappeared as a military office and one of the three decuriones became the commander of the unit as a whole.

> *Turma*, a troop of cavalry is from *terima* (the E changed to a U), because it is composed of three times ten troopers, each ten raised from each of the three tribes; that is the Titenses, Ramnes, and Luceres. The leaders of each

7

group of ten cavalry [*decuria*] are called decuriones from this and even now there are three to each *turma*.

Light cavalry?

6 VARRO, *ON THE LATIN LANGUAGE 7.57*

Varro is the only source that calls the *ferentarii* "cavalry." In the second century the term was used of a type of light infantry. There is a grave stone from Clusium in Etruria which shows a rider armed with a javelin, but with no body armor, and seems to portray a light cavalry trooper. It is possible that the figure is a *ferentarius*. Plautus is the famous Roman comic playwright who wrote at the beginning of the second century. The shrine mentioned was the only temple of Asclepius (originally a Greek god of healing) in Rome, on the Tiber Island and built in the early third century.

> [Plautus] writes in his play the *Trinummus*: "I see that a *ferentarius* friend has been found for you." *Ferentarius* is from the verb *fero*, that is empty and without profit: or because cavalry were so called who bore only those weapons which are used up such as the javelin. I have seen cavalry of this type in an old shrine of Asclepius and they are labeled *ferentarii*.

Changes in cavalry forces before the mid-sixth century

The tradition concerning the increase in the Roman cavalry before the reign of Servius Tullius is confused and uncertain. The problem is centered on the reigns of two kings, Tullus Hostilius, the third king, and Tarquinius Priscus, the sixth. There is a much greater probability that Tarquinius is historical, but many scholars also accept the historicity of Tullus and the reality of certain events of his reign. Hostilius is presented as the incarnation of the warlike sprit in the sources. He is a counterpart to the first king, Romulus, and a foil to the peaceful Numa, who preceded him. The core event that can be accepted to his reign is his successful war against Alba Longa, southeast of Rome in the Alban Hills, whose early archaeological history is closely related to that of Rome. Tradition made it the mother-city of all of the Latins. The site continued after its conquest by Rome as the religious center of the Latins. If we accept the historicity of the war, although not its course as described by the sources, then it is possible that around this period Roman forces were increased as a result of the acquisition of immigrants from Alba. This increase is to some extent supported by reports that Tullus added new regions to the city.

7 LIVY, 1.30.3

The acquisition of population is to some extent supported by independent attestation that certain noble Roman families such as the Julii, the family of Julius Caesar, claimed an Alban origin, as well as by the fictitious sequence of Alban kings who were ancestral to those of Rome. Some ancient sources assign the increase to Romulus' reign.

> In order to increase the strength of all orders with the addition of new population, Tullus added ten *turmae* of cavalry from the men of Alba, and created supplements for existing legions, as well as creating new ones.

Tarquinius Priscus

Priscus is the first Roman king claimed to be of Etruscan origin. His father was supposedly an immigrant Greek, Demaratus, and his mother, Tanaquil, is said to have been from Tarquinii in Etruria, though it has reasonably been suggested that the family actually came from Caere because of the much fuller archaeological attestation of a family of the same name there. However, given doubts about whether the family from Caere was related it is probably safer to accept the ancient tradition.

The tradition records that two of the last three of the Roman kings were Etruscan and there are hints that Servius Tullius, the sixth king, was Etruscan as well. It has been natural to see the last century of the monarchy as dominated by an Etruscan dynasty, and some scholars have even claimed that the Etruscans conquered the city. However, there is no trace of such a conquest in our sources nor is there any need to postulate it. Given Rome's position as a frontier city at the borders of Etruria and Latium, as well as the hill peoples living to its northeast, it must have had a mixed and open aristocracy from the start. That one of its elements was Etruscan should occasion no surprise.

The traditional dates for the reigns of the last three kings are marked by major construction in the city, including the start of the Capitoline temple to Jupiter and the draining and first paving of the Forum. There are hints as well of growth in population and of at least some Roman military successes in Latium and its vicinity. These developments form a plausible context for the cavalry reform ascribed to the first Tarquin, even if the historicity of the numbers given cannot be established.

8 CICERO, *DE RE PUBLICA* 2.36

The core of this passage is formed by the explanation of a statue and stone in the Forum supposedly of Attus Navius, as Livy's parallel account makes clear. It is also an explanation of the importance of augury or the taking of omens in political affairs. The number and names of centuries remained constant for these six cavalry centuries for the rest of the Republic. They became a special voting group as the native Roman cavalry lost its military functions. The story is an attempt to explain the fact that three are called prior and three are called posterior centuries.

Then [Tarquinius Priscus] organized the cavalry in the form which it retains to the present. He was not able to change the names of the three centuries, Titenses, Ramnes, and Luceres, because Attus Navius that most renowned of augurs would not agree ... nevertheless, he added additional troops to the centuries and doubled their number to twelve hundred.

9 FESTUS, 247 L

Festus, a second-century AD writer, draws on an antiquarian writer, Verrius Flaccus, a grammarian of Augustan date, who is a learned, if not always accurate, source. Given the general ignorance of our sources on the realities of early warfare it is hard to assess the truth of this passage.

Paired horses: that is the two horses that the Romans were accustomed to use in battle, so that they could change to a fresh horse when their first mount began to sweat.

10 GRANIUS LICINIANUS, 26.12

Granius is probably a writer of the mid-second century AD. The use of multiple horses is known elsewhere, and later additional pay was awarded to cavalrymen who maintained multiple mounts. There appears to be some archaeological evidence of this style of fighting. An archaic frieze from the Roman Forum shows several riders apparently galloping to the attack. The riders are arranged in pairs, with an armored rider paired with an unarmored one. This would seem to imply that the armed rider was a groom who rode and then held the second horse in readiness. A possible argument against the validity of this passage is the fact that the state later granted the individual trooper only a single mount.

In the earlier parts of this work I have spoken of the names and numbers of the legions as well as the armament of the infantry, so I will not omit to mention the cavalry, whose number Tarquinius doubled so that the prior cavalry should join battle with two horses.

Other combat groups

The gens *or clan*

There is some evidence that clans or *gentes* (*gens* is the singular), groups of families linked by real or fictitious descent from a common ancestor and their associated clients, acted as military units. It is not impossible that the institution of the tribal army in the seventh or sixth century was an attempt to curb and organize these units, which formed the original fighting force of the community. There is some evidence during the Republican period for *gens* members and their clients functioning as fighting units.

11 DIONYSIUS OF HALICARNASSUS, *ROMAN ANTIQUITIES* 5.40.3–5

This is the most cited example of the migration of an aristocrat and his following. The number given for his following, also repeated in other sources, is clearly too high for this period. These groups must have been relatively small. Perhaps they numbered in the tens for less important chiefs and in the hundreds for leading figures. Fidenae lay on the left or eastern bank of the Tiber, approximately five miles north of Rome. The passage should be viewed as evidence for the open nature of Roman and Italian aristocracies in this period.

> There was a certain Titus Claudius, a Sabine, from the city of Regillum, well born and wealthy, who went over to the Romans. He brought with him many kinsmen, friends and clients with their whole households. They totaled not less than five thousand men capable of bearing arms. The necessity that compelled him to move was said to be the following: The leading men of the most distinguished cities were opposed to him because of their political competition with him and were bringing charges of treason against him because he did not favor conflict with Rome ... So taking his wealth and his associates he joined the Romans, providing a major increase in strength to them in this situation and in doing so he was considered the principal cause of Roman success in this war.

The clan as a fighting group

The single case of a clan functioning as an independent fighting unit is the narrative of the disastrous defeat of the Fabian *gens* by the men of Veii at the Cremera River, a small stream flowing through the territory of Veii and joining the Tiber near Fidenae.

This episode is part of one of the three wars waged between Etruscan Veii and Rome after the regal period. Unlike the situation confronting the Romans in other theaters, where they fought tribal groups, the war against Veii pitted large and successful city-states against each other. The goal of each was to gain control of the enemies' possessions on the opposite bank and so completely control the river. The first war, which lasted from 483 to 474, ended in a stalemate.

The sources give the number of clan members as either 300 or 306. It is no accident that the number recalls the number of Spartans who supposedly died at Thermopylae, and to some extent the description of the destruction of the Fabii seems colored by Greek accounts of that battle. Nonetheless, as was mentioned above multiples of three are a feature of Roman military organization, and the origin of the number may be a result of that preference. In addition to the members of the Fabian *gens* there were a number of clients. Clients appear in other military actions of the period. Their presence can be accepted as historical, but their number is far too large. It may be that the number 300 included clients, and this would be in line with the number postulated for the entourages of important noblemen in this period.

The historicity of the incident is supported by the disappearance of the Fabii from the consular lists after this incident until 467 and their obscurity over the next half-century. The most common date given by the sources for the incident is July 18 (477). A certain suspicion attaches to this date, as it is the most famous date in Roman history. It was the day on which the Romans were defeated by the Gauls in the battle of Allia that led to the capture of the city in 387.

12 LIVY, 2.48.6–50.11

The Fabian force was raised as a *coniuratio* or irregular force, bound presumably by an oath. In any case the Senate could not declare war; that was a function of the popular assembly.

> So it seemed that war with the men of Veii could neither be ignored nor brought to a conclusion. Also there were other wars that were either imminent or in the offing against the Aequi and Volsci ... However, Veii was a persistent rather than a serious enemy and it was the insults that rankled more than any danger. They could not be disregarded or turned away. In this situation the Fabian *gens* approached the Senate. The consul [Kaeso Fabius] spoke on behalf of his clan.... "It is our intention to wage this war as a family matter at our own expense. Let the state be free from providing soldiers and financial support in this cause." The Senate enthusiastically voted an official thanks ....
>
> Never did an army smaller in number but more talked about and admired march through the city. There were three hundred and six soldiers, all of patrician rank, belonging to a single clan. You would not have rejected any as a leader and they would have constituted a first-rate Senate at any time. The strength of a single clan was threatening destruction for all of the population of Veii.
>
> They set out for and arrived at the Cremera River, a suitable place to construct a fortification.... As long as it was only a question of raiding the Fabii could protect the area, but they were also able by movement through the Etruscan territory where it bordered the Roman to render their own land safe and to make the enemy's dangerous for him by their forays on both sides of the border.
>
> Again, there was the struggle of the Fabii with the Veientines. It took place without any preparation for a major war. There were not only raids on farmers' fields and forays against Etruscan raiding parties. Sometimes there were regular encounters in the open field and a Roman clan was often the victor in the contest with one of the wealthiest of the Etruscan cities.

At first the Veientines were bitterly resentful and so devised a plan born of circumstance for trapping the fierce enemy by an ambush. The Veientines even took pleasure when they saw the boldness of the Fabii increase because of their frequent successes. So they sometimes drove herds in the way of the invaders, as if by chance, the fields would be left desolate by the flight of the country folk and troops of soldiers sent to bring aid by repelling the invaders would often flee in simulated flight. The Fabii were now at the point that they so despised the enemy that they believed themselves invincible so that the enemy could not stand up against them at any time or place. Their expectations carried them to the point that when they saw a herd widely separated from the Cremera by a broad open field they ran down to capture it ignoring the appearance of widely scattered enemy forces. Carelessly, in a disordered rush they passed beyond the place on the road where the ambush had been laid. They wandered about in every direction to seize the animals that as happens when they become fearful had scattered. Suddenly, the enemy in ambush rose up and there were enemies on every side. First, the shouting in every direction terrified them; then weapons fell upon them from every side. The Etruscans closed ranks, and an unbroken ring of armed men surrounded the Fabii. As the enemy increased his pressure on them, they were forced in proportion to draw in their own circle, which revealed how few they were and how many were the Etruscans whose columns had been multiplied by the narrowness of the space.

The Fabii stopped the struggle, which they had waged with equal intensity in all directions and turned as a group in one direction. There they forced a way through in wedge formation by force of arms. The road led up to a small hill. There, at first the Romans put up resistance, since the elevation of the spot had given them a breathing space and time to collect themselves. They even forced back the troops advancing against them and despite their small number would have prevailed because of the advantage of the high ground, but for the Veientines who had been sent around by a ridge and had made their way to the crest of the hill. Once again the enemy had the advantage. The Fabii were slaughtered to a man and their fort taken. The general opinion is that three hundred of the Fabii died, leaving one young boy to perpetuate a clan that would be the greatest support of the Roman people in dangerous times at home and in wartime.

13 THE LAPIS SATRICANUS

The Latin town of Satricum lay in the area of the Pomptine Marshes in southern Latium. It was sited on one of the main routes that connected Latium and Rome to the rich and fertile area of Campania to the south and lay close to Antium, one of the few ports in Latium. A statue base has been found there dating from the end of the sixth century with the inscription given here in a heavily restored version. The term *suodalis* (singular) can be used either as a general term implying "comrade" or "friend" or more narrowly to signify a member of a formal corporation or group. Its earliest use refers to sworn groups of comrades often assembled for military purposes. One can see these groups as military fellowships bound by oath. There is no direct attestation of such a group at Rome but there is a parallel in the clan army of the Fabii in **12**. On the most likely interpretation the inscription is a dedication of the *suodales* (plural) of Publius Valerius to the god of war and so may represent a military fellowship. It is tempting to identify the Publius Valerius of the inscription with the well-known figure of Publius Valerius Publicola, one of the consuls of the first year of the Republic (509) and a major figure in early Republican history. There is a very good chance that this inscription represents another form of war band, based not on ties of kinship but on voluntary association. It is important to remember that one of the most important functions of early warfare is the accumulation of wealth through booty won in battle. Groups of this nature are widely attested in other cultures.

The *suodales* of Publius Valerius have erected this as a dedication to Mars.

How the archaic army fought

Archaeological evidence is our only source for reconstructing Rome's earliest fighting methods. From the early tenth century through to the first half of the seventh century Etruscan material provides the best parallels. The extent of Etruscan influence and the position of Rome on its southern fringe point, as well as the clear cultural links between Rome and the southern Etruscan cities, are a sufficient basis to use Etruscan material, as there are few finds of this period at Rome. In the early Iron Age the spear predominated as the main offensive weapon, both the heavy thrusting variety and javelins. Swords appear later and in general function as a secondary armament. The sword's presence in certain burials may be more indicative of its role as an expensive marker of status rather than as a crucial implement of war. Defensive equipment seems limited to a bronze helmet, the pectoral or chest protector, and a shield probably of wood, perhaps with a metal guard or *umbo* over a central handgrip. The predominance of the heavy thrusting spear would argue for some sort of close formation. It need not have been a very regular one. Warfare was probably conducted by small bands following a better-equipped leader who perhaps often carried a sword.

Until 600 BC there is no basic change in the types of weapons available, although there does seem to be a greater variety of them. Presumably, the tactical organization implied was unchanged except for the development of true cavalry by 600 BC. Their presence implies in theory a more complicated command structure, with the need to coordinate two different types of troops if the cavalry fought mounted.

The introduction of the phalanx in central Italy

The Etruscans

By the latter part of the eighth century there is a notable cultural transformation in Etruria in conjunction with increasing urbanization and social change. There is a substantial increase in luxury, visible in burials and in the large-scale importation of luxury objects from the eastern Mediterranean. It is hard not to see this change as associated with contemporary Greek colonization in southern Italy, which had a profound effect on the culture of both Etruria and Latium. The influence of Greek culture was intense and widespread; it included not only artistic styles and techniques but also other crucial phenomena such as the growth of literacy in Etruria.

Accompanying these vast social and cultural changes was a phase of Etruscan expansion on land and sea. From the eighth century there is evidence for Etruscanizing elements in the culture of Campanian cities, although the chronology and the nature of Etruscan penetration are uncertain. There is no evidence that this was done in any unified or conscious manner. Rather it seems to have been the work of individuals and small bands from different Etruscan states. The Etruscans also expanded to the north into the Po valley. But their movement to the south was of particular significance for Rome because of the deep cultural impact it made. Rome of the late seventh century was an open and ethnically fluid society in which Etruscans played an important role. It may even have had a bilingual elite. However, it was Roman and not Etruscan.

The Etruscans were strongly influenced by Greek weaponry and tactics. In the period between about 675 and 650 the city-states of central and southern Greece were developing a new mode of warfare based on a phalanx of heavily armed infantrymen. The Greek phalanx was a rectangular formation of heavily armored infantry, usually ranged eight men deep. Each warrior was armed with a heavy thrusting spear which was his main offensive weapon, cuirass, metal helmet and the most distinctive piece of equipment, the great round hoplite shield. This was an extremely convex shield made with a wooden core and either rimmed or later completely faced with bronze. Its most distinguishing characteristic was its grip, which consisted of two parts: a curved metal band into which the arm was inserted up to the elbow and a cord often made of leather, which was threaded around the perimeter of the shield and grasped by the hand. This grip limited the usefulness of the shield in single combat, but was extremely effective when used in a tight formation, where the soldier to the right could cover the right side of the warrior to his left.

In Greece the adoption of this mode of fighting seems to have been closely tied to the adoption of a city-state, a form of community in which all citizens were liable to service, but only those who could afford to do so served in the phalanx, providing their equipment at their own expense.

The evidence for the adoption of phalanx-style warfare in Etruria is of two types: weapons found in grave deposits and pictorial representations. From the middle of the seventh century Greek hoplite equipment begins to appear in Etruscan burials.

15

The bronze bell corselet arrives just at this time. More significantly the hoplite shield also appears. The pattern is not one of consistent and thoroughgoing adoption of Greek equipment. Native types persist side by side with hoplite equipment.

The earliest pictorial representations of what seem to be hoplites appear at the same time. From the beginning of the sixth century representations of hoplites become very frequent. The evidence seems to indicate that Etruscan warriors had begun widespread adoption of Greek-style equipment from the mid-seventh century, not long after the Greeks themselves had developed this form of warfare. However, unlike the Greek example, in Etruria native equipment persisted. This may point to a slightly different development of the phalanx in Etruria from that in Greece.

The uniformity of the Greek phalanx is to some extent a product of a certain leveling of the Greek citizen body in the period of the adoption of the phalanx. It is linked to a general decline of aristocratic privileges and the limitation or elimination of the aristocracy's former determining role in government. This in turn was connected to a wider distribution of wealth and an increase in power of those citizens whose wealth was above a fixed property minimum. The situation in Etruria was very different. From the eighth century Etruscan society became organized in large kin groups similar to the Roman *gentes*. These groups were characterized by strong economic inequalities, which were also mirrored in the unequal distribution of power. These groups seem to have consisted of a clan chief and other elite members of his family along with a large number of clients and slaves.

These social divisions may explain a major difference in the distribution of weapons and portrayals of war in Greece and Etruria. There is a direct correlation between hoplite equipment and wealthier tombs. So it appears that it was the aristocracy that first adopted Greek weaponry, although in a piecemeal fashion. This fact has been used to argue against the use of such equipment as evidence for fighting on the Greek model in a phalanx formation. Given the disparity of wealth and the long history of the use of the thrusting spear as the primary offensive weapon, it may be that the reason such equipment was adopted was that it was advantageous in a pre-existing, close-packed, phalanx-like formation. The development of phalanx warfare at Rome forms an illuminating parallel.

Roman equipment in the seventh and sixth centuries

In this period there are few finds at Rome. A few scattered pieces of equipment and some fragmentary representations of Greek equipment from which little can be inferred are all that have been found. This is a characteristic not only of Rome, but of Latium in general. There is a significant general decline in grave goods in this period. Since in other ways it appears to be a time of substantial growth, this impoverishment of burials seems best explained as a deliberate change in disposal of the dead. It may be as has been suggested that, in this first period of monumental construction and urbanization in Latium, wealth that had formerly been deposited with the dead was now directed towards public building and display.

Given the paucity of evidence little can be deduced directly from the Roman material. In view of the general cultural similarities between Rome and southern Etruria there is every reason to expect that Roman fighters duplicated in their equipment and tactics the style of fighting prevalent in Etruria, and that the standard heavy infantry was composed at least in part of hoplites by the sixth century.

The adoption of hoplite tactics and equipment at Rome

14 INEDITUM VATICANUM 3

This Greek fragment was discovered at the end of the nineteenth century in a manuscript that contained writings by fourth-century AD Christian authors. It is part of a collection of historical anecdotes designed to illustrate a particular maxim or adage. On the basis of language the work appears to be of the late first or second century AD. The author is unknown. The context is a meeting between the Roman envoy Kaeso and an unknown Carthaginian at the beginning of the First Punic War.

Certainly the Romans did borrow some of their military equipment from their enemies. One example is the so-called Spanish sword that became the standard legionary short sword at the latest after the Second Punic War, which was most likely patterned after a sword type found among the tribes that the Romans fought in Spain. But the way the passage envisions these developments is too stereotypical to be true. The borrowing of the phalanx from the Etruscans is probably incorrect. It is far more likely, as has been suggested, that the change to the Greek phalanx style of fighting spread to most of the city-states of west central Italy by pressure from neighboring cities in Latium and Etruria.

The statement about the Samnites seems equally inauthentic. The little we know of Samnite equipment points to differences from the Roman (see pp. 43f.). Further, the development of the manipular army seems to have been a long, slow process and not a simple borrowing. The long and difficult training such a formation required could hardly have been undertaken during wartime. Further the notion that the Romans fought only in infantry formations prior to the Samnite wars is extremely doubtful.

> Kaeso said "Our nature is such that [I will only mention examples that are beyond dispute, so that you can report it to your city] we engage our enemies on their own terms and we have, as far as foreign methods go, surpassed those who have had long experience in them. The Etruscans used to wage war against us armed with bronze shields and arrayed in a phalanx, not arranged in maniples. We changed our equipment and adopted theirs, and arraying ourselves in battle against them overcame them, though they had long experience of fighting in a phalanx formation. The Samnite *scutum* was not our ancestral shield nor did we have the javelin. We fought with the round shield and the heavy thrusting spear. We were not strong in cavalry; either all or the majority of our army was infantry.

But when we were at war with the Samnites we armed ourselves with their shields and javelins and were constrained to fight on horseback. By emulating foreign arms we made subject to ourselves those who had a very high regard for themselves."

Falerii, modern Città Castellana, lay in southern Etruria not far north of Veii, and Fescennium seems to have been located close by and may originally have been dependent on it. Both Pliny and Dionysius ascribe a Greek origin to it, though it was originally a native settlement of a people known as the Falisci, who came under strong Etruscan influence and were culturally and politically part of Etruria. The reference to Greek military equipment is part of Dionysius' attempt to prove a Greek origin for this area of central Italy to support his view that the Romans were originally Greeks. The presence of such equipment, perhaps in the main temple of Falerii dedicated to Juno Curitis, indicates nothing about the ethnic origin of the citizens. However, Dionysius' remark about the presence of Greek military equipment receives some support from statuettes of the fifth and fourth centuries from Falerii with Greek military equipment. Argive shields are the round hoplite shield.

Falerii and Fescennium were still inhabited by the Romans in my day. In those cities there remained many of the old Greek customs that survived for a very long time such as the type of military equipment, Argive shields and heavy thrusting spears.

Servius Tullius and the reform of the Roman army

The most important change in Rome's military forces during the regal period is ascribed to Servius Tullius, Rome's sixth king, whose traditional dates are 578–534. The reform resulted in the development of the first hoplite army on the Greek model.

Modern scholars generally accept him as an historical figure as well as the traditional date of his reign and other important political and military reforms ascribed to him. The date appears to be supported by archaeological evidence for the spread of hoplite weaponry in Etruria and Latium in this period.

Many elements in the traditional picture of the king, which occur in the accounts of Livy and Dionysius, fit contemporary developments in central Italy. In the traditional picture of his reign Servius Tullius plays a crucial role in the early development of the city, appearing as a second founder of the city. He is said to have enlarged the city and surrounded it with a defensive wall, created a new tribal system which served as the basis for his army reforms and created a new basis for citizenship with the institution of the census.

The clustering of myth around this figure is indicative of his importance and serves as a foundation charter for what the Romans perceived as crucial alterations in the nature of their state and society. Servius seems to have been used a precedent for both conservative and popular political programs in the later Republic.

The sources give divergent accounts of his origins. It is not impossible based on Etruscan evidence that he began his career as a member of a war band that settled at Rome and obtained the kingship by some sort of coup. Part of tradition mentions him commanding Latin auxiliary forces and then the Roman cavalry for the previous king, Tarquinius Priscus.

The Servian reforms

The centurionate system

All of the sources ascribe a major change in the basis of citizenship and a new form of military organization to him. The foundation of this new system was a census of all citizens and their property and then the creation of a new army based on it. The institution of an assessment (however it was carried out) of property as a means of assigning citizen rights and responsibilities was an important departure from the existing system based on kinship and residence. Inherent in this reform is a new idea of citizenship. Rather than having an individual's political standing mediated through the power and standing of his kin group, the citizen now stands in a direct relationship to his community and is assigned his rights as an individual and not as a member of a group. Aspects of Servius' reforms have striking similarities to contemporary reforms in Greek Italy and in Greece itself.

The reform of the army

16 LIVY, 1.42.5–43.10

The same basic schema is also found in our other two sources for the Servian army, but with some minor differences. Dionysius assigns shields, swords, and thrusting spears to class IV as opposed to Livy's assignment of only the heavy thrusting spear and the *verutum*, a short throwing spear, the implication being that this class was not part of the battle line. Dionysius explicitly assigns it to the rear of the phalanx. In class V Dionysius has javelins in addition to the slings mentioned by Livy. The most striking difference between the two is over the centuries assigned to support troops. Dionysius allots two centuries of weapons makers and engineers to the second class. He has two centuries of musicians including trumpeters, horn players, and other musicians whose task it was to signal in the field. He attaches them to the fourth class. Livy assigns his two centuries of engineers to the first class and appears despite some difficulties with the text to add three more centuries to the fifth class consisting of attendants, trumpeters, and horn players.

In a brief discussion in his *Republic*, Cicero mentions a century of wood workers assigned to the fifth class. This seems to support Livy's version of the distribution of centuries. However, Cicero seems to be describing the centuriate assembly as it emerged from a reform which brought it in line with the tribal assembly in 241.

It seems likely that the description of all three authors ultimately descends from a single source. Their differences center on the weaponry assigned to the classes with the lower census ratings. The fact that Dionysius ends the phalanx with the fourth class and Livy with the third is a result of the equipment assigned to each class. Given the importance of organization by threes in both the earlier tribal system and the later manipular army, Livy's assignment of the first three classes to the heavy infantry seems preferable.

The major difference between the first class and the other two classes is the possession of the round hoplite shield. Some have conjectured that the phalanx was confined to this class alone and so have estimated the size of the Servian phalanx as 4,000 men disposed in forty centuries. This argument has been made that the phalanx could only have consisted of men uniformly armed in the manner of the Greek hoplite, which is the equipment of the first class. But there is contemporary and later Etruscan evidence that various types of shield were in use and that there was more variation in equipment in central Italy than among Greek hoplite armies. The *scutum* is an early Italian shield type that might well have preceded the adoption of Greek equipment and been used by the less wealthy. In this way the Servian reforms may have built on the characteristics of clan armies where the elite possessed a complete hoplite panoply while clients and followers had to content themselves with the less expensive *scutum*. They would have served to support and add mass to the elite phalanx.

The extension of the duty to serve as heavy infantry to all who possessed the hoplite census may also have had political implications. Servius is credited with reforming the Roman tribal system and expanding the boundaries of the city. Most scholars accept the fact that Servius was responsible for the creation of the four urban tribes, but there has been much controversy over whether he created rural tribes and how many existed under the monarchy. It seems likely that a number of rural tribes were created under the monarchy and perhaps by Servius Tullius. This tribal reformation together with the reform of the army has been correctly seen as an attempt to enlarge the community and provide a new basis for citizenship and social bonding. This was a series of reforms designed to weaken the traditional kin groups and their leaders and strengthen the central government. This might also be a factor in the heterogeneous composition of the army, with Servius trying to dilute the power of the clan chiefs by diluting the heavy infantry core with a wider section of the community.

It is thus possible to accept a certain variation in equipment, but except for the *scutum* it is harder to see the justification for the differences between the second and the third class. It is probable as has been suggested that the differences in equipment are the product of antiquarian speculation. The small changes in weaponry of each class have no obvious purpose and seem to reflect later developments when the centuriate system had become the basis for a political assembly designed to give more weight to the votes of the wealthy. It is not likely that this was the original distinction between census groups. There is good literary evidence for what was a simpler distinction between those with full hoplite equipment, the *classis*, and those who served as light-armed or in some other capacity, the *infra classem*.

The army created by the Servian reforms was a crucial development in Roman military history. It may not have marked the introduction of hoplite tactics so much as the creation of a military community, a community recognized by the importance accorded to the army in its political role as an assembly, the *Comitia Centuriata*. It institutionalized military service to the state as part of a set of communal obligations and communal rights.

The figures for property values cannot be original. The valuations in both Livy and Dionysius are based on the sextanal as, a bronze coin of two ounces which was introduced around the year 211. So the original source used by both writers must date after this year. It is not impossible that the figures are recalculations in terms of the new coinage of earlier values and that this system of classes is far earlier. The tremendous stress on manpower produced by the Second Punic War might well have stimulated renewed interest in the system.

It is impossible to assign absolute values to these figures; all that can be said is that the first class was well off by the standards of the first century BC and those below minimum property rating were poor. The figures in both authors agree with one another except for the fifth classes, to which Livy assigns 11,000 asses and Dionysius 12,500. One drachma is equal to 10 asses and a mina was worth 100 drachma.

[Servius] instituted the census, a most beneficial measure for a future imperial power of such great magnitude and from this point on the duties of citizens in war and peace were assigned in accordance with their wealth and not as before without distinction. He then organized the centuries and classes according to the arrangement which follows which was suitable for both war and peace.

From those whose property rating was 100,000 asses or above, he created eighty centuries, forty of men of military age (17–46) and forty of older men (47–60). All of these centuries were known as those of the first class. The older men were to be available for guarding the city and the younger for campaigns in the field. He ordered this class to equip themselves with helmet, a round shield (*clipeus*), greaves, and a breastplate, all of bronze. This would be their defensive equipment; against the enemy they would use the heavy thrusting spear (*hasta*) and the sword.

He added to this class two centuries of workmen who would perform their military service unarmed; they were assigned to construct engines of war.

The second class was formed of those whose rating was between 100,000 and 75,000 asses and from these were enrolled twenty centuries, ten of younger and ten of older men. They were to carry the rectangular

THE REPUBLICAN ROMAN ARMY

shield (*scutum*) in place of the round one and except for the corselet all their other equipment matched that of the first class.

The rating of the third class was 50,000 to 75,000 asses. They were to have the same number of centuries as the second and the same distinction between younger and older men. Their armament was the same as the second except greaves were omitted.

The fourth class was rated at 25,000 to 50,000 asses and had the same number of centuries, but their equipment was different. They carried only the heavy thrusting spear and the *verutum* [a short throwing spear].

The fifth class was larger as it consisted of thirty centuries and it carried slings with stones for missiles. Attendants, buglers, and trumpeters belonged to it and were divided into three centuries. The class was rated at 11,000 to 25,000 asses. The multitude whose property was rated at a lower value were placed in one century and excused military service.

17 DIONYSIUS OF HALICARNASSUS, *ROMAN ANTIQUITIES* 4.16.1–18.1

After he [Servius] had received the census valuation of all the citizens and had determined their number and the size of their estates he introduced the wisest of political measures and of greatest benefit to the Romans as events showed. The measure was as follows. He chose from all of the citizens that category whose property valuation was the highest being not less than 100 minae. He grouped them into eighty centuries and ordered them to bear the following arms: Argive shields [the round hoplite shield or *clipeus*], heavy thrusting spears, bronze helmets, cuirasses, greaves, and swords. He divided them into two groups, forty centuries of juniors whom he assigned to the field army and forty of seniors who were to remain in the city and guard the walls when the juniors went off to war. This was the first class, and in time of war it occupied the front line of the whole phalanx. Then from those who remained he separated off another section whose property rating was less than 10,000 drachma, but not less than 75 minae, and he grouped it into twenty centuries. He instructed them to equip themselves in the same way as the first class except that he took from them the cuirass and gave them a rectangular shield (the *scutum*) in place of a round one. He also divided them into two groups, separating off those who were older than forty-five from the men who were of military age. He created ten centuries of younger men and ten of older ones whom he assigned to guard the walls. This was the second class. In battle they were deployed behind the fighters in the first ranks. He formed the third class from those remaining who had property valued at less than 75,000 drachma but not less than fifty minae. He removed from their equipment not only cuirasses as he did for the second class but also greaves. He arranged them in twenty centuries as well and divided them according to age as he had done for the first two classes, assigning the juniors ten

22

centuries and the seniors ten. The post and position of these centuries in battle were after those arrayed behind the fighters in the front of the phalanx.

Once again he chose from the remainder a group consisting of those whose property was less than 50,000 drachma but more than 25 minae. He also divided these into twenty centuries, ten for those at their physical peak and ten for those who were beyond it in the same way as before. He instructed them to be armed with the rectangular shield, sword, and heavy thrusting spear and to take their position at the rear of the phalanx. The fifth class, which consisted of those whose property was between twenty-five and twelve and one-half minae, he divided up into thirty centuries. He also divided them according to age. The older men were assigned fifteen centuries and the younger also fifteen. He ordered them to carry javelins and slings and to serve outside of the phalanx. He instructed four centuries to follow those who were armed. These consisted of two centuries of armorers, carpenters, and other professions whose business it is to prepare things useful in war. The other two were made up of those who played the trumpet, horn players, and others who play instruments for signaling in warfare. The craftsmen were attached to the second class and divided by age, one of their centuries following the older and the other younger. The trumpeters and horn players were brigaded with the fourth class, one century attached to the older and the other to the younger centuries. The bravest men of all were chosen as centurions who being the best in war rendered their men obedient to orders. This was [Servius'] arrangement for the infantry consisting of the phalanx and the light-armed.

The classis

Early Latin had various expressions to designate the Roman army, among which was the word *classis*. Its basic meaning is an appeal to or summons. It was used to designate the army in the field or in the new centuriate assembly.

The dominant view is that the distinction between the *classis* and the *infra classem* that appears in the following passages represents the initial division of the army under Servius Tullius, the *classis* being the heavily armed hoplite infantry and the *infra classem* (literally below the *classis*) the light-armed. If the term applied only to the first class it would mean that the phalanx of the Servian reforms numbered 4,000. The further distinctions between classes in the accounts of later writers would be the product of the army's role as a political assembly and the later growth in manpower.

But there is no definitive evidence that *classis* in the early period exclusively referred to the first Servian class. It may well have signified the members of classes I to III whose equipment represents variations on that of the heavy infantry. In favor of this view is the fact that the later Roman system consisted of three lines and the earlier division by threes in the previous tribal army. The use of a

23

hoplite-style mode of battle is not incompatible with the use of the rectangular *scutum*. As late as the last part of the second century BC, the last line in the Roman army retained the heavy thrusting spear, while there were significant changes in the front lines.

It seems best to take the early distinction, that is *classis* and *infra classem* as distinguished between heavy and light. That distinction was between the first three and the last two classes, not between the first and the rest. The limiting of the term to the first class may well be a later development and perhaps grew out of its commanding position in the centuriate assembly rather than its military role.

Was Rome in the sixth century capable of fielding an army of 6,000 heavy infantry with cavalry and light-armed support? It was by far the largest city in Latium, with a territory two to three times that of the next largest communities. The most reasonable population estimate for Roman territory is between 35,000 and 40,000 by the end of the monarchy about 500 BC. Such a population could support a military force of close to 9,000 men. This is congruent with the figures arrived at through the most likely reconstruction of the Servian reforms.

18 AULUS GELLIUS, *ATTIC NIGHTS* 6.13

Aulus Gellius was an essayist and commentator of the mid- to late second century AD. He often preserves valuable antiquarian material and shows strong interest in the meaning and use of words. The passage below is an explanation of the use of the terms *classicus* and *infra classem* in a speech by the elder Cato of the mid-second century BC. Clearly, the way Gellius defines the term shows that by his time it was no longer used. The implication of Gellius' explanation is that behind the complicated accounts of the Servian system in the historians there was a simpler system, that is the army of Servius was divided into two parts: the *classis*, or heavy infantry, and the *infra classem*, who served as light infantry.

> Not all of those in the five classes are called *classici*, but only men of the first class whose census rating was 125,000 asses or more. Those who are called *infra classem* are the men who belonged to the second class as well as all the other classes, whose census ratings were below that of the first.

19 FESTUS, 100 L

Sextus Pompeius Festus, a grammarian of the late second century, abridged a work by the Augustan writer Verrius Flaccus entitled *On the Meaning of Words*. The abridgment preserves much valuable early antiquarian learning. The usual view is that the census rating found in the historians was that assigned after the change in about 211 to a bronze coinage with six asses to the Roman pound of twelve ounces. Polybius, a Greek historian contemporary with Cato, also gives the census rating of the first class as 100,000 asses. There are various possible solutions to this problem, but it may simply be that the grammarians are giving a later figure for the first class.

Perhaps a devaluation of the bronze coinage in 141 led to a new valuation for the census of the first class.

The term *infra classem* refers to those whose census rating is less than 120,000 asses.

20 FESTUS, 48.32 L

The *clipeus* was the round hoplite shield. This passage has been taken as evidence that the phalanx was the only early heavy infantry, but it may well be that the phalanx was the most important section of the heavy infantry and the name was used of all heavily armed troops.

The ancients used the term *classes clipeatae* for what we now call armies.

21 LIVY, 4.34.6

This incident belongs to the war against Veii that broke out in 437 after the murder of a group of Roman ambassadors. This was the second in a series of three major conflicts that ended in the capture and incorporation of Veii in the Roman state in 396. At issue was the control of traffic along the Tiber and from the river into the interior. Fidenae was a crucial Veientine bridgehead that threatened Roman control of the left bank of the river. Fidenae was finally captured in 435. This passage is in reference to the campaign of 426 under the dictator Mamercus Aemilius. It ended in the total destruction and permanent Roman occupation of the site. There are some doubts about the historicity of these events. Nonetheless this account of the campaign must have developed early, since *classis* is used in an archaic sense of heavy infantry. In classical Latin it has the meaning of "fleet," and this is the source of Livy's perplexity in the passage.

Some historians record that the *classis* also fought near Fidenae with the men of Veii, but it is difficult to believe this. For the river [Tiber] is not now wide enough and was at that time as the ancient writers tell us narrower. But it may be the case that there was a massing of some ships in an attempt to prevent a crossing of the river and the importance of this action was exaggerated, as often happens, in the desire for the empty claim to a naval victory.

22 DIODORUS SICULUS, 12.64.3

The sources assign the dictatorship of Aulus Postumius Tubertus to 431. His only other attested office is that of *magister equitum* (master of the horse) during the second dictatorship of Mamercus Aemilius in 434. Though the historicity of this post has been questioned there is no reason to do so. His dictatorship, perhaps, in 431 was according to Livy the result of disputes between the consuls, which led to paralysis in the face of a war against the Aequi and Volsci. Under Tubertus a decisive victory was achieved over both of these peoples at the Mount Algidus pass near the important Latin city of Tusculum southeast of Rome. The details of the battle have been elaborated in the later tradition, but there is no reason to doubt the historicity of the battle or its importance.

Both Diodorus and Livy express disbelief about the dictator's execution of his son. There is a later and more widespread version of the same story told of one of the consuls of 340, T. Manlius Torquatus. It seems likely that both stem from independent family traditions. This passage has been used as evidence for the use of the hoplite army, whose success depended on keeping position in battle. However, such an interpretation is hardly compelling. This anecdote, as well as the version involving Manlius, and the earlier traditions about the sons of Brutus the Liberator are at base examples of appropriate behavior between fathers and sons. At the core of each is the moral imperative to place duty to one's own country above family obligations. Support for this view is visible in the fact that both commanders are successful in serious battles that have momentous consequences for the community. There is nothing to link the Tubertus episode with the use of a hoplite formation. Any mass formation requires some form of order, and the Romans presumably used ordered formations before they adopted the phalanx as they did after they discarded it.

> They say [Postumius] did something strange and totally unbelievable. During the battle Postumius' son leapt out in front of the battle line that his father had established because of his eagerness to engage. Observing ancestral custom his father executed him on the charge of deserting his post.

Servius Tullius and the reform of the cavalry

23 LIVY, 1.43.8

The account of this cavalry reform in our sources is extremely confused. This is surprising, as it would be the part of Servius' reform that the elite would be the most interested in and so likely to preserve most accurately. The general ratio of cavalry to infantry among Mediterranean states is ten infantrymen to each cavalry trooper, and this ratio seems to be implied in the cavalry reform ascribed to Tarquinius Priscus (see **8**). If the increase of twelve centuries is accepted for the Servian reform this would produce a cavalry of 1,800, both light and heavy, which stands at a ten-to-one ratio to the 180 centuries of heavy and light infantry produced by Servius' arrangements. For purposes of comparison the later Roman Republican legion had 3,000 heavy infantry and 300 cavalry, giving a ratio of ten to one. If the phalanx was composed of the first class as some suppose or more likely the first three classes, this would produce a ratio of two and one-half or three and one-third to one. These ratios are far too small to be believable, and this provides further evidence that the phalanx included more than the first class.

The number of centuries given in our sources represents the number of units assigned to the cavalry that were created for political not military reasons as the *Comitia Centuriata* evolved. This seems to be supported by what appear to be anachronistic payments for the purchase and maintenance of the mounts. Given the usual assumption that all of the infantry provided their equipment it would appear doubtful that at this stage the aristocratic cavalry would have received support from the state.

> He [Servius Tullius] enrolled twelve centuries of cavalry from the leading men of the city. He likewise created six other centuries under the same names, which had been consecrated by augury, three of which had been established by Romulus. He gave the cavalrymen 10,000 asses each. Unmarried were assessed to pay 2,000 asses per year each to provide food for the mounts.

Phalanx in action

The battle of Lacus Regillus

The turmoil surrounding the expulsion of Tarquinius Superbus, Rome's last king, affected the Latins, who seem to have resented the dominance that Rome had acquired. A further cause for resentment was Rome's expansion in Latium under Superbus. The Latins joined together to try to end or reduce that dominance. The sources name their main leader as Octavius Mamilius of Tusculum, the son-in-law of the last Tarquin, who was acting at the instigation and in the interests of his expelled father-in-law. It has been argued that this struggle with the Latins was a continuation of a more wide-ranging conflict involving not only Rome and the Latins, but also the Etruscan king of Clusium, Lars Porsenna, and Aristodemus, the Greek tyrant of the Cumae.

Lacus Regillus was the decisive engagement in this conflict. The sources offer two different dates for it, either 499 or 496, and there is too little evidence to decide between them. The location of the battle is uncertain. It seems to have been fought in the hilly country near Tusculum. Livy and Dionysius are the main sources for the encounter. The Roman force fought under the command of the dictator A. Postumius Albinus, with Titus Aebutius as his master of the horse. The Livian account is markedly different than that of Dionysius. It is told as a series of Homeric encounters between the leaders of the opposing forces fighting from horseback. The terminology Livy uses in referring to the opposing forces betrays the fact that he is describing the later manipular army and not the phalanx. The decisive role in the battle is played not by the infantry but by the dictator's elite cavalry guard who stiffen the line and the Roman cavalry who dismount in response to the order of the dictator and continue the battle on foot. Though the cavalry also play a crucial role in Dionysius' version, nothing is said about their dismounting to fight. Rather it is the cavalry charge of the dictator and the loss of their leaders that lead to the rout of the Latins. Some scholars have seen this and other instances in Livy when the cavalry dismount to fight as evidence that early Roman cavalry like their Greek counterparts rode to battle but fought on foot, that is they were mounted hoplites.

It does seem that whether mounted or dismounted the cavalry played a role of significance in the battle. Our accounts of the battle claim that Postumius as the result of his victory vowed a temple to Castor and Pollux, who were supposed to have brought the news of the victory to Rome. These deities are closely associated with the cavalry and its rituals.

The importance of Dionysius' description of the battle lies in his use of the term "phalanx" to describe the formation of the Roman heavy infantry. The battle certainly does not in any way resemble the normal portrait of a Greek hoplite encounter in which the heavy infantry were the decisive arm. The term is not used to describe a particular form of heavy infantry formation but seems to be used by Dionysius simply for any heavy infantry formation. It appears in his descriptions of various battles under Romulus and the first Tarquin before the Servian reforms.

We have no description of a Roman hoplite army in action in the ancient authors. They all describe the manipular formation of the middle Republic. It is the manipular army's javelins and swords that figure in their accounts, not the hoplite's heavy thrusting spear. The Servian reform and hoplite equipment seem to have been a discovery of an antiquarian not an annalistic tradition. That antiquarian reconstruction was accepted by the historians, but never thoroughly integrated into their accounts.

24 DIONYSIUS OF HALICARNASSUS, *ROMAN ANTIQUITIES* 6.5.4–12.6

The totals for the troops of both sides are impossibly high. The use of anachronistic terms such as "legate," a position that only appears in the second century, shows that the account has been elaborated by later writers.

> When the signal for battle was raised on both sides, both armies advanced to the space between their camps. Their orders of battle were the following: On the Latin side, Sextus Tarquinius commanded the Latin left wing, Octavius Mamilius commanded the right, while Titus one of the sons of the exiled king commanded the center where the Roman deserters and exiles were stationed. The Latin horse was divided into thirds, two units were on the wings and a third was stationed in the center of the phalanx.
>
> On the Roman side, the master of the horse, Titus Aebutius, commanded the left wing opposite Octavius Mamilius. Titus Verginius the consul led the right wing opposite Sextus Tarquinius. The dictator Postumius held the center of the phalanx and was intending to oppose Titus Tarquinius and the exiles. The number of forces assembled for battle on the Roman side was 23,700 infantry and 1,000 cavalry. The Latins and the allies totaled about 40,000 infantry and 3,000 horse....

After both sides had received the agreed-upon signal from their leaders, trumpets sounded the charge. They raised their war cries and rushed forward. First came the cavalry and the light-armed of both sides, then the phalanxes armed and similarly arrayed. And there began everywhere an intense hand-to-hand struggle. Things had turned out contrary to expectations as neither side had expected that a battle would be necessary, but assumed they would rout the enemy with the first onslaught. The Latins trusted in the number of their cavalry, supposing that the Roman cavalry would not withstand their assault. The Romans thought that by reckless and blind assault they would throw their enemies into consternation. Although they supposed that this would be how things would develop at first, the opposite resulted....

First, the dictator with his picked horse was in the middle of the Roman phalanx, and fighting in the front lines he pushed back the enemy line opposite to him .... The commanders of the Roman phalanx on either wing, Titus Aebutius and Mamilius Octavius, fought most brilliantly of all, routing those who opposed them wherever they advanced; they rallied their own men wherever they had become disorganized. Then Aebutius and Mamilius challenging each other came to close quarters and after they had dashed together they exchanged fierce but not deadly blows. The master of the horse drove his spear point clean through Mamilius' corselet and into his chest, while Mamilius had driven his spear through the middle of Aebutius' right arm.

[Postumius] summoned the other legate [assistant], Herminius, who commanded a body of horse to ride around the back of the Roman phalanx and to turn back those who were fleeing, and to kill those who did not obey. The dictator with his best men pressed forward against the mass of the enemy. When he neared the enemy, he, first of all his men, drove violently at the enemy. Since the Romans charged en masse and their charge was unnerving, the enemy was unable to endure their wildness and fury, were routed and many of them fell....

Sextius Tarquinius in command of the Latin left was resisting in the midst of these difficulties and was pushing back the Roman right. When he saw Postumius and the select cavalry appear he abandoned all hope and rushed into the midst of the enemy. There, surrounded by the Roman horse and foot, bombarded by missiles from all sides like a wild beast, but not without killing many that came to close quarters, he died. After the death of their leaders the Latin flight became general ...

Rome and the Latin League

In the period after 900 BC the area between the Tiber and the Anio, and flanked by the Apennine foothills and Monte Lepini, seems to have formed a linguistic and cultural unity. The result of these uniformities was the development among the communities of this area of a common identity as Latins and it found expression in shared religious cults. Apparently one of the earliest of these communal celebrations was the *Feriae Latinae*, a festival held in the spring in honor of Jupiter Latiaris, the eponymous god of the Latins, on the Alban Mount. The number of participating communities is said by later authors to be thirty, and each community contributed to and was required to have a share in a communal meal. Unfortunately, there are problems in identifying known Latin states with the list we have. This celebration may well be the origin of the ancient view that at one time Alba dominated the Latins as the Romans were later to do. There were other sites as well at which similar rites were celebrated, such as the grove of Diana near Lake Nemi, the festival of Diana at the Latin town of Aricia, and a further festival at Lanuvium.

In addition to the sharing of religious rites the Latins also shared social and political rights that in part were the result of a common ethnic identity. Citizens of one Latin community could contract a legal marriage with a citizen of another, as well as the rights to engage in commerce, to conclude a legal contract, and to change residence, becoming a full member of another Latin community. These too are a reflection of an original ethnic unity that was not forgotten with the rise of separate city-states, perhaps strengthened by the apparent ease of elite migration in Etruria and Latium in the archaic period. Little is known about the procedure at these ceremonies. At a later period the ritual was presided over by the Latin cities in turn.

There is no evidence that prior to the end of the monarchy the league had any functions other than religious ones. If anything, the sources report constant warfare between Latin communities, and that explains the fact that, as in many ancient religious celebrations, the *Feriae Latinae* were accompanied by a truce among the Latins for the duration of the festival. Although the association was a religious one it could have political implications. It is in this context that the establishment of a temple to Diana by Servius Tullius to act as a competing cult center for the Latins must be viewed.

Rome is portrayed as acting as a separate power, fighting other Latin states, and never appears as involved on an equal footing with them when they act in common for political or military purposes. The Roman sources claim that Rome already exercised a sort of hegemony in the mid-seventh century. True or not, it seems that by the later half of the sixth century Rome had gained the dominant place in Latium. The evidence for this is provided by a treaty, which the mid-second-century BC Greek historian Polybius cites and dates to the first year of the Republic (509). Although there has been debate as to the authenticity and date of this treaty, most scholars now accept it as genuine. It provides collaborative evidence for the situation in Latium at the end of the monarchy at Rome. In the treaty the Carthaginians are forbidden to harm certain peoples named as subject to Rome, as well as the remainder of the Latins. The parallels with the sections which concern Carthaginian interests make it clear that the Romans are claiming a general supremacy over Latium.

It appears that a combination of Roman pressure and the general dislocation of central Italy at the end of the sixth century resulted in the Latin League's metamorphosis into a political and military alliance under the leadership of Tusculum. The attempt to shake off Roman domination ended in failure at the battle of Lacus Regillus (see **24**). During the course of the next few years the situation was, as Livy tells us, one of neither a firm peace nor open war. The Latins continued to maneuver against Rome, but pressure from the surrounding hill peoples who were pressing upon Latium finally led to the conclusion of a treaty with the Romans that was to define Romano-Latin relations for the next century and a half. The *Foedus Cassianum* or Cassian treaty specified that the contracting parties, Rome and the Latins, were equal. It established perpetual peace between them and at the same time instituted a defensive alliance as well as providing for the settlement of commercial disputes. It also allowed for an equal division of spoils between Rome and the Latins resulting from wars undertaken in common. The question of the command of joint Roman–Latin expeditions is unclear (see **27**). What does emerge from the terms of the treaty is that the overwhelming predominance of Rome in Latium had been reestablished.

25 DIONYSIUS OF HALICARNASSUS, *ROMAN ANTIQUITIES* 4.49

This passage gives the fullest extant account of the *Feriae Latinae* or *Latiar*, the festival of the Latins in honor of their tutelary god, Jupiter Latiaris. The main tradition ascribes the foundation of the festival to either the first or the second Tarquin; this type of confusion occurs concerning other matters as well. This may be the result of the view of our sources that the Latin League was from the beginning both a religious and a political association. Since the sources describe the second Tarquin as holding political hegemony over the Latins it would have been natural to ascribe its foundation to him. The fact that Rome later dominated the festival may also have contributed to this error. Antiquarian sources ascribe the origin to the so-called *Prisci Latini*, that is the Latin-speaking inhabitants of what the ancients called Latium Vetus or Old Latium which ran from the Tyrrhenian sea in the west to the foothills of the Apennines in the east. It was bounded on the north by the Tiber and Ario rivers. To the south it extended towards Campania with no fixed boundary. Pliny, a first-century AD source, gives a list of the thirty Latin peoples who participated, but there are difficulties in identifying the peoples he specifies and it is probable that membership varied over time.

It seems to have been only one of a number of early religious rites common to the Latins. Other celebrations are mentioned at Lanuvium, Gabii, the Lucus Ferentinae and Nemi among other sites. In the case of this festival it seems to have been a prerequisite for being considered a Latin state. The details about the truce between Latin states and the types of food and sacrificial animals brought by the participants found in the passage seem to be accurate, including the most important sacrificial animal, the bull.

More surprising is the inclusion of non-Latins in Dionysius' account in what is clearly a Latin festival. Again, it may have been the result of Dionysius' view that it was an expression and symbol of Roman domination. The peoples listed are the ones that Dionysius specifies as subdued by Tarquin. Another possible explanation is that by the early imperial period when Dionysius was writing Latin status no longer denoted ethnic affiliation, but rather a legal status that could be held by anyone whether he was ethnically Latin or not.

> Tarquinius [Superbus], with the intention that the alliances with these peoples would endure forever, decided to appoint a temple in common for the Romans, Hernici and those Volsci who had subscribed to the alliance as a place to assemble yearly, and there to hold a festival, a common banquet and to participate in common sacred rites. His actions were gladly accepted, and Tarquinius decreed the place where they would gather; it was a high mountain, which overlooked the city of the Albans and which was situated in the center of these peoples where they would hold their yearly festival and he laid down that there would be a truce and common sacrifices and banquets held in honor of the so-called Jupiter Latiaris. He specified what each state had to provide for the sacred rites and that portion of the sacrifice that each could receive. There were forty-seven cities that participated in the festivals and sacrifices. The Romans are still celebrating these festivals and rites at present calling it the Latin Festival. Some of the participating cities bring lambs, some cheeses, some a certain measure of milk, and others a type of cakes to be offered to the gods. A bull is sacrificed by them in common and each city receives its due portion. They sacrifice on behalf of all the contributing states and the Romans superintend the sacrifices.

26 CATO, *ORIGINES* II.28. 28C

Cato's *Origines* or Origins was the first history to be written in Latin. Its seven books began with the origins of Rome (I) and the Italian cities (II and III) and ended in the year of the author's death in 149. The first three books, which are at issue here, were patterned on a Greek form of history writing which dealt with the origins of cities. Unlike many other Roman writers, Cato seems to have conceived of Roman history as a part of the overall history of Italy. The shortness of the citation gives no clue as to the context of the quote.

The context of the passage is generally dated to around 500 BC, the very time when Rome had lost its dominance in Latium and was trying to restore control. Thus it may refer to the transition of the league from a religious into a political and military alliance of the Latins to resist Roman pressure. It may also have been a symbolic rejection of the Latin center set up by Servius Tullius on the Aventine. This grove of Diana appears to have been on the edge of Lake Nemi and the territory of Aricia, and held several other religious sites important to the Latin League such as the grove of Ferentina (a grove sacred to the river spirit). The title of Baebius may well have had military connotations, as it did at Rome, though it is found in Latin cities as a title of an ordinary magistrate. The leading role ascribed to Tusculum, not only supplying the dictator, but also named first in the list of participants, would fit the context of the end of the monarchy at Rome, when Tusculum played a leading role in supporting the expelled Tarquin.

The list of participating peoples is probably not complete. Dionysius mentions that the membership eventually included the traditional number of thirty. Tusculum's prominence is probably owed to its leading role in the war against Porsenna and the victory of the league at Aricia in 504. Aricia had played a leading role among the Latins in the last years of the monarchy at Rome and as well was the center of several important Latin cults. Lanuvium was also the center for the cult of Aeneas and lay on the southern side of the Alban Mount, while Aricia lay east of it and Tusculum to the north. The Laurentes are something of an enigma. They are associated with Lanuvium in later inscriptions and it may well be that they were a local group of villages that were absorbed into its territory. All were to come under heavy pressure from other Italic peoples, and this may explain in part their membership in the league. Pometia lay in the area of the Pontine Marshes; it was subject to pressure from the neighboring Volsci, who controlled it by 495 BC. It had disappeared by the first century BC. Ardea, in the lowlands of Latium and about four and a half kilometers from the sea, was the chief city of the Rutulians, who play a prominent part in the myths surrounding the origins of Rome.

Cato the Censor in the [Second Book] of his *Origins*: Egerius Baebius from Tusculum as Latin dictator made a dedication in the grove of Diana in the Arician wood. The following peoples were assembled: the Tusculans, the Aricians, the people of Lanuvium, the Laurentes, the people of Cora, those of Tibur, Pometia, the Rutulians of Ardea.

The Foedus Cassianum

27 DIONYSIUS OF HALICARNASSUS, *ROMAN ANTIQUITIES* 6.95.2

There is no reason to doubt the historicity of this treaty. Cicero claims to have seen a copy inscribed on bronze. The text preserved in Dionysius omits many important points that must have stood in the original treaty. For instance there is nothing about which state would hold command or any details about the type of the troops each side was required to provide. The treaty is a defensive alliance and must have been concluded under the threat posed by the pressure of the Aequi and Volsci as well as Roman success in reimposing its control over Latium. This is clear from the fact that Rome was not a member of the league, but contracted as an equal with all of the league's member states. The imposition of a prohibition against mutual conflict is unprecedented and can be viewed as an extension of the truce provisions found connected to various Latin festivals. The question of the division of booty seems clear, but later practice does not bear it out. The addition of private rights in such a document is the result of an attempt by the Latins to safeguard pre-existing rights (see p. 30). The clause concerning the prohibition on bringing in or allowing safe passage by either side to enemy forces is not found in other Roman treaties. The treaty remained in force until the end of the Latin League in 338.

> The following was the text of the treaty: "There shall be peace between the Romans and the cities of the Latins, as long as the sky and the earth shall remain in their same positions. They shall not engage in warfare with one another nor shall they bring in foreign enemies, nor shall they allow passage to enemy forces. They shall aid those who are attacked with all of their strength. They shall share equally in the booty and plunder from wars they wage in common. Judgments concerning private contracts shall be rendered within ten days. Nothing may be added to or deleted from these terms unless by agreement of the Romans and all the Latins."

28 FESTUS, 276.19-L

The traditional date of Alba Longa's destruction is in the mid-seventh century. The reference is to one of the major battles, the Veseris, of the final Roman conflict with the Latins that led to the dissolution of the league. It has often been taken to imply that the Latin cities and Rome alternated in command of the combined army. However, it is possible to interpret it to mean that in years when military campaigns were necessary a Roman commander always commanded the joint army. Certainly, the Roman historical tradition preserves no record of a Latin commander, but it is hard to gauge whether Rome's later dominance influenced this portrayal. It is a theoretical, but attractive, hypothesis that at first the command was shared between the two contracting parties, but as Rome grew to overshadow the league it came to supply all commanders for allied expeditions. The Latin complaints about the lack of equality in the 340s can be taken as some confirmation that such a state had existed previously.

> After the destruction of Alba until the consulship of Decius Mus [340] the Latin peoples were accustomed to consult in common and manage the problem of military command by taking common counsel. And so, in the year in which a Roman commander had to be sent to the allied army at the request of the Latins, many of our commanders used to take the auspices at sunrise.

Roman and Latin colonies

Early Latin and Roman colonization was ethnically based. Rome was a participant, but the colonies were Latin and not Roman. Livy, our most accurate source, claims that several colonies such as Signia to the east of the Monte Lepini and Cora on the other side of the same mountains were founded as early as the 490s. Given that Rome was a major Italian power at the end of the monarchy this claim may well be true. These colonies were clearly directed against the Volsci (see p. 43), who in the wake of the fall of the monarchy and the temporary weakness of Rome were able to quickly expand into this area. It may be that the Volscian threat had existed under the kings but they were strong enough to contain it.

These as well as the many colonies founded in the fifth and fourth centuries were Latin colonies founded with Rome as a participating member. Livy labels them Roman, but the fact that their legal status was Latin shows that this was not strictly true. The sources portray the Romans as acting unilaterally, which is probably a reflection of Roman dominance. The process of decision-making is so obscured by our sources that it is impossible to reconstruct it. Certainly the Cassian treaty presupposes equality between Rome and the Latins and that must have been reflected in their common colonization projects.

The colonies of the period such as Norba, Signia, and Nepet ringed the borders of Latium and the sources are clear that whatever the other motives were for colonization the major purpose was military. The colonies were sited at strategic points to guard Latium and to control its territory. The most pressing need of the period was to stem the tide of invasion by the Volsci and Aequi from the hill country surrounding Latium on its east and south. For instance Norba, founded in 492, was as Livy tells us founded on an easily defensible height to stand guard against the Volsci, who were advancing into the southern coastal plain of Latium at that time. Labici, fifteen miles northeast of Rome, was founded in 418 to exclude the Aequi from access to the Mount Algidus pass. In 383 a colony was established at Nepet to control the route into Umbria and guard against a possible Gallic threat.

In all, fourteen Latin colonies are known for the period down to 383/382, which was then followed by a hiatus that lasted for about forty years, and colonization was only resumed under the direction of Rome after its success in subjugating the Latins in the war of 340–338. In part, the cessation may be explained by the simple fact that by the beginning of this period there was little available space for new colonies in Latium, and Roman success against the Aequi and Volsci had greatly reduced any threat from them. There may also have been increased alienation from the Latins as witnessed by the break in relations with Tibur and the references to the fact that the Latins were allied with the Volsci against the Romans in 386, 385, and once again in 377.

All of our evidence concerns the Roman role in colonial foundation, and must have been influenced by Rome's role after 338. Nonetheless, there should be some correspondence with earlier practice. Formally, the foundation of a colony was dependent on the passage of a law by the people, most likely in the *Comitia Centuriata*, since the colony always had a quasi-military aspect. However, the sources claim, and it may well be true, that the Senate had the major role in deciding on the founding, size, and location of the colony. An elected commission normally including three senators oversaw the surveying of land and the recruitment of colonists. The Latin colonies could be sizeable enterprises. At a later period they varied from 1,500 to 6,000 settlers. A substantial proportion of these settlers were Roman citizens, but sizeable additions were drawn from populations that were neither Latin nor Roman. For example, at Ardea many of the local inhabitants who were Rutulians were enrolled in the new colony. Emigration for a Roman meant the loss of citizenship and taking the citizenship of the new foundation. Latin colonists did possess significant rights at Rome. They could contract formal legal marriages

35

with Roman citizens, make legal contracts and carry on commercial activities. Significantly, they could, if they were willing, take up residence at Rome and thereby acquire Roman citizenship. The possibility of a return to Rome if the colony were less than a success must have been attractive, but probably the single most important draw was the sizeable land grants given to colonists. These ranged from ten to thirty acres. Lots of this size would have allowed Romans too poor to qualify for military service at home to be enlisted in the colonies. This may also explain why the Roman government was willing to tolerate a substantial loss of manpower. What mattered in the end was not the total population of the city but the part that could be called upon to fight.

The colonies played a vital role in Rome's expansion in Italy. They provided permanent garrisons that controlled vital strategic links that made Roman domination possible. They also allowed the Roman state to sizeably increase its reserves of manpower. These reserves were to be vital factor in future Roman military success in Italy and overseas.

The Roman view of the function of a colony

29 CICERO, *ON THE AGRARIAN LAW* 2.73

In 63 the tribune P. Servilius Rufus brought forward a massive piece of agrarian legislation. Its centerpiece was the creation of a commission of ten to supervise the purchase and assignment of public lands in Italy, including areas previously untouched by this type of legislation. Colonies would be founded and lots of six or seven acres were to be distributed to 5,000 citizens. This number seems rather low for multiple colonial foundations, as citizen colonies now numbered in the thousands. In response to this bill Cicero, while consul, delivered four speeches against the proposal. The passage cited here comes from one of his speeches to the assembly. Disingenuous or not, Cicero's condemnation of the bill was successful and it was withdrawn.

Of more importance is the view of early Roman colonization presented by Cicero in this passage and also echoed in other sources. By the mid-first century Italian colonization no longer had a military purpose, as Rome's position in Italy was secure and south of the Po all free Italians possessed Roman citizenship. Latin colonies still existed in the area of Italy between the Po and the Alps, but they were to have only a transitory existence in this status as by the end of the 40s they had become citizen municipalities. The colonies of this period had other than military functions. They owed their foundation to social, political, and economic considerations such as the relief of the urban poor or rewards for veterans.

> In this matter as in other affairs of state it is worth remembering the care shown by our ancestors who founded colonies in various locations at the hint of danger so that these were not so much towns in Italy as the ramparts of empire.

30 APPIAN, *THE CIVIL WARS* 1.7.26

The following passage is from Appian's general work on Roman history written in the early second century AD. It comes from the section dealing with the civil wars that eventuated in Augustus' rule. It is part of a larger discussion of Roman public land, which played a central part in the opening phase of the civil war and which the Romans had divided to found their colonies as well as making assignments of land to individuals. His view is essentially that expressed by Cicero in the preceding passage, but he makes a strange distinction between founding cites and enrolling colonists, which appears to be a misunderstanding of the fact that some Roman colonies were simply re-foundations of existing states, such as the one at Velitrae.

> The Romans subjugated one part of Italy after another by war, and in the course of this conquest they founded cities or enrolled their own colonists for cities already established. They planned these foundations to serve in place of strongpoints.

31 LIVY, 4.11.3

The founding of a colony at Ardea by senatorial decree was done on the basis of a motion of both consuls of 442. The decision to found the colony according to Livy arose out of an unjust decision of the popular assembly given in 446 concerning a local dispute between the Ardeans and Aricia that converted the holdings of the inhabitants of Ardea, a Rutulian town, into Roman public land. Livy claims that, although the colony was publicly announced as directed against Volscian attacks, it was really a means to redress this unfair though popular decision. The civil strife in Ardea and the Volscian attack in the following year lend plausibility to Livy's picture of the situation.

Unlike the broad general statements of Cicero and Appian, which claim that the establishment of colonies was a defensive measure, in this case the main reasons in our source are political and moral. Certainly, in the case of other early Latin colonies such as Velitrae the sources also record economic motives. However, purely military motives should not be excluded from consideration. Ardea was sited about twenty-two miles southeast of Rome and about three miles from the coast at the foot of the Alban Mount. It served as a barrier to the southern approaches to Rome, and its strategic location served as a defensive position against Volscian expansion north into southern Latium, which is evidenced by the many attacks of this highland people against it.

The three-man commission elected by the assembly is the normal mechanism used to found colonies. These men were invested with *imperium* because the foundation was a quasi-military venture. The names in the text are probably authentic. In general, Livy seems to have used archival sources as the basis for his notices on colonial foundations.

The Senate issued a decree that, since the city of Ardea had been reduced to a few inhabitants on account of civil strife, settlers were to be enrolled to form a defense against the Volsci. This decree was published to deceive the tribunes and people to the fact that the [previous] judgment was being rescinded. However, the consuls privately agreed that a much greater number of Rutulians would be enrolled in the colony than Romans and that no land would be divided among the colonists except that which had been set aside previously under that disreputable decision and that no land would be given to any Roman before it had been distributed to all the Rutulians. And so the land was returned to the Rutulians. Agrippa Menenius, Titus Cloelius Siculus, and Marcus Aebutius Helua were elected to the three-man land commission in charge of founding the colony.

Military tribunes with consular powers

One of the most difficult problems in the history of the early Republic is the appearance of military tribunes with consular powers as replacements for the consuls as chief executive and military officers beginning in 444. Even the official title of these magistrates is uncertain. Livy, who provides the only continuous account of the period, varies in his references to them. Most frequently he simply calls them military tribunes, but he also refers to them as military tribunes with consular powers and more rarely as consular tribunes. The office manifests striking variations in the number of office-holders and in the frequency of its appearance.

Almost all aspects of the office are controversial. In part, this is due to the ambiguous nature of evidence. In part, the sources that we depend upon have no very clear understanding of the institution and their narrative is often distorted by the projection of later political developments into the politics of the fifth and fourth centuries. Further difficulties result from the fact that the office disappeared after 367.

In origin they seem to have been the military tribunes of the legion invested with special competences. It is significant that in 362, within five years of the final disappearance of military tribunes with consular powers, the tribunes of the legion, who had earlier been selected by the consuls, were elected by the people. This change can be seen as a concession to a popular demand to have a greater voice in the choice of their officers in parallel to that which they had had with the election of consular tribunes. Establishing a connection between these different types of tribunes is made easier by the fact that military tribunes, at least in the later periods, had general duties and were not linked to specific units within the army.

It might be expected that these magistrates, as consular replacements, must have had *imperium*. Many modern scholars have denied it. However, this seems an impossible position. How could the Roman state have functioned for extended periods without magistrates with *imperium* or how could the military tribunes with consular powers have held independent command as they did? In addition, Livy provides clear evidence despite contrary interpretations that they were elected by the *Comitia Centuriata*, the same assembly that elected consuls and later other magistrates holding this power. They must also have had the right to their own auspices, that is the right to ascertain the will of the gods with respect to state-sanctioned activity. This right was crucial to the independent exercise of *imperium* in general and of military command in particular.

The major objection to the possession of full consular *imperium* by the tribunes is the absence of any record of triumphs celebrated by military tribunes. One late source claims that they did not possess the right to this supreme military distinction. However, this evidence is of questionable value. Given the fact that they must have had the same *imperium* and auspices as the consuls, the absence of consular tribunes from the *Fasti Triumphales* or list of those who had triumphed, set up in the Augustan period, is not as strong an objection to their right to triumph as it might seem. According to its editor the list has a large gap precisely in the period when there were military tribunes. In addition, it appears clear that during those years a serious military situation of the type that might lead to a triumph for a victorious commander was usually met either by the election of consuls, except after 406, or by the appointment of a dictator. A further point of some interest is that the record of the tribunes was less successful than that of the consuls. Especially in the early years of the new office, divided command and internal disputes often led to a lack of success on campaign. Given the limitations of our evidence it seems more reasonable to accept that military tribunes had the right to triumph just as consuls and dictators acting under their own auspices did.

Perhaps the most difficult question concerning the consular military tribunate is why it existed at all. The ancient sources predominantly assign political reasons for its creation. They represent its creation as a stage in the struggle of plebeians for admission to the consulship. Livy claims that the tribunes of the plebs had brought their agitation to such a point that the levy could not proceed and in desperation the patricians agreed to the creation of this office, which would be open to plebeian candidates as a way of avoiding pollution of the consulship with non-patricians. Against this explanation is that very few of the known consular tribunes have plebeian names. In addition, the strange variation of numbers and the alternation with consulship do not fit easily with a political explanation.

Livy introduces as an alternative explanation, which he does not support, that there were simply too many wars for two consuls to handle and so a new magistracy was required with more members to meet these pressing tasks. These responsibilities included not only military command but also administrative and other duties at home. However, there are serious problems in positing any relationship between military needs and the office of military tribune. First, the decision to hold an election for them would have taken place before the opening of the campaigning season and so the Senate, which appears to have made the decision each year whether or not to appoint them, could not have known what the coming year's military demands were going to be. Second, the need for military leadership in critical situations was regularly met until 406 by the appointment of consuls or a dictator. The varying numbers of tribunes also present a problem. The fluctuations do not seem to accord with the annalists' report of the dangers threatening Rome. Finally, the mostly dismal record that the military tribunes compiled in the field would have done nothing to recommend the continuation of the office for military reasons.

It has been suggested that the variations in time and numbers is to be explained not by a single cause but by the supposition that the office met a variety of needs over time. Nevertheless, in some years we have tribunes appointed, but the annalistic record preserves nothing of any note, as Livy indicates, for 369. The regularities after 405 in numbers and in the appearance of the post make an *ad hoc* explanation unlikely.

Growing administrative needs have also been used as an explanation for the institution of the office, and when the consulate was restored the number of magistrates was increased. The fluctuating numbers are an objection to this explanation, as they are to the one based on military needs. There is no doubt that state business increased during this period, and this would be particularly so with the beginning of the final war against Veii in 406. However, in the following period the sharp variation in military needs of which we have some idea does not fit this changing pattern even assuming some constancy in internal administrative needs. Further, this explanation takes no account of the restoration of the consulship in 367 and later. If need alone was the determining factor the reversion is a problem.

In the end there is no clear solution as to why the Romans first used and then discarded this office. Much of the plebeian–patrician conflict in which it is embedded in our accounts appears to be fictional. But two points stand out. Immediately before the introduction of consular military tribunes a tribune of 445 passed the Lex Canuleia. The law removed the barrier to intermarriage between patricians and plebeians, which had been put in place by the Decemvirate five years previously. At the termination of the office in 367 the Licinian–Sextian Laws formally opened the consulship to plebeians, though there in fact seemed to have been no legal bar. Whatever the fictions in the historical record it is hard not to see a connection to the struggle of the orders. The fact that so few plebeians were elected is less of an objection than it seems. As one scholar has recently pointed out, having access to office is not identical with actually being elected. The traditional methods used to attain electoral success were in patrician hands. It was they who had military experience. It is then less surprising that plebeians were rarely elected even when there was an opportunity to do so.

No explanation can meet all of the problems that the history of this office engenders. The record is too tendentious and fragmentary to allow us to see clearly the factors at work. There are no definitive solutions, only possibilities.

The creation of military tribunes with consular powers

32 LIVY, 4.6.5–8

Livy precedes this account with a passage depicting a political meeting at which one of the tribunes asks the consuls why plebeians could not hold the consulship.

The reply was that plebeians were not entitled to exercise the auspices, without which independent military command was impossible. Despite this statement, repeated in other sources, there seems to have been no bar to plebeians using the auspices. Certainly, after the opening of the consulate to plebeians in 367 the issue was never raised. Indeed, there appears to have been no legal bar to a plebeian's holding the consulate, and in the early Republic plebeians had done so. Rather, it seems that the special religious prerogatives of patricians as well as their wealth and influence allowed them to create a *de facto* monopoly where no legal impediment existed. Canuleius was tribune in 445.

> Canuleius became influential because of his victory over the patricians and through popular favor and this incited the other tribunes to fight with all their resources for their proposal [to open the consulate to the plebeians] and though there was a daily, growing rumor of impending war to hinder the levying of troops. When nothing could be accomplished in the Senate because of the tribunes' interruptions, the consuls held a meeting of the leading men in private. It appeared that victory would have to be conceded either to their opponents at home or to their external enemies....
> The result of their discussions was that they would allow the election of tribunes with consul powers who were either patricians or plebeians, but there would be no change to the status of the consulship. This ruling satisfied both the tribunes and plebs as a whole.

The first election of military tribunes in 362

33 LIVY, 7.5.9

Some scholars have connected the introduction of elective military tribunes with the end of the consular tribunate in the sense that this was an alternative concession to the people. The five-year interval is not necessarily worrisome, as the changes in the consulship of 367 might well have slowed further changes as the system adapted itself to this new situation. The true origin of the term *Rufuli* was unknown to the later antiquarian tradition, but presumably came from the red band worn on their tunics to distinguish them from their elected colleagues.

> In that year [362] it was decided for the first time to elect the legionary military tribunes. Before that commanders selected them just as is now the case with those military tribunes they call *Rufuli*.

2

THE DEVELOPMENT OF
THE MANIPULAR ARMY

The iron century

The end of the Roman monarchy at the close of the fifth century opened a period of internal instability and external threat that was to endure until the Gallic sack of the city in the early fourth century and its immediate aftermath.

Internally a struggle for power that the ancient sources characterize as a struggle between patricians (see pp. 4–5) and plebeians emerged as the central issue in domestic politics. The narratives of this conflict are not to be trusted in detail, but an overall picture emerges of a struggle by a diverse movement of those outside the elite, centered on the issues of land, debt, military service, and access to political power. Certainly, some of those involved in the dispute with the patricians must have been men of substantial property as the struggle for political office and the use of the army as a political weapon against the patricians indicate.

The economic difficulties that figure so prominently in this clash of interests were exacerbated by a possible economic decline visible in central Italy in the course of the first half of the century. There are a number of indicators of this economic deterioration. There is a general decline in the quantity and quality of Roman and Latin material in this period. Of more significance is the fact that, though the sixth century opens with significant temple building, there is a hiatus after 484, continuing until the last third of the century. The apparent accuracy of the sources in reporting such undertakings renders their silence more important. Further support is provided by archaeological evidence for building at Rome, which is virtually non-existent for the fifth century.

In addition, Livy and Dionysius record pestilences and food shortages at Rome in the course of the fifth century. These epidemics were serious enough so that at times there were not enough men available for a levy. Reports of food shortages or famines cluster in this period. They are concentrated in the years from 509 to 384, whereas after this period until the first century they are relatively infrequent.

Rome's internal problems were in part brought on by an almost continuous series of conflicts. Two of these dominate the tradition, the wars with the Etruscan city of Veii ten miles north of Rome and the wars with a series of Italic peoples, the Sabines, Aequi, and Volsci.

42

The latter were part of a movement of Apennine peoples, who at the beginning of the fifth century began a prolonged migration into the Tyrrhenian plains of central and southern Italy. What differentiates this movement from earlier ones appears to be its extent and the large-scale military action it generated.

These peoples ringed Latium in a broad semicircle extending from the northeast to the Tyrrhenian Sea. The territory of the Sabines, who some ancient sources saw as the ancestors of the Sabellians of the south, lay northeast of Rome and stretched from the western side of the upper Tiber valley northeast into the Apennine highlands above the Tiber. The land of the Aequi extended south from Sabine country. They were concentrated on the upper Anio (a tributary of the Tiber) and in the Tolerus valley. South of the Aequi the Hernici inhabited the Trerus valley, with their territory extending to the eastern border of Latium. Finally, to the southeast and south of Latium lay the territory of the most formidable of these tribes, the Volsci, who originally seemed to have had their center in the Liris valley.

We possess almost no information about the internal political organization of these peoples. Presumably, as with the Samnites, their highland settlements were organized on some sort of cantonal arrangement with village headmen and perhaps tribal assemblies. Their economy probably consisted of herding and mixed farming. The need for pasture for their animals must have meant that they had been in constant contact with the inhabitants of the plains. Infiltration and settlement in the plains must have been going on for centuries.

At the beginning of the fifth century the situation seems to have changed dramatically. What had been a constant interchange of people and goods became an invasion that resulted in fighting for most of the fifth century. The reasons for the movements of these Apennine people at the end of the sixth century are far from clear. The most frequent explanation offered has been that of overpopulation. But it does seem unlikely that all of these tribal groupings would suddenly have been affected by increasing population simultaneously. There were probably other factors that remain hidden from us by the nature of our sources. The waves of the movement seem often to have proceeded in accord with the rite of the Sacred Spring, which functioned as a sort of communal sacrifice to avert disaster. Everything born in the spring following the vow was to be sacrificed. However, children born at that season were not literally immolated. They were dedicated to the god of war and then on reaching adulthood were forced to leave the community and seek a new home. It seems likely that one function of the rite was to drain off excess population. Such practices led to constant small-scale warfare and raiding, though it seems clear that, as with the Samnites in the fourth century, large expeditions could occasionally be mounted.

Our knowledge of the equipment of these sixth-century warriors is limited. The most that can be said is that the most common finds of protective equipment are helmets and the so-called chest protector or *kardiophylax*, which is essentially a disk of bronze measuring seventeen to thirty-five centimeters in diameter. It was affixed by a strap or metal band over the shoulder and attached to a back plate. There are parallels for it in Etruria and Latium. No shields have as yet been found. Probably, the majority were made of perishable materials such as wood and hide.

Spearheads have been found in this area; all are made of iron, as are the spear butts. They display a range of sizes that could indicate the use of thrusting spears and javelins. The other major offensive weapon was the sword. Swords are made of iron and reproduce the characteristics of the Greek hoplite sword, that is a short iron sword whose blade widened toward its point. The Italian specimens are two-edged.

More difficult to assess is the evidence for the use of Greek hoplite equipment. Finds of actual Greek equipment are rare. The bulk of evidence for the use of hoplite equipment is pictorial. Given the expense of hoplite equipment and its circumscribed use at Rome it would seem extremely doubtful that it was widely used by these peoples. It may have been confined to a small proportion of the elite. In addition, given the small-scale nature of much of the warfare in this period, phalanx fighting is unlikely to have played a significant part.

It is generally agreed that the sources for this period must be assessed critically. This holds true especially in the domain of warfare because of its close connection with the political and social standing of the elite. The reliability of the general framework of these wars seems to be supported by elements in the tradition. First, despite a number of anachronisms about the nature of these wars, the annalists' accounts contain an indication of the true nature of these conflicts, which is that much of the fighting was not done by large forces but mostly consisted of mutual raiding. The locations of and the foundation dates for various colonies yield a reasonable outline for these wars. It seems that the tradition preserved the general outline of events as well as some significant episodes, but that the narrative of individual events is untrustworthy.

The course of the wars against the Sabines, Aequi, and Hernici

The hostilities of this period manifest a very different character than later Roman wars. While the latter often had political or expansionist aims, the primary goal of these struggles was the survival of the Roman state against what appear to have been unfavorable odds. The seriousness of the struggle is apparent from the internal political difficulties and the economic problems of this period. In addition, on Rome's northern border the fifth century was punctuated by serious wars with Veii. The Sabines and Veii presented the most direct threat to Rome, as there were no intervening peoples to act as a buffer. However, members of the Latin League and other Latin states stood between Roman territory and the Aequi and Volsci. Moreover in 486 the Romans concluded a treaty with the Hernici, separating the Aequi and Volsci, which gave them control of a portion of what later became the *Via Latina*. Almost nothing is known of the Hernici beyond the remains of a few polygonal structures in their territory and the possibility that they may have had some form of communal government centered at the strategically important site of Anagnia. The treaty is said by our sources to be essentially the same as the treaty of 493 between Rome and the Latin League. The alliance brought the Romans a number of benefits. First, it provided an additional buffer against the Aequi and Volsci as well as a wedge between their territories which made combined operations by them more difficult. Further, it opened a route around the north side of Monte Lepini that allowed the Romans to threaten the Volsci from the northeast. The annalistic narrative indicates that for most of the fifth century the Hernici provided the Romans and the Latin League with dependable support.

The course of these wars, which consisted for the most part of mutual raiding, is hard to trace. The crucial battle of the war with the Aequi came at the Algidus pass in 431. Though the details of the battle cannot be trusted there is no reason to doubt the importance of the battle or its outcome. It ended the forward pressure of the Aequi and they were slowly forced back into the Apennines. Fighting continued in a desultory fashion until the 380s. By the beginning of the third century they had ceased to exist as an independent people.

The Volsci proved to be the most difficult of Rome's adversaries. It was to the Romans' advantage that most of the fighting took place in the area of southern Latium outside of their own territory. The annalists present a rather confused account of the fighting that is difficult to follow. In the fifth century the Romans and Latins made deep incursions into Volscian territory so that by 400 Volsci power was waning, and by 300 they had become so acculturated that they seem to have disappeared as an identifiable ethnic group. In the course of these conflicts Rome's former allies the Hernici were also brought under control.

Rome's victory in these wars was made possible by a number of factors. Despite occasional problems stemming from the pressure of the military levy the Romans possessed the necessary reserves of manpower in conjunction with the Latins and the Hernici to deal with what turned out to be a century and a half of a war of attrition. Also Rome's geographical position was favorable. It was in the north and northeast that Roman territory fronted on its enemies. In the principal theaters of war against the Aequi and Volsci it was the Latins and Hernici whose territory was directly menaced and who bore the heaviest share of the fighting. Finally, from the beginning of these conflicts the Romans seized and colonized strategic points that controlled access to Latium from the enemy territory.

The migration of the hill peoples: the Ver Sacrum or Sacred Spring

34 STRABO, *GEOGRAPHY* 5.4.12

Strabo came from Amaseia in Pontus in north central Asia Minor. Born about 64 BC, during the reign of Augustus (27 BC – AD 14) he wrote a geography in seventeen books, which is our most important geographical source for the Roman Empire. He wrote at least part of the work in the reign of Augustus' successor, Tiberius (AD 14–37). This passage occurs in the section of Strabo's survey of Italy that deals with the lands and peoples of the Apennines from north to south as well as Campania. More immediately he is describing the origins of the Samnites of the southern Apennines (see pp. 42f.). His account seems to reflect the migration of various peoples and the expansion of settlement in the Apennines in this period.

The Opici mentioned by Strabo appear to have been an early group that inhabited a substantial portion of the Apennines before being displaced by the migrating Sabellians.

It seems reasonable to assume from the ancient evidence that Sacred Springs were a major mechanism by which Sabellian communities expanded and produced new community and tribal groupings. The Sacred Spring's function has generally been seen as a mechanism to relieve problems of overpopulation: in essence a religious act designed to respond to communal calamities and stress.

> The Sabines were at war with the Umbrians for a long time and made a vow, just as some Greeks do, to dedicate everything born in the course of this year. After their victory they sacrificed some of them, and dedicated others. When a food shortage ensued, someone said that it was also necessary to dedicate the children born in that year; they did this and called the children born at that time sons of Mars. When they had reached adulthood the community sent them out to settle elsewhere with a bull as their guide. It came to rest in the country of the Opici, who lived in villages scattered over their territory. They expelled the natives and settled there and sacrificed the bull to Mars, the god who had given them rule in accordance with the pronouncement of their prophets.

35 LIVY, 6.12.2–6

Livy raises an important point; over a century of warfare was required until the Aequi and Volsci were subdued. Livy's discussion is in the context of a major Roman expedition under A. Cornelius Cossus, dictator in 385. The annalistic narrative in both Livy and Dionysius gives what is basically an anachronistic picture based on traditional battle description and stock themes. Behind these accounts lay a tradition that recorded place-names and military actions along with the names of commanders and other important figures. Using this bare structure, elaborate battle narratives conforming to general Hellenistic rules of battle depiction were elaborated. The passage describing the mutual raiding between the Sabines and Romans (36) must have been typical of the vast majority of the fighting.

> I have no doubt that in addition to satiation that must occur to those reading about these constant wars with the Volsci through the course of so many books the question will suggest itself which has occurred to me in my amazement while reading those writers who lived closer in time to these events: from what source did the Aequi and Volsci, defeated so many times, get their troops? What explanation can I give, since these early writers have passed over this matter in silence? It seems most probable that it was the result of the intervals between the wars just as is now

the case in Roman levies, that different age groups were drafted time and again for the frequent beginnings of wars, that the armies were not always enrolled from the same peoples, although it was always the same tribe that waged war, or that there was a huge population of free males in those areas that now are a meager seedbed for soldiers and are only kept from being a wasteland by gangs of Roman slaves.

36 LIVY, 2.26.1–4

This raid was part of the continuing struggle with the Sabines begun in 505 and which lasted with some intensity to 449. The picture presented is probably typical of the type of encounter most frequent in the war, the mutual raiding that predominated in the struggle against the mountain peoples. This particular episode took place in 495. A. Postumius is A. Postumius Regellenis, who had been the victor at Lacus Regillus. P. Servilius Priscus was the first of his family to be consul and was victorious in the same year over the Aurunci.

At the beginning the Sabines also struck fear into the Romans, but it was a hostile incursion rather than a war. It was announced in the city during the night that a Sabine army engaged in a raid had advanced as far as the Anio and that farmhouses in that area had been everywhere plundered and burnt. A. Postumius, who had been dictator in the war against the Latins along with the consul Servilius, was immediately dispatched with a picked body of troops. The Roman cavalry surrounded the enemy who were wandering through the fields, who put up no resistance to the Roman infantry. They were worn out by their nocturnal march and plundering, and many of those in the villas were stuffed with food and drink. They scarcely had the strength to flee. Within a single night the war against the Sabines was announced and brought to an end.

37 LIVY, 4.27.1–29.4

The major military action of 431 was a combined campaign of the Aequi and Volsci against the Romans. In Livy's narrative it takes place against a background of internal strife between the Senate and the plebeians as well as between the two consuls. Livy paints a picture of a city weakened by internal strife and the plague using all of its resources to meet a determined enemy attack. Given what must have been a paucity of details, this narrative is certainly embroidered. It illustrates one of Livy's most fundamental themes: the ability of the external enemy to bring the state together and stir Roman patriotism.

Doubts have persisted concerning the historicity of the battle. Most have centered on the dictatorship of Postumius Tubertus. But it is now generally accepted. There seems to have been some confusion about the date, though this seems to stem from uncertainty rather than deliberate fabrication. In addition, Tubertus is given a triumph in the *Fasti*, which suggests the battle was mentioned in very early sources. A strong argument for the authenticity of the battle is that the campaigns that follow, which resulted in the driving out of the Aequi from the Algidus valley, only make sense on the assumption of a prior major victory.

The Algidus pass figures frequently in the account of the Roman struggle with the Aequi, perhaps most famously as the site of the victory of Cincinnatus as dictator in 458. It is a natural conduit for an invasion from Aequian territory into southern Latium. By 418 it was garrisoned and closed to the Aequi. The account of the battle is constructed for the most part of heroic commonplaces focusing on the Romans, although Latin and Hernician troops fought on the Roman side.

> After he had divided his army with the consul Quinctius, the dictator [A. Postumius Tubertus] made his way to the enemy [encampment]. In parallel with the two enemy camps which were separated from each other by a small space the dictator and the consul set up their camps about 1,000 feet from those of the enemies. The dictator's camp was closer to Tusculum while the consul's lay nearer to Lanuvium. So there were four camps in the middle of the plain, which was not only suitable for small sorties, but also had sufficient room for setting up battle lines.
>
> From the moment they set up camp the Romans were engaged in incessant small-scale encounters with the enemy. The dictator willingly allowed these engagements to imbue his men with an expectation of total victory by comparing their own forces with those of the enemy through the continuing results of these engagements.
>
> The enemy, having no hope of success in a fair fight, attacked the consul's camp during the night, risking an uncertain outcome. The enemy's shouts not only alerted the guards at the consul's camp but also the dictator and the entire army.
>
> The consul lacked neither the courage nor the plans that the situation required. He reinforced the guard at the camp's gates with a part of his troops, and with the rest he safeguarded the top of the palisade. In the other Roman camp, since the situation was less serious, more attention was given to what had to be done. Help was immediately dispatched to the consul's camp under the command of the legate Sp. Postumius Albus, and then the dictator with a portion of his troops by means of a small detour sought a position totally separated from the action from which he launched an unexpected attack on the enemy rear. His legate Q. Sulpicius was left in charge of the camp while he assigned his cavalry to his legate M. Fabius.
>
> He ordered his men not to move before dawn since it would be difficult to move a force at night during such confusion. Everything that a prudent and energetic commander might order or execute was done by him. He gave a splendid example of his courage and planning by an act meriting no ordinary praise. He sent M. Geganius with select cohorts to attack the

enemy camp, which he had learned was now under strength since the majority of the enemy's force had left it. After he had attacked the enemy troops who were fixed on the outcome of their fellows' peril and not watchful of their own safety and who had neglected their own watches and guard posts, he almost captured the camp before the enemy knew it was under attack. Then as had been agreed a smoke signal was sent so that the dictator could see it and he ordered there to be a general announcement that the enemy camp had been captured.

It was now dawn and there was a clear view of the action. Fabius attacked with his cavalry and the consul made an assault from the camp against the now frightened enemy. In another part of the field the dictator attacked the enemy's second line and reserves. Victorious with both his cavalry and infantry the dictator pressed upon an enemy beset by wild shouts and sudden disruptions.

So being hemmed in on every side the entire enemy force would have paid the price of their rebellion to the last man unless a Volscian, Mettius Valens, a man distinguished in deeds rather than birth, had shamed his men, who were already crowding into a circle, by saying "Will you offer yourselves to the weapons of the enemy without striking back and unavenged? For what purpose do you bear arms and why have you, men unruly in peace and sluggish in war, begun this war voluntarily? What hope is there for you standing here? Do you think some god will protect you or snatch you away from here? The route to safety lies through cold steel. Follow where I have gone, if you want to see your homes, parents, wives, and children. Follow me! You are armed and your way is barred not by a wall or a palisade but by armed men. You equal them in strength and courage, but are superior because of necessity, which is the final and ultimate weapon."

They renewed their shouts and emulated him in word and deed. They pressed back the cohorts of Postumius Albus where they faced them. The Romans were forced back until the dictator arrived after his men had returned, and this spot became the central point of the battle. The success of the enemy rested on Mettius alone. On both sides there were wounded men everywhere and slaughter to match. Even the Roman commanders fought while wounded. Only Postumius left the battle line, when hit by a rock, as his skull was fractured. But neither the dictator's wounded shoulder nor Fabius having his thigh almost pinned to his horse or the consul's loss of an arm took these commanders out of the battle line.

Messius' attack with his band of fearless young men brought them through the enemy dead to the Volscian camp, which had not yet been captured. It was on this point that all the Roman forces focused. The consul pursued the dispersed enemy to their camp, and then attacked it and its palisade; there, too, the dictator moved his forces. The assault was undertaken with the same energy as the battle. It is said that the consul also took the Roman standard and cast it into the camp to make his men more eager in their assault, and the first break in the camp's defenses was made in an effort to recover it. Then the dictator breached the palisade and carried the fight into the camp.

At this point the enemy began to throw away their arms and surrender. After the capture of these men and their camp all were sold into slavery except for the senators. A part of the booty was returned to the Latins and Hernici who could recognize their own goods and the rest was put up for sale by the dictator.

Rome and Etruria

To its north Rome directly bordered potentially hostile territory. Against the Aequi and Volsci the Latin states and the Hernici served as buffers. But, on the border with Etruria, Rome possessed only the barrier of the Tiber, which was easily fordable.

Etruria itself was divided by geography and topography into three main areas. The northern portion, bounded by the natural frontier of the Apennines to the north, was marked off from southern Etruria by the Fiora valley on the south, and on the west it fronted the Tyrrhenian Sea. This region abounded in metal-bearing ores, especially iron, that from the eighth century had attracted Greek traders. Southern Etruria, delimited by the Tiber on the east and the sea on the west, offered more attractive conditions for farming. The landscape was less hilly and the volcanic soil richer. Finally, the inland area lay up against the Tiber and the upper Arnus (Arno) rivers, with major settlements at Clusium, Orvieto, and Perusia.

The Etruscans also expanded outside of their heartland. To the south, probably from the late seventh century, they established settlements in the fertile Campanian plain. To the north, perhaps at the same time, the Etruscans expanded into the Po valley.

Etruscan expansion in these areas was not a concerted effort, but the work of individual leaders and their followers. Despite a common language and cultural identity the Etruscan cities appear to have rarely acted in concert. We have evidence for a league of twelve Etruscan cities that met at the as yet unidentified site of Fanum Voltumnae, which probably lay in the territory of Volsinii in the south. Though some of the sources mention the league making political decisions and even the existence of a league army, the narrative of annalists reveals a picture of independent military and political action by Etruscan cities and only temporary alliances between them.

By 500 most of the Etruscan cities seem to have been ruled by oligarchies whose members were linked in close family units. However, the literary tradition asserts that at an earlier period kings were the norm. In fact, we hear of a king at Veii as late as the 430s or 420s (see p. 52), but this appears to have been an exceptional situation that angered other Etruscan states. Given the scanty evidence available, these states seem to have been marked by sharp social and economic cleavages between the ruling elite and the rest of the population which must have limited the military effectiveness of the Etruscans.

We know almost nothing about Etruscan military practice beyond the type of tactical formation and equipment they used. Command appears to have been exercised by monarchs or their relatives. Presumably in oligarchical states the chief magistrates performed the same functions.

We know more about Etruscan military equipment. From the mid-seventh century hoplite equipment began to spread in Etruria, though at different rates depending on region. But this adaptation of Greek equipment was not uniform. The evidence presents a much more varied picture of Etruscan weaponry than we find in Greece. Helmet types include both native and Greek types. There are representations of different shield types, including a shield that looks like the Roman *scutum*. It appears that native and non-Greek equipment types remained in use beside Greek equipment.

The evidence for Etruscan tactics has already been discussed (see pp. 15f.). Given the presence of the heavy thrusting spear in iconography and in weapons finds it is probable that they fought in a phalanx-like formation as the Roman sources claim. A much more divided social structure based on a sharper distinction between the elite and the rest of the population should have produced a relatively small number of men who could serve as hoplites and limited the poorer classes to service as light-armed and in support roles.

Rome and Veii

Rome's earliest military problems in Etruria involved its closest neighbor to the north, Veii. The city was situated on a high plateau in an extremely strong position. On all sides except the northwest the site was bounded by steep cliffs and in addition surrounded by the Cremera River (Valchetta) on the western side, while a tributary of the Cremera bounded the plateau on the east. It was only about 450 that these natural defenses were supplemented by the construction of a defensive wall, perhaps as a result of Roman pressure.

Veii's territory was larger, healthier, and more fertile than Rome's. North of the city there was an extensive series of rock-cut tunnels which seemed to have formed part of an elaborate drainage system, which would later play a role in the city's fall to the Romans at the beginning of the fourth century. This system supported an extensive occupation of the countryside. In the later sixth century Veii appears to have had a prosperity mostly based on the wealth of its countryside.

Veii lay along some crucial lines of communication. It commanded two routes across the Tiber. Control of these two routes allowed Veii to command the north–south traffic between Etruria and Latium as well as access to salt pans on the Tiber. In the fifth century Rome disputed Veii's position in a struggle centered at first on the town of Fidenae, which formed a bridgehead for Veii on the Roman bank of the river. Rome's desire to expand its available agricultural land area also played an important role.

There are traces of earlier conflicts with Veii under the kings. However, in the fifth century three major wars took place, in 483–474, 437–425, and 406–396, if the traditional chronology is accurate. One decisive step for Rome was the capture of Fidenae in 425, which eliminated Veii's bridgehead on the Tiber's southern bank. The third and final war seems to have been the result of Roman aggression. The climactic phase of the war was a prolonged siege of Veii itself. The narrative in our sources has been heavily influenced by coloring drawn from the siege of Troy.

The turning point came in 396 with the election of M. Furius Camillus as dictator. Despite the accretion of legend there is no reason to doubt the historicity of the role he played in this war or in the later conflicts in the course of a career that spanned thirty-five years.

The capture and destruction of Veii was of tremendous significance to Rome. The most obvious benefit was the addition of a large and fertile territory. It added approximately 562 square kilometers to the estimated 822 square kilometers the city possessed at the end of the monarchy. The land was incorporated and distributed to individual citizens. This was especially feasible as it was contiguous with Roman territory. Possession of Veii's territory allowed the Romans to control the trade routes that ran north to south across the Tiber and northeast into the Apennine foothills and valleys.

The final attack on Veii

38 LIVY, 5.21.10–14

This excerpt from Livy's description of the fall of Veii is typical of his treatment of military actions. He tends not to be interested in the technical details of the siege, but rather focuses on the emotional state of the participants, especially the besieged. The aim is to create pathos and tension in the reader rather than enlighten him on the actual course of events. Often, as here, there are sudden changes in the situation or the emotions of the participants that create dramatic effects. There seems to have been little or no detail that lay behind this account and much of it stems from Hellenistic precedents that focused on emotion and drama rather than factual material.

The fact that the Roman mine exited into the temple of Juno seems a detail too good to be true, and the preceding paragraph contains a prayer (*evocatio*) by Camillus asking the goddess to abandon her city and take up residence at Rome. The goddess was probably the Etruscan goddess Uni, who served as a city guardian and was equated with the Roman Juno. There is on the southern part of the plateau on which Veii stands in the Piazza d'Armi the remains of a small temple approximately fifty by twenty-six feet which has been identified as the most likely site for the Juno temple. At Rome and in other Latin cities Minerva possessed the epithet Regina or queen. In the Capitoline temple she was associated with Jupiter and Minerva in the central cult of the Roman state. In their wars in Latium and southern Etruria the removal of the protecting deity of the enemy city and its domestication at Rome seem to have been a common feature. Camillus vowed a temple to Juno in 396 at the conclusion of the war, and it was finally dedicated in 392. The family of Camillus may have established a special relationship with Juno Regina, as fifty years later his son dedicated a temple to Juno Moneta, a deity related to Regina of the Capitoline triad.

> The water channel filled with picked troops suddenly poured forth these armed men into the temple of Juno which was located on the citadel. A section of them attacked the enemy stationed on the walls from behind. Another group tore off the bars of the gates. A further section, in response to a bombardment of house roofs of tiles, stones, and rocks, brought fire against them. The whole city was filled with the cries of the fearful and their attackers mixed with the laments of women and children.
>
> In a moment the Veientine troops were thrown down from the walls, the city filled with enemy troops, and the gates lay open. Some of the Romans in formation rushed in, while others mounted the now deserted walls. The city was filled with the enemy and there was fighting everywhere. Then after great slaughter the fighting began to subside. At this point the dictator [Camillus] ordered the heralds to inform the troops to spare the unarmed. That was the end of the bloodshed. The unarmed began to surrender and the dictator gave the troops permission to disperse in search of plunder.

Rome and Etruria after the fall of Veii

The Gallic sack of 390 (see p. 56) seems to have been only a temporary setback for the Romans, but the years that followed were a time of constant warfare with numerous enemies. There were the final struggles with the Aequi and Volsci and confrontation with former allies such as the Hernici and some of the most important Latin cities, such as Tibur and Praeneste.

The north seems to have presented less of a problem. The Romans had by the mid-380s created an acceptable defensive line for themselves and were preoccu-pied elsewhere with campaigns against the Volsci, Gauls, and various Latin cities. The inaction of the Etruscans is harder to explain. It may in part have been due to Gallic pressure. Little is heard of the Gauls until the raid of 367 and the campaign against them in 359, but their appearance in the sources tends to reflect Roman concerns.

The clash in 359 took the form of a plundering raid by Tarquinii, which occupied a high plateau about fifty-five miles northwest of Rome and about three miles inland from its port of Gravisca. A rich and flourishing city in the early period, with close ties to Rome, it had gone into economic decline after 500, though it was still a major Etruscan power. There had been some earlier troubles with the Romans. Livy reports a raid by Tarquinii on Roman territory in 389, but it seems to have been of little consequence. The raid of 359 seems to have been on a larger scale, reaching as far as the Tiber. In response the Romans declared war in 358. Other

Etruscan cities joined the conflict against Rome, but within five years the Romans had been able to assert their primacy, though without any territorial gain. Rome's omission to press the issue further may well have been the result of its engagement elsewhere.

After the conflicts of the 350s Etruria was quiet. It is doubtful whether the Etruscans had the strength to mount a successful attack, and the Romans were involved in serious struggles, first with their Latin allies and then with the Samnites to the south. However, in 311 a new conflict erupted in Etruria. The reasons for it are not clear, but it may be significant that this was at the time when the balance in Rome's war with the Samnites, its most important enemy, had decisively shifted in Rome's favor. Further, 311 was the date at which Rome seems to have doubled its military forces from two to four legions. The latter development points to a more expansive policy. It may be that the Etruscans feared that with the Samnites no longer a major threat they would be the next victims.

The war ended inconclusively in 308, but with Rome in a favorable position for further operations in Etruria and poised to move northeast into Umbria. There was a further series of wars, which by 292 had ended serious Etruscan resistance. There were noticeable differences in the treatment of northern and southern Etruria, with treaties regulating relations in the north, while various degrees of incorporation and expropriation of land took place in the south. Rome was now firmly established in both Etruria and Umbria. Although the process of Romanization through colonization and finally by cultural assimilation seems to have been a long and rather slow process, it was mostly completed by the last century BC.

Rome and the Gauls

The people whom the Romans called Galli or Gauls and the Greeks Keltoi impinged dramatically on Roman consciousness at the beginning of the fourth century. In 387 they sacked Rome and were to be an important psychological if not military factor until the first third of the second century BC.

They were the first transalpine peoples with whom the Romans came into direct contact and their different physical appearance and especially their customs were to leave a lasting legacy of prejudice visible even under the Empire. They can best be characterized by their common language related to Italic and their shared artistic traditions. At its greatest extent the area of Celtic culture stretched from the Atlantic to Asia Minor. The archaeological evidence as well as later Greco-Roman literary evidence points to a highly stratified society in which warriors had a central role. Elite burials are accompanied by the warriors' military equipment such as spears and swords, and religious dedications are often of military equipment. Later literary sources paint a social hierarchy in which warrior chiefs dominated bands of clients, sometimes of very large size.

In the fifth century the Celtic peoples of France and Germany enjoyed extensive contact with the Mediterranean, especially with the Greeks and Etruscans, through elaborate trading networks.

The timing of the Celtic movement into northern Italy as far south as the Apennines is a matter of controversy. The ancient tradition presents us with two dates separated by two centuries, around either 600 or 400. It seems most likely that there had been constant Celtic movement into the area during the sixth century but that this was probably in small-scale warrior bands. However, about 400, large-scale migrations began and resulted in extensive settlement by Gallic tribes in northern Italy.

At the entry of the Gauls into northern Italy the Etruscans dominated the Po valley. Their control of the area evaporated under Celtic pressure. The migration probably unfolded in waves, and Livy knows of at least four of them, of which the most recent were the Senones, who settled on the Adriatic coast. The most important tribes as far as the Romans were concerned were the Insubres north of the Po, with their capital at Mediolanum, the Boii, particularly noted for their savagery by Greco-Roman writers, between the Po and the Apennines, the Cenomani, centered on the lake district, and the Senones. Though these were the areas of major settlement it is clear from archaeological discoveries that the Celts penetrated, on at least a small scale, much farther south in peninsular Italy. The most southerly Celtic find is a helmet from Canosa in Apulia, and we hear of Celtic bands operating even farther south. The initial migration was not the last; there was continued migration into Italy, northern Europe and parts of the eastern Mediterranean. It was only by the second century that the area of Celtic settlement in northern Europe and the Mediterranean began to contract.

The basic economy of these Celtic communities was the typical ancient combination of stock raising and agriculture, with craft production in the characteristic forms of Celtic art. But raiding and mercenary service for various Mediterranean powers also played an important role in the Celtic economy.

The first large-scale encounter of Gaul and Roman ended with the sack of Rome in 387. The Roman sources portray this as the result of a tribal migration, but it was more likely a mercenary band on its way to take service in southern Italy and not averse to raiding and plundering along the way. During the fourth and third centuries Gauls were employed as mercenary troops by major Hellenistic powers also in the eastern Mediterranean. This would explain why the Gauls were so far south as well and explains the absence in the sources of any reference to women and children accompanying them.

The initial battle with the Romans was fought at the Allia, a tributary of the Tiber, which lies on its left bank at the eleventh milestone from the city. Whatever the truth about the course of the battle, it was no doubt a disastrous defeat. Its date is certain, July 18, which was marked as an ill-omened day in the Roman religious calendar. Rome was sacked and despite Roman propaganda to the contrary the garrison on the Capitoline ransomed itself by a large payment of gold. The myth of Rome's redemption from the attack focused on M. Furius Camillus, the conqueror of Veii. But the absence of any references to his victory in our earliest sources make it likely that it was a face-saving legend.

Livy, Plutarch, and other writers describe widespread burning and destruction, which led to extensive rebuilding. However, no archaeological trace of such a burn level has been found. It seems that what the Gauls were interested in was movable plunder, and once the Roman field force had been defeated the lightly fortified city was a tempting target. The lack of evidence for destruction and the rapid recovery of Rome are confirmation of the limited physical effect of the sack. Its psychological consequences were far more profound. The building of a strong fortification wall enclosing the seven hills of the city is only the most concrete manifestation of the anxiety caused by the attack.

Though engaged in fighting the Volsci, Aequi, Hernici, and several Latin towns of which the most important were Praeneste and Tibur, Rome seems to have easily dealt with the Gauls. Gallic raids followed in the 360s and 350s without any serious consequence.

Serious problems seem to have developed at the beginning of the third century when a fresh movement of Transalpine Gauls into Italy led to a coalition between the newcomers and the Gauls of the Po region. The major encounter with the Gauls came in 295 when they fought the Romans as part of a combined Gallic–Samnite army. After an initial Roman defeat and the loss of a praetor, the opposing forces met at Sentinum in Umbria in what was probably the largest battle fought in Italy up to that time, which ended with a decisive Roman victory.

In 232 Gallic territory was annexed by Rome and distributed to colonists. The sources allege this as the reason for the massive confrontation with the Gauls in the following decade, and there is reason to believe them. The initiative had clearly passed to the Romans, and the land distribution made clear to the Gauls the possibility that they would be granted no accommodation by the Romans but would be expelled from their lands. In 225 a major battle took place between a Celtic army assembled from various major tribes and a Roman force of four legions at Telamon near the Tyrrhenian coast in central Etruria. The outcome was the total defeat of the Gauls. This battle marked an essential turning point in Rome's relation with them. From this point on Rome seized the initiative and it was only other military problems that delayed the final subjugation of the Po valley.

The outbreak of the war against Hannibal diverted the Romans from their preoccupations with the Gauls and northern Italy. However, in 200 at the end of the war against Carthage the Romans began a relentless advance in a series of campaigns made more brutal by the fact that Gallic contingents had fought with Hannibal. The major tribes were subjugated and a series of Roman colonies such as Bononia and Aquileia were established to serve to control the area.

A Greco-Roman view of the Gauls

39 STRABO, *GEOGRAPHY* 4.4.2–5

For Strabo, see **34** above. The Greeks had developed a set of standardized descriptions of foreign peoples and places. Ethnographic description covered a number of standard topics, such as location, geography, physical appearance, economy, manner of making war, and psychological characteristics. Much of the material was made up of commonplaces, and the same descriptions were used to characterize very different groups.

There is a particular set of attitudes visible in the descriptions of the peoples of northwestern Europe, and they are used for both Celts and Germans, whom the ancients thought were closely related to each other. As Strabo makes clear, they were struck by the size of the northerners, and other writers mention their whiteness, as striking physical characteristics. Cultural differences are always measured against a Greco-Roman standard, and any deviations from that norm are deemed inferior. Even those characteristics that are thought admirable, such as the warlike nature of the Celts, are balanced against negative traits such as lack of planning and extreme emotional reactions especially in battle. The Celts because of their relations with the Romans excited unusual ferocity on the part of the Romans.

The picture of the Gauls as simple warriors who thoughtlessly deploy for battle is part of the notion of the noble savage and is not borne out by the sources. The few descriptions we have of Romans and Celts in battle, including those of the Allia and Telamon as well as the later account of Caesar (see p. 96), display a grasp of tactics that contradicts Strabo's view.

Strabo mentions three groups of experts. The best known are the Druids, whom the Romans in the imperial period did their best to suppress as agents of resistance to their rule. The Druids controlled all sacrifices, both public and private, and ruled on religious matters. They were also called on to decide disputes, as Strabo points out, though his attempt to assimilate them to Greek philosophers displays the limitations of ancient ethnology. The functions of the other two groups are less than clear.

By the fourth century Celtic craftsmen were subject to a variety of influences from the Mediterranean that profoundly affected their work. Nonetheless, a definable Celtic style emerged especially in the making of jewelry, which particularly struck Mediterranean observers. Celtic male jewelry because of its appearance on the battlefield made a definite impact. For the Greeks and Romans the most striking piece was the Celtic torque, essentially a thick, rigid necklace formed by twisting a band or strip of metal to fit the wearer's neck and heavily decorated. Its use in battle may have had a religious significance, as Celtic gods are often portrayed with the torque.

Head hunting is well attested in the literary sources as well as in Celtic art. Keeping parts of the enemy's body is a custom known in other areas of the ancient world. It is probably to be connected with the idea that possession of the head also gives control over the spirit of the enemy, which can be used to enhance the warrior's power. The other function mentioned in Strabo's description and found in other ancient authors is that the head functioned as a trophy, giving visible proof of the warrior's prowess.

> The people who are now called Gallic and Galatian are mad for war. They are high-spirited and quick to fight, but are straightforward and not malicious. On account of this disposition, if they are roused to anger they

assemble for battle; they do so openly and without considering it in advance. The result is that they are easy to cope with for those who wish to defeat them by guile. So, if someone wants to provoke them by some pretext at any time or place, they are ready to join battle, bringing nothing to the contest except their strength and daring.... Their strength is in part the result of their large size and in part the result of their numbers....

Among all of the Gallic groups in general there are three groups of men who are especially esteemed: the bards, seers, and Druids. The bards are singers and poets, the seers conduct sacred rites and study nature, and the Druids practice moral philosophy in addition to studying nature. The Druids are considered by them to be the most just of men and for that reason are trusted to decide private and public disputes. Previously they acted as arbitrators in warfare and stopped armies arrayed for battle from fighting. The Gauls especially turned over to their judgment cases involving murder.

In addition to their simplicity and liveliness, they display thoughtlessness and are boastful and extremely fond of ornaments. They wear gold ornaments: torques about their necks and chains around their wrists and ankles. Their men of standing wear brightly colored clothes sprinkled with gold. A consequence of this shallowness of character is that they are unbearable when victorious and stricken with terror in defeat. In addition to this simplicity there is also a barbaric and inhuman custom among most of the northern tribes; after battle they hang the heads of their enemies from the necks of their horses and when they arrive home they nail them to the entrances to their houses.

Celtic military equipment

40 DIODORUS SICULUS, 5.30.2–4

Diodorus gives our most detailed description of Celtic military equipment apart from Caesar. The archaeological evidence indicates that he exaggerates the size of the Celtic shield. Extant examples unearthed appear to have been about three and one-half feet long and two feet wide. They are constructed of wooden planks and then covered with hide and have central bosses of various shapes. The animals Diodorus mentions must have been part of the boss. The most frequent shape is oval but other shapes such as square or hexagonal are known. In many ways they resemble Italian shields. Helmets of bronze predominate in the examples found, but iron is also used. The most frequent types in northern Italy are variations of the jockeycap type, which is essentially a metal cap with a peak-like projection designed to protect the wearer's neck, and the Coolus type, which has a more distinct and flattened peak-like neck guard. Both were used by the Romans and other Italic peoples. Specimens of Gallic helmets had been found with sockets for attaching the projecting figures that Diodorus mentions.

Celtic war trumpets appear on the famous Gunderstrup cauldron from Denmark, and actual examples have been found. They are animal-headed with movable jaws.

The use of body armor is infrequent. The sources refer to a group of warriors called the Gaesati who made an especial impression on the Greek and Roman writers. They appear to have been some sort of tribal group living in southern France. The references to them indicate that they served as mercenaries. They are often described as fighting naked. The nakedness may have been ritualistic. This implies that the other Gauls normally did not fight in this manner. Diodorus clearly indicates that they wore clothing. In fact there is archaeological and statuary evidence for chain mail by the third century. Its use appears to have been confined to the nobility because of the expense.

The Celtic warrior who appears in the sources is primarily a swordsman. There are references to the great size and the inferior workmanship of the Celtic sword. Polybius mentions the frequent bending of this sword in battle, which made its owner vulnerable to the short thrusts of which the Roman sword was capable. Archaeological examples indicate that Celtic swords were in fact of high quality, and there is no easy explanation for the bending observed by Greco-Roman authors.

Diodorus does not exaggerate about the size of the Celtic spearhead. Remains of spears as much as eight feet in length have been found. Also a variety of head types are attested, including the serrated head that Diodorus notes. These are too heavy to be used as javelins so that there must have been Celtic spearmen as well as swordsmen in the battle line. Javelin heads are also extant. Arrowheads have also been found, but in general there is little evidence for the use of the bow in battle.

> The Celts employ a man-size shield decorated in a manner that is peculiar to them. The shields are embossed with figures of animals skillfully made with a view to decoration and utility. They wear bronze helmets with large embossed figures which project from the helmet and give the impression that the wearer is of great size.
>
> Some helmets are decorated with horns so made as to give the appearance that they form a single piece .... Some wear iron cuirasses made of chain mail while others satisfied with the protection nature has given them go into battle nude. In place of the short sword they carry long slashing swords which are suspended from iron or bronze chains and worn on the right side. Their spears called *lanceae* have iron heads eighteen inches or more in length; their swords are almost the length of the javelins of other peoples and the heads of their javelins are longer than the swords of others. Some of these missiles come straight from the forge, while others are twisted into spirals for their entire length so as to not only pierce the flesh but mangle it as well. When they are withdrawn they further tear the wound.

The Celtic chariot

41 DIODORUS SICULUS, 5.29.1

Coin representations show chariots whose sides are in the form of double hoops, while the back and front of the vehicle are open. By the time of Caesar the chariot seems to have disappeared on the continent, but it was still a formidable weapon, as Caesar discovered among the British Celts. A later source of the mid-first century mentions a chariot group of three warriors: the fighter and two grooms, one of whom served as a groom and could take the warrior's place if he were killed or wounded.

When traveling and in war they use two-horse chariots which carry a driver and a warrior. On meeting the enemy on battle they cast javelins at them and then descend from the chariot and fight on foot with their swords.

The Celts in battle: the battle of Telamon, 225 BC

42 POLYBIUS, *HISTORIES* 2.27.7–30.8

The battle was fought near the Etruscan city of Telamon situated near the mouth of the Osa River, which flows out into the Tyrrhenian Sea. Polybius, our best source, claims that the reason for the Gallic attack was the distribution of the land that had earlier been confiscated from the Senones to Roman citizens in 232. It convinced them that the Romans no longer aimed to subjugate them, but rather to exterminate them. It has been suggested that the Romans were less interested in colonization than in forming a forward base to serve as a staging point for the conquest of the plain of the Po. Certainly, as soon as danger from Carthage had passed after the Second Punic War they began a thirty-year campaign that ended in the very conquest whose possibility had so frightened the Gauls in 232.

In response the Gauls sought to inflict a decisive defeat on the Romans that would keep them from confiscating their lands. In addition, they hired Gallic mercenaries, the Gaesati. Polybius claims that the army that finally marched into Etruria numbered 50,000 foot and 20,000 horse.

Rome reacted with speed and decisiveness. They brought in supplies and began enrolling legions to confront the Gauls. In all, ten legions of about 5,200 men each were levied, of which eight were for use in Italy: two for each of the consuls, L. Aemilius Papus and C. Atilius Regulus, and four as a reserve stationed at Rome. Polybius says that accompanying both consular armies there were 30,000 allied infantry with a further 2,000 cavalry. So at the crucial battle the Romans had a slight preponderance in infantry, but in cavalry Roman and allied forces totaled 3,200 while the Gauls had over six times as many.

Pappus and his army were stationed at Arminium to defend the recently confiscated lands, while Atilius was dispatched to Sicily. A praetor and allied troops were posted at the borders of Etruria. Polybius claims that the praetor had 50,000 allied foot and 4,000 horse, but these numbers seem far too large for a force commanded by a praetor.

The Gauls crossed the Apennines without difficulty and were able to overrun Etruria unopposed. When they reached Clusium in Etruria they discovered that the praetor and his army were approaching. In response they moved north and engaged the praetor. The battle resulted in a Roman defeat with heavy casualties. Pappus learned of the disaster and managed to bring his army up to the Gallic encampment. His arrival led to the decision by the Gallic leaders to retreat north along the coastal road, as they were too heavily encumbered with booty to fight effectively. The arrival of the army of Atilius from Sardinia at Pisa to the north allowed the double-sided attack described in the following passage.

Several interesting points emerge in Polybius' account. The most important point is the ability of the Celts to deploy their army to meet an unanticipated situation as well as Polybius' notice of their well-deployed battle line. This strongly contradicts the usual picture of the Celts as wild and undisciplined fighters. Further, this is the last mention of the use of the chariot by the Celts in continental Europe. It was replaced by the use of cavalry. The chariot continued to be used in Britain and presented Caesar with problems during his invasions in 55 and 54 BC. Further, this is one of the few Roman battle descriptions that highlights the effectiveness of the light-armed in battle.

Polybius claims that 40,000 Celts were killed and a further 10,000 were captured, which would amount to the practical destruction of the entire force. In fact, this was perhaps the largest engagement in Italy up to that time. The Gauls never again were able to mount a force of such size.

> At this time Gaius Atilius, the consul, had sailed from Sardinia to Pisa and was making his way with his men to Rome. His line of march was in the opposite direction to that of the [Gauls]. When the Celts neared Telamon in Etruria, their foragers fell in with an advance party of Gaius' and were captured. Under questioning by the consul they explained what had happened and signaled the presence of the two armies, stating that the Gauls were quite close and that behind them was Lucius' army. Astonished at what had happened and filled with hope because he seemed to have caught the Gauls between two armies while on the march, he instructed the tribunes to ready the army to advance at a marching pace as far as the ground would allow. Luckily the consul noticed a hill lying above the road, which the Celts must pass by. Taking the cavalry he hurried to take the height and begin the encounter, convinced that in this way he would gain most of the credit for the result.
>
> At first the Celts were unaware of the arrival of Atilius and his army, and guessed that the cavalry of Aemilius had ridden round their flank during the night and gained control of the area. They immediately sent out some of their cavalry and light-armed to contest control of the hill and the

surrounding area. Then, quickly learning of Gaius' presence from prisoners who had been brought in, they lost no time in drawing up their men for battle. They arranged them so that they faced both back and front, as they knew from report and with their own eyes that there were two armies following them, which they expected to meet face to face, and that they were approaching at the same time.

Aemilius' men had learned of the voyage of the other army to Pisa but had no idea that they were so close to it. Then they realized from the battle around the hill that the other Roman army was quite near. So they immediately sent their cavalry to help those struggling around the hill, and drew their infantry up in the normal battle order and advanced against the enemy. The Celts deployed with the so-called Gaesati from the Alpine area in front and the Insubres behind them to face the rear, which was the direction they expected Aemilius to appear from. Against those attacking from the front they arrayed the Taurisci and the Boii from the north bank of the Po, facing in the opposite direction to the former facing Gaius' direct frontal advance. They positioned their chariots and wagons on both wings. They assembled their booty on hills nearby and posted a guard. This battle line was not only formidable in appearance but it was also practical. The Insubres and the Boii wore trousers and light cloaks, but the Gaesati because of their love of glory and courage discarded their garments and fought naked in the front rank with nothing but their weapons. They thought that they would be more effective because some of the ground was covered with brambles and would catch their clothes and hinder their use of their arms.

At first, the battle was confined to the hill and visible to all with so many cavalry from both armies furiously engaged there. At this point the consul Gaius fighting admirably in a hand-to-hand struggle lost his life. The Gauls cut off his head and carried it to their chiefs. The Roman cavalry after a difficult struggle finally gained control of the hill and overcame the enemy. The infantry of both sides were now close to each other, and it was a remarkable and unusual spectacle not only to those present but also to those who could picture it from the accounts they heard. First, it was a fight involving three armies and it was clear that the appearance and action of the armies marshaled against each other would be unusual and extraordinary. Second, how could one not be in doubt either now or at the time of the battle as to whether the Celts were deployed in a dangerous position with two enemy armies advancing on them at the same time, or whether they held the more effective position since they were able to fight both forces simultaneously and at the same time were able to assure the safety of their rear in each direction while most significantly they were absolutely cut off from any possibility of retreat to the rear and any hope of safety by flight? This is characteristic of any formation that faces in both directions. On the other hand, the Romans were encouraged at the enemy being caught in the middle and surrounded on every side, but the Celtic army's shouting and good order terrified them. The Celts had a large number of horn blowers and trumpeters and as the entire army was shouting its war cries it seemed as if the entire countryside had taken voice from them. Equally frightening was the appearance and movement of naked men in the front ranks who were in their prime and of exceptional appearance. All the Celts who formed the front companies were adorned with gold torques and bracelets. The sight of these things both terrorized the Romans and at the same time drove them on by hope of gain so that they were twice as eager to fight.

The light-armed advanced from the Roman armies as usual and launched frequent and effective attacks with their weapons; the Celts in the rear were well protected by their trousers and cloaks, but the naked men in front contrary to their expectations found themselves in a distressing and difficult position. The Gallic shield does not cover the whole body and to the degree that they were naked and large in size, to that extent the missiles struck home. Finally, unable to drive off the javelineers because of their distance and the numbers of missiles falling on them, they were in extreme distress and at a loss. Some of them in mindless rage without plan or purpose fell upon the enemy, exposing themselves and readily died; others retreated step by step, and threw the ranks behind them into confusion because of their open display of fear. In this way the spirit of the Gaesati was broken by the javelin men. The main body of Insubres, Boii, and Taurisci after the Romans had received the javelineers back into their ranks fell upon the Roman maniples, attacking them, and a fierce hand-to-hand struggle took place. Though being cut to pieces, the Celts held their ground. Their courage equaled the enemy's, but both their organization and weapons were inferior. The Roman shields provided more protection and their swords were more effective; their enemies' swords were useful only for thrusting. After the Roman cavalry had attacked them fiercely from higher ground and on their flanks as they rode down from the hill, the Celtic infantry was cut down where it stood and their cavalry turned to flight.

The development of the manipular army

Between the end of the fifth century and the middle of the third century a profound revolution in Roman military tactics took place. Before this the main striking power of the army had been provided by a phalanx of heavy infantry dependent on the heavy thrusting spear and the momentum of their charge to defeat the enemy. This single formation was supplanted by a number of small phalanx-like units known as maniples. These units were now arranged in three distinct lines and within each line intervals separated each of these units and allowed them to operate independently of each other. The Romans now gave battle by deploying their lines successively instead of committing all of their troops at once. This created a flexibly organized reserve that not only could offer support to threatened units but also could be deployed as the encounter developed.

Accompanying this tactical change was the adoption of new equipment; a short sword and a large oval or rectangular shield that provided better protection and enhanced mobility replaced the heavy thrusting spear and the round hoplite shield. In addition, troops were armed with a missile weapon, the *pilum*, that was thrown before contact with the enemy. These changes were accompanied by lightening of body armor that further increased mobility. These developments placed a higher premium on the individual soldier's technical skills, especially in the use of the sword, which must have resulted in a greater need for training and continued practice.

Polybius, writing in the 160s, with personal experience of Roman fighting methods, had pointed out in his comparison of the Macedonian phalanx with Roman battle tactics that the phalanx suffered from severe limitations. For effective deployment it needed open and level ground. Surface irregularities and obstacles such as trees and shrubbery hindered its ability to maintain the cohesion crucial for success. The formation was vulnerable to attacks on its flanks, especially on the right or unshielded side, and on its rear, and by its nature was poorly designed to respond to them. These limitations had become apparent to the Greeks by the end of the fifth century BC, and during the fourth they had experimented with supporting the phalanx with lighter and more mobile forces. The Macedonian armies of Philip II and Alexander the Great, though based on the phalanx, relied for victory on the operation of combined arms. Pyrrhus of Epirus had brigaded troops armed in the Italic fashion with his phalanx during his confrontation with Rome between 280 and 275. However, since the phalanx remained an integral part of such tactics its limitations still greatly affected the outcome of an engagement. The change in Roman tactics gave them all of the advantages of these combined armies while removing the limitations that continued use of the phalanx entailed.

These changes in tactics and equipment were accompanied by changes in the levying of troops and in conditions of service. Pay for military service was introduced, although its scale indicates it was viewed as compensation for service rather than as a wage. A military tax called the *tributum* was introduced which entailed a new view of how the financial burdens of military service were to be met. Linked to this was substitution of the state for the individual as the provider of military equipment. Such compensation and the much cheaper new panoply of the Roman heavy infantryman resulted in the ability to utilize a far larger part of the citizen body and so resulted in changes in the social composition and perhaps political orientation of the army. The basis of the levy shifted away from the Servian census qualifications and became based on the tribes. The unity that had bound the century in its political aspect to its military functions was broken, and this must have further contributed to social and political change.

The chronology, manner and reasons for this change have been the subject of frequent debate. The reasons for this uncertainty lie in the nature of our literary evidence. As mentioned earlier, Roman historical writing as a genre began at the end of the third century at a time when the manipular army had already become standard. The annalistic accounts assumed it had always existed, as they did with so many other Roman institutions. Though war and politics were the major themes of their writing, their descriptions concentrated on psychological states and the actions of commanders rather than on the organization of war. How troops were armed and functioned in battle was of minimal interest. Roman historians tended to avoid technical details for their own sake. Most of the information we have on such changes originates from antiquarian speculation or ethnographic description and not from the historical tradition. But even in these traditions the interest in technical matters appears late.

It is illustrative that the important change in the basic tactical unit from the maniple to the cohort in the course of the second century, though occurring in a period when historical writing was well established at Rome, is never explicitly dealt with by our sources.

Transition from the phalanx to the manipular army appears to have taken place slowly and gradually so that the stages of development were already obscure by the second century. The magnitude of the changes as well as the need to develop new forms of military training must have taken considerable time. Clear evidence for the slowness of the process is provided by the nature of the terminology for the three lines of the army and its constituent parts. Perhaps the most striking example is the name given to troops of the second line, the *principes*. In normal usage such a name should designate troops of the first line as the leading element in the army. Ancient writers found this a difficulty, with some postulating that the troops of the two lines had changed places. Over time the original meaning of the term had become obscure. The same may be said of the name of the first line, *hastati*, which would normally designate troops who used the heavy thrusting spear.

Polybius supplies the fullest and most comprehensive description of the manipular army. He appears to be describing the Roman army as it existed between 220 and 170, although there are anachronisms and mistakes in his account. Even at this late stage the manipular army was still evolving. The third line of the army, the *triarii*, still carried heavy thrusting spears, which were only to be replaced by *pilum* and sword by the end of the second century.

There is some evidence that the developed use of manipular tactics was in place by the first quarter of the third century. However, it is the earliest stages that remain the most confused. But some indications in our sources can provide some sense of the timing and pace of development.

Fourth-century Rome was more belligerent and expansive than it had been earlier. It was able to field a number of armies in different theaters of war simultaneously and with great success with the help of its allies. This is all the more remarkable given the fact that it was engaged simultaneously in conjunction with the Latins in large-scale colonization. From 362 Rome was able to double the number of legions annually levied to two. In 311 that number was doubled to four.

Despite the effects of colonization this large increase in military manpower cannot be explained by natural growth in the population alone, although the subjugation of Veii in 396 more than doubled Roman territory. Even the introduction of state pay at the end of the fifth century could not have substantially enlarged the pool of available manpower, since it functioned as compensation for expenses incurred rather than as actual pay. This increase seems to have been the result of the lowering of the minimum census figure necessary for service in the heavy infantry made possible by the change to the less expensive equipment required by the manipular system.

Thus we have at least some tentative evidence that the process began in the first half of the four century. A hint of what might have happened emerges from Polybius and Dionysius of Halicarnassus. As was mentioned above, the third line of the army, the *triarii*, still retained their heavy thrusting spears as their main offensive weapon. Dionysius, narrating the Pyrrhic War, mentions that the *principes* still fought with spears as their main offensive weapon. This would seem to indicate that the abandonment of the phalanx formation was gradual, with the change to the new weaponry and tactics starting at the front of the army and then gradually moving backwards. This would make sense if the introduction of these new tactics was first seen as a more effective way of weakening the enemy prior to the charge of the phalanx. Thus, there would have been an intermediate stage, a manipular phalanx with combined manipular and phalanx formations in the same battle order. Its descendant is visible in the legion of the Middle Republic when the *triarii* still operated as a phalanx.

The origin and meaning of the term "maniple"

The maniple was the basic tactical unit of the new army. It consisted of two centuries, totaling 120 men in the first two lines, the *hastati* and the *principes*, and containing 60 in the third line. They were arranged so that each line consisted of ten of these units. Each maniple was commanded by two centurions (see pp. 106f.), one in overall command stationed on the right of the maniple and the second more junior centurion on the left, acting under the senior centurion's orders and able to replace him if he were wounded or killed in battle. The unit also had two standard bearers who functioned in the same way as the centurions. Its size seemed to have been dictated by the fact that a single century was too small to act as an independent unit in battle.

43 OVID, *FASTI* 3.115–117

One meaning of the term "maniple" is "sheaf" or "bundle," and the metaphor comes from rural life, as does "cohort," another important term for a military unit. Its basic meaning is "a handful." By the first century AD this seems to have been the normal explanation of the term. There seems to be no other evidence for this standard, and it is not impossible that the standard never existed and that Ovid, a first-century AD poet, or his source has derived it from the common Roman notion about the simplicity and agricultural character of the early Romans.

> Their standards were of hay, but there was as deep a reverence as the eagles now possess.
> They carried these suspended in bundles [*manipulos*] on a long pole and it is for this reason that the soldier is called a *manipularis*.

44 VARRO, *ON THE LATIN LANGUAGE* 5.88

Varro provides evidence of the maniple as the basic tactical unit.

> Maniples are the smallest military units that follow a single military standard.

The origin of the manipular army

45 DIODORUS SICULUS, 23.2.1

This passage repeats a commonplace that Rome was able to conquer its enemies by surpassing them at their own game (see p. 17). This idea also occurs in Polybius' discussion of the Roman equipment.

> The Romans as pupils always surpassed their teachers. In ancient times they used rectangular shields. The Etruscans who fought in a phalanx with round bronze shields forced the Romans to adopt their equipment and as a consequence were defeated by them. Later again, peoples using the same shields as the Romans now do and fighting in maniples were conquered by those same Romans who had imitated these excellent methods of fighting and of arming themselves.

Samnite military equipment

46 LIVY, 9.40.1–3

Our knowledge of Samnite military equipment is very meager. Livy's description of it does not match the equipment found in excavations. It seems likely that they did carry a form of *scutum*, oval in shape, though Samnites are more frequently represented with a round shield and with helmet forms that seem to be based on Greek models. They are frequently depicted with a broad leather belt covered in bronze which must have served to protect their midsection and sometimes with a breastplate in the form of a triple disc. They are also depicted wearing two greaves and not the single greave in Livy's description. Their main offensive weapon appears to have been a javelin with throwing loops, and occasionally they used the heavy thrusting spear.

On the basis of such evidence it appears very unlikely that either the *scutum* or the *pilum* was borrowed from the Samnites. It is certainly not impossible given the poor state of our evidence that some borrowing took place, but at present it seems unlikely.

The equipment that Livy describes belongs not to fourth-century Samnites but to Samnite gladiators in the Roman arena. His description is meant to convey Samnite luxury in contrast to Roman simplicity.

> The war against the Samnites was attended by a danger that was equaled by its glorious outcome. The Samnites, besides their other military equipment, had taken steps to make their army resplendent with new and magnificent arms. There were two armies, one adorned with shields decorated with gold and the other with silver. These shields had a straight edge at the top where they were broadest to protect the chest and shoulders and they were tapered towards the bottom to increase mobility. Each man wore a "sponge" [perhaps a pectoral or chest protector] as protection for his chest, and his left shin was protected by a greave. He had a crested helmet to make him look taller. The troops with golden shields wore multi-colored tunics while those with silver shields had bright white linen ones.

Other views

47 LIVY, 8.8.1–4

Livy's digression on the introduction of manipular tactics occurs in his narration of the Latin revolt that lasted from 348 to 340, which ended in a total Roman victory and the dissolution of the Latin League. It forms a prologue to his account of the battle of the Veseris River in 340. His source is probably antiquarian and not historical.

There are serious errors in Livy's account of the legion, especially in his description of its third line. He seems to have envisioned the change to the manipular legion as a single event. Livy's chronology is very imprecise on the relationship between the introduction of pay and the change in tactics, although his sequence makes sense. Pay must have been introduced first to allow army expansion. The description implies a period when the maniples were brigaded together without internal line divisions. On the face of it this seems unlikely.

> The Romans employed a round shield and then, after military pay was introduced, they used the *scutum* instead. They had employed a phalanx formation similar to that of the Macedonians, but afterward adopted a battle formation based on the maniple. Finally, they arranged the maniples in several lines.

48 PLUTARCH, *CAMILLUS* 40.4

Plutarch dates these military innovations to Camillus' fifth dictatorship in 367. The passage has been used to argue that Gallic attacks and the inadequacy of the phalanx led to the development of the manipular system, although the Greeks were successfully able to meet later Gallic invasions with that very formation. The passage appears to be of little value. The Celts did introduce new types of iron helmets into Italy, but bronze continued in use in the Roman army into the imperial period. The same type of anachronism appears in supposed innovation in shield construction. The Romans were already familiar with the use of bronze rims to strengthen the edge of a shield before Camillus. Polybius reports the use of the *pilum* to ward off blows of the long Celtic sword at the battle of Telamon in 225 (see pp. 63ff.) and this seems more plausible for this tactic. The Camillus passage will not bear the weight that has been put on it. It provides no real evidence for significant changes in tactics and is filled with inaccuracies. It provides no evidence that the Gallic attacks after 400 played a role in the change to the manipular formation.

He was aware that the barbarians' swords were their most effective weapon and that they used them in a barbaric manner without art, slashing downward especially on the head and shoulders [of their opponents]. He had helmets forged completely of iron for the majority of his men and had them polished about their circumference so that sword blades would slide off or break. Further, he had the shield rims encircled by a strip of bronze since the wood itself was incapable of resisting the enemy's sword blows. He instructed the soldiers in how to use long javelins with their hands to receive the sword strokes of the enemy and turn them aside.

The three lines of the maniple

Polybius and Livy provide us with our fullest descriptions of the manipular army. Polybius' account most likely refers to the period 220–170 BC. The date of Livy's account is more problematic. As mentioned earlier, it is closely tied to his description of the battle at the Veseris in 340 and meant to illustrate the army at that period. But if the development of the army outlined above (pp. 65f.) be accepted, the description cannot represent the Roman army as it stood in the mid-fourth century. Despite differences between Polybius' and Livy's accounts the army they describe is essentially the same force. Its first two lines are armed with typical manipular weapons, while the third carries the heavy thrusting spear. This would place the army that Livy describes after 270 and there seems no reason not to see it as belonging to the same period as the Polybian one.

Nevertheless, there are important divergences. Most striking is in the number of maniples of each line. Polybius has ten and Livy fifteen. Thus Polybius has a total of thirty maniples or sixty centuries for all three lines. Livy's total is forty-five maniples and ninety centuries. Polybius must be right; as far as we know the Roman legion always consisted of sixty centuries. The origin of Livy's mistake is difficult to understand. His total for the first two lines in fact equals Polybius' for the entire legion. Interestingly, the forty-five maniples add up to ninety centuries so that the normal Roman multiple of three is present. If Polybius is right about the assignment of light-armed troops to all three lines, then that would make an additional thirty units, which Livy may have mistaken for the centuries of heavily armed infantry and so thought there were ninety centuries or forty-five maniples to a legion.

Further, Livy assigns light-armed troops to the first line only, while Polybius attaches them to all three lines. Again, Livy is probably wrong. His 300 light-armed troops are far too few to support a legion of 4,000 or more heavy infantry, which is generally accepted as the normal complement of a legion in this period. This is another one of Livy's mistakes that is difficult to explain. One possibility is that the total is a mistaken deduction from the normal number of legionary cavalry at this period. It was normally 300, and we know that light-armed and cavalry did operate together, so this may be a mistake that arose from limiting the light-armed to those who operated with the cavalry.

Perhaps the most striking difference is in the composition of the third line. In Polybius it consists only of the *triarii* armed uniformly with the heavy thrusting spear in place of the sword and *pilum* of the first two lines. Livy claims that the third line is divided into three smaller units of different troops and in addition that the third line has more men than the other two lines. These problems will be dealt with in greater detail below. Despite attempts to save Livy's credibility by claiming his description is of the army at a stage earlier than Polybius or attempting to show that such a structure is compatible with generally accepted legionary strengths, the system seems unlikely in theory and was probably unworkable in practice.

However, Livy does provide valuable additional material omitted in Polybius. After the passage translated in **50**, he notes in describing the army in battle that the *triarii* kneel. This fact is well attested elsewhere, and some of the names for troops of the third line though incorrect in themselves occur in other authors as designations for early troop units. Further, the portrait he provides of the army in action seems to be basically reliable.

The unknown source he used had a reliable picture of the legion's basic framework, but introduced military terms which he did not fully understand. Varro, writing in the mid-first century BC and one of the greatest of the antiquarian writers, displays similar problems. Matters are made worse by textual difficulties which complicate our understanding of the passage.

49 POLYBIUS, *HISTORIES* 6.21.7–23.16

This section of Polybius is the single most important source for the divisions of the manipular legion and its equipment despite the presence of some mistakes. It forms the basic framework of modern accounts of the legion of the mid-second century. The equipment will be dealt with on pp. 76ff.

When the recruits arrive on the appointed day, they [the tribunes] divide them up. The youngest and poorest form the *velites* [light-armed]. The group next to them is assigned to the *hastati*. Those in the prime of life make up the *principes* and the oldest men are allotted to the *triarii*. These are the differences within the four groups in the Roman legion that differ in name, age, and equipment. They divide them in the following manner [in each legion]: the oldest men called the *triarii* number 600, the *principes* 1,200 and they assign an equal number to the *hastati*. The remainder who are the youngest are the *velites* [light-armed]. If a legion larger than 4,000 men is required they increase the number of men in each line in proportion except for the *triarii*. These always number 600.

They order the youngest men to carry a sword, javelins and the *parma*. The *parma* is strongly made and its size provides sufficient protection. It has a round shape and is three feet in diameter. They also wear a plain helmet, which they sometimes cover with a wolf skin or something similar for protection and to distinguish them so that subordinate commanders can recognize whether they are conspicuous in the fighting or not.

The wooden shaft of these javelins is about thirty-six inches long and about an inch in width. The javelin head is about four inches long and is hammered out to such a fine point that it bends after the first throw and the enemy cannot throw it back. If it were not designed this way both sides could use it.

The *hastati*, the next in seniority, are required to be fully equipped as heavy infantrymen. The Roman version of this equipment consists of the following: the *scutum*, which is convex in shape and two and one-half feet wide and four feet long, and its thickness at the rim is about four inches. It consists of two planks fastened together with glue. The outer surface is wrapped in linen and that in turn is covered with bull's hide. It has iron edging on its upper and lower sections which protects it against slashing sword strokes above and below when resting on the ground. It has an iron boss attached to it, which protects against hard blows from stones, pikes, and heavy javelins. They also carry a sword. It is worn on the right side and known as a Spanish sword. It has an excellent point for thrusting and cuts well on both sides because its blade is strong and rigid.

In addition to this they carry two *pila*, a bronze helmet, and a greave. There are two types of *pila*, heavy and light ones. Some of the heavy ones are round and are four inches in diameter, and some are square-sided. The light ones which they carry in addition to the heavy are similar to moderate-sized hunting spears. The shafts of all *pila* are about three and one-half feet long; each shaft is fitted with a barbed iron head equal in length to the shaft. They insure the head's firm attachment and usefulness by securely driving it into the wooden shaft halfway up its length and fixing it with many iron rivets. The result is that in battle the head shatters before it can

71

come loose since they take such care with the join, although its thickness at the bottom where it joins the wood is only an inch and a half.

In addition to all the equipment just mentioned they wear as an ornament on their helmets a circle of feathers made of three black or red feathers that add to a man's height. The feathers on his helmet together with his other equipment make a man appear double his true height. He is an impressive sight and strikes fear into the enemy.

The majority of solders also wear a bronze breastplate four inches square which protects the chest and which they call a heart protector [*kardiophylax*]. This is the whole of their equipment. Those whose property is rated about 10,000 drachmas or above wear a cuirass of chain mail instead of the chest protector. The *principes* and *triarii* are armed in the same manner except that the *triarii* carry a heavy thrusting spear in place of the *pilum*.

50 LIVY, 8.8.5–8

The number of maniples in each line was ten (see pp. 69f.). The maniples were arranged in three lines in quincunx fashion. The maniples of each line were arrayed in the gaps between the maniples of the line in front of it. There has been much debate as to the size of the gaps and whether they were maintained when the line closed with the enemy. It has been argued that this would have been impossible and that the gaps were closed before actual contact was made.

Livy and Polybius both make it clear that by the end of the third century the Servian classes no longer provided the basis for recruiting. It had now become tribal and for the most part age had replaced census ratings in determining military functions, though some traces appear to have remained. Polybius and other sources mention that those above a certain property rating had to wear a mail shirt instead of the chest protector. This must have been supplied at the owner's expense and recalls the differences in equipment required at individual expense in the Servian system.

Livy explains the term for the first two lines, *antepilani*, as due to the fact that the first two lines were stationed in front of the standards, though elsewhere he uses an equivalent term only for the *hastati*. The word itself is very rare, and the normal term is *antesignani*, that is, those in front of the standards. It has been argued that this term *antesignani* refers not to the first two lines but only the *hastati* on the basis of passages elsewhere in Livy. But Livy must be right here. It is reasonable to assume that both lines had their *signa* at the back when in contact with the enemy. The Roman system allowed for the retreat of either line in case of trouble. Given that, it seems reasonable to suppose the ensigns of both lines were to the rear of the battle line to stabilize the line and to guide the retreat if necessary. That is, Livy's explanation is in fact incorrect. The term he uses signifies something different, and that is that the *triarii* were arranged in maniples formed as columns. Such a formation would have allowed the third line to form gaps through which the other two lines could retreat and then close up for a final charge by the closed formation.

The most troublesome part of Livy's explanation is his account of the rearmost line. He states that it consisted of three units of sixty-two men. He adds that each unit consisted of sixty soldiers, two centurions and a standard bearer, which in fact totals sixty-three. These figures result in a total of 189 men for each of the fifteen maniples. He describes each of these three rear units as consisting of three different types of troops. In front are the *triarii*, behind them the *rorarii* and finally the *accensi*. Such an arrangement seems impossible. For one thing, centurions are always counted within the unit, that is each subunit should total 60 including centurions. The evidence for the *rorarii* points to their being light-armed and not part of the heavy infantry. The term *accensus*, which also occurs in Livy's description of the Servian army, should normally mean a servant or attendant, and in Cato, our earliest source, that is its meaning. Other writers mention that they picked up the weapons of the fallen and took their place on the battlefield. Despite the confusion in our sources over these terms, what does seem clear is that these groups have been wrongly included in the heavy infantry by Livy's source and that Livy himself had no real understanding of the army he was describing. What is especially odd is the fact that he places the *accensi*, whom he claims are the weakest and most unreliable element in the army, in the rear. It was standard Greek practice to place men of proven courage and discipline in the rear to maintain the cohesion of the phalanx. This sensible measure must have been true of the Roman army as well. It may well be, as has been suggested, that Livy's description of five different classes of soldiers is an artificial link to the five classes of the Servian army. The proverb that Livy quotes here, that if matters have reached the *triarii* the situation is desperate, seems to imply that the *triarii* were the last line of the army. Finally, it is hard to make sense of Livy's view of the number of men in the legion. Various calculations have been offered, but there are too many uncertainties for it to be possible to reach a firm conclusion.

The first line was called the *hastati* and was arranged in fifteen maniples which stood at a moderate distance from one another. Twenty light-armed were attached to each maniple, while the rest of the troops carried the *scutum*. However, those troops who carry light javelins and heavy javelins are classed as light-armed. This is the rank at the front of the battle line and it was made up of the flower of the young men who were coming of age for military service. The *principes*, who are older and are also arranged in fifteen maniples, form the second line. All carry the *scutum* and have especially magnificent equipment. They call these thirty maniples the *antepilani* because another fifteen maniples are stationed under the standards. Each maniple was made up of three sections; a section consisted of sixty soldiers, two centurions and a standard bearer. The total for the company was thus 186 men. The standard of the first section was followed by the *triarii*, veteran soldiers of proven courage, the second by the *rorarii*, who were men of lesser strength and accomplishments, and the third were the *accensi*, who were the least reliable group and who for that reason had been placed in the rear of the battle line.

The names of elements of the manipular army

The reasons for the names of the first two lines of the manipular legion seem to have been lost by the first century BC. The antiquarian sources who deal with the origins of the names are clearly unaware of their original meaning. One obstacle to their understanding was their ignorance of the long process of change that lay behind the birth of a fully developed manipular organization. Another was the concentration on equipment rather than function. They seem to have envisioned the change as centered on equipment rather than tactics. The *scutum* appears to have been seen as a diagnostic mark of the change in most authors regardless of when they placed the transition and what origin they assigned to the equipment. Given the visibility of the shield this is hardly surprising.

The fact that the *hastati* precede the *principes* in the Roman order of battle has produced the most difficulty for ancient as for modern writers. The usual derivation of their name from the heavy thrusting spear seems contradictory. However, some of the earliest evidence makes it clear that the term *hasta* could also be used of a missile weapon. In fact, the light-armed troops carried a number of javelins which the Romans called the *hasta velitaris* or *hasta* belonging to the light-armed. It is a reasonable supposition that makes sense of the available evidence if the first line was called the *hastati* because they were the first section of the legion to adopt the *pilum*. The term *principes* can then be explained, as has already been suggested, as troops at the front of the phalanx formation still used by the rest of the army.

51 VARRO, *ON THE LATIN LANGUAGE* 5.89

Varro was the greatest of Rome's antiquarian scholars in the breadth of his learning and in his analytic ability. His work on the Latin language was originally published in twenty-five books, of which books 5 to 10 are extant. The passage is illustrative of the weakness of the antiquarian tradition in this area. He appears to derive the name of the *hastati* from their use of the heavy thrusting spear. His explanation of the *pilani* or *triarii* is clearly derived from his etymology of the term and the usages of the army of his time. The explanation of *principes* is equally fallacious and seems to imply that the other lines did not possess the sword, which cannot have ever been true. Only the last section, in which he gives an alternate name for the *triarii*, is correct.

One calls those soldiers *hastati* who first engaged the enemy with their *hastae*, and *pilani* those who fought with the *pilum*, and *principes* those who fought in the first line with their swords. The *pilani* are also known as *triarii* because they were deployed in battle in the third line at the rear as a reserve. Since they served in the reserve they were also known as "the reserve," from which derives the line of Plautus "Stir yourself; give me your support as the *triarii* do."

52 VEGETIUS, *HANDBOOK OF MILITARY AFFAIRS* 1.20

Vegetius is the author of the only surviving complete Roman military treatise. The four books were composed either in the second half of the fourth century AD or in the first half of the fifth. He cites earlier sources, among them Cato. But in this case he seems to have been working on the basis of etymology rather than any direct information. He quite naturally assumes that the *principes* fought in the first rank and the *hastati* in the second. It is a desperate expedient that has on occasion found modern support.

Armed in this manner they called those who fought in the first line the *principes* and in the second the *hastati* and in the third the *triarii*.

The hastati

53 LIVIUS ANDRONICUS, FRAGMENT 35 MOREL

Livius, a freedman, is the earliest known writer of literary Latin. He lived sometime in the mid-third century BC. He wrote hymns and plays and translated Homer's *Odyssey* into Latin. The passage below probably comes from his translation of Homer and makes clear especially with the epithet "swift" that he used the term *hasta* for a missile weapon and not a heavy thrusting spear.

But the flying steel of the swift *hasta* tore into his chest.

54 ENNIUS, *ANNALS* 284 V

Quintus Ennius, who immigrated to Rome from southern Italy, is the greatest of early Roman poets. His dates are 239–167. The fragment translated below is from his epic poem the *Annales*, which dealt with Roman history from the founding of the city until his own time. As in **53**, *hasta* is clearly used of a missile weapon.

The *hastati* showered their *hastae*, a storm of steel.

The triarii *or* pilani

55 DIONYSIUS OF HALICARNASSUS, *ROMAN ANTIQUITIES* 8.86.4

Dionysius' description of the *triarii* occurs as part of his narrative of a battle against the Volsci in 484. The battle may well be fictional, as there were no *triarii* in the

Roman army at this date which still fought as a phalanx. Nonetheless, he gives a good general picture of the *triarii*. The earliest extant reference to them is in a play of the early-second-century BC writer Plautus. It makes clear the role of the *triarii* is as a reserve.

Varro (**51**) notes that the other name for them was *pilani*. He wrongly derives this from the *pilum*, the very weapon they did not carry. The term was persistent, and even in the imperial period the senior centurion of a legion was the *primus pilus* or first centurion of the first maniple of the *triarii*. The basic meaning of *pilum* is "pestle." The long thin shape recalls the Roman javelin, but since the *triarii* did not use it the name must refer to something else. The most likely possibility is the arrangement of *triarii* in battle. Their maniples were arranged as columns until they closed up to form a phalanx. The reason was the greater need for depth in a phalanx rather than lateral extension. Unlike the situation with a normal phalanx there was less need to extend the battle line to match that of the enemy, as the troops of the other two lines could provide flank protraction. In desperate situations the *triarii* were to function as a rallying point for the rest of the legion and if possible break through the enemy line and so extricate the legion.

> Then behind the [cavalry] came the so-called *triarii* who had closed ranks. These are the oldest soldiers in the army to whom the safety of the camp is entrusted when the army moves out to battle. The army falls back on these troops whenever the Romans suffer catastrophic loss of the men in their prime and lack any other support.

The equipment of the manipular army

The shield

The adoption of the *scutum* was the change in equipment that most struck ancient authors. It was certainly closely associated with the change in manipular tactics. The round hoplite shield with its peculiar grip was not suited to the new tactics. The soldier was now required to operate as swordsman and needed a shield that could be maneuvered quickly and offer maximum protection for him. These requirements led to the adoption of a shield that was both long and convex.

The *scutum* of the manipular legion traced its ancestry back to an old Italic type that first appears in the mid-eighth century in Etruscan art and spread throughout central and northern Italy. Like the later Roman *scutum* the shield possessed a central boss over the handgrip as protection for the hand and a central spine as reinforcement for the shield.

The introduction of hoplite tactics led to the spread of the round hoplite shield at its expense. However, the *scutum* had spread from Italy to Gaul and then was widely dispersed in Europe. It reemerged in Italy in the fourth century. The types found reflect a combination of native types influenced by the Celtic equipment. Its importance at Rome is clear from its appearance on a type of early Roman currency.

Given the perishable nature of the materials out of which the shield was made, the available evidence is not as complete as one would wish. The most comprehensive ancient literary description is that of Polybius (see **49**). There are also scattered references and two reliefs that provide us with representations of the shield from the mid- and late Republic. These are the monument of Aemilius Paullus dedicated at Delphi to celebrate his decisive victory over the Macedonian king Perseus at Pydna in Thessaly in 168 and a monument erected by C. Domitius Ahenobarbus at Rome, probably made in the late second or early first century BC. Both of these show long oval shields with a central spine and umbo. Perhaps the most striking evidence is provided by an actual example found in the Fayum area of Egypt at Kasr el-Harit. The date is uncertain and may be as late as the reign of Augustus, when the rectangular cylindrical shape replaced the oval. The shield is 4.2 feet long and approximately 2 feet wide, which confirms Polybius' figures. It is made in three layers of laminated birch. A horizontal layer of planks is sandwiched between two vertical layers and the layers are glued together and covered in wool felt. It has a boss and spine but of wooden not metal construction. Also absent is a metal rim. The handgrip is mounted horizontally behind the central umbo. A reconstructed version weighs approximately twenty-two pounds, which makes it too heavy to have been consistently wielded with the handgrip, and it has been suggested the in the charge it must have been rested on the shoulder, and the same may have been true in close-quarter battle.

56 VARRO, *ON THE LATIN LANGUAGE* 5.115

Varro (see **51**) gives a substantially correct description of the construction of this shield.

> The name of the *scutum* is derived from the act of cutting [*secuta*] because the shield is constructed from boards cut into small pieces.

57 LIVY, 9.41.17–19

This passage is from a description of a battle against the Umbrians in 308. The weight and size of the *scutum* meant it could be used effectively in battle to unbalance or topple an opponent. This maneuver was especially effective with a metal boss.

> Then before the order could be given the Roman troops attacked the enemy in a rush to the blare of trumpets and horns. They charged as though they thought they were attacking unarmed men. It was remarkable. First they began to snatch the enemy's standards from their bearers, and then the bearers themselves were dragged before the consul; even fully armed soldiers were brought over from the enemy's battle line to their own. Wherever the fighting flared up, the contest was fought not with swords

but with shields [*scuta*]. The enemy was laid low by blows from the bosses of their shields and the Romans' right arms.

58 LIVY, 30.34.2–4

Livy is describing the final and decisive battle of the Second Punic War at Zama.

The battle line of the Romans was firm and pressed with the weight of the men's bodies and their equipment upon the enemy. On the other side there were repeated charges at great speed, but with less power. So at the first rush the Romans immediately forced the [Carthaginian] line back. Then beating with their shoulders and their shields, the Romans stepped forward as if there was no resistance and forced them back some way. The rear of the Roman line added its weight as soon as it sensed the enemy's line had given way, and this added much force to driving the enemy back.

The helmet

Despite a number of helmet finds from the fourth century there is no definitive evidence about what helmet was used in the Roman army. The most common type found in Italy from the mid- to late Republic is the so-called Montefortino type. This is also the commonest helmet type in the fourth century BC and, though there is no direct evidence for its use by the Roman army, the frequency of the finds as well as its similarity to later Roman helmets makes it a likely candidate for the standard heavy infantry helmet of the period. It belongs to the family of jockey-cap helmets widely used in the Roman army throughout the imperial period. All jockey-cap helmets were essentially bowl-shaped metal caps with a neck guard at the back of the helmet that gives the impression of a modern jockey cap worn backwards with the peak reversed.

The helmet was made from a beaten copper bowl, often with a knob to which a crest or feathers could be attached. The helmet is probably of Celtic origin and can be traced back to cemeteries in France and Austria as early as the fifth century BC. It was furnished with detachable cheek pieces in triple-disc form, to be succeeded in the third century by scallop-shape cheek pieces.

Polybius (**49**) mentions that the knob was used to affix feathers to add height and to help in identification. He says that Romans used three black or purple feathers about one and one-half feet long.

The neck guard was enlarged over time and this must be a function of the way in which Roman infantry fought. There is evidence that in fighting the Roman soldier crouched, and this would have exposed his neck to slashing sword blows.

The greave

The greave or shin protector had long been used in Greek hoplite warfare and was introduced into Italy at the same time as other hoplite equipment. It became popular in Etruria and central Italy in the sixth century. As in Greece, there was a general replacement of greaves that were attached by lacing with snap-on models. Given the nature of the hoplite shield they protected that part of the leg left exposed by the shield and helped prevent the shield from chafing the thigh. The greave is listed among the equipment of the first two Servian classes.

Polybius mentions greaves in his description of Roman heavy infantry equipment. It is of some significance that he uses the singular. It has been thought that this reflected Roman practice, with a greave worn only on the left leg, which was thrust forward in battle, and there is some late evidence that this was so. Livy (see **46**) claims that they wore only one greave on their left shin. Later writers also refer to the use of the greave, and Arrian in the mid-second century AD (see **59**) mentions the use of the single greave. The greave was abandoned soon after the period of Polybius. It may be that its cost as well as the limitations it placed on mobility outweighed its value as protective armor.

59 ARRIAN, *THE ART OF TACTICS* 1.3.5

Flavius Arrianus, serving as governor of Cappadocia in 131–137, had in 132 to deal with a threatened invasion of his province by the Alans, a tribe who lived near the eastern coast of the Black Sea to the north of Arrian's province. Besides his famous account of Alexander's campaigns and many other works, he also wrote two works of military importance: *The Expedition against the Alans* and *The Art of Tactics*. The latter was perhaps composed in 136 and is a surprisingly derivative work combining an account of Greek and Macedonian infantry tactics with description of Roman cavalry tactics. The helmets mentioned in the passage may have been made of either leather or metal. Metallic helmets are the more likely. What exactly the author meant by qualifying helmets as Spartan or Arcadian is not clear, though there is some possibility that it refers not to a type of helmet but rather to a place known for the excellence of the equipment it produced. This is not unlike the reference to Spanish sword work in the early modern period.

> Those who wear full hoplite equipment also have a helmet, either the Spartan cap or the Arcadian, and greaves as were worn by the ancient Greeks or the ancient Romans, who wore a single greave on the leg that was thrust forward in battle.

Offensive weapons

The pilum

Polybius offers us the most detailed description of the *pilum*. His interest in the technical details of military equipment, a subject ignored by most ancient historians, provides invaluable information. There are some additional details in other sources, but the most important evidence apart from Polybius is archaeological.

There are important finds at Vulci and Telamon (see **42**) in Etruria, but the majority of material comes from second-century military camps in Spain, of which the most important are at Numantia and nearby at Renieblas.

The *pilum* is basically a mass-produced javelin, and the name was applied to various missile weapons. Polybius mentions two types, heavy and light. Polybius describes the head as barbed, but heads of pyramidal shape also occur. The heads vary in length from about two inches for the heavy *pilum* to about three-quarters of an inch for the light. The shanks also vary a great deal, from approximately nine inches to about three feet. The head and shank either were attached to the wooden shaft by a tang or were socketed. The lighter *pilum* was usually socketed, while the heavier normally was attached by a tang. According to Polybius the shank was driven halfway into the wooden shaft and then fixed with rivets. Great attention was paid to assuring the attachment of the metal and wood, and Polybius claims that the join was so firm that it was more likely that the metal would break before the wood and metal became separated. The *pilum* was about seven feet long, which is approximately the length of the Greek hoplite spear and probably the spear used by the *triarii*.

Some scholars have expressed doubt about the practicality of the heavy *pilum*. It has even been suggested that it was an experimental weapon introduced by Polybius' friend Scipio Aemilanus and never actually used. Heavy *pila* have been reconstructed with a weight of nearly twenty pounds. A weapon of this weight could never have been thrown. The most reasonable solution is to assume a tapering of the shank, which would reduce the weight of a heavy *pilum* to about ten pounds and a lighter one to less than half that weight. The fact that the heavy *pilum* continued to be used in the imperial period is evidence of its functionality.

The *pilum* seems to have had a natural tendency to bend on impact and this is borne out by excavated examples. This was a significant advantage for the Romans as it could not be simply picked up by the enemy and thrown back. In the early first century BC the sources claim that the Roman commander Marius had the metal rivets that bound the shank to the shaft replaced with wooden ones to facilitate the bending on impact, but later battle descriptions mention enemy forces returning *pila*, and it is possible that this change did not take place.

In essence the *pilum* substituted for other missile weapons such as the bow, as a means of causing casualties and of disorganizing enemy formations before closing for close combat. The design of the head maximized its ability to penetrate, and modern experiments have shown it capable of penetrating three-quarters of an inch of plywood at a distance of sixteen feet. The maximum range of the light *pilum* was about thirty yards.

There has been debate about the origins of this weapon. Various ancient sources claim a Samnite, Gallic, Spanish, or even Etruscan origin. Various modern scholars have favored one or the other, especially a derivation from a Samnite or Spanish prototype. A Samnite origin is extremely unlikely (see pp. 67f.), but there is better evidence for a Spanish origin. A third-century AD author, Athenaeus, explicitly says that the Romans learned the use of the *pilum* from the Iberian tribes. Certainly, hand-thrown missile weapons similar to the *pilum* had long existed in Italy. In fact, manipular tactics are inconceivable without the *pilum* and sword. So, if we posit the beginning of the transition to manipular tactics in the early fourth century, a javelin of some type must have existed quite early on. This of course does not rule out changes in the Roman *pilum* as a result of encounters with Spanish mercenaries fighting for the Carthaginians in the First Punic War, though it may be significant that Polybius states that the legionary sword is Spanish, but is silent about the *pilum*.

60 POLYBIUS, *HISTORIES* 1.40.11–13

This passage is from a description of the battle of Panormus (Palermo) during the First Punic War in 250. This is the earliest definite reference to the use of the *pilum*.

> [Caecilius] ordered the lower-class civilian population to bring up mis-
> siles and to set them down outside by the base of the [city] wall, while he
> took up position with his maniples at the gate facing the enemy's left
> wing, constantly sending reinforcements to his light-armed troops who
> were attacking the enemy with missiles. While the struggle became more
> intense the elephant drivers, vying in displaying their prowess before
> Hasdrubal and in their desire to win the battle by themselves, charged the
> foremost troops of the enemy and, routing them easily, drove them into the
> trench. When the elephants encountered the trench they were wounded by
> arrows shot from the walls and bombarded by a rapid and dense hail of
> javelins and *pila* thrown by the fresh troops arrayed in front of the trench.
> Struck in many places and wounded, they quickly lost cohesion and
> turned on their own troops.

The use of the pilum in battle

There is little ancient evidence for the use of the *pilum* in battle. Most authors confine themselves to the bare statement that they were thrown before the Romans drew their swords and closed. By far the best source of the use of the *pilum* in battle is Caesar's *Gallic War* and *Civil War*. His material should be valid for the earlier period, as there is no evidence and little likelihood that anything dramatically changed over the long history of the *pilum*'s use. However, even with the evidence of Caesar we have no clear idea of the tactics employed. Any reconstruction must be based on probabilities and physical possibilities.

The problem of reconstruction is rendered more difficult by the fact that we have no firm idea about the depth of the maniple in battle. This is of crucial importance given the limited range of the *pilum* (about thirty yards) and the need to avoid casualties caused by friendly fire. Polybius (see **49**) assigns two *pila* to the first two lines, with the implication that these were both carried into battle, though it has been argued this would be too difficult given the other equipment a Roman soldier had to carry, but there is good evidence for it. This mostly consists of prolonged discharges of *pila* such as that at the crucial battle of Zama in 202 that ended the Second Punic War. Livy notes the special preparations that the Roman commander Scipio took to deal with the large number of Carthaginian elephants facing his men. One of the results of his actions was that the elephants were continuously bombarded by the missiles of the Roman light-armed and also by those of the *hastati* and *principes*. In his *Civil War* Caesar provides another example from his fight against Pompeian forces at Ilerda in Spain in 49 of a prolonged encounter waged with missile weapons by legionaries. This must mean that each of the first two lines must have carried two *pila*. One of the *pila* was presumably held in the right hand ready to throw while the other must have been held together with the shield in the left hand. This would present no problem, as the *pila* would have been discharged before the use of the sword required full mobility in the employment of the shield.

Since the effective range was only thirty yards the *pila* must have been discharged successively as each line joined the battle. Some have doubted that this would have been done as it would have caused the legion to lose its forward impetus. But this was much less important for a formation that depended on the effect of sword and shield than it was for a phalanx where forward momentum intensified the effect of the heavy spear thrust. The discharge must have been done in open order to allow the room necessary for throwing. This would have been less of a problem for Roman tactics, as their use of the sword required a relatively open deployment. The depth of the maniple as already mentioned is uncertain, but if it was between six and eight men deep and each man was allowed six feet for throwing room this would have allowed all six to eight lines to discharge their missiles before contact with the enemy.

The discharge of the *pila*, given their penetrating power, the dense mass formations normal on ancient battlefields, and the closeness of the enemy, could be extremely effective. The passage from the *Gallic War* (**61**) illustrates a phenomenon often noted. Even if the enemy was not wounded or killed they could still hinder his movements in the hand-to-hand phase of battle. Occasionally we hear of enemy formations broken by discharges of *pila*.

The *pila* could also be wielded as the equivalent of a heavy thrusting spear, as Plutarch's description (**63**) of a phase of the battle of Pharsalus makes clear. The same tactic is also visible at the battle of Telamon against the Gauls in 225 BC (see **42**). But it was always a secondary weapon. As Polybius makes clear it was the Roman sword that normally decided battles.

The pilum *as a missile weapon*

61 CAESAR, *GALLIC WAR* 1.25.1–4

These events belong to Caesar's first major campaign against the Helvetii in 58.

> Caesar first removed his own horse from sight and then all of the others to end any expectation of flight by putting all in equal danger. Then, after

encouraging his men, he began the battle. The soldiers from their elevated position easily broke the enemy phalanx by the discharge of their *pila*. After the enemy formation had broken they drew their swords and attacked them. The Gauls were greatly hindered in their fighting because the *pila* had passed through their shields and locked them together. When they bent the shanks they could not pull them out or easily fight with their left arms weighed down. Many of them, after they had shaken their arms for a while [in an attempt to dislodge the *pila*] preferred to throw away their shields and fight unprotected.

62 CAESAR, *GALLIC WAR* 1.52.3–4

This encounter also took place in 58, but this time the Romans were fighting Ariovistus, king of the German tribe of the Suebi, who controlled a number of Gallic tribes in the Rhine region. It resulted in the collapse of the German army and the flight of Ariovistus and his army.

> At the signal our men made a violent attack against the enemy. Likewise the enemy moved forward so suddenly and at such speed that there was no room to launch the *pila* at them. Our men threw down their *pila* and fought with their swords at close quarters.

The pilum *used as a thrusting weapon*

63 PLUTARCH, *THE LIFE OF POMPEY* 69.2

This incident belongs to the decisive encounter between Pompey and Caesar at Pharsalus in Thessaly in the late summer of 48 BC, which destroyed Pompey's army and his reputation and resulted in his assassination within a few months. Pompey had counted on his superiority in cavalry to bring him victory. Caesar countered this by stationing a reserve of six cohorts obliquely behind his line with instructions to use their *pila* to counter the Pompeian horse. The passage makes clear that the *pilum* must have had sufficient rigidity to be used as a heavy thrusting spear. It was also used in this manner against infantry, as at Telamon.

> For at this point almost all the cavalry had assembled on the Pompeian left to overwhelm Caesar and to cut down the Tenth Legion, which had a reputation as the fiercest of Caesar's troops. Also Caesar usually took up his position with them and usually fought with them. Seeing the left wing of the enemy enclosed by such a great number of horse and fearful of such a brilliant array of arms, Caesar sent six cohorts from the reserve and stationed them behind the Tenth Legion. He ordered them to remain quiet and unseen by the enemy. He told them that whenever the enemy's cavalry charged they should run out through the front ranks, though without

casting their *pila* as the best soldiers usually did in their eagerness to draw their swords, but to strike upwards with their *pila* and wound the eyes and faces of the enemy.

The legionary sword

The basic offensive weapon of the manipular legion was the short thrusting sword. The most detailed ancient description of it is again given by Polybius. He remarks on the strength of the blade and its suitability either for stabbing or for slashing. He says that it was known as the Spanish sword. Most scholars have assumed that it was adopted from the Celtiberi of southern Spain who served on the Carthaginian side in both the First and Second Punic Wars. The Second Punic War, given the long Roman exposure to Celtiberian mercenaries, would seem the likelier period, but there is some evidence that the Romans were using what appears to be the identical sword by the mid-220s and so it is possible that the sword was adopted during the First Punic War.

Unfortunately, aside from some depictions of the sword in various artistic media there have been until recently no Republican finds of such swords. The last twenty or so years have added at least two possible examples. One was discovered in the mid-1980s on the island of Delos in the central Aegean and dates from the sack of the island in 69 BC. The other comes from southern France and perhaps dates from the last years of the second or early first century BC. Both of these examples are similar. They measure about thirty to thirty-one inches, with a blade having two parallel cutting edges and a long sharp point. This type remained in use from the mid-third until the first century AD.

There is less evidence for the sword the Romans used prior to the adoption of the Spanish weapon. It may well have been similar to Etruscan sword types that have been found. Many of them are of iron and short, about two feet in length, and related to Greek types.

In his survey of the equipment of the legion Polybius omits any mention of a dagger. Daggers had a long history in Italy and were used by legionaries in the imperial period, so this is surprising. Specimens have been found in some second-century military camps (see pp. 135f.). These weapons are about six to eight inches in length, with a central midrib and a waisted blade with a large swelling handle. The obvious uses of the dagger and its long history as a weapon in central Italy make the historian's omission surprising. It may be that in the Republican period the dagger was not part of the standard repertory as it was to be under the Empire.

The origin of the legionary sword

64 *SUDA*, ENTRY: THE SWORD

The *Suda* is a Byzantine lexicon composed about 1000 AD. The Celtiberian homeland lay in northeastern Spain. Celtic groups are known in Spain through the literary sources as early as the fifth century. They are singled out by the classical writers for their ferocity in war and the excellence of their weaponry. There appear to have been three types of Spanish swords in use: the *falcata*, which was a saber with an undulating blade; a straight sword with a handle ending in two antennae; and a type almost identical with the Roman sword. The resemblance is so close that it is often difficult to tell the difference between them.

> The Celtiberians far excelled others in the making of swords. The swords have a sharp point and the cutting edge of the blade is effective with either hand. As a consequence from the war with Hannibal the Romans discarded their traditional swords and adopted those of the Iberians and they also copied its form but they could in no way reproduce the excellence of the metal nor the other elements of production.

The sword in action

65 LIVY, 31.34.1–5

The passage describes the burial of cavalry who had fallen in the battle between Philip V (221–179) and the Romans at Cynoscephalae in Thessaly in 197.

> To win the affection of his people and thinking to do something to make them more eager to undergo danger on his behalf, Philip undertook the burial of all of the cavalry who had fallen on the campaign. He ordered the bodies to be borne into camp so that their funeral honors would have the widest public exposure. But nothing is as uncertain and unpredictable as the attitude of a group. This act which he thought would make them more eager to endure any struggle inspired fear and aversion. Men who were accustomed to fight with Greeks or Illyrians and had seen wounds made by thrusting spears, arrows, and the occasional lance, after they had seen the work of the Spanish sword, the headless corpses, arms with the shoulder sliced away, heads with necks attached cut off, viscera laid open, and other horrific wounds, were struck by a general fear when they saw what weapons and men they had to face.

Roman sword-fighting technique

After the discharge of his *pila* the Roman soldier depended upon his sword-fighting skills to bring victory. Its use must have required a long and thorough training, but we know little about it. The large shield as well as the sword required extensive space to be effective. Polybius claims that the maniple opened up to prepare for sword fighting so that each soldier occupied a frontage of six feet. From this must be subtracted the width of the soldier himself, perhaps a foot and a half. So if the six feet were measured from the right shoulder of the man to his left to the left shoulder of the man to his right there would actually be a gap of approximately two feet on either side to allow the movement necessary to face an attack from any direction. This appears to be correct.

On the other hand some scholars have followed Vegetius' claim of a three-foot separation. This is far too small to be suitable for sword fighting. In Vegetius' case, measurement is not an issue as he clearly assigns a total of three feet to each man measured from the left shoulder of the man to the soldier's right to the right shoulder of the soldier to the man's left. This would give a theoretical maximum of eighteen inches on both sides. Such a distance is too small for effective fighting.

Polybius also mentions the Roman tactic of taking a step backward after engaging the enemy to allow room for sword play after the first rush. The possibility of such a tactic has been questioned but not only do we have the authority of Polybius for it but there are examples of non-Roman armies in Caesar's account of his campaigns in Gaul that were able to accomplish this very maneuver. It is important to keep in mind that such order would not last for long at the front of the battle line. The impact of meeting the enemy's line and the ensuing struggle would dissolve these rigid alignments fairly quickly. It also has to be borne in mind that sword fighting would be intermittent. The physical wear and tear of such fighting probably limited the actual fighting to bursts of about twenty minutes followed by a period of rest and, in addition, the shield would be used not only as protection but also as an offensive weapon to ram and try to unbalance the opponent.

66 POLYBIUS, *HISTORIES* 18.30.6–8

Polybius admits that a phalanx of pikemen on a level, delivering a frontal attack, is unstoppable. He sees the superiority of the Roman formation in its flexibility, especially its capability to adapt itself to any terrain, and its ability to meet an attack from any direction.

> The Romans with their equipment are also spaced three feet apart, but in this method of fighting each man moves separately because of the need of each to protect himself with his *scutum*, constantly turning to meet the threatened blow, and cutting and thrusting with his sword. It is clear that they require a looser order and an interval between them. So they must have a three-foot separation from the man to their rear and to the side if they are to be of use.

67 VEGETIUS, *HANDBOOK OF MILITARY AFFAIRS* 3.14

Though a late writer (see **52**), Vegetius had access to some early sources, including Cato the Censor writing in the mid-second century BC. However, he tends to mix early material with later practice and to employ a rather mechanical approach reminiscent of Hellenistic manuals on warfare, as perhaps he does here. It appears that his calculation starts from the number of troops in a line and, since this fits

Polybius' statement about the distance between soldiers prior to opening for sword play, it is possible that he has confused the two stages of the battle.

> However, individual soldiers arranged in a straight line were accustomed to have three feet between them. That is, in a distance of 5,000 feet there were arranged 1,666 soldiers in line so that the battle line could not be seen through and there would be space for them to use their arms. But between one line and the next the desired space was six feet so that those fighting would have room to go forward and backward. That way *pila* could be thrown at a run while jumping forward.

68 VEGETIUS, *HANDBOOK OF MILITARY AFFAIRS* 1.12

The Romans favored using the sword as a stabbing weapon, but the description given by Livy (**65**) as well as archaeological evidence drawn from skeletal remains indicates slashing blows were frequently employed. Polybius' description of the Spanish sword (see **49**) praises its ability to be used effectively for either type of stroke.

> In addition, they learned to deliver a stabbing blow and not a slashing one. The Romans not only easily overcame those who fought with a slashing blow, but even laughed at them. For a slashing blow, despite the force with which it is delivered, often does not kill, since the vital organs are protected by armor and bone. However, a thrust that penetrates two inches deep is fatal. For it is necessary that whatever penetrates deeply will pierce a vital organ. Also, when a slashing blow is delivered it exposes the right arm and side. But the stabbing blow is delivered with the body protected and wounds the enemy before he can see it. So it is agreed that the Romans used this type of blow especially.

The light-armed troops of the manipular legion

In both Greek and Roman armies the heavy infantry was the decisive force. Although light-armed troops were present, they rarely played a crucial role on the battlefield. The lightness of their protective equipment hindered them from engaging heavy infantry directly, but they could harass and wear them down. In general, they were used for reconnaissance, for foraging, to drive off opposing light-armed troops, to screen the movements of their own forces from the enemy, and in pursuit once the opposing army had broken. They were also used to extend the battle line in cases where the wings rested on broken and uneven ground not suitable for heavy infantry. They seem to have been especially effective in dealing with the elephant on the battlefield, after its appearance on Italian and western battlefields in the course of the third century. From this period we often find them operating with cavalry in reconnaissance and pursuit, and occasionally in battle. They seem most effective when operating in mixed formations with other types of troops.

In the mid-second century Polybius in his review of the Roman army mentions that the light-armed were recruited from the youngest and poorest of the citizens. Livy in his account of the Servian army (see p. 22) also states that the light-armed were drawn from those with the lowest census ratings. This was also the Greek practice. It explains the relative inattention of classical writers to such troops. Given this state of affairs, it is scarcely surprising that the literary tradition contains much confusion about the nomenclature and tactical disposition of these troops. Before the later third century it appears that a light-armed soldier was called a *rorarius*, and this term is attested as current as late as the mid-second century in poetry, though this does not prove it was current.

Livy records the creation of a body of light-armed troops called the *velites* in 211. Their name seems to have been derived from their swiftness. This development signals only a change in title not a major alteration in tactics or equipment. It has been suggested that the formation of the *velites* should be connected with a lowering of the census requirement necessary for service between 214 and 212 and that a reorganization then occurred with the entry of a previously ineligible group. The only traces of this are certain minor equipment changes.

Polybius states that the forty *velites* were assigned to each maniple in the three lines of the legion, totaling 1,200 in all. What this meant in practice is harder to determine. The assignment of a unit of *velites* to a maniple may only have been for administrative purposes. The standard recommendation of ancient writers was to station the light-armed on the wings with the cavalry. However, the gaps between maniples made it possible for the *velites* to be stationed with the maniples in battle line and charge out through the gaps. At Zama in 202 Scipio placed his light-armed in the gaps between the maniples, but this was dictated by the special circumstance that Hannibal had a strong force of elephants. It may be that there was no standard placement for the *velites*, and after their skirmishing they may well have often been placed on the wings to cooperate with the cavalry.

We are equally ignorant of the command structure of these troops. Officers are never mentioned but they must have existed below the level of the higher command. The mobility and various uses to which the light-armed were put required direct leadership. Their detachment from their maniples during fighting excludes the possibility that the maniple's centurions could have exercised command over them in battle.

The names of the light-armed

69 NONIUS MARCELLUS, *ON TYPES OF MILITARY EQUIPMENT* 552 M

Nonius is the early-fourth-century AD author of an encyclopedic dictionary from which the following passage is drawn. Particularly valuable are the quotations of fragments of Republican writers. Gaius Lucilius wrote in the later second century BC. This is a reference to the rain of missiles showered on the enemy by these troops.

Those soldiers are called *rorarii* who, before the battle lines had met, began the battle with some javelins. This is derived from the fact that light rains precede heavy ones.

Lucilius in the fifth book of his *Satires* gives the following lines: "Five javelins, the golden belted light-armed skirmisher."

Again Lucilius in Book X: "In the rear the light-armed skirmisher was standing."

Varro in the third book of his *On the Life of the Roman People*: "They are called *rorarii* because light rain usually comes before heavy showers."

70 NONIUS MARCELLUS, *ON TYPES OF MILITARY EQUIPMENT* 552 M

Varro refers to the round shield of the *velites*, the *parma* (see pp. 90f.).

Velites: light-armed troops.

Varro: "But you will not stand fast for the sake of money." "The light-armed *velites* who with their round shields pursue him."

The origin of the velites

71 LIVY, 26.4.3–10

This incident belongs to the war against Hannibal. In late 216 after the great Roman defeat at Cannae in Apulia, Capua in Campania, the second most important city in Italy, defected from Rome along with other important Campanian towns. In the autumn of 212 the Romans were able to completely invest the city and despite a desperate march by Hannibal on Rome they refused to be drawn off. It fell at the end of 211.

That during occasional sallies by the besieged Capuans the Romans were worsted in cavalry battles is hardly surprising; Campanian cavalry had a well-earned reputation for being an effective force. The Roman response to use light troops to add to the effectiveness of the cavalry could hardly have been a new tactic, though we hear little of it.

Livy cannot be right about the reasons for the institution of the *velites*. The story links the introduction to a special tactic which is only occasionally repeated by later Roman commanders and was not among the normal functions of the *velites* although we hear often of light-armed and cavalry troops operating together (see 63). The reasons for the origin of the *velites* have much more to do with census changes and the expansion of the available pool of manpower (see p. 66). For the *hasta velitaris* see 72.

[The Campanians] in the many cavalry actions they had with the Romans were generally successful, while they were defeated in infantry engagements. But in no way did the pleasure gained in such victories by the

Romans compensate for discomfort caused by being in any way worsted by an enemy under siege and also defeated. Nevertheless, a plan was devised by which deficiencies in strength could be compensated for by technique. From all of the legions young men were selected who were especially quick because of their physical strength and lightness. They were equipped with a *parma* that was somewhat smaller than those of the cavalry and with seven javelins about four feet in length with iron heads like those on the *hasta velitaris*. Then each cavalry trooper taking one of these men on his horse trained them to ride behind and to immediately dismount on command.

After these men seemed sufficiently confident on account of their daily practice, they advanced into the plain which lay between the camp and the city walls to confront the Campanian horse.

When the forces came within range the light-armed dismounted. Then the line of infantry made a sudden run at the enemy from the line of horsemen, bombarding them with missile after missile. Throwing everywhere at both horses and men, they wounded many. The fear induced by a new and unexpected attack and the charge of the Roman horse against an already demoralized enemy resulted in flight and a slaughter that extended up to the gates of the city. From that point on the Romans were also superior in cavalry battles and *velites* were now added to the legions. The tradition holds that Q. Naevius, a centurion, was the originator of the idea of mixing infantry and cavalry and he was honored for it by his commander.

The equipment of the light-armed

72 POLYBIUS, *HISTORIES* 6.22.2

In Livy's account of the Servian army the light-armed carry not only javelins but also slings. Whether they ever carried them is questionable. The Romans seem to have had a strong preference for the javelin and to have paid little attention to other missile weapons. In the later Republic their need in these areas was supplied by foreign troops.

The round shield or *parma* was also employed in a different version by the cavalry. We know little about it beyond literary descriptions, as no specimens have survived. Most likely it was made of some light material, wood or perhaps plaited willow branches, and covered with skin or felt. The sword they carried was the standard Spanish weapon used by the heavy infantry. The *galea* or unadorned helmet of the *velites* may have been made of leather or felt. The use of a wolf skin covering probably had more to do with telling Roman troops from the enemy than with marking out bravery.

The javelin of the *velites* or the *hasta velitaris* appears to have developed from earlier javelin types and may be related to Gallic or Samnite models. It was a long, thin weapon similar to the *pilum* of the legionaries in construction. It had a shaft of about three feet long and a head ten to twelve inches in length designed to pierce shield and body protection. The *velites* seem to have carried a number of them. Livy claims they carried seven, whereas the passage from Lucilius (**69**) mentions five. There must have been some means to resupply them after the discharge of their missiles, as we hear of repeated discharges of missiles over a prolonged period. Occasionally the sources also mention their engaging the enemy with their Spanish swords, but such references are rare.

> The youngest men are instructed to carry a sword, javelins, and a round shield called the *parma*. The *parma* is strongly made and is of sufficient size to provide protection. It is round and three feet in diameter. They also wear an unadorned helmet and sometimes they cover it with a wolf skin or something similar. They wear the skin to provide protection and as a distinguishing emblem so that those who energetically take risks on the battlefield are conspicuous. Their javelin has a wooden shaft three feet long and two inches wide. The head is four inches long and hammered out to such a fine point that it is bent by its first impact and cannot be thrown back by the enemy.

The velites *in battle*

73 POLYBIUS, *HISTORIES* 3.113.3–5

This disposition of forces is that of the Roman consul of 216 before the crucial battle of Cannae. The *velites* were used here in their usual role as skirmishers, opening the battle and screening the movements of the heavy infantry. Cavalry was normally placed on the wings. The battle illustrates the usually indecisive outcome of the encounters of light-armed troops. After no clear decision had been reached the *velites* withdrew through the maniples and seem to have played a minor role in determining the outcome of the battle, which was a devastating Carthaginian victory.

> C. [Terentius] stationed the Roman horse on his right wing right by the river. He placed the Roman infantry next to them and on the same line. He deployed the maniples closer together than usual, arranging them so that their depth greatly exceeded their frontage. The allied cavalry was on the left wing and he positioned the light-armed some distance in front of the whole force.

74 POLYBIUS, *HISTORIES* 11.22.8–10

This episode is part of the crucial battle by Scipio Africanus against Carthaginian forces under Hasdrubal in 206 at Ilipa in southern Spain near Seville. The appearance of the light-armed on the wings was part of a complicated maneuver in which Scipio marched his Roman troops on his left and right wings so that they, including the cavalry and light-armed, were able to attack the Carthaginian flank. It is an unusual use of light-armed troops as part of the vital phase of a battle.

> With the Roman cavalry coming up to the palisade of their camp and the rest of their army forming up in full view, the Carthaginians were hardly given time to arm themselves. With no time to eat they were forced to form up their men on the spur of the moment and without preparation. They sent off their light-armed and cavalry to engage the enemy on the plain and drew up their heavy infantry on level ground not far from the foot of the hill, arranging the infantry in their accustomed manner. For a while the Romans maintained their position, but when the day was far advanced the fighting between the light troops of both sides was indecisive, as those who were worsted fled to their respective phalanxes and then wheeling about renewed their attacks.
>
> Scipio received the light-armed through the gaps between his maniples and distributed them on each wing, behind the neighboring formation, with the *velites* in front and the cavalry behind.

75 LIVY, 31.35.5–6

This encounter took place during the Second Macedonian War between P. Sulpicius Galba, one of the consuls of 200, and the Macedonian king Philip V in 199. Note once again the close cooperation of cavalry and light infantry which was a hallmark of Roman light-armed tactics as it was of Greek. Greek light troops tended to possess more varied weapons than their Roman counterparts. These included the sling and the bow and arrow as well as the javelin. They also frequently fought without helmet or other defensive armor besides their shield.

> The *velites* discharged their javelins and fought at close quarters with their swords, while the cavalry as soon as they rode up to the enemy reined their horses in. Some fought from the backs of their horses while others dismounted and joined the infantry, fighting on foot. The king's cavalry was inferior to this force, as it was unused to fighting in position, and his infantry were accustomed to skirmishing in open order and wore little protective equipment and were not equipped as were the Roman *velites*, who carrying both the *parma* and a sword were equally able to defend themselves and attack the enemy.

Legionary cavalry

Each legion had a complement of 300 citizen cavalry, organized in ten *turmae* or squadrons. The squadrons were subdivided into three units of ten horsemen each.

The ten horsemen consisted of eight troopers and two officers, the decurion and his handpicked subordinate, the *optio*. In each *turma* one of the three decurions commanded his unit as well as the entire squadron. The other two served under him and commanded their subunits. There was no designated overall commander of the cavalry. In normal situations a consul or legate could command the cavalry in addition to the legionary infantry.

The cavalry remained a preserve of the rich and well born. It had, however, expanded its membership in comparison to earlier periods. According to Livy, at the end of the fifth century and as result of the war with Veii cavalry troops who had not been granted a public horse began to serve with their own mounts. Although these men apparently did not participate in the special ceremonies and honors accorded to those who served with a horse bought at public expense, they still belonged to the wealthiest groups in Roman society.

Despite the social status of the cavalry it remained a secondary arm, although its role was exaggerated by historians. Since the size of a military force was in general the determining factor in military success, cavalry could play only a limited role. It was the difficulty and expense involved in raising horses that made them a socially potent symbol of status.

Greek and Roman horses were smaller than later European warhorses. However, for general cavalry fighting this was no impediment. It is the carrying capacity and endurance of the horse that counted, and for these purposes it is build and not size that is the determining factor. Even speed during the charge is less important than it at first sight seems to be. Unlike infantry, cavalry units did not directly collide with their opponents, though of course accidents did happen. Horses will not willingly crash into a solid object such as an infantryman or another horse, but will seek to find a way around it. A solid line of heavy infantry cannot be broken by cavalry. The charge's function is rather to intimidate the infantry in order to make them lose cohesion. In the case of cavalry attacking cavalry, wheeling or formations opening and riding through each other were the normal practice in antiquity and in later periods. The inability to break dense formations of heavy infantry severely hindered the ability of cavalry to dominate the battlefield.

A further limiting factor was the absence of stirrups, which did not appear in western Europe until the medieval period. Their absence affected the ability of the cavalry trooper to maintain a firm enough seat for heavy shock tactics. However, a recent examination and reconstruction of the Roman saddle of the imperial period provides evidence that at least from the first century AD Roman cavalry were to some extent capable of shock tactics. But our material evidence prior to this period is almost non-existent, and there is no compelling proof that Roman cavalry in the Republic used saddles of this type. Greek cavalry did not. The Aemilius Paullus monument of the mid-second century BC shows cavalry without saddles. In the absence of such equipment, the Republican cavalry must have had only limited shock capabilities.

The normal position of the cavalry was on the wings out of the infantry's way. Their main role was to skirmish prior to battle, either by themselves or in the Roman case in conjunction with the *velites* (see pp. 91f.). Secondly, they were useful in reconnaissance and to harass dispersed enemy troops engaged in such vital duties as foraging. Thirdly, they protected the infantry's flanks and rear either by driving off the enemy cavalry or through a holding action. The converse of this was the opportunity once the enemy cavalry had been driven from the field to attack the enemy infantry's flanks and rear, which proved decisive in a number of encounters. Finally, they were particularly effective in the pursuit that normally followed a successful battle. It was at this point, against isolated and fleeing soldiers, that they could do the most damage. It was precisely in this phase that the majority of casualties were suffered by the defeated army.

The equipment of the cavalry

76 POLYBIUS, *HISTORIES* 6.25.3–11

Unfortunately, we have almost no archaeological evidence to serve as a check on Polybius' description of Roman cavalry equipment. But given the accuracy of Polybius' description of other elements of the contemporary Roman army there is no reason to doubt his account. The change in equipment that Polybius describes is a more difficult matter. The historian's description of the cavalry prior to the adoption of Greek equipment implies that earlier Roman cavalry was essentially a light cavalry. The date of the change to heavy cavalry and the adoption of Greek equipment is problematic. Dates during the Second Punic War or in the aftermath in the first half of the second century have been proposed. The most plausible period is that of the Second Punic War when the Romans faced massive cavalry forces, some of whom fought in the Greek manner, and suffered a string of defeats which came to an abrupt end by approximately 211 when Roman cavalry appear able to face and defeat their opponents.

Contemporary Greek heavy cavalry normally wore corselets, open-faced helmets, boots, and occasionally a leather apron as protection for the thighs. There is less certainty about the use of a shield, and earlier Greek writing on cavalry warfare recommended against it, but Polybius says that cavalry normally carried it. The annalistic tradition, which uses the army of this period as its model, points to the use of a circular shield, a *parma*, slightly larger than three feet in diameter and similar to the shield of the light infantry (see p. 91). The cavalry probably wore the chain mail corselet that was also worn by infantry belonging to the highest census rating.

Any mention of a sword is strangely omitted from Polybius' discussion of cavalry equipment. Certainly, Hellenistic cavalry had it. Given the repeated Roman engagements where Roman cavalry dismounted to fight, it seems impossible that they did not carry swords, and the annalists mention them in various cavalry engagements.

At the close of this passage Polybius singles out the Roman readiness to adopt more effective equipment from others so often mentioned by other writers.

The armament of the cavalry is now like that of the Greeks. Earlier, they did not have breastplates, but went into battle protected only by a belt and so they were able to dismount and mount their horses quickly. But in close combat they were exposed to danger because of their lack of protective armor. Their lances were deficient because they made them so light and flexible that they were not able to aim them effectively, and before the iron tip became fixed in anything the vibration caused by the motion of their horse caused most of them to break. In addition to this, they were made without a butt-spike and so they were only able to deliver a single blow with the point, and after this, if they broke, they were useless. They had a shield of cowhide similar in shape to the round bossed cakes used at sacrifices. It was of no use in attack as it was not rigid enough. In rain the skin peeled off and decayed, and if it was useless before it was even more so after this. Since these arms were unsatisfactory they quickly began to replace them with arms made according to the Greek pattern, which assured that the first thrust of the spearhead would be well aimed and effective because the spear was constructed so as to be stable and firm. It was also useful for a steady and effective blow when reversed because of the addition of a butt-spike. The same applies to the Greek shield, which with its stable and firm construction is effective. The Romans after they noticed this immediately adopted it. It is one of their virtues that the Romans more readily than others adopt new practices and imitate what they see are best in those of other peoples.

Cavalry in battle: a contrast in styles

77 DIONYSIUS OF HALICARNASSUS, *ROMAN ANTIQUITIES* 20.2.1–2

Pyrrhus, king of Epirus in northwestern Greece, arrived in Italy in 280 at the request of the people of Tarentum, the most important Greek city in southern Italy, which was losing its war with Rome. An excellent commander, but too daring and impetuous, Pyrrhus brought a sizeable army of approximately 22,000 foot and 3,000 horse in addition to twenty elephants, the first seen in Italy. In 280 he defeated the Romans near Heraclea, which lay to the southwest of Tarentum along the Gulf of Tarentum and near the Siris River. After fruitless negotiations Pyrrhus renewed the conflict and defeated the Romans at Ausculum in Apulia near the Aufidus River. The following passage is taken from an account of the battle.

Dismounting to fight is mentioned in connection with other battles as a usual Roman tactic. Such a tactic allowed the cavalry trooper more freedom of movement and stability than fighting on horseback. It may be that the importance of battle scars as evidence of courage on the battlefield among the elite may have also served as motivation.

The cavalry of both armies was stationed on the wings, and aware of those tactics in which they were superior to the enemy they resorted to them: the Romans to hand-to-hand stationary fighting and the Greeks to wheeling and flanking movements. When the Romans were pursued by the Greeks, the Romans wheeled their horses about, and reining them in would fight on foot. But the Greeks, when they saw the Romans wheeling to the right and wheeling through their own ranks, turned their horses to the front and applying their spurs charged the enemy.

78 CAESAR, *GALLIC WAR* 8.28.1–29.3

Caesar's narration of this encounter belongs to 51. In the wake of his rapid conquest of Transalpine Gaul a series of revolts against Roman domination broke out in 54. After a difficult struggle Caesar spent 51 in mopping-up operations. Gaius Fabius, one of Caesar's senatorial commanders, had been sent to put down opposition in the far west of Gaul.

The use of infantry in support of cavalry is attested among the Germans and Gauls as well as the Romans. Pursuit is one of the most important activities for the cavalry and when they could be especially effective, as the enemy had lost cohesion. It was the point in the battle when the majority of casualties were inflicted on the losers. The office of prefect of the cavalry only appears in the late Republic. Dumnacus was a chieftain of one of the lesser Gallic tribes, the Andes.

On the following night Fabius sent forward his cavalry to engage the enemy and delay them until his army arrived. Q. Attius Varus, the prefect of the cavalry, a man of unusual intelligence and courage, informed them of his orders. He caught up with the enemy and, deploying some of his cavalry squadrons in suitable positions, he sent the rest into battle. The enemy fought with more than their usual intensity because they were buoyed up by their infantry coming up in support, as the whole column had stopped which was supporting their cavalry against the Romans. The battle was a fierce contest for our troopers who were contemptuous of men whom they had defeated the day before, aware of the legions coming up in support, and were anxious to finish the battle on their own. The enemy from the experience of the previous day thought the Roman cavalry would receive no further support and that they now had a chance to destroy them.

When the fierce struggle had been going on for some time and Dumnacus had drawn up his battle line to support his cavalry as the occasion demanded, the legions suddenly appeared in close order. At the sight, the cavalry squadrons of the barbarians as well as their battle line were struck with terror and cried out and turned to flight in every direction, disrupting their baggage train in the process. Our cavalry, who had a little while before courageously fought them, elated by the joy of victory and raising a loud cry, rode around the retreating Gauls, their slaughter of them limited only by the strength of their horses and their own right arms.

Command in the manipular legion

Overall military command remained confined to magistrates with *imperium*, the consuls, and the dictator. The use of *imperium* entailed responsibilities towards the gods of the state as well, especially to Jupiter Optimus Maximus, the chief god of the Roman state and the deity most closely linked to military command and the exercise of magisterial powers. It was the commander's responsibility to maintain a correct relationship with the gods. If he did not do so, he ran the risk of endangering not only his own enterprise but also the welfare of the state. On the morning of his departure from the city he was required to mount the Capitol and ascertain the will of Jupiter towards his expedition. To do so he relied on a complicated system of signs, either natural phenomena or the appearance and actions of birds and other animals. The omens did not generate a prediction of what to do, but rather whether the gods were favorably disposed.

The auspices and an accompanying prayer were repeated prior to any major engagement and could be repeated until the gods returned a favorable answer. These acts were indissolubly linked to the exercise of military command, and texts and inscriptions before the first century BC attribute the commander's victory and honor to the actions of the gods. In 367/366 a new magistracy with *imperium* of a more restricted type, the praetorship, emerged.

In essence, *imperium* was a general competency to act on behalf of the community in every sphere, and it was especially linked to command in war. Its absolute character was tempered by the fact that magistrates who possessed it were limited normally to an annual tenure or less and operated with a colleague of equal authority. The only exceptions to the rule of collegiality were the dictatorship and the praetorship before the later increase in the numbers of praetors. However, in the case of a dictator a shortened tenure of office limited to a specific task or six months compensated for the absence of an equal authority. The praetor remained limited by the superior *imperium* of the consuls.

The employment of the collegial principle, in spite of its usefulness as a check on the untrammeled authority, created problems of its own. In theory a consul could check an action of his colleague by a veto, but mechanisms were developed to ease such conflicts. Normally, consuls did not campaign together; one remained at Rome while the other commanded in the field. In cases such as the battle of Cannae in 216 BC where both consuls were operating simultaneously, command was rotated on a daily basis. Other methods such as prior agreement or the use of the lot were used to dampen disagreements and differences.

Though the elite character of command remained the same as it had been in the early Republic, the group which supplied that elite changed in the course of the fourth century. A combination of economic, social, and political problems led to important changes in political organization and social structure which had a pronounced effect on the army. At the level of supreme command the most striking result was the creation of a new elite from which the consuls and later in the century the praetors were drawn. This change was the result of the opening of consular office to elite plebeians after 367/366. The first plebeian dictator held office in 356, and the first plebeian praetor held office exactly twenty years later. Plebeians were gradually allowed access to the other state offices so that, by the end of the fourth century, they no longer suffered from any bars to holding public office. As a result of these developments a new mixed patrician–plebeian elite emerged.

However, there were certain residual barriers between patricians and plebeians within the new elite. The best evidence for them is the delay in granting plebeians triumphs. The first did not occur until 306. This expansion of the ruling group also led to increased competition for political office. It is surely no accident that the pace of military operations picked up in the last half of the fourth century.

Military command must have become more complicated in this period, owing to the increasing numbers of troops and formations army commanders had to deal with. In addition, the numbers of independently operating groups increased as simultaneous campaigns were carried on in several theaters. The election of military tribunes for the legions levied during the year provides evidence for the increasing scale of operations. They were first elected in 362 and totaled six. In 311 Livy notes that sixteen tribunes of the four legions were elected by popular vote. The remaining eight were nominated by the consul conducting the levy. Livy presents this as a popular victory, and that implies that a higher percentage of the tribunes were now elected. Thus it is not unlikely that by 362 the normal annual levy was two legions and that prior to 311 the number of legions had doubled to four. Since each legion was accompanied by at least an equivalent force of allies under Roman command (see pp. 125ff.), there was a corresponding increase in allied forces as well. During the Second Punic War as many as twenty-five legions were enrolled, with an average of approximately twenty legions in service every year between 218 and 202. The vast increase in troop strength and the need to operate in separate theaters led to the development of new methods to increase the numbers of commanders available (see pp. 110ff.). In the areas of logistics and daily administration there must have been a vast increase in complexity, but the nature of the legionary formation, with so much of its tactical command devolved to small units and junior officers, simplified the task of commanding in battle.

The yearly alteration of magistrates created problems. Differences of policy and personality might make maintaining a consistent course of action difficult. To some extent the need for popular agreement for a formal declaration of war and shared values among the elite tended to promote stability. The most important factor in supporting such consistency was the Senate, which had emerged as the leading organ of state by the first quarter of the third century BC. Membership in the Senate was lifelong. Senators were appointed by the consuls until 312 and then by censors. Over time, membership in the Senate usually followed for a senior magistrate after his term of office, despite the fact that the consuls were not legally bound to choose such ex-magistrates. Though empowered only to offer advice in the form of resolutions, the Senate represented the collective opinion of leading aristocrats who could affect a consul's political future. Moreover the fact that the consul would one day again be a member made the consul sensitive to senatorial opinion and conferred an authority on the Senate that it did not legally possess.

The Senate in the third century also possessed formal powers that could create problems for consuls who disregarded it. The Senate controlled the state treasury as well as all state revenues and expenditures. The Senate's permission was needed by the consuls to conduct troop levies and to grant discharges. Further, the Senate assigned the consuls' spheres of action or *provinciae*. It played a central role in relations with foreign powers, and normally its consent was necessary for the declaration of war. These powers severely reduced magistrates' independence. Despite these limitations consuls and proconsuls sometimes ignored the senatorial authority. That authority rested on fragile foundations, as the last century of the Republic would show. Nevertheless, in the third and second centuries the Senate was able to exercise a general oversight of military and foreign policy, providing a consistency which annually changing magistrates could not.

The consuls

79 POLYBIUS, *HISTORIES* 6.12.1–8

This passage is from Polybius' description of Rome's constitution, designed to illustrate the reasons for its emergence in a very short time as the most important Mediterranean power. Polybius envisions the Roman constitution as a mixed constitution consisting of three parts: monarchical, aristocratic, and democratic. In his view the consuls are the monarchical element. Although containing much useful information, Polybius' analysis fails to mirror much of the reality of Roman politics.

By the mid-second century the authority of the consuls was more circumscribed than it had been earlier. Praetors had taken over much of the judicial business formerly undertaken by the consuls. The censors, especially after 311, assumed important functions in the area of public finance, especially for the assessment of the *tributum*, the extraordinary levy that financed military campaigns. They now enrolled new members of the Senate, which must have altered the relationship of the consuls to that body.

On campaign the consul's authority was legally subject to no restriction, as Polybius mentions. Within Rome, perhaps as early as 449 but certainly by 300, a magistrate's legal decision was subject to a right of appeal to the popular assembly. In the field the consuls retained the right to execute citizens without appeal.

The obligations of Roman allies were fixed by treaty but Rome could and did make demands for men above and beyond the specified numbers when the situation demanded it.

The consuls, while exercising their authority at Rome before leading out the legions, are in charge of all public matters. The other magistrates are subordinate to them and obey them except for the tribunes of the plebs.... Further, they have an almost absolute authority in all matters concerning the preparation for war and the conduct of a campaign. They can issue appropriate orders to the allies. They are able to appoint military tribunes and they have the authority to draw up the register of those liable to military service and to select those who are suitable for service. In addition to these powers they are able to punish anyone they wish and in any way while a campaign is in progress, and they have authority in the field to spend as much as they see fit of public moneys. For this reason they are accompanied on campaign by a quaestor ready to carry out their every order.

Alternation of command

80 POLYBIUS, *HISTORIES* 3.110.4

The disagreement mentioned in the following passage forms part of the preliminaries to the Roman disaster at Cannae in Apulia in 216. It was one of the worst defeats in Roman history (see pp. 150ff.). It illustrates one of the conflict-limiting mechanisms in a collegiate magistracy, devised to prevent disagreement from paralyzing action. The same approach appears in other facets of the consulship. The most graphic example is that of the lictors alternating monthly.

The two consuls were Gaius Terentius Varro and Lucius Aemilius Paullus. Paullus was later to die in the battle.

On the following day the consuls broke camp and marched their army to where they had heard that the enemy was encamped. On the second day, coming upon them, they set up camp about six miles from them. Lucius, seeing the surrounding area was flat and bare, said that they should not attack, since the enemy was superior in cavalry, but draw them on to a place where conditions for an infantry battle were favorable. However, Terentius, because of his lack of military experience, was of the opposite opinion. So quarrels and difficulties arose between the consuls, the worst thing that can happen in such circumstances. The command reverted to Varro for the following day because of the Roman custom that the consuls should alternate command daily.

The praetorship

In 367/366 the Licinian–Sextian Rogations opened access to the consulship to plebeians and created a new office, the praetorship. Livy describes the new office as a concession to the patricians and claims its function was the administration of justice. It appears that Livy was correct about its being a concession to the patricians, as a generation passed before a plebeian praetor held office, Q. Publilius Philo in 336.

The reasons for the creation of the office are less certain. It has recently been asserted that the origin of the office lay in the need for additional military commanders rather than in the area of civil administration. The paucity of our sources on praetorian activity makes any firm conclusion impossible. However, some points can be made. The fourth century was a time of both intense military activity and territorial expansion for Rome. These factors led to the absence of the consuls in the field and therefore to the inability of these chief magistrates to perform their urban judicial duties. The praetorship would act as a remedy for this difficulty. The creation of a single praetor instead of a college to parallel that of the consuls is in itself unusual and makes more sense as a device to fulfill a singular and specific need.

The praetor's possession of *imperium* allowed him to exercise military command in a subordinate capacity when needed, but it is unlikely to have been the main reason for the creation of the office. The military activity of the praetorship is first mentioned in 350, when a consul placed a praetor in command of a reserve force. The second praetor, created in 242, who heard suits between foreigners or between foreigners and citizens, is often found commanding the fleet.

The praetor's *imperium* was of the same nature as the consuls', and he was elected in the same assembly. However, his insignia of office made clear that his power was subordinate to that of the consuls.

The quaestorship

On campaign the consul was always accompanied by a quaestor. The latter's importance is made clear by the fact that at the center of the Roman military camp the quarters of the quaestor were in a separate building adjoining the consul's. In theory, the relationship of the consul to his quaestor paralleled that of a father to his son. The direct dependence is made more evident by the fact that the quaestor's tenure of office was dependent on that of the consul. The main duties of the quaestor were financial and logistic. He was in charge of the campaign treasury and saw to the provisioning of the army. At the end of the campaign it was the quaestor's responsibility to submit his accounts to the state for auditing. But the range of his activity extended far beyond these matters, and in practice he could be used for any task. If the consul died or was incapacitated the quaestor assumed temporary command until the arrival of a replacement.

The tradition claims that quaestors existed under the kings and at the beginning of the Republic. It is more likely that quaestors were first appointed early in the fifth century as Rome's finances became more complex. Probably they were originally assistants to the consuls in financial matters. By the second century it was the Senate that selected their individual spheres of action. From 449 the two quaestors were elected by the tribal assembly. Although by the early second century BC they were required to have ten years of military service, they were not given *imperium* and so were incapable of exercising independent military command unless the consul delegated some task to them. In 421 two more quaestors were created to accompany the consuls on campaign. The number of quaestors increased as tasks multiplied. The formation of provinces led to further increases, and by the first quarter of the first century BC the number of quaestors was raised to twenty.

Dictatorship

81 PLUTARCH, *FABIUS MAXIMUS* 4.1–9.1

The first known dictator was appointed in 501 to meet a military emergency. In general, dictators were elected by the assembly after being nominated by one of the consuls to meet military crises, but they also performed many other political and religious tasks. The term of office was limited to six months or to the completion of the task for which they were chosen. Unlike other magistrates, they held power without a colleague. By the early third century, men who had previously held the consulship were chosen for this office. The period after 302 witnessed the gradual demise of the office, with the sources mentioning dictators only for 301, 249, and Fabius Maximus in 217. The last two appointments occurred in periods of severe crisis, with a single theater of operations dominating all of the others. The disappearance of the dictatorship seems to be the result of an attempt by the aristocracy to restrain the power of its members by limiting access to important offices. In addition, the use of promagistrates (see pp. 110ff.) as military commanders and the increase in the number of theaters where military campaigns were taking place reduced the need for an overall military commander.

The Fabius of the passage is Q. Fabius Maximus Verrucosus, who had already held the consulship twice, in 233 and again in 228. The defeat at Lake Trasimene in 217 led to the revival of the dictatorship, which had been in abeyance for over thirty years. Fabius laid down his office after six months at the end of 217.

The extent of the limitation of the dictator's right to use a horse is not clear. Presumably, the limitation only applied to use on the battlefield, given the advanced age of many dictators. Various explanations for this limitation have been offered. Its purpose remains obscure.

> After his appointment as dictator Fabius named as his master of the cavalry Marcus Minucius. His first request of the Senate was to be allowed the use of a horse on campaign, for such use was not permitted because of an ancient law, either because the Romans considered their strength to lie in their infantry and so thought that the commander ought to remain with the phalanx and not leave it behind or because the power of a dictator is tyrannical in nature with respect to the rest of the state and so in this at least they wished to make it appear that the dictator had need of the people.

The magister equitum

Though the original functions of the office are the subject of debate, it is clear that it must have had some political purposes, as dictators were required to appoint one even if they were elected for non-military reasons. They possessed an *imperium* that was subordinate to the dictator's, which parallels the relation of the praetors to consuls, and their term of office was limited to that of the dictator who had appointed them.

After an important defeat of Roman forces under Gaius Flaminius at Lake Trasimene in 217 and the death of the consul in battle, the Romans revived the antiquated office of dictator. In an unprecedented step the appointment was made by popular vote instead of by the remaining consul. The reasons alleged for this anomaly are hard to credit and it is difficult to resist the idea that Fabius and his supporters were behind the unprecedented turn of events. This irregularity was carried one step farther by the election of Minucius as Fabius' master of the horse. Such a procedure vitiated the fundamental relationship between the dictator and his master of the horse. Traditionally, the master of the horse had been a direct subordinate of the dictator and handpicked by him as a means to insure a minimum of conflict. The separate election of Minucius is evidence that the dictatorship had ceased to function as it had earlier. The situation was made worse by the constant friction between Fabius and Minucius, and it seems likely that from the start Minucius was a political opponent of the dictator.

Fabius pursued a strategy of attrition and refused to engage Hannibal in set battle. In the circumstances this was probably the correct strategy to adopt, but the lack of tangible success and the traditional Roman preference for the offensive and for a decisive battle made the dictator's conduct of the war extremely unpopular. During the absence of the dictator in Rome, Minucius, despite explicit orders not to engage Hannibal, won a minor victory. This precipitated a major development at Rome. On the motion of a tribune of the plebs, Minucius was voted *imperium* equal to that of Fabius. The two men were unable to cooperate, and Fabius' army was divided between them. In effect these developments meant the end of the traditional dictatorship. Military emergency in the past had made the office of dictator an efficient response when Rome was engaged in wars that were fought in Italy and on a smaller scale. As the nominee of the consul and approved by the Senate the dictator could act with the support of a generally united aristocracy behind him. The changes in the nature of Rome's military commitments and increased competition among the aristocracy meant that such a consensus was now no longer possible. The dictatorship and the master of the horse survived for functions other than military command until the end of the century. In fact, election to the dictatorship was again resorted to in 210. But for all intents and purposes the dictatorship and the master of the horse disappeared. When these offices were revived in the first century BC by Sulla and Caesar they served very different purposes.

82 LIVY, 22.8.5–6

Since the consul by whom the dictator could alone be nominated was absent and could not easily be contacted either by messenger or letter because of the Carthaginian military presence in Italy, a thing that had never happened before, the people elected Q. Fabius Maximus dictator and M. Minucius Rufus as master of the horse.

83 LIVY, 22.11.1–3

The dictator consulted the Senate on which legions he should take and how many of them to confront the enemy. The Senate decreed that he should take over the army of the consul Gnaeus Servilius and he should enroll as many horse and foot as he deemed best. After these were levied by his master of the horse he ordered them to assemble at Tibur on a specified day.

Military tribunes

Six military tribunes were assigned to each legion. They served in pairs for two months each in rotation, and there may have been a daily rotation of the tribunes parallel to that of the consuls, though we have no specific evidence. They were the equivalent of staff officers. The remaining four served on the consul's staff as advisors while they were not on active duty. Their term of office was annual.

Given the close relationship with their commander, the tribunes were initially selected by the consul or consuls, but starting in 362 the six legionary tribunes were probably elected in the tribal assembly. In 311 the number was raised to sixteen and finally by 207 twenty-four were elected. These were the tribunes of the four urban legions, raised in campaign years, which were the equivalent of two consular armies. Their election by the tribal assembly meant that the tribunate had now become a normal annual magistracy.

The tribunes as senior officers of the legion were separated by a rigid divide from the centurions and other non-commissioned officers. They were of at least equestrian birth and many were members of important senatorial families. Polybius states that they were required to have prior military service. Fourteen had to have five years' experience, while the other ten had to serve for ten years before their election. Until the first century men who had served as senior magistrates often served as tribunes after they left office. The death toll of the battle of Cannae in 216 included twenty-nine military tribunes, among whom were men who had been consul or praetor.

It is difficult to be certain how far these formal requirements for this office were respected. It appears that at least in some cases the known individuals were simply too young to have gained the required amount of prior service. By the first century BC the qualifications for the military tribunate had changed fundamentally. The rules on prior service were no longer in force. There is evidence that men chosen for the office had little or no military experience and that other factors determined their selection. Ex-magistrates no longer served, and tribunes were recruited almost exclusively from equestrians, who often did not pursue a senatorial career. This development is to be connected with the increasing use from the early second century of legates (see pp. 112f.), men of senior rank chosen by the Senate on the recommendation of the commander.

Polybius provides our most extensive evidence for the duties of the tribune, although most of it relates to administrative duties. Besides specific duties such as playing an important role in the military levy, tribunes selected the site for the daily marching camp and were responsible for aspects of guarding the camp and administering military justice. More generally, in their task as elected magistrates they had a responsibility to see to the health, interests, and general welfare of the troops.

From sporadic references in Livy and elsewhere it is clear that the tribune did play a role in battle. We hear of tribunes setting the battle line in order, performing reconnaissance and making reports to the consul, sitting on the commander's military council, and commanding detachments. In the late Republic there is even evidence for their command of individual legions. Here, as in the case of the praetor, the concentration of sources on the highest echelon of military command obscures military activity at lower levels.

The duties of the military tribune

84 *DIGEST* OF JUSTINIAN, 49.16.12.2, ON MILITARY MATTERS

This selection comes from the *Digest* of Justinian (emperor 527–565). The *Digest* issued in 530 was a compilation from the writings of earlier legal authorities. Though late, its list of the tribunes' duties accords with the outline of some of the responsibilities given in Polybius, although large areas such as the activity of the tribune in the levy are omitted.

Polybius provides some information of the tribunes' legal duties. He mentions the tribune's responsibility to serve at court martials and to order punishment in cases where a night watch neglects its duty.

> The duties of military tribunes or others who have military command are to: keep the soldiers in camp, to lead them out to training, to receive the keys to a camp's gates, to check the guards at intervals, to attend to their fellow soldiers' food supply, to keep fraud by those who measure out the food supply in check, to punish wrongdoing in accordance with their authority, to be present frequently at headquarters, to hear the soldiers' complaints, and to inspect the sick.

The tribune in battle: Cynoscephalae

85 POLYBIUS, *HISTORIES* 18.26.1–3

For the battle between Philip V and the Romans in Thessaly in 197, see pp. 171ff. This is one of the few instances in which we find a tribune exercising command on the battlefield. The other recorded instances are late. The tribune's role is unclear.

Was he in command of the entire legion, as is occasionally attested later, or simply the twenty maniples that formed the first two lines? Was the movement of the troops done on his own initiative or did he first consult the consul? At least Polybius makes clear that the reading of the tactical situation was his own.

> The majority of the Romans cut them down in pursuit. One of the tribunes who was with them having twenty maniples with him and perceiving on the spur of the moment what needed to be done contributed greatly to the success of the entire battle. He saw that the men with Philip had advanced far in front of the others and were pressing back with their weight the Roman left. Leaving the Roman right which was now clearly victorious, he turned towards the left wing and coming up from behind fell upon the Macedonian rear.

The centurion

The sixty centurions of the legion formed a crucial link between the high command and the common soldier. They were the equivalent of non-commissioned officers and exercised tactical command of their units in battle. Their experience allowed the normally rather loose chain of command to function successfully. Their name implies that they commanded a group of a hundred men and presumably dates to the creation of the centuries system under Servius Tullius if not earlier, since the extant references to the earliest Roman army depict a decimal organization.

According to Polybius, during the annual levy the military tribunes acting under consular authority selected ten men of proven military experience from each of the three lines as prior or senior centurions and then a second thirty as posterior or junior centurions. In practice, patronage as well as merit must have played a part. Centurions normally had prior service as common soldiers. Until the Empire the centurionate was the highest rank to which citizens who were not members of the elite could aspire. There is some evidence that in the late Republic this social barrier was occasionally breached.

The century remained an important administrative unit, but, as mentioned earlier, on the battlefield the main tactical unit was the maniple of two centuries. Each of these units was commanded by the prior and the posterior centurions. Polybius mentions the first as commanding the right of the unit while the posterior commanded the left. He further states that the prior was in command of the entire unit, with the posterior acting as his subordinate and replacement if necessary.

All of the centurions of a legion were graded by rank. The centurions of the *triarii* maniples were the most senior, followed by those of the *principes*, who were in turn senior to the centurions of the maniples of the *hastati*. In each of the three lines seniority increased as one moved from left to right. Added to this was the distinction between prior and posterior centurions within the maniple, so that the posterior centurion of the maniple of the *hastati* at the far left of the line was the most junior centurion in the legion while the prior centurion of the maniple of the *triarii* on the far right of the line was the most senior. The latter centurion was known as the *primipilus*, since from the second century the *triarii* were often known as the *pilani* because of their column-like formation.

The seniority of the centurions of the *triarii* may at first seem surprising, as according to the Livian description of the manipular army in battle these maniples were only used in an emergency. However, this meant that they were the last to engage in battle and thus their centurions could issue commands for the maniples in front of them without the distractions of combat. In both Greek and Roman warfare the right side of the line was not only the most dangerous, since it was unshielded; it also held primacy ideologically, and these factors probably explain the rank of the *primipilus*. In addition, centurions commanded the *velites* in the field.

There has been a great deal of controversy as to how the system of promotion worked. This is complicated by the fact that, until the Romans maintained large-scale overseas forces, the legions were recruited annually and thus there could have been no formal hierarchy. But it is clear from the evidence that men who had served as centurions in certain grades expected to be reappointed at that rank or above. Certainly, by the last century of the Republic the existence of a semi-professional army must have made promotion possible, although how this was done is far from clear. Also, within this graded hierarchy there existed a small group of elite centurions. The ancient sources identify them as the *primi ordines*. As a mark of their status they sat on the commander's war council and could influence crucial military decisions. It is difficult to identify which centurions belonged to this group. The most likely candidates are the prior centurions of the maniples on the right of the line. The important advantages in pay and privileges that the centurions enjoyed, which included double pay at the least, must have acted as a strong incentive among the troops, since valor in action was an essential avenue to promotion.

In addition to their role on the battlefield and in administration, centurions were central to maintaining unit discipline. Their emblem of office was the *vitis* or staff of vine wood which symbolized their ability to inflict corporal punishment. In accounts of disturbances centurions were often the first targets on whom the disgruntled soldiers vented their rage.

To carry out his numerous tasks the centurion appointed an assistant, the *optio*. This officer's main function appears to have been to relieve the centurion of many of his administrative duties, but as was more generally the case in the Roman system of command he could also be used in whatever capacity his superior chose. The centurion also appointed two *signiferi* to carry the maniple's standard. The second would act as a substitute should the first be unable to carry out his duties.

The qualities of the centurion

86 POLYBIUS, *HISTORIES* 6.24.9

[The Romans] want their centurions to be not so much bold or risk takers, but rather wished them to be capable of command, steady and controlled.

They want them to attack when the issue is in doubt, or to open the battle, but to hold fast even when the battle went against them and they were hard pressed, and to die at their post.

The career of a centurion

87 LIVY, 42.34.1–11

The following speech by Spurius Ligustinus comes from Livy's description of the levy of 171 in preparation for the war against King Perseus of Macedonia. We are told that the consuls conducted the levy with more than normal severity, enrolling men who had previously served as both rankers and centurions. They enrolled former centurions as they came, presumably assigning posts in that order. As a result, twenty-three former holders of the primipilate appealed to the tribunes on the grounds that they should not be assigned a lower rank than they had held previously, and as a result an investigation was begun.

This is an extraordinary document, though its source must remain uncertain. However, there is no reason to doubt the outlines of the career Spurius sets out in his speech.

Spurius' career was probably unusual in both his length of service and the degree of success he achieved. Normally, Roman infantry were required to serve sixteen years before the age of forty-six, according to Polybius, although the number is not totally certain. But there must have been enormous variation, as in this case, where the consuls were permitted by the Senate to enroll men up to the age of fifty-one. As Livy indicates, there were men on this campaign who sought to enroll because the prospect of the rich booty the war was expected to produce.

Spurius' tribe, the Clustumina, lay north of the old Latin town of Fidenae along the Via Salaria. He was clearly brought up in rural poverty as the size of his farm is meant to stress. Peasants provided the main source of recruits.

His career opens with the Second Macedonian War in 200, and he remained in service until its conclusion in 196. He then served as a volunteer in Cato's successful Spanish campaign in 195, and then again in the East against Antiochus III between 191 and 188. His second sequence of Spanish campaigns fell in the late 180s and early 170s. In fact, his career forms a list of the major Roman wars of the period. It illustrates both the continuity of the Roman command structure at the level of the centurionate and the possibility for what amounted to a semi-professional career made possible by constant campaigning and the prolongation of service by the growing number of campaigns fought outside of Italy.

After the consul had spoken as he intended, Spurius Ligustinus, who belonged to the group summoned by the tribunes, asked permission of the consul and tribunes to say a few words to the people. Then with the agreement of all he spoke as follows: "Fellow citizens, I am Spurius Ligustinus, belonging to the tribe of Clustumina. I come from the Sabine land. My father left me less than an acre of land and a little hut in which I was born and brought up, where I still live.... I began my military service when P. Sulpicius and C. Aurelius were consuls. I served as an ordinary soldier in the army which was transported to Macedonia to fight King Philip. In my third year of service, on account of my bravery, T. Quinctius Flamininus made me a centurion of the tenth maniple of the *hastati*. After the defeat of Philip and the Macedonians, when the army returned to Italy and was released from service, I set out for Spain as a volunteer in the army of the consul M. Porcius. And those who through long military service have served under Cato and other commanders know there is no commander alive who is a more critical observer or sharper judge of courage. This commander appointed me prior centurion of the first maniple of the *hastati*. I served my third tour of duty as a volunteer in the army sent against the Aetolians and King Antiochus. The commander M. Acilius named me as prior centurion of the first maniple of the *principes*. After the expulsion of Antiochus and the defeat of the Aetolians, we returned to Italy, and next I served two annual campaigns. I then went on to serve twice in Spain, the first time under Fulvius Flaccus and the second time with the praetor Tiberius Sempronius Gracchus in command. I was among those whom on account of courageous conduct Flaccus brought back for his triumph. I was called back to the province by Tiberius Gracchus. Within a few years I held the position of *primipilus* four times and I was decorated thirty-four times. I received six civic crowns. I have completed twenty-two campaigns and am now more than fifty years old."

The centurion in battle

88 CAESAR, *GALLIC WAR* 2.25

The following incident took place during Caesar's campaign against the tribe of the Nervi in northeastern Gaul in 57 BC. Sextius Baculus, though perhaps not fully recovered from his wounds, appears twice more in heroic roles in Caesar's account. In 56 one of Caesar's lieutenants, Sergius, encamped in a narrow valley and was surrounded by the enemy. It was only on the advice of Baculus and a tribune that a sortie was made that ended the encirclement. Finally, in 53 as a convalescent he valiantly rallied the defenders during an attack on a camp and was again severely wounded. It is likely that he died soon after as a result.

The portion of Baculus' career that appears in Caesar's narrative serves as an excellent illustration of the centurion's role. He directs his men in battle and just as importantly maintains their fighting spirit especially in difficult circumstances. The latter is a recurrent motif of the portrayal of the centurion in the annalists. In part, this may be due to the moral cast of ancient battle narrative in which human character is often more important than technical skill. Baculus is shown as acting as an advisor in his capacity as *primipilus* and so an automatic member of the commander's war council. What is lacking here as well as elsewhere is any sense of the functions of a legion's centurions as a whole throughout the course of a major engagement or in the routine of camp life.

> Caesar, after encouraging the Tenth Legion, set out for his right wing where he saw the Twelfth Legion under pressure. Their standards had been gathered in one place and the soldiers were so packed together that they got into each other's way as they fought. In the fourth cohort all of the centurions had been killed, and the standard bearer had fallen, with the loss of the cohort's standard. In the remaining cohorts the centurions had all been killed or disabled. Among the latter was P. Sextius Baculus, the *primipilus*, who was an extremely brave man and so afflicted with serious wounds that he could not stand erect. The remaining men were tiring, and some of those at the extreme rear of the unit had given up the battle; they had withdrawn from the battle and kept clear of the enemy's missiles. The enemy in front was advancing against them from low ground and pressing them on both flanks. Our troops were in great danger and there was no relief possible that could be moved up. Having snatched a shield from one of the soldiers at the rear of the formation, Sextius moved to the front line. After appealing to the centurions by name, and then encouraging the soldiers, he ordered an advance and instructed the maniples to open up to allow freer sword play. His arrival rekindled the men's hope and restored their spirits. The enemy attack was slowed, as each man, no matter how desperate his situation was, wanted to do all that he could in the sight of his commander.

Promagistrates

By the closing decades of the fourth century the pace of Roman warfare accelerated as Rome pursued an expansionist policy. One of its consequences was the need for a larger number of military commanders than earlier. Further, given the magnitude of the Roman military commitment, there was also the need to maintain a supply of men of proven competence.

The number of annual magistrates was not equal to the task. There were only three, the two consuls and the praetor, and there was the further limitation of annual tenure. This limitation and several others had been put in place as safeguards against the abuse of power, but in the face of increasing demands they had created a problem. One solution might have been to enlarge the number of offices that possessed *imperium*. Such a solution was attempted in the previous century with the creation of military tribunes with consular powers (see pp. 40f.) and found unacceptable. The need to retain commanders of demonstrated ability presented another dilemma. The elite's own interests dictated the need to maintain restricted access to the highest offices and to thereby limit the possibilities of outside competition as well as limiting the success of its own members to avoid imbalance. Since military office was so vital to prestige and political success, it remained the area where restricted access was particularly important.

Though in theory the powers of the consuls in their military and civilian aspects were integral parts of their office, in practice by the mid-fifth century the idea had developed that a number of the consul's tasks could be split off and assigned to other magistrates. Not only various duties but magisterial power could also be conceived as separable. This was especially true of *imperium* because of the nature of its conferment on the magistrate. Election to the consulship did not automatically grant the magistrate *imperium*; a separate vote by the *comitia curiata* was necessary, though given automatically. This temporal separation of *imperium* from office led to the view that it had an existence separate from office-holding. This made possible a solution which preserved the balance among the elite while providing the necessary number of commanders: the conferral of *imperium* on non-magistrates.

Until the Second Punic War (218–201) these grants were of a limited nature except during the crisis of the Second Samnite War. During the war the grants were for a single year, although for the first time extended to the praetorship. The known grants were limited to extending a magistrate's military authority after the expiration of his annual term of office. But after this crisis, from 291 to 218, in the absence of compelling need the practice disappeared.

It was only with the grave emergency of the Second Punic War that the promagistracy enjoyed a remarkable resurgence, with approximately six prorogued commands a year. The constant need for multiple commanders to fight on many fronts brought about several changes. Grants of proconsular and propraetorian *imperium* were now made for a number of years. They first extended to men who had previously held a magistracy with *imperium* and then finally to private individuals who had held no prior office. Perhaps the best-known example of the latter is that of P. Scipio Africanus, who in 210 was granted a proconsular command in Spain as a private citizen. He had previously held only a minor office.

The growing empire that resulted from Rome's military success in the eastern and western Mediterranean and the gradual annexation of these areas as provinces led to proconsuls being appointed as governors, though initially there had been an increase in the number of regular magistrates. The adding of provinces, however, made this an impractical solution. Nevertheless, attempts were made to limit the concentration of power in any of these promagisterial offices by limiting tenure of most to a single year.

The procedure for assigning a proconsular or propraetorian command gradually became formalized. Originally we have several references to consuls themselves assigning such commands in the field. The procedure that developed involved both the Senate and the popular assembly. The Senate chose the recipient and set the time limits for his command and the sphere in which it could be exercised. A consul then presented the Senate's decree to the assembly, whose assent was necessary for it to have the force of law. At the center of the whole process stood the Senate, which exercised a close control of the procedure. It was within this body that debate on these commands was held and bargaining until an acceptable candidate was chosen. The Senate so dominated the process in this period that Livy and some other authors simply omit the passage of the enabling law in the popular assembly. It was only when the Senate began to lose control of the process that such commands became a danger to its aristocratic government.

The first formal assignment of a proconsular command

89 LIVY, 8.23.10–12

The notice that this was the first instance of such prolongation of command beyond a magistrate's year of office appears accurate. There are earlier cases mentioned but they seem to be anachronisms or errors. The measure was clearly taken as a practical step to meet a difficult situation. Publilius was engaged in a siege of the Greek city of Naples in Campania and close to capturing it when he would have normally been recalled to Rome to hold elections and then to complete his term of office. The vote to extend his command until the fall of the city was the result of these circumstances. We have later instances of extended commands for the performance of specific tasks. Philo's extraordinary record of political and military success must also have been a factor in the decision. By the time of his promagistracy he had already held the consulship twice and he was to go on to hold it twice more, a record which stood until the first century BC. He had been dictator, *magister equitum*, and censor although of plebeian rank. He had also an established reputation for military success. After his capture of Naples, Philo celebrated the first triumph held by a proconsul. Until the extension of empire made prolongation of commands regular and necessary, proroguing of command remained essentially a device designed to deal with specific situations. Palaeopolis was a suburb of Naples.

> Publilius by opportunely occupying a position between Palaeopolis and Neapolis (Naples) deprived them of the ability to mutually support each other. Since the time for elections was drawing near, and it was not in the public's interest to summon home Publilius, who was threatening the enemy's walls and was expecting to capture their city any day, the Senate persuaded the tribunes that they should bring before the assembly a proposal that, when Q. Publilius Philo finished his magistracy, he should conduct operations as proconsul until the defeat of the Greeks.

Legates

The structure of Roman military command at its summit had a serious weakness. There existed no system for automatic substitution in cases where the holder of *imperium* was absent or when there was a need for army detachments to operate independently. On occasion, military tribunes could be used, but they were closely tied to individual legions and were often deficient in military experience. After the end of the Second Punic War the Romans devised a system of standing legates or lieutenants to increase the personnel available to exercise command and perform other functions. As opposed to other commanders, legates did not possess *imperium* themselves, nor were they magistrates or promagistrates. They were essentially deputies whose power was derived directly from the holder of *imperium*. Though military command was a central function, they could execute any task on the instructions of the commander, and their status as legates ended with the completion of their tasks.

The annalists assign to them an important role from the early years of the Republic, though scholars have expressed doubt about such an early origin for the institution. A crucial piece of evidence has been the casualty list given by Livy of Roman officers who perished at the battle of Cannae in 216. Since a major portion of the force was destroyed it should provide solid evidence for the absence or presence of legates by that date. In fact, Livy omits any mention of legates among the dead. The notice does provide evidence for the absence of standing legates, but there is no reason to doubt that they were used occasionally earlier and seem to have been chosen from among the existing officers of the army such as military tribunes. It is usual to date the transition to the legate as a standing officer to the period between the Second Punic War and the 190s. By Polybius' time in the mid-second century BC they are a normal part of the command structure. The creation of standing legates changed the character of the holders of this office. Though *equites* were earlier occasionally chosen as legates, the post was now often filled by senior senators, sometimes of consular rank. For those at an earlier stage in their career it became a faster and surer path to advancement, and the importance of the military tribune diminished accordingly. The creation of standing legates also affected the process of their appointment. The Senate now assumed control of the process by appointing them at the beginning of the political year when they assigned spheres of activity to the consuls and other magistrates. The appointment by the Senate might be seen as an attempt to limit the independence of commanders, but it seems often the legate was chosen upon recommendation of the commander himself and was often a close associate who would probably aid rather than restrain his superior officer.

For a century, standing legates were used only in overseas campaigns and then as assistants to the governors of a growing list of provinces. It was not until the war between Rome and its Italian allies in the 90s and 80s of the first century BC that they were used in Italy. By the 50s, under Caesar, legates appear to regularly command legions or expeditionary forces. When Caesar distributed his forces throughout Gaul in 54 to conserve food supplies his legates commanded the various legionary camps and their surrounding area. However, these arrangements were temporary and dictated by the situation. It was not until the Empire that the position of legates was formalized and they became the main commanders of Rome's military forces as deputies of the emperor.

The preparations by Lucius Aemilius Paullus, consul in 168, for his campaign against Perseus provides a summary of some of the tasks carried out by legates prior to the actual campaign.

> It was immediately apparent to all that Aemilius would conduct the war energetically. Among other evidence, it was clear from the fact that he devoted his exclusive attention to it day and night. First of all, he requested the Senate to send legates to inspect the army and fleet, and to report back based on first-hand knowledge what military and naval forces were required and, in addition, to find out what they could about the king's forces, how much territory the enemy controlled, and how much was controlled by Rome; whether the Romans were encamped in difficult country or had cleared all the passes and reached level ground; which allies were loyal, which were doubtful and waiting on events, and finally who were openly hostile. Further they were to ascertain the amount of supplies assembled and land and sea resupply routes. Finally, what were the results of this year's land and sea campaigns?

These events belong to 171 and the initial operations against Perseus. Legates could command independent forces, as Lucretius does here, as well as exercise important subordinate commands, as Domitius Ahenobarbus acting as legate to Scipio Asiaticus did at the battle of Magnesia in 189 against Antiochus III. Haliartus lay in central Boeotia.

> At about the same time Gaius Lucretius, the praetor in charge of the fleet at Cephallenia, ordered his brother Marcus to sail to Chalcis past the Malian promontory ... Marcus reached Chalcis when he heard that Haliartus was being besieged by Publius Lentulus. In the name of the praetor he ordered Lentulus to abandon the siege. The legate had undertaken it with that part of the Boeotian troops who were allied to the Romans. The end of this siege gave way to a new one; Lucretius surrounded Haliartus with 10,000 marines and 2,000 of the king's troops under Athenaeus.

Logistics

Though technical and often ignored in modern studies of warfare, logistics are a crucial part of any army's ability to fight. Napoleon's dictum that "an army marches on its stomach" is not the whole truth; rather, all military operations depend on the adequate provision of supplies. Without them sickness and desertion destroy armies. Since the nineteenth century the art of military supply has been labeled as "logistics," a term that basically covers all aspects of army movement and supply. Interestingly, though there are Latin terms referring to various aspects of supply there was no Roman term embracing all aspects of supply that corresponded to logistics.

The study of ancient Roman logistics is complicated by the fact that ancient historians rarely refer to normal Roman practice. It is generally only when the system breaks down or some extraordinary event occurs that it is mentioned. Much has to be inferred with the help of analogies, the calculations of general human requirements, and other variables that cannot always be based on reliable information. Nonetheless, it is possible to arrive at a general idea of the Roman system during the mid- and late Republic relying on such calculations and particularly on Livy and Polybius.

Crucial to the understanding of these problems is the character of the terrain in which military operations take place: whether it is mountainous or level, the availability of food and firewood, and most importantly the accessibility of water, which is by far the most crucial element.

The land and climate of the Mediterranean area in which most of the Republican campaigns took place present their own special problems. The terrain is often rocky and hilly, hindering access and increasing the difficulty of using supply trains, and hence the importance of pack animals in the carrying of military supplies. When possible the Romans sited their supply bases at seaports or rivers, owing to the ancient limitations in land transport.

The Mediterranean climate also posed serious problems. Many rivers in the area were not navigable for their entire length and became little more than streams or totally dried up during prolonged summer droughts. Variability of rainfall led to considerable fluctuations in harvests that could severely affect the availability of local food supplies and make it difficult to import food from the outside. The rhythms of the agricultural year governed ancient warfare in general. The need for food and fodder normally restricted campaigning to the late spring and summer months. These restraints were eased to some degree in the late Republic when the Romans began to campaign in northern Europe.

Food, forage, and firewood accounted for approximately 90 percent of the total weight of army supplies. The amount of food required by a Roman army in the Republican period is difficult to estimate, since the size of the legions varied considerably. Polybius claims that the normal legion consisted of 4,200 men and could be increased to 5,000 in a crisis. We do not have figures for individual consumption, but based on modern figures and allowing for differences in ancient armies a figure of about 3,000 calories per day seems reasonable as a normal ration, although armies could and did operate for extended periods on reduced rations.

Our basic ration figures are provided by Polybius writing in the mid-second century, and there seems to be no reason to assume any change in these amounts during the Republic. The only item mentioned by Polybius is the grain ration which formed the most important element in the soldier's diet. On a convincing calculation the figure for an infantryman works out at approximately two pounds of wheat a day. Normally eaten in the form of bread made by the soldiers themselves, it contributed perhaps 60–70 percent of their total calories. Barley was not normally used for human consumption, but rather was given to troops as a punishment ration. In addition, the troops were supplied with meat, legumes, olive oil, cheese, and salt. Water, wine, and vinegar were drunk. Besides those actually fighting, servants, probably about 500 per legion, had to be provided with rations. Food had also to be supplied to the allied forces that accompanied the legions.

Each legion also fielded 300 cavalry, and Polybius informs us that cavalry received a monthly ration of three times the amount of wheat given to an infantryman, as well as approximately 600 pounds of barley. The increased wheat ration is to be explained by the fact that Roman cavalrymen had two servants who also needed to be fed. The Roman practice of having the troops cook their own food meant as well that large amounts of firewood had to be provided.

Further, food had to be provided for the animals accompanying the army. In addition to cavalry horses and remounts, amounting to 500 horses, pack animals had to be fed. Estimates vary, but perhaps 1,000 or more pack animals per legion is a reasonable figure. These animals required grain, straw, and adequate pasturage as well as sufficient water. Pasturage would normally be available locally, but 30 pounds of other fodder had to be provided by the army.

The vast amount of supplies entailed a large baggage train that marched behind the legion to which it was attached. In addition, the troops carried a heavy pack that included equipment and rations and that may have weighed close to a hundred pounds. The ancient sources contain a variety of figures for the number of days for which rations were carried. Livy mentions thirty days. However, a more likely maximum is seventeen days. The amount would vary in relation to a force's mission. When organized as a flying column, troops were required to carry all of their own supplies.

Polybius claims that Rome's military success was due largely to the availability and abundance of its supplies. An army has various strategies open to it for obtaining supplies. Foraging, requisitioning, plundering, and supplies sent from its territory were possibilities. Though Cato the Elder claimed that war should nourish itself, foraging and plundering were generally not sufficient to meet an army's needs, especially if it had to remain in place. Foraging was necessary for certain needs such as fodder, firewood, and water, but the Romans seem to have rarely used foraging to supply all of their cereal needs. Plundering, though an organized activity, was not a regular means for insuring an army's food supply. Local supplies were simply not available at various times of year. Ripened grain would only be available in the fields for a short portion of the campaigning season and the yield in the Mediterranean simply too uncertain to be relied upon.

Two systematic methods were normally employed. Either supplies were requisitioned from the local population or nearby allies or supplies were brought in from outside the theater of operations. Such supplies could either be gathered by soldiers or brought to the army by the locals, who had to bear the cost of transport. Procurement of this type was crucial to the operation of all pre-modern armies. Local food sources were so important that they could determine whether military operations could be carried out. The availability of local food supplies often played a crucial part in determining military operations. In 199 BC the proconsul Sulpicius Galba, campaigning in Illyria on the northwestern border of Macedonia, was able to remain in the area, which was fertile because of the abundance of local resources, but had to withdraw at the onset of winter for lack of supplies. This was a particularly serious problem in the conduct of siege operations when armies were forced to remain stationary for long periods and quickly exhausted the surrounding countryside.

To counter the limitations of local resources the Romans developed a logistical transport system. A convincing recent argument has been made that the system depended on two types of bases, an operational base which served as a major conduit for supplies in a theater of operations, and a tactical base in the area of actual operations that changed its position with army movements. The main base was usually located at a population center on the coast or on a navigable river, as moving massive amounts of material by water was the cheapest and easiest mode of transport. The tactical base had to be supplied by pack animals and wagons, but the Romans could normally rely on local transport for much of the task. This arrangement was supplemented by strategically located magazines at least from the Second Punic War. With the expansion of the Empire, the Romans were able to rely on provincial resources closer to campaigning areas.

The major role in the gathering and transporting of grain supplies has long been thought to have been carried out by large-scale equestrian contractors, the *publicani*, but a convincing argument has recently been made that the major burden was borne by the Roman state itself, though such contractors did supply other items such as horses and uniforms. The Senate appears to have played the major role in authorizing provisioning which was then carried out by military personnel. The sources of the grain varied. Grain could serve as a diplomatic tool, and the sources mention gifts of grain from Carthage and Syracuse as well as other states to Rome. Allies were called upon for contributions and purchases made from Italian sources.

The addition of the provinces of Sicily and Sardinia in the late third century must have eased supply problems for armies operating in the West and lessened the burden on the state since this grain was in the form of taxation. In the course of the third century BC and later, enormous numbers of Roman and allied soldiers led to a supply organization that was perhaps the most developed of Rome's governmental institutions.

92 APPIAN, *PUNIC WARS* 14.100

This passage is part of Appian's narrative of the opening stages of the Third Punic War (149–146). The two consuls of 149, Marcius Censorinus and Manlius

Manilius, were sent to Africa with an enormous army, which may have totaled 84,000 men, consisting of eight legions and an equal number of allies. Manilius was in command of the infantry while Censorinus was in charge of the fleet. From the start, Manilius was plagued with supply difficulties because of the size of his forces and his distance from his sources of supply. The units sent out to forage consisted of a legion and its attached allied forces as well a large cavalry force. Collection of a large amount of grain from the countryside was not a normal practice and extremely hazardous. Cavalry were especially necessary, as enemy cavalry were normally employed to disrupt foraging and to pick off stragglers. The men involved in harvesting would be unarmed.

Scipio Aemilianus was serving as a military tribune in 149 and so would have been one of the commanders of the expedition. Though Appian presents the later conqueror of Carthage in an extremely laudatory fashion, the measures he took to guard his foragers are paralleled in standard military manuals.

> Manilius began fortifying his camp more strongly, encircling it with a wall in place of a ditch and constructing a fort by the sea at the point where his supply ships came in. Then turning inland with 10,000 infantry and 2,000 cavalry, he ravaged the countryside gathering grain and fodder and collecting provisions. The foraging parties were led by military tribunes in rotation. Phameas, the cavalry commander of the Africans, who was young and eager for battle, had horses that were small and fast and ate grass when there was nothing else, and endured thirst and hunger when necessary. Hiding in thickets or ravines, Phameas made surprise attacks like an eagle on the careless. Inflicting damage, he then withdrew. But when Scipio was in command he never appeared. For Scipio always led his soldiers in formation with his cavalry mounted. He did not open his formation before the field in which the harvesting was to be done was surrounded by cavalry and infantry. He continuously made the round of the cavalry formations and if any of the foragers scattered or passed out of the circle he punished them severely.

93 [CAESAR], *THE AFRICAN WAR 75*

The African War survives under Caesar's name, but its author's name is unknown. It was written by one of his officers, as were the accounts of the civil war in Egypt and Spain.

Caesar began his campaign against the surviving supporters of Pompey in Africa in the winter of 47/46 BC. He brought over a force of eight legions, and at Thapsus on the coast southeast of Carthage he defeated Metellus Scipio and his own former legate Titus Labienus. The following passage is from the preliminaries to the final encounter at Thapsus.

Pre-modern armies were accompanied by servants and large numbers of camp followers. It has been estimated that in early modern Europe camp followers might number anywhere from 50 to 150 percent of the number of combatants. Roman armies used slaves and civilians for logistical support. The slaves appear to have been owned both by private soldiers and by the state. By the second century BC they were armed and were used to defend the camp.

Army buying power attracted private merchants who accompanied the army with their wagons and sold to the army as well as to individual soldiers. They could hinder army movements and when the troops formed for battle the baggage and these merchants were stationed in the rear. The term *lixa* (plural *lixae*) is something of a problem. The word is normally translated as "sutler," an individual who sold supplies directly to the soldier, but in some of the sources the word appears to mean "servant." At least some of the texts mention that the *lixa* followed the army in hope of gain, and it may be that the distinction of *lixa* and merchant reflects small and larger-scale enterprise.

> Caesar ... moved his camp to Sassura, which Scipio had garrisoned with Numidians and to which he had brought grain. When this move was noticed by Labienus he began to attack the rear of Caesar's formation as well as the *lixae* and merchants who were carrying their goods on carts among the cavalry and light-armed. Encouraged because he had intercepted the baggage, Labienus with daring approached the legions more closely. He thought that the men would not be able to fight since they were loaded down with baggage and exhausted by the march.

94 LIVY, 25.20.1–2

This passage forms part of Livy's narrative of the events of 212 leading to the Roman capture of Capua, the richest and most important city in Campania, which had joined Hannibal after Cannae. Casilinum lay two miles to its north, both cities being situated on the Volturnus River. It emphasizes the importance of sea and river transport in supporting military forces. This would have been especially important when siege operations were undertaken, as no army could supply itself if it remained stationary for any length of time. In 153 in Spain the loss of a supply base at Ocilis compelled the consul Fulvius Nobilior to abandon the siege of the important city of Numantia.

> The consuls took up the siege of Capua once again, and pressed it with the utmost force. They prepared and assembled supplies for the task. Grain was collected at Casilinum; at the mouth of the River Volturnus, where the city now stands, a fort built by Fabius Maximus had its defenses strengthened. It was garrisoned to command the coast and the river. Grain which had recently been sent from Sardinia and which the praetor Iunius had bought in Etruria was brought from Ostia and stored at these strongpoints to feed the army over the winter.

Recruitment and the levy

At Rome military service was a fundamental part of citizenship. It was both the duty and the privilege of every male citizen. The close association is evident in the prohibition of military service for slaves. It was only at exceptional moments, as in the aftermath of the enormous losses sustained at Cannae in 216 BC, that slaves were enrolled, and the prohibition remained in effect until the early fifth century AD. A parallel ban excluded those citizens convicted of serious crimes or in debt. Participation in it could be a heavy burden for a citizen, demanding on both his person and his property in the form of a war tax (see p. 140) and in the need to supply his own equipment.

The obligation to serve was linked to the census (see pp. 20f.) and based on a declaration by adult male citizens of their citizenship and property. Its results were used to determine voting rights, taxation, and the individual's military obligation. Though in theory all male citizens under the age of sixty were liable to service, the type of service was dependent on their personal wealth. For legionary or cavalry service a minimum property rating was necessary. Exemptions from service were granted for illness or other reasons. The military character of the census is apparent from the fact that it was held in the Campus Martius where military training was undertaken and where the centuriate assembly met. A further factor is military in determining military status was age. Men between the ages of seventeen and forty-six were classified as *iuniores* and those from forty-seven to sixty as *seniores*. Those in the second group were normally not subject to service in the field except in emergencies and were deployed as a home guard or reserve.

The Romans had a comparatively large pool of men from which to draw for military service. The census records preserved in the literary sources are of varying reliability. For the period prior to 225 they are unsound, but after that date, if not exact, they provide generally internally consistent figures which appear to have a factual basis. For the second half of the second century the figures for registered citizens vary between approximately 380,000 and 480,000. Of this total approximately three-fourths would be *iuniores* and eligible for service in the field. Even allowing for the fact that for various reasons segments of this population were not available, the levy that Polybius describes, the raising of four legions for two consular armies, should not have been an undue burden. But often far more than four legions were in the field in any one year. The peak of military effort was reached during the Second Punic War when in 212 twenty-two legions were in the field, each legion normally consisting of 4,200 infantry and 200 cavalry, though the infantry could be increased to 5,000 and the cavalry to 300 if necessary.

The levy began by the consuls submitting an estimate of the men and money they would need for the impending campaign to the Senate. The Senate then passed a decree which allowed the levy to go forward. An edict was published allowing thirty days for the enrollment to take place and requiring that those drafted appear at Rome on a specific day.

The process of raising an army consisted of two steps. The first was the levy and the second the distribution of the enlistees to various legions. Plausibly, the annalists inform us that originally conscription was done on the basis of the century. But this method had limitations. It was a cumbersome procedure because of the number of units involved, and it placed an unusually heavy burden on the richer citizens, as they formed the majority of centuries. In addition, over time the increase in territory and the formation of new tribes must have further complicated the process. At some uncertain date the basic unit of the levy changed from the century to the tribe. The modification may have taken place by the time of the Second Punic War. Not only did it simplify the conduct of the levy but it also spread the burden over a far larger percentage of the population. Part of the motivation for the change may have come from the institution of some form of military pay, traditionally at the end of the fifth century and from the development of the manipular army, which required simpler and less expensive equipment than the hoplite phalanx. The origin of the procedure may have lain in the emergency levy which had developed to deal with Italian or Gallic threats and was essentially a levy en masse which included the *seniores*. It also embraced the *capite censi*, those below the minimum census requirement, who were normally exempt from military service and whose first enrollment is attested in 281/280, and who were called up during the First and Second Punic Wars.

Polybius, our main source, places the levy at Rome on the Capitoline hill, but this seems impossible. By 225 the number of men eligible for active service from Rome, the municipalities, and the colonies of Italy was of the order of 240,000, a number far too large to be accommodated in the city. It is more likely that individual colonies and municipalities levied men locally and those selected were then sent on to Rome for assignment to specific units on the basis of their census rating. It has been suggested that conscription may still have occurred at Rome for residents of the city and its surrounding territory. Even in the context of the tribal levy, wealth and age still played a part in the assignment to the various lines of the legion.

The draftees assembled at Rome on the specified day, with the consuls presiding. The names of those eligible were called out from the census list and those present were required to answer; those failing to do so were liable to various punishments. It was at this point that the enlistee was permitted to ask to be excused from service for valid reasons, including physical incapacity and political or religious office, or a record of exceptional service. The tribunes of the plebs could intervene to stop the levy or to exempt individuals, but this could be circumvented by the declaration of an emergency levy.

Volunteers were raised. Men with a sufficient reputation and personal prestige could raise substantial forces. In 134 Scipio, the conqueror of Carthage, was able to attract 4,000 volunteers for his campaign in Spain. Despite such examples and the importance of warfare in Roman ideology, an element of compulsion was generally present, as the punishments for failure to appear for conscription evidence. Reluctance to serve in the army varied during the middle Republican period depending on the theater of operations. It was far easier in the second century to attract recruits to serve in the eastern Mediterranean with its prospects for rich booty than to recruit them for campaigns in Spain, where guerilla war was being waged and there was little prospect of booty. The problem worsened as the Empire expanded in the second century. Most military service was now overseas and for an extended period. It was no longer possible for soldiers to campaign annually and then return. Despite all of these problems the Romans had a vast pool of manpower for military service drawn from their own citizens and their allies that was unmatched by any of their opponents.

The levy

95 POLYBIUS, *HISTORIES* 6.19.5–21

Polybius' account of the levy, probably written about 160, presents several problems. A striking feature of his account is the omission of the consuls' role in the levy. Though Polybius had dealt with their rights as far as conscription was concerned, he did so only in passing, in contrast to the detailed description he offers here. A second problem with his account is the implication that all eligible men had to present themselves at Rome and be enrolled there. Clearly, this is a logistical impossibility, and Livy informs us that recruiting occurred elsewhere than in Rome.

Contradictory evidence and internal difficulties make it more than likely that what Polybius presents is not the whole levy but rather the assignment of men already conscripted to the legions.

A further problem is presented by the cumbersome nature of the process. The levy is obviously for the four legions for two consular armies of two legions each. That would mean that there would have to be 4,200 separate rotations of four men each to make up the total necessary. This must have taken place over several days. Polybius gives no indication for the length of the process. The levy is conducted on a tribal basis rather than on the centuries. This procedure may have been introduced in the late third century, but there is no hint of the assignment of the men to the various lines of the legion. It must be assumed that the three lines of the legion were sorted out after each legion was enrolled from the tribes. However, it is hard to believe that wealth was evenly distributed among the existing thirty-five tribes. Despite these difficulties this is the most detailed account of this part of the levy that we possess.

The source of Polybius' passage is disputed. It seems more likely that the account comes from a set of procedural instructions for military tribunes charged with conducting this process.

Finally, Polybius oddly ends with the levy of the cavalry, which he describes as previously held last but who were now chosen first. Various explanations have been offered for this change. The earlier procedure implies that the cavalry were selected simply on the basis of their census rating. The shift is best seen as one of a number of attempts in this period to elaborate distinctions among citizens.

When the consuls in office wish to hold a levy they announce to the people that day on which all men of military age must assemble. This is done each year. On the appointed day, when those fit for service have arrived in Rome and after they have assembled on the Capitoline, the more junior tribunes divide themselves up in the order in which they were elected or appointed by the consuls into four groups, because the primary division of their force is into four parts. They assign the four tribunes elected first to the first legion, the next three to the second, the following four to the third and the last three to the fourth legion. The first two senior tribunes are assigned to the first legion, the next three to the second. Then two are assigned to the third and the last three to the fourth. Such is the division and assignment of the tribunes that each legion has the same number of tribunes.

After this, the tribunes have separated and been grouped according to the legion to which they are assigned. They summon the tribes one by one according to lot. From the first tribe they select four young men as like each other as possible in age and physical condition, The four are brought forward and the tribunes of the first legion select one of them, then those of the second legion choose the next, then the tribunes of the third legion make their choice and finally those of the fourth make their selection. Then another four are brought forward and the tribunes of the second legion have first choice and so forth with the tribunes of the first legion choosing last. After this another four men are brought forward and the tribunes of the third have first choice while those of the second have last choice. So with this rotation of choice it results that the men in each legion are approximately the same. They continue until they reach the required number of men, that is 4,200, sometimes 5,000, when the situation is especially serious. They used to choose the cavalry last; now they do it first, and the selection is now done by the censor on the basis of wealth, with 300 assigned to each legion.

The sacramentum

After the completion of the levy Polybius describes an oath administered by the military tribunes to the new recruits. The use of an oath at Rome called the *sacramentum* draws on a custom that seems to have been common to Italic peoples. The oath had a religious basis and functioned as a ritual of initiation to promote group solidarity by invoking religious sanctions. The Romans considered military service to be a consecrated activity. The oath seems to have been considered as a necessary preliminary to any active military service. Without it the soldier was not permitted to use his weapons or engage in fighting. It also appears to have been valid only for the impending campaign. Under new commanders the oath had to be repeated.

The tradition seems to indicate that the oath changed over time. According to Livy initially an oath was sworn to assemble on the day specified by the consuls and not to depart unless permitted to do so. He claims that the soldiers customarily swore among themselves not to desert because of fear or to leave the battle line except under special circumstances. Livy claims that in 216 just before Cannae this oath ceased to be informal and was taken over by the tribunes as the standard military oath. However, Livy's near contemporary Dionysius of Halicarnassus records an earlier oath to follow the consuls against any enemies that bound the men not to desert or act illegally. This may be a simple reflection of later practice but it is hard to believe that an oath of this nature was not formally instituted until the last decades of the third century.

One other oath is recorded in Polybius and in a citation from a third-century source. It concerns discipline in the camp. The tribunes administer it to all, both slave and free, who swear not to steal. The details differ somewhat in the two versions we have, but in essence it forbids stealing within the camp and its vicinity.

96 DIONYSIUS OF HALICARNASSUS, *ROMAN ANTIQUITIES* 10.18.2

The speaker is the consul suffect for 460, L. Quinctius Cincinnatus. The speech occurs in the context of the struggle between patricians and plebeians, an episode which attracted much invention by the annalists.

> When the tribunes [of the plebs] hindered him from carrying out the levy, [Quinctius] called the people to the assembly and said that they had all taken the military oath to follow the consuls in whatever wars they should designate and not to desert the standards or to do anything else contrary to the law. Since he had taken up the consular power he held that they were all bound by their oaths.

97 LIVY, 22.38.1–5

In contrast to the writer of the last passage, Livy dates the new type of oath to 216 after the battle of Cannae (see pp. 150ff.). The episode is plausible and is explicable given the crisis the state was going through. Nonetheless, it is hard to believe that the oath had only been customary and privately administered to this point.

> After the levy was completed the consuls delayed a few days until the arrival of the allied and Latin troops. Then the tribunes administered an oath to the soldiers, something which had never happened before. Until this day there had been no oath other than to assemble at the order of the consuls and not to leave without permission. Previously after they had joined their unit, the cavalry in their decuriones and the infantry in their centuries had sworn voluntarily not to flee in flight or fear or leave the ranks unless it was to pick up or find a weapon or to attack the enemy or to save a citizen's life. This oath, which had started voluntarily, was taken up by the tribunes and became official.

98 AULUS GELLIUS, *ATTIC NIGHTS* 16.4.2

This version of the oath against stealing in the camp differs somewhat from Polybius' in extending the range of the oath to a radius of ten miles beyond the camp. It is possible that the oath would be repeated at each new camp. Gellius dates the oath to 190. Military necessities are exempted from its provisions.

> In ancient times when a levy was held and the soldiers had been conscripted, the military tribunes bound them with the following oath dictated by the magistrate: "In the army of the consuls Gaius Laelius, son of Gaius, and Lucius Cornelius, son of Publius, and for ten miles around it, you shall not steal, intentionally and with malice, either alone or in company with others, goods worth more than a silver denarius each day, except for one spear, spear shaft, wood, fruit, fodder, bladder, bag, and a torch, and if you find or carry off what is not yours and which is worth more than a silver coin, you must bring anything you have found or carried off maliciously either to the consul Laelius or to the consul Cornelius or to whomever they shall appoint within the next three days or return it to the owner whose possession you think it is to act as you should."

The Roman allies

A vital factor in Rome's military success was its ability to mobilize massive reserves of manpower. It was able to sustain casualties that would have crippled most ancient states. In the course of the Second Punic War (218–202) approximately 120,000 citizens lost their lives, yet Rome was able to continuously field armies in multiple theaters despite these losses. Rome's ability to do so depended not only on the expansion of its citizen body through enfranchisement, but on its policy of building a system of alliances that extended to all of peninsular Italy south of a line drawn from Arminium on the Adriatic to Pisa on the Tyrrhenian Sea. Polybius and other sources report census returns from Rome and its allied states gathered in preparation for a Gallic invasion in 225. The figures as recently emended show the Romans had available for service about 250,000 infantry and 23,000 cavalry, while its allies could provide 330,000 infantry and 31,000 cavalry. In the period from 225 to the beginning of the first century BC the allies supplied from one-half to two-thirds of Roman forces.

Rome and its allies were not bound together in any systematic fashion. Rather the alliances were concluded in a piecemeal way as a result of Rome's expansion. The allies were linked to Rome by a series of bilateral treaties containing different provisions and conditions. Some were drawn up on terms of equality, while the majority recognized Rome's predominance. The only stipulation that appears to have been present in every treaty was the provision of military aid at Rome's request. The system appears to have taken shape in the fourth and third centuries BC. Rome's settlement of the Latins after the war of 340–338 appears to have set a precedent for future alliances and settlements. Rome ended all mutual ties between the Latins and dissolved the Latin League. Bilateral treaties were concluded with the proviso that the only direct substantial burden the Latins would bear would be to provide Rome with troops and to supply them while in the field. Because of close ethnic and historical ties these communities were given commercial privileges at Rome as well as the right to conclude a legal marriage with Roman citizens and migrate to Rome and once in residence become full citizens. These privileges set the Latins apart from other Roman allies and they remained a separate category. Some of the Latin communities were absorbed into the Roman citizen body although allowed local autonomy. The founding of Latin colonies by Rome after 338 created another source of manpower, created through the act of foundation. By 265 this system extended through almost all of peninsular Italy.

There was no consultative or governmental body to regulate the structure of the system. Rome's overwhelming power meant that all effective decision-making remained in its hands. However, this did not mean that the allies were bound to Rome solely by force. Rather, what maintained these relations was the exchange of mutual benefits between the Roman and local elites. These local elites were the means by which Rome maintained its control. From a very early period (see p. 11), Rome had followed the pattern of freely admitting and absorbing elite members of other Italic groups. This policy led to the development of ties to other elite groups through intermarriage and resettlement. Ruling members of various Italian towns often had a branch of the family that had settled at Rome, with members in the Senate. Roman senators were appointed as patrons by the local elite to support its interests in Rome or to provide help in case of disputes between towns. In addition, Rome could protect these local grandees against their own lower classes. The absence of central machinery meant that dominant local groups were allowed a broad sphere of independence in managing their communities.

There were advantages as well for those outside the ranks of the notables. Allied soldiers were probably less heavily burdened by military service than Roman citizens. While serving on campaign their rations were provided free, while legionaries had their food deducted from their pay. They received booty though in lesser amounts. Rome, its colonies, and its allies were bound to each other in a nexus that above all rested on Rome's overwhelming power and a net of obligations that joined the Italians to it.

At least from the Second Punic War each year the Senate passed a decree detailing the state's military needs. It authorized the raising of the legions and specified theaters of operations and the assignment of commanders. It also included the number of allied troops needed for the year. The consuls issued an edict to the allied communities detailing the number of troops each would have to raise. The numbers demanded were based on the *formula togatorum*, which was a list probably arranged by geographical areas specifying the maximum numbers of soldiers each community was obliged to provide. These numbers were probably computed on the basis of local censuses. Given the variations in population and size of communities, there must have been a great deal of difference in the numbers of soldiers each

126

community contributed. Most often allied forces appear as single ethnic units, but it seems likely that smaller towns must have pooled their limited sources and produced mixed units.

Allied units were organized differently than Roman ones. The basic infantry unit was the cohort of 400–600 infantry, which may have been more an administrative than a tactical unit, though the Romans were later (see pp. 199ff.) to reorganize their own army on that basis. Centuries and maniples are not explicitly mentioned, but they must have existed. Such a division would have helped to make food distribution to the soldiers easier and would parallel the Roman system. There is no conclusive evidence for a division into three lines paralleling Roman infantry formations. It seems likely that allied tactical organization changed over time. By the battle of Magnesia in 189 Livy describes allied formations as being indistinguishable from Roman ones. Whether there were light-armed troops attached to the heavy infantry remains unknown.

A consular army would have had two *alae* or wings, each composed of ten cohorts, with one *ala* assigned to each of the legions. These were normally arrayed on the flank of each legion. The number of allied troops attached to each legion varied with the percentage of allied to citizen infantry. It has been estimated that the normal infantry complement would have been approximately equal to that of the legions, as Polybius states.

In addition to supplying heavy infantry the allies were required to supply cavalry units that totaled three times the normal number of Roman cavalry. A consular army normally had 600 cavalry in this period so that allied horse would have numbered 1,800. Given the expense involved in maintaining cavalry units this must have been a heavy burden. They were organized in *alae* as well. Each *ala* consisted of 300 men and was in turn subdivided into five double *turmae* of sixty men each. The *turma* of thirty troopers was also the basic tactical unit employed by Roman cavalry. These units do not appear to have been homogeneous, but were often composed of cavalry from different communities.

Polybius informs us that the consuls selected one-fifth of the allied infantry and one-third of allied cavalry to serve as *extraordinarii* or select troops on the basis of fitness. How this was done is not clear. Perhaps many of these men had a prior record of service to which the consuls could refer. If that is the case, it would imply some sort of Roman state archive. In camp the *extraordinarii* were brigaded separately, and on the march they were assigned to exposed positions, which implies a high confidence in their loyalty.

Overall command of these units was vested in Roman officers, the *praefecti socium* or officers in charge of allied forces. Three were assigned to each legion. The men selected appear often to have been of senatorial background. Their duties paralleled those of the military tribunes (see pp. 105f.), but unlike many of the military tribunes they were all appointed by the consul. It is not clear whether they rotated periods of service as the military tribunes did or whether they served continuously. Select officers from the allied communities exercised command as subordinates of the *praefecti socium*.

A proportion of the allied states supplied ships and their crews rather than land forces. These were primarily the Greek city-states of southern Italy. It used to be thought that they formed a separate category of allies but there is no evidence to support this view. Presumably their treaties of alliance were the same as the other allies', though the Romans required them to supply ships and crews rather than land forces. At an early period they seem to have been under a specially appointed quaestor, but as Roman naval forces increased, especially during the First Punic War and after, they were often commanded by consuls or praetors (see pp. 238ff.).

In battle the allied infantry was brigaded on the right and left wings, while the allied cavalry was usually stationed on one wing, as at Cannae. The sources indicate no difference in style of fighting or equipment that serves to differentiate allied infantry or cavalry from citizen forces. It is possible that, by the mid-fourth century, the Latins at least had the same equipment as Roman soldiers. By the early second century this was probably true for the majority of the allies and would certainly have made commanding the army much easier.

The allied presence, although necessary, created certain tensions. From the figures we possess it seems that the allied forces suffered disproportionately heavy casualties and that Roman commanders were more willing to risk their lives than those of their fellow citizens. There is also a hint in the sources that rivalry existed between Roman and allied forces which may not always have been beneficial. The potential rewards for allied soldiers were less than those open to Roman soldiers despite the fact that they underwent the same risks. In addition, it must have been a heavy burden for local communities to supply their forces given the unrelenting character of Roman warfare. The increasing numbers of allies used after the Second Punic War, when twice as many of them were serving as Romans, must have considerably aggravated the burden. Nonetheless, until the outbreak of the Social War in 90 we hear of few revolts by allied communities. This may in part have been due to the overwhelming military power of Rome, but the most significant factor was surely the mutually beneficial ties established between the Roman elite and those of the allied communities. There may, as well, have been a reciprocal effect on the Romans. It has been argued that this system of alliances promoted warfare, as the use of allies' troops was the most visible symbol of Roman dominance. Against this view it has been claimed that the Romans engaged in almost constant warfare before the Italian allies were a significant factor. This is certainly true. It was not the desire for war that these alliances changed but rather the opportunity. The Romans had a pool of manpower larger than their own, which served at no expense to the state. This allowed them to undertake military ventures that they could not have done on their own.

Service with the Roman army had important long-term effects. The gradual spread of Latin in the peninsula owed something to the enormous number of Italians drawn into military service over more than three centuries. The same may be said of the expansion of Roman institutions in Italy. Not only were allied soldiers exposed to them, but the local elites with close ties to the Roman elite had a powerful incentive to assimilate Roman practices. In the end the division of

Roman and Italian was to be erased by the extension of Roman citizenship to all of the peninsula.

The consul and the allies

99 POLYBIUS, *HISTORIES* 6.12.5–6

This and the following passage come from Polybius' description of the civil and military powers of the consuls. The extent of the consuls' powers in war is best illustrated by the fact that on campaign Roman citizens could be executed without the right to appeal.

> In preparations for war and the conduct of operations in the field the [consuls] have almost unlimited power; they can issue orders to the allies as they see fit and select military tribunes, enroll soldiers, and choose those fittest for service.

Allied officers

100 POLYBIUS, *HISTORIES* 6.21.4–5

The officers appointed are the native prefects serving under the *praefecti socium*. The names of a few are mentioned in the sources, such as Dasius of Beneventum, who served as commander of the garrison of Clastidium in 218. The garrison must have been composed of allied troops, as non-Romans would not have commanded legionaries. Presumably the allied paymasters were under the supervision of the *praefecti socium*, but they must have also reported to the quaestor on financial matters.

> At the same time the consuls issue orders to the governments of the allied cities they have selected to contribute troops to the expedition, clearly stating the number of troops they must provide, and they specify when and where the men should assemble. After the allies have carried out their levies according to the instructions and administered the oath they dispatch their men, having appointed a commander and a paymaster.

The prefects of the allies and the extraordinarii

101 POLYBIUS, *HISTORIES* 6.26.5–9

For a discussion of the *praefecti socium*, see p. 127. These prefects were probably first instituted after the dissolution of the Latin League in 338, though they are first attested during the Samnite Wars. Given the need for aristocratic Romans for military service they are often men of high birth.

After the allied forces have assembled together with the Roman army, men are selected by the consuls, twelve in number, who are called prefects, to organize and command the allies. First, they select on behalf of the consuls the fittest of the allied infantry and cavalry, who are called *extraordinarii*, which can be translated as "select." The total number of allied infantry is about equal to the Roman. The number of allied cavalry is three times that of the Roman. A third of the allied cavalry and a fifth of the allied infantry are assigned to the *extraordinarii*. They divide the remainder into two parts, which they call the right and left wings.

Allied military equipment

102 LIVY, 37.39.7

The following excerpt is a description of the Roman army at the battle of Magnesia ad Sipylum near modern Manisa in western Turkey in mid-December 190 to fight against Antiochus III, the Seleucid king. The army was under the command of one of the consuls, Lucius Scipio, and the battle ended in a decisive Roman victory. This is a normal consular army of two legions plus allies, though the legions had more than the normal complement of 4,200 men. The maximum number of men serving in a legion appears to have risen after 200 to 6,000.

The importance of the passage lies in its description of allied equipment and organization. Especially important is the apparent division of the allies into the same three lines as the legions. This implies that allied troops on the battlefield were indistinguishable from the Romans in their style of fighting as well as equipment.

There were two Roman legions and two composed of the allies and those of the Latin name. Each of these units had 5,400 men. The Romans held the center of the line and the allies were on the wings. The standards of the *hastati* were in front, behind them were those of the *principes*, and those of the *triarii* closed up the rear.

103 LIVY, 29.15

In 209 twelve of the thirty Latin colonies declared they could no longer furnish men or supplies to the Roman war effort. At this point in the Second Punic War the tide in Italy had clearly shifted in Rome's favor, which makes it likely that these colonies were simply exhausted by the demands of the war. Remarkably, these colonies were not dealt with until 204, the date of the senatorial decree described in this passage.

Unlike other allies, Latin colonies do not appear to have had a treaty obligation to support Rome militarily, but such support was an automatic consequence of the foundation of the colony. The passage makes clear Rome's overwhelming position. It also reveals that each of the colonies and the other allies was obliged to supply the

Romans with fixed numbers of troops and that these were raised by local magistrates using their own procedures for conducting the census. The imposition of the property tax, based on capital not income, is a punishment, as normally the only financial obligation would have been to furnish supplies to a city's own troops. The dispatch of these forces outside of Italy was clearly meant as further punishment.

While supplements for the legions in the provinces were being discussed, it was suggested by certain senators that the time was right, since they had been freed from fear by the kindness of the gods, to put an end to that situation that had been tolerated while the war hung in the balance. With the full attention of the Senate they stated that the twelve Latin colonies, which in the consulship of Quintus Fabius and Quintus Fulvius refused to provide soldiers, had enjoyed for almost six years an exemption from military service as though it was an honor and a favor, while good and faithful allies in return for their loyalty and devotion to the Roman people had been exhausted by levies year after year. This speech not so much recalled to the memory of the senators a matter almost forgotten as it stirred up their anger. They demanded that this be the first item of business before the house and decreed that the consuls should summon the magistrates and ten leading men to Rome from Nepet, Sutrium, Ardea, Cales, Alba, Carseolis, Sora, Suessa, Setia, Circei, Narnia, and Interamna, for these were the colonies at issue. They should order them to supply double the number of the infantry which they had supplied from the time of the entrance of the enemy into Italy as well as 120 cavalry each. If any of them could not fulfill the quota for cavalry, they could make up the deficiency by substituting three infantrymen for each cavalryman. The wealthiest of the infantry and cavalry shall be chosen and they should be sent to wherever replacements are needed outside of Italy.

If any of the colonies should refuse [to comply with these terms], their magistrates and ambassadors are to be detained and they shall be denied an audience before the Senate until they have carried out these orders. Besides, a property tax of one-tenth percent shall be collected yearly from these colonies, and the census in these colonies will be conducted according to the procedures used at Rome.

The naval allies

104 LIVY, 36.42.1–2

Gaius Livius Salinator commanded the fleet as praetor in 191. In that year he scored a great naval victory over the fleet of Antiochus III that prepared the way for the invasion of Asia Minor by the Romans. Locri and Rhegium were among the Greek city-states allied with Rome. It has been conjectured that the states which supplied naval forces in place of troops were a separate category. They are absent from

Polybius' list of allies in 225, and from this the separate nature of this category has been inferred. However, there is no reason this should be so. Polybius' interest was in the land forces the Romans had available to confront the Gauls, who had no major naval forces, so it would have been natural to neglect allied states in that category. There is no reason to think that the treaties of naval allies would have been significantly different. These treaties must have specified the number of ships, crews, and the amount of supplies that had to be provided in the same manner that other treaties specified forces and supplies. The Lacinian promontory lay to the south of another important Greek city, Croton.

The undecked or open ships referred to in the passage were smaller warships.

> Gaius Livius, the commander of the Roman fleet, set out from Rome for Naples with fifty warships. He had ordered the allies on this coast to assemble there with the undecked ships which they were required to provide according to treaty. From there he made for Sicily, sailing through the straits of Messana. After he had picked up six Carthaginian ships that had been sent and others from Rhegium and Locri and other allies with the same treaty obligations, he performed a lustration of the fleet at the Lacinian promontory and then put out to sea.

On the march

For any army marching in formation, local conditions play a critical role. The possibilities that a reasonably flat open valley offer differ from those of broken and hilly terrain. Speeds will vary partly as a function of terrain, the condition of the men, and the speed of the army's baggage train. The threat of a possible attack will also affect marching formations. So there are bound to be a number of variations in marching formations. Despite these variations the Roman army of the Republic, like every other army, possessed a number of basic patterns that could be adapted to circumstances. Polybius describes the basic patterns but he omits a number of variations known from other sources.

In the standard marching formation the legions were placed in the middle, with allied infantry formations both in front and behind. The select allied cavalry led the entire column, while the remainder of the cavalry either marched to the rear of the formations to which they were assigned or rode along the sides of the column, herding the animals of the baggage train. Such a sequence was designed to allow the army to move from column to battle line with a minimum of difficulty. The normal battle line placed the allies on the wings, with the legions in the center, and this was replicated on the march. The arrangement of cavalry could be more flexible because their greater speed made it far easier for them to move into position. If the Republican army pattern was analogous to that of the later imperial armies, the men would have marched six abreast, which would imply that that was also the depth of each maniple in battle formation. This would mean that they marched in maniples, and it is probable that the maniples of each line followed the other, so that first marched maniples one to ten of the *hastati*, followed by the same sequence of the maniples of the *principes*, and ending with the ten maniples of the *triarii*. This would allow a fairly simple movement of the maniples behind each other when forming up for battle.

When there was a threat of an enemy attack, the basic change if there was sufficient room was to have the maniples march in parallel lines so that they could rapidly swing into formation. The formation outlined by Polybius assumes an attack from the left. From the Roman commander's point of view this would have been the best possible outcome, as the men could form up with their shielded side to the enemy. If the enemy were sighted on the right, some adjustments had to be made, and this is presumably what Polybius refers to when he talks of the *hastati* having to wheel, that is the line would have to form up so that these maniples were in the front of the line. There were other marching formations when danger threatened not mentioned by Polybius. The most common alternate formation in our sources is the square formation where the troops form a square with the baggage in the middle.

The location of the baggage also played a role in the change from column to line. Normally it was placed behind units, but in dangerous situations it preceded each element in the column. When speed was necessary and the enemy close, columns were sent out without the baggage train, with the troops carrying their own supplies.

Pioneers also accompanied the column, usually in front to clear paths through wood areas or bridge rivers, in the imperial period. Cavalry and infantry were used for scouting purposes.

Roman marching formations

105 POLYBIUS, *HISTORIES* 6.40

For the Roman camp, see pp. 135ff. The wheeling of the *hastati* had to take place if the enemy attacked the side of the column opposite to them.

There is some difficulty in understanding Polybius' description of the formation used in dangerous situations. He appears to mean that each maniple marched with its baggage preceding it.

> They break camp in the following manner. At the first trumpet blast they take down the tents and pack their gear. The soldiers are not permitted to take down or set up their tents before those of the military tribunes and the consul. At the second trumpet call they load their belongings on to pack animals. Finally, at third call the first maniple advances and the whole camp is set in motion. They place the *extraordinarii* in the vanguard and then next to them the right *ala* [wing] of allies, followed by the baggage of these units. Next follows the first Roman legion, with its baggage immediately to its rear, and then the second legion, again with its baggage together with the baggage of the left *ala*, forms the rear of the column. Sometimes the cavalry rides in the rear of the units to which it is assigned;

at others times it rides along the flanks of the baggage train, herding and guarding it. If an attack is expected from the rear, the other units keep their position in line, but the *extraordinarii* take up a position on the rear of the line. Each day the allies and legions change position so that they can share in the advantages of fresh water and food.

They use another marching formation in times of danger if there is enough open ground. The *hastati*, *principes*, and *triarii* of each legion advance in three parallel columns with their baggage in front. The second group of maniples also has its baggage to its front, as does the third and so on. In this order of march, if some danger should threaten, then turning to the left and sometimes to the right they disengage the maniples from the baggage in the direction of the enemy. So in short order and with a single movement they form their infantry battle line, unless the *hastati* have to wheel around the others. The baggage and its attendants, protected by the infantry, have their proper place in times of danger.

The marching order in times of danger

106 CAESAR, *GALLIC WAR* 2.19

The Belgae were a confederation of tribes living in what is today northeastern France and Belgium. The Nervii were members of this tribal confederation, occupying the northern area of Belgium. Notice that, unlike the situation in the description of the Roman march formation in proximity to the enemy in Polybius, the baggage is placed at the rear of the column. This reflected Caesar's awareness that the enemy was to his front and that attack on the baggage in the rear was unlikely.

> Caesar followed the cavalry he had sent ahead with all of his forces, but he had changed the plan and order of his march. The Belgae had informed the Nervii of these changes. As was usual as he approached the enemy, the legions were without their baggage, as he had placed the baggage behind all of the legions. Two legions conscripted locally closed up the rear of his line and guarded the baggage.

107 SALLUST, *THE WAR AGAINST JUGURTHA* 46.6

In his struggle for the control of the North African kingdom of Numidia, Jugurtha, a member of the royal family, pursued a course that led to war with Rome. The war broke out in 112 and was incompetently waged by the Romans until the arrival of Caecilius Metellus, the consul of 109. The following account describes Metellus' initial invasion of Numidia. The formation he adopted was determined by the fact that the main strength of his opponents lay in light cavalry. To counter this he placed his light-armed troops armed with missile weapons at the head of the column. His cavalry dispositions were directed to the same end. This passage makes clear, as does the preceding one, the flexibility of Roman marching formations. The prefects of the cohorts were the prefects of the allies.

> Metellus, acting as if the enemy was present, proceeded with his column well protected. He scouted the country far and wide. He believed that the signs of surrender were only a ruse and that the enemy was looking for a place to ambush him. He headed the column of cohorts ready for action, with a select group of slingers and archers. The rear of the column was in the hands of his legate Gaius Marius with the cavalry, while on the flanks he had assigned auxiliary cavalry to the military tribunes and prefects of the cohorts. Mixed in with them were light-armed troops to repulse the enemy horse wherever it should appear.

108 PLUTARCH, *LIFE OF CRASSUS* 23.3–4

Plutarch is describing the preliminaries to Crassus' disastrous defeat by the Parthians east of the Euphrates near the city of Carrhae in 53. The square was a common marching order when there was fear of the army being outflanked, in this case by Parthian cavalry. The Romans were in this case handicapped by facing a mounted enemy in open country.

Although the square provided an excellent defense against attacks where the enemy closed, it did not provide security against the repeated missile attacks of the kind that were to destroy the Roman army at Carrhae. Plutarch refers to the cohorts which had now become the basic tactical unit in the later Republic in place of the maniple.

> [Crassus] changed his mind and formed his troops into a deep square facing in all directions, with twelve cohorts on a side. Near each cohort he placed a squadron of horse so that no part of his line would lack cavalry support. Protected on all sides he marched forward to combat.

The Roman camp

It was normal Roman practice to encamp at the end of each day's march. This was not an invariable rule. Sallust, in his account of the war against Jugurtha (112–105), describes the arrival of a new general, Caecilius Metellus, to take up the command against the Numidian king, faulting previous commanders for failing to fortify their camps. The sources also note other occasions on which the Romans failed to construct fortified camps, but these were normally in situations where the army was engaged in a difficult retreat.

A detailed account of the construction of these temporary camps is provided by Polybius (see 109) but given the general lack of interest by ancient writers in technical military details it is difficult to check the accuracy of his account. Some archaeological evidence is provided by a series of camps constructed by Roman generals between the mid-second century and the 80s BC at Renieblas near the ancient Celtiberian town of Numantia (see pp. 237f.), which lies close to the modern city of Burgos in northeastern Spain. Of particular interest is the third camp, which has been identified as that of Quintus Fulvius Nobilior, consul in 153, who unsuccessfully campaigned against the Celtiberians in that year. The date is roughly contemporary with Polybius' description, and this provides some control for his account. There are also camps dated about twenty years later built by Scipio Aemilianus for his siege of Numantia in 133. Though traces of a number of marching camps from the imperial period have survived, especially in Britain, the Republican evidence is very sparse. This is the result of the nature of these camps, which were usually built for temporary use and made of perishable materials. Since the legions were raised annually, the construction of long-term camps was unnecessary, though there are exceptions. Nobilior's camp at Renieblas has stone fortifications, presumably because it was occupied over the winter of 153/152, and was not simply a marching camp. These camps as well as those of the imperial period show that the Romans were not rigidly bound by camp plans such as the one laid out by Polybius but adapted their camps to the local topography and to their immediate military needs.

Camp construction was done under the general supervision of the military tribunes and directly overseen by centurions. The layout of the camp appears to have been done by surveying specialists. Construction and fortification were assigned to allied and legionary units. The fortifications were relatively simple and consisted of three parts. The first was the excavation of a ditch (*fossa*) around the perimeter of the camp, normally five feet wide and three feet deep. The second element was an elevated walkway (*agger*) made of the earth removed from the ditch. Finally, a *vallum* or palisade was constructed of wooden stakes driven into the top surface of the *agger*. A large open space was left around the perimeter between the fortifications and the actual troop encampments to allow for additional troops or animals to be brought within the walls and it also served as protection against missile weapons. In all, for a two-legion camp the square created was about 2,000 feet on a side based on Polybius' figures. The camp had four gates. Unmentioned by Polybius are the gate fortifications. These defenses consist either of an obstacle erected in the middle of the gate or of an extension of both sides of the defenses in a semicircular pattern so that an attacker would have to expose his side to the defending troops.

Within the camp the crucial buildings were the *principia* or commander's tent, with an open space or forum on one side, and the quaestor's tent on the other side of the *principia*. To the front of this block were the tents of the Roman infantry and cavalry flanked by those of the allies, in exactly the same position as these units would have occupied in the battle line. Behind the command center were the tents of the *extraordinarii* and auxiliaries. It has been estimated that the entire construction process would have taken about three hours and could easily have been completed in the afternoon after a morning's march.

Camp defenses were not especially strong, and the sources record the breaching of the defenses and the capture of camps, though the result of a Roman defeat in the field. In part, this can be explained by the nature of Roman warfare in this period. It was offensively minded, and so the strength of the camp remained of secondary importance. It did, at least, provide a minimum of security and gave the Romans some time to respond to enemy attacks. Further, it served to restrict the number of deserters, a problem that plagued all pre-modern armies on a large scale. In addition, its value as a symbolic exhibition of Roman discipline for Roman troops and of Roman power to its opponents should not be underestimated.

109 POLYBIUS, *HISTORIES* 6.27.1–32.8 (SELECTIONS)

Some Roman handbooks of camp construction such as that of Hyginus (second century AD) have been preserved, but this long and detailed digression on camp construction in a historical work is unusual. It seems similar in character to the description of the levy which precedes it, and it is probably dependent on a military tribune's handbook. This is basically a template for a model camp. The origins of this plan are probably to be sought in religious ritual and town planning. The method of laying out the camp bears some similarities to methods used for creating certain religious spaces.

There is a basic problem with the account. The difficulty arises from the author's statement that, when the consuls camp separately, that is in a two-legion camp, the headquarters buildings and the market are placed between the two legions. This arrangement is not borne out by the camp of Nobilior at Renieblas. It has been suggested rightly that Polybius' description of a two-legion camp is really a description of one-half of a four-legion camp. In other aspects Nobilior's camp fits the Polybian model closely.

They employ the following method in building their camp. Once the site has been chosen the commander's tent occupies the position best suited for general observation and for the issuing of orders. They fix a flag at that spot and with it as a center they measure out a square whose sides are one hundred feet from the flag so that the total area equals 40,000 square feet.

The Roman legions are encamped as follows along the side of the square that provides the best opportunities for foraging and for access to water. There are six military tribunes in each legion, as I just mentioned, and each of the consuls always has two legions, so it is clear that each consul has twelve military tribunes. They place the tribunes' tents in a line parallel to the selected side of the square and fifty feet from it to allow room for the horses, baggage animals, and the rest of the tribunes' gear. The tents are pitched in a parallel line away from the square facing the outside of the camp, a direction which I will always call the front. The tents are equally spaced from each other so that they extend along the entire space occupied by the legions.

They measure another hundred feet from the front of all the tents, and then starting from this distance parallel to the tents of the tribunes they begin to encamp the legions in the following manner. They bisect the line I have just mentioned, and from this spot they draw a line perpendicular to the first, and along it they encamp the cavalry of each legion facing one another and fifty feet apart. The manner of encamping the foot and horse is similar; the entire space occupied by the maniples and the *alae* is square. This square faces one of the streets and is one hundred feet long, and generally the depth of the square is equal to it in length except in the case of the allies. Whenever they construct a larger camp they increase the square proportionately.

The cavalry camp has something like a street running down from the tribunes' tents and at right angles to them and to the space in front of them. The whole system of lanes through the camp is like a network of streets, as troops of horse or units of infantry are encamped along them. Behind the cavalry are the *triarii* of each legion, with a troop of cavalry next to each maniple in a manner similar to the rest of the infantry, but with no gap between them and facing in the opposite directions. They make the depth of each maniple half of its length, since these units are only half the strength of the other maniples. The result is that, although the number of men is often unequal, all of the units are of equal length because of the differences in depth. Then fifty feet from the *triarii* of each legion they place the *principes*, and they face the abovementioned space between themselves and the *triarii*. In this way two streets are created at right angles. These start from the same line, that is one hundred feet from the tribunes' tents, and run down to the *agger* opposite to the *principia* on the side we agreed was to be called the front of the camp. After the *principes* at no interval they encamp the *hastati* back to back with no space between them. Since these units are all composed of ten maniples, the streets are all of equal length and they end at the front wall of the camp in a straight line. At this point the last maniples are turned to face the front of the camp.

Again, fifty feet from the *hastati* they place the allied cavalry facing them, starting from the same line and ending at the same line. As I mentioned, the allied infantry are the same in number as the legions, but the *extraordinarii* must be subtracted, while the number of cavalry is double after deducting a third for the select cavalry. For this reason they increase their depth to make their length equal to that of the legions. They face the *agger* and the sides of the camp in two directions....

Behind the tents of the tribunes on both sides and at right angles to them are the tents of the *extraordinarii* cavalry and some volunteers serving at the discretion of the consuls. These are placed along the sides of the camp, in one case facing the quaestor's depot and on the other the market place.... Back to back to them and facing the *agger* the *extraordinarii* infantry perform the same services as the cavalry.

The form of the entire camp is a square. The layout of its streets and other arrangements give it the appearance of a city ....

> Whenever the four legions and the two consuls are encamped together, one need only imagine two camps, formed as I described, joined together back to back at the two encampments of the *extraordinarii* of each camp, whom we mentioned as facing the rear of their camps. The shape of the camp is now rectangular, with twice the area and with a circumference one and one-half times as large.

110 POLYBIUS, *HISTORIES* 6.42.1–5

Our knowledge of Greek camps is very limited. Defensive works for classical Greek camps seem to have been rarely used except under special circumstances; ordinarily guards and pickets were used in their place. In the Hellenistic period fortifications appear more regularly.

The contrast that Polybius draws between the Roman methods of artificial camp construction and the Greek preference to adapt a camp to the natural advantages of its position is greatly overdrawn.

> In this matter the Romans seem to be pursuing a course of convenience opposite to that of the Greeks. The latter think that the most important point in encamping is to adapt to the natural strength of a place, because in the first place they shirk from the labor of entrenching and, secondly, because they do not consider man-made fortifications superior to the natural strength of a position. So they are compelled to constantly change the form of their camp in accordance with the natural configuration of the ground and to have to move units to unsuitable positions, and the result is that individuals and units are uncertain of their location in the camp. On the other hand, the Romans prefer the fatigue of entrenching and other defensive works because of the convenience of having a single form of camp, familiar to all.

Military pay

Though some sources claim that pay for military service was introduced under the kings, a more acceptable tradition, found in both Livy and Diodorus Siculus, links it the last of the wars against Veii, on Livy's date in 406. Livy connects it to the struggle between patricians and plebeians and represents it as a concession granted by the Senate to the plebs. The historian interprets it as a way to relieve the economic pressure of military service on the less wealthy section of the population. Some scholars have questioned the early date assigned to this reform on the basis of the lack of a coinage, which was not minted regularly at Rome until the early third century. Since pay could have been given in kind, this does not seem a compelling objection. Others would date the introduction of pay as late as the First Punic War, but this seems improbable given the number and size of earlier Roman armies. A date around 400 for some form of compensation seems acceptable.

The reform did not introduce pay as such but rather a form of compensation that allowed those who barely qualified by census rating for enrollment in the legions to serve. It is best seen as a mechanism to allow the state to mobilize greater numbers of its citizens for military service. Rome was under heavy military pressure in this period, and in this situation the need to increase manpower would have been imperative. Such an increase might help to explain the relatively rapid recovery of Rome and its expansion in the course of the first half of the fourth century.

Inextricably linked with the introduction of pay was the imposition of a method to pay for it – the *tributum*. It was not a tax in the formal sense, but a mandatory loan levied to meet military expenses including supplies and other necessities which in theory would be repaid from war profits. Its specifically military nature is revealed by the few years such as 347 when, with no military operations, the *tributum* was not levied and by the few references to the *tributum* being repaid from booty. Not all citizens paid the *tributum*. For instance, those whose property was less than the minimum rating required for military service were exempt. In essence, it served to spread the military burden to all of those liable to military service, including those not called up for service. The *tributum* seems to have been levied on the basis of tribes and centuries; they may have been responsible for collecting it and then turning it over to the state. The amount must have varied in proportion to the anticipated expenses of different campaigns. The same sort of system must also have been used by the allies when they levied their own troops. The *tributum* came to an end in 167 when the booty from foreign conquests allowed the state to carry on military operations without it.

The introduction of military pay

111 LIVY, 4.59.11–60.6 (SELECTIONS)

The introduction of compensation for military service not only enlarged the pool of potential recruits but allowed the army to be kept in service for longer periods. This would have been of particular importance in the war against Veii, as it involved a prolonged siege of the Etruscan city.

The detail about the use of carts to convey the unworked bronze ingots to the treasury certainly fits the period and has a ring of authenticity in an obviously tendentious account. *Aes grave* were cast irregular ingots of bronze. It seems more likely that compensation was paid in kind, given the clumsiness of *aes grave* as a medium of exchange.

In a later notice Livy connects the introduction of pay with the introduction of the manipular formation (see **47**). This cannot be correct, as the transition to the manipular formation extended over a number of decades.

Then [406] all of the leading men conferred an extremely timely benefit on the whole citizen body. Without any prior reference to it by a tribune of

140

the plebs the Senate decreed that soldiers should receive pay. Prior to this measure each man served at his own expense. It is said that no measure was as happily received by the plebs as this one. The plebeians were pleased that the benefit of this measure would at least allow their property to remain intact while their persons were at the service of the state.... And because coined money did not yet exist [the senators] conveyed *aes grave* in heavy wagons to the treasury as conspicuously as they could.

112 POLYBIUS, *HISTORIES* 6.39.12–15

Polybius' pay rates and grain allotments are those of the mid-second century given in Greek measures. There are six obols to the drachma, and it is probable that Polybius' drachma is equal to a Roman denarius, a coin originally worth ten asses. This would mean that the infantry received a denarius every three days, a centurion two denarii every three days, and the cavalry a denarius per day. More difficult to determine is the value of the pay. We have no idea of how it compares to contemporary wages of the civilian population. The most that can be said is that the sources do not mention insufficient pay as a problem. It is best to see it as a supplement to meet the cost of food, clothing, and equipment. The real opportunity for profit lay in the distribution of booty at the end of a successful campaign, and later figures indicate that this could be a substantial amount.

The *medimnus* was a dry measure of about 40.5 liters. Based on Athenian figures this would be enough grain to last about a month. The large ration of grain given to the cavalry probably supported a groom and the trooper's mount.

> The foot soldiers received two obols a day, the centurions twice that amount, and the cavalry a drachma. The infantry are allotted about two-thirds of an Attic *medimnus* a month, the cavalry seven of barley each month and two of wheat. The allied infantry receive the same as the Roman, and the allied cavalry one and a third of wheat and five of barley. The grain is distributed free to the allies, but the quaestor deducts charges for grain, clothes, and weapons from their pay, if necessary, at a fixed rate.

The tributum

It is clear from the sources that it was levied in proportion to a citizen's census rating and was a percentage of the total value of his property. The exact proportion is unclear, though one-tenth of 1 percent has been suggested as the rate. But the rate must have varied on the basis of expected military expenditures. The tax was confined to those actually eligible for military service, and so the *proletarii* were exempt from it. Some of the burden imposed was met by repayments out of booty and indemnities.

113 VARRO, *ON THE LATIN LANGUAGE* 5.86

The *tributum* is so called because the amount which has been assessed on the citizens is collected from each by tribe and in accordance with their individual census rating.

114 DIONYSIUS OF HALICARNASSUS, *ROMAN ANTIQUITIES* 4.19.1–4

The passage is anachronistic, dating the introduction of pay to the mid-sixth century, but it probably gives a reasonably accurate picture of the calculation of the *tributum* and distribution of the burden, although omitting the role of the tribes.

Following this arrangement [Servius Tullius] levied troops according to the division of the centuries and assessed the war tax according to property ratings. So whenever he needed 10,000 or 20,000 troops he would divide that number among the 193 centuries and then order each century to supply its quota. Calculating how much money was necessary for provisioning the army and other military expenses, he would divide it in the same way among the centuries, ordering each man to pay his share according to his rating. The result was that the wealthier, being fewer in number and spread over a greater number of centuries, were obliged to serve more often and to pay more tax than the others. Those of middling or small wealth, distributed in fewer centuries in greater numbers, served less often in rotation and paid a smaller tax; those who fell below the minimum census rating were excused all burdens.

The manipular army in battle

Rome and Carthage

Carthaginian forces

Founded at the end of the ninth century, Carthage became one of the most powerful states in the western Mediterranean. The city was situated on a triangular peninsula projecting into the western side of the Gulf of Tunis. Admirably placed for commerce, the site had strong natural defenses. The city's immense prosperity rested on an extremely rich agricultural hinterland and its commerce both in its own products and as a transit point for Mediterranean trade. Particularly important for the latter was the ability of Carthage to dominate commerce with the western Mediterranean and serve as the only large-scale outlet for its products.

Carthage had expanded its territorial control in two directions. Within Africa it built up a large empire. By the mid-third century it controlled the coast of Africa from Cyrenaica in the east to the Atlantic Ocean, including the Cape Bon peninsula and the fertile valley of the Bagradas River (the modern Oued Medjerda).

Carthage's empire and influence extended outside of Africa. It had colonies on the southern coasts of Spain, though it is unclear how far inland its influence extended. It also controlled much of Sardinia and Corsica. Sicily, a rich prize, remained the major area of Carthaginian military operations outside of Africa. From the fifth century, Sicily witnessed a series of seesaw struggles between Carthage and the Greek cities, which were mostly located in the eastern half of the island. The most important Carthaginian centers such as Motya and Panormus (Palermo) were in the western half of the island. Victory and expansion alternated with defeat and contraction.

The organization and equipment of its military forces are far from clear, as our sources contain little on these topics. They seem mostly to have consisted of mercenaries and forces drawn from subject peoples. The steadiest infantry troops were the African infantry, who appear to have fought in the fashion of Hellenistic phalanxes and were heavily armed. The method of recruitment of these men is unknown, but it is possible that contingents were supplied by the Libyo-Phoenician cities. Africans may also have provided light-armed skirmishers armed with a small shield and javelins.

After the Carthaginian expansion in Spain in the wake of the First Punic War, large Spanish contingents make their appearance in Punic armies. Some of the groups must have served as mercenaries earlier, but by the late third century they were serving in allied units. These troops fought as both light and heavy infantry. Celtic (for their equipment, see pp. 58f.) mercenaries were also used, though in Hannibal's forces in Italy, Celtic tribes fought as allied contingents often under their own leaders. There were also mercenary forces of mixed origins.

The Carthaginians employed both light and heavy cavalry, often of a high standard, which were mostly drawn from Celtic, Spanish, and Numidian sources, though occasionally native Carthaginians served as well. The Celts and Spaniards fought as shock cavalry in the manner of traditional Hellenistic heavy cavalry, while the Numidians supplied by allied kings functioned as particularly effective light cavalry.

In addition the Carthaginians used elephants in warfare. These were usually ridden by a driver mounted in a howdah and carried light infantry armed with javelins. However, it was the elephant's charge that was its most effective weapon. If successful, it could destroy the cohesion of the imposing infantry.

The Carthaginian system of command was significantly different than the Roman.

The exact method of appointment for senior commanders is unknown. By the Second Punic War there is some evidence that generals could be chosen by the armies they commanded. As opposed to the normal Roman practice of yearly commands, the practice for Carthage's generals seems to have been that they served either for an unlimited tenure or to the completion of the task for which they were chosen. Given the mixed origins of most Carthaginian armies, command and coordination must have been more difficult than they were for Roman generals, but long-term service would have allowed the general a greater opportunity to develop close ties to his troops.

A further difference between the Roman and Carthaginian military systems lies in their approach to war. Carthage, as was the case with most of the Hellenistic states, waged a limited type of warfare. It was not directed at the annihilation of the enemy, but it was fought to compel the enemy through exhaustion or lack of further resources to surrender on reasonable terms. Its corollary was that Carthage was prepared to fight only as long as gains outweighed losses. The Romans approached war as struggle to the finish. Not only was war waged offensively, but it was fought until the enemy was beaten into total submission. Rome only began to negotiate after it had secured this result. One of Carthage's weaknesses in both the First and the Second Punic War was its failure to understand how Rome waged war.

The First Punic War

Relations between Rome and Carthage had traditionally been friendly. Their earliest known treaty dates to 509, the first year of the Republic. This was followed by later treaties during the fourth century and early third century. These treaties highlight the divergent interests of both parties. In essence the treaties established a separate sphere of influence for each, with little possibility for a clash of interests.

Rome's victory in the war against Pyrrhus and a resurgence of Carthaginian military successes in Sicily changed that situation. With the capture of Tarentum, Rome now dominated southern Italy, and for the first time its control extended to the narrow Sicilian Straits that separated the tip of southern Italy from Sicily. This opened up the possibility of friction with Carthage.

The immediate cause of the outbreak of the first war between them was the result of local events in Sicily. Campanian mercenaries, the Mamertini, had seized control of the city of Messana in the 280s. Its site was of great strategic importance, as it formed one of the two points of control of the Sicilian Straits, the other being Rhegium on the Italian side, which was now in Roman hands. Hiero, the ruler of Syracuse, the most powerful of the Greek cities of Sicily, had finally succeeded in bottling the Mamertini up in Messana after a decade of war. In response the Mamertini had accepted a Carthaginian garrison to protect the city, and in response Hiero withdrew. With the immediate threat of Syracuse over, an internal dispute broke out among the Mamertini over the presence of the Carthaginian garrison. A faction that wanted its removal appealed to the Romans for help.

The Senate was divided on its answer to this appeal and referred the matter to the people. Appius Claudius, consul in 264, argued for action to be taken on the grounds that Carthage was a potential threat and held the prospect of rich booty before the people. The exact political steps that followed are unclear but Claudius was authorized to aid the Mamertini. However, it is unlikely that at this stage either party envisioned anything more than limited action. Neither side recognized that in the end there was no compromise possible given the Roman attitude to warfare.

Certainly by 263 the Romans had taken Messana, and Hiero, realizing Roman strength, concluded a treaty with them by which he retained his kingship and the control of a small territory. Late in 262 the Romans attacked the main Carthaginian headquarters at Acragas and after a difficult siege took it in 261. The sacking of the city and the selling of the inhabitants into slavery antagonized many of the Greek cities, who joined the Carthaginians.

Polybius states that it was this development that determined the Romans to expel the Carthaginians from Sicily. It must have been clear that the only way to do so was through the construction of a major war fleet, which won its first victory off Mylae in northeastern Sicily. Naval encounters, which were mostly Roman victories, as well as mostly unsuccessful sieges of the remaining Carthaginian strongpoints in western Sicily, mark the last eighteen years of the war. A final encounter off the Aegates Islands in 242 ended in a Roman victory and the exhaustion of Carthage, which signed a treaty of peace in the next year. For Roman naval developments, see pp. 183ff.

The Second Punic War

The origins of the Second Punic War are closely tied to the results of the first (264–241). That twenty-two-year struggle had deprived Carthage of an effective navy for military use and of its control of Sicily. Relations were worsened by the Roman seizure of Sardinia and Corsica in 238 while Carthage was preoccupied with a revolt of its mercenaries.

Perhaps drawn by the prospect of Spain's manpower and its productive mines, Carthaginians began to greatly extend their presence in the Iberian peninsula. In 239 Hamilcar Barca and his son Hannibal landed in Spain, and the father began a consistent policy of expansion in southern and southeastern Spain. Hamilcar was succeeded by his son-in-law Hasdrubal, who continued the Carthaginian offensive, campaigning in the north and building the city of New Carthage (modern Cartagena) on the east coast as Carthage's new headquarters in Spain. Hasdrubal had concluded an agreement of uncertain character with Rome, probably in 226, that supposedly set the limit of Carthaginian expansion at the Ebro River. The purpose of the treaty is unclear, as Carthage's territory lay far south of the Ebro and Rome had no obvious interest in Spain at this point beyond safeguarding the interests of its longtime ally Massilia on the French coast. In 221 Hasdrubal was murdered because of a private dispute. He was succeeded by Hamilcar's son Hannibal, who also had his position ratified by the army.

Hannibal resumed the expansionist policy of his father. In a little more than a year he had brought central Spain under control. It is difficult to know what to make of these conquests; he might simply have been enlarging the empire begun by his father or building up resources for a possible war with Rome.

It was during Hannibal's drive to the north that a problem arose. The native town of Saguntum lay about one hundred miles south of the Ebro. Saguntum had earlier experienced an internal struggle between pro-Punic and pro-Roman factions which had been settled by an appeal to Rome. By this action the Romans created a lasting, though probably informal, relationship with Saguntum. The Romans viewed Saguntum as connected to them by *fides* or trust. References to *fides* occur often in the history of Roman foreign relations. The obligations inherent in this bond were ill defined and varied depending on circumstances. Its most important consequence in this case is that Rome felt that such a bond gave it the right to intervene on behalf of Saguntum if it chose to do so.

The sequence of events is unclear, but by 220 the Saguntines were afraid of an attack by Hannibal. They appealed to Rome, and an embassy was sent to instruct Hannibal to keep away from Saguntum. Hannibal's claim that the Saguntines had attacked a neighboring tribe friendly to Carthage generated popular support for an assault on the town. The attack was launched during the early spring of 219 and it fell after a siege of eight months. In response, in March 218 a final Roman embassy was dispatched to Carthage to demand the surrender of Hannibal and his staff and to threaten war if this was not done. The Carthaginians refused, and after a twenty-year interval they found themselves once again at war with Rome.

Why both sides so easily decided on war is not totally clear. It may be that the Romans thought that the declaration of war would be met with the same response as in 239 and that Carthage would back down. At the worst, they probably thought they could confine the conflict to Spain, as they had done with the fighting in Sicily in the first war, and that their superior resources would wear the Carthaginians down and force them to sue for peace. In that case, it would be a continuing demonstration of superiority to Carthage and a further warning if it persisted in challenging Rome's authority.

Hannibal's response to Roman demands may have developed from the same considerations. By taking the position it did on Saguntum, Rome had limited his freedom of operations and made it clear that it was ready to interfere when and where it chose in Spain. The example of Sardinia and Corsica was also surely not lost on him. He could not predict Rome's future actions, and given his success in expanding the area of Carthaginian control he must have thought that sooner or later a conflict with Rome was inevitable. He must have judged that his resources in hand as well as those he could assemble later gave him the possibility of success. The speed of his preparations also hints at the fact that he had already thought about the possibility of war with Rome and had devised a plan for it.

In formulating his plan Hannibal had to take into account two problems that Carthage would face in any conflict with Rome. The first was Rome's overwhelming superiority on the sea. This meant that an invasion of Italy by sea was impracticable and that receiving reinforcements on any scale while in Italy by sea would be impossible. This meant that if he planned an invasion of Italy it would have to be by land. Secondly, it must have been clear to Hannibal that fighting a campaign in Spain similar to the one fought by Carthage in Sicily during the first war would turn into a campaign of mutual attrition and that in such a conflict Rome's superior resources of manpower meant that it would win. Victory would have to be based on effectively robbing Rome of the capacity to fight and that meant depriving it of its apparently limitless sources of manpower. The only way to accomplish this was by striking at its Italian allies. The hostility of the Gauls of northern Italy increased the possibilities for the success of such an attack. They could provide him with a secure base and recruits for the coming conflict.

These factors must have determined Hannibal to act. It was a daring plan that had serious difficulties. The passage to Italy over the Alps was bound to take a toll of his men and once he arrived in the north Italian plain he would be totally dependent on local sources for supplies and additional manpower for his initial attack.

Hannibal probably set out on his march to Italy in June of 218 with 90,000 infantry, 12,000 cavalry, and thirty-seven elephants. The need to establish garrisons and the crossing of both the Pyrenees and the Alps resulted in severe losses. On his arrival in Italy, Hannibal's force now consisted of 20,000 infantry and 6,000 cavalry.

The Ticinus

115 POLYBIUS, *HISTORIES* 3.65

Publius Cornelius Scipio, one of the two consuls of 218, had tried to intercept Hannibal in Gaul, but failed to do so and so returned to Italy. The situation was complicated by a Gallic rising, perhaps fomented by Hannibal. This unbalanced the Roman forces, which were forced on the defensive. Scipio marched north from Pisa into the Po valley to confront Hannibal. He probably crossed to the northern bank of the river at Placentia and marched west to the Ticinus River, a tributary of the Po which flowed past Patavium, and bridged it. Hannibal's victory persuaded a number of Gallic tribes to give him support. It is probable that the Numidian cavalry controlled their horses with their legs and did not use bridles.

The next day both Hannibal and Scipio advanced along the river [Po] on the bank nearest the Alps, the Romans with the river to their left and the Carthaginians with the river on their right. On the next day the armies learned from their scouts that they were close to one another; they then encamped and halted. On the following day both commanders, taking all of their cavalry and Publius also his javelineers, advanced through the plain with the intention of scouting each other's forces. When they neared each other and saw a rising cloud of dust, they straight away deployed for battle.

Publius, placing his javelineers and his Gallic cavalry in front and the rest of troops to their rear, advanced slowly. Deploying his bridled cavalry and all of his heavy cavalry in front and arranging his Numidians on either wing for an encircling maneuver, Hannibal moved to meet the enemy.

Both the generals and their men were so enthusiastic for an encounter that at the first shock the javelineers had no time to cast their missiles but gave way and fled back through the gaps in their cavalry, struck with terror at the charge and frightened that they might be ridden down by the cavalry. The cavalry of both sides clashed head on. For a long while the struggle was equal. It was a fight of horsemen and men on foot, as many of the cavalry fought dismounted.

But when the Numidians had encircled the Romans and fell on them from behind, the javelineers, who had at first fled the cavalry charge, were trampled by the numbers and impetus of the Numidian charge. The cavalry who had faced the Carthaginians from the start of the battle suffered heavy casualties, although they inflicted even more. Now attacked from the rear they turned to fight, some scattering in all directions and others rallying round the general.

The Trebia

116 POLYBIUS, *HISTORIES* 3.72.1–74.8

Wounded during his defeat at the Ticinus and in fear of a Gallic uprising, Scipio withdrew eastwards to his camp, and then learning of Hannibal's advance to the Trebia, another tributary of the Po, he encamped on its western bank. The further advance of the Carthaginians and the desertion of a large Gallic contingent persuaded Scipio to cross the river and build a new camp on its eastern bank.

The arrival of Hannibal in Italy shocked the Senate into action. It summoned the other consul of 218, Tiberius Sempronius Longus, who had been operating in Sicily, back to Italy. Longus arrived in northern Italy in December 218 and linked up with Scipio. The consuls now commanded a force of four legions and allies. An attack by Roman light-armed and cavalry against Numidian and Gallic cavalry was taken by Longus as a victory and increased his eagerness to fight. Both sides wanted a battle. Hannibal needed a victory to solidify his position with the Gauls, and it was to his advantage to face recently recruited and inexperienced Roman troops. Longus was impelled by the normal Roman desire to force a confrontation and by the need to reestablish Roman control in the area.

As soon as Tiberius saw the Numidian horse approaching he sent out his own cavalry with orders to close with the enemy. Then he sent off 6,000 javelineers and began to move the rest of his forces out of camp, confident because of the size of his force and the previous success of his cavalry. He thought the mere sight of his men would decide the matter.

The flat land west of the Trebia was ideal for cavalry and it was there Hannibal decided to fight. A river with steep banks provided an ideal spot for an ambush, and Hannibal stationed 1,000 infantry and 1,000 cavalry. The next day Hannibal sent his Numidian cavalry across the river to lure the Romans to the west bank. The bait was taken, and Sempronius crossed the river with his double consular army.

No figures survive for the losses on either side. The battle displays many of the characteristic elements of Hannibal's tactics. His ability to read his opponent's mind is striking. The use of both light and heavy cavalry to expose the flanks of a superior infantry force and then encircling would be the pattern for the far greater victory at Cannae.

The time was about the winter solstice and the day was very cold and snowy. Both men and horses had left the camp without food. At first, they were sustained by their eagerness and enthusiasm, but arriving at the crossing of the Trebia, which had become swollen during the night by a storm higher up the valley than the camp, the infantry had severe difficulty in crossing, since the water was chest high. The result was that as the day advanced the men suffered from both cold and hunger.

The Carthaginians, who had both eaten and drunk in their tents and prepared their mounts, anointed and armed themselves around their camp fires. Hannibal waited for his opportunity and, when he saw the Romans crossing the river, he moved forward his spearmen and slingers as a covering force, numbering 8,000, and led out his army. Marching about a mile from his camp he deployed his 20,000 infantry made up of Spaniards, Celts, and Africans in a single line in the center of his formation. He divided his cavalry, which numbered more than 10,000 including his Celtic allies, and placed them on either wing. He also located his elephants on each wing so that his wings were doubly protected.

At the same time Tiberius recalled his cavalry, seeing that they were ineffective against their opponents, as the Numidians easily retreated and scattered and then wheeled around and attacked the Romans with great boldness. This is the normal way the Numidian cavalry fights.

He deployed his infantry, 16,000 Romans and 20,000 allies, in the usual formation. This is their complete army for offensive operations when both consuls chance to be operating together. Then Tiberius placed his 4,000 cavalry on the wings. Tiberius then advanced in an impressive manner on the enemy, making his approach in order and at a slow pace.

Now that both sides had neared each other the light-armed on both sides began the fight. The Romans had in many ways the worst of it during the fight, as the Carthaginians were more proficient, since the Romans had fared badly in the morning and had used most of their javelins against the Numidian cavalry. Those they had left proved useless because of the continued wetness. The cavalry and indeed the whole army did no better, but the Carthaginians had the opposite experience. The men in their formation were in excellent condition and fresh, and did what had to be done effectively and with enthusiasm. So when the light-armed had retired through the gaps and the heavy infantry engaged one another the Carthaginians on both wings quickly forced back their opponents since they were superior in numbers and in better shape and with their horses, as I mentioned, still fresh. After the Roman cavalry had fallen back and exposed the wings of the infantry, the Carthaginian spearmen and the majority of the Numidians, passing their own troops arrayed in front of them, fell on the Romans from the flanks, inflicting great damage and preventing them from fighting those to their front.

The frontline heavy infantry in the middle of the army on both sides fought in close formation for a long time, with the advantage to neither side. But at this point the Numidians emerged from ambush and attacked the enemy's center from the rear, leading to great disorder and confusion on the Roman side. Finally, both of Tiberius' wings, pressed on the front by the elephants and on the flanks by the light-armed, gave way and were pursued to the river in their rear. After this, those in the rear of the Roman center suffered heavily from those attacking from the ambush, while those in front, forced to advance, overcame the Celts and a portion of the Africans, and after killing many of them cut their way through the Carthaginian line. Seeing that their own wings had been driven off they were unable either to help them or to retreat to their own camp, as they were afraid of the numerous enemy cavalry and hindered by the river and the strength and the force of the downpour. Maintaining their order, they made their way back to Placentia in safety. The majority of the rest were killed by the elephants and cavalry near the river. Some of the infantry and the majority of the cavalry made their way to the main body and together they returned to Placentia.

Victorious at the Ticinus and Trebia in the north Italian plain, Hannibal now moved south towards Etruria and probably crossed the Apennines in May of 217. A Roman army was ambushed and defeated at Lake Trasimene near Perusia with heavy losses.

Defeat in two major battles with large losses had undermined Roman confidence, and in the emergency a dictator, Q. Fabius Maximus, was appointed. Fabius adopted a strategy which relied upon not meeting Hannibal in battle but wearing him down and denying him access to supplies and recruits, but there was still a strong faction who favored decisive action on the battlefield. Fabius dogged Hannibal, harassing his foraging parties and attacking stragglers, but refused to engage in battle. Though this strategy was contrary to the normal aggressive Roman campaigning style it allowed time to prepare for a future battle of encounter. Fabius laid down his office at the end of 217.

The battle of Cannae

The two new consuls for 216, C. Terentius Varro and L. Aemilius Paullus, took office after a heavily contested election. The dispute at issue centered on the conduct of the war: whether to attempt to prolong Fabius' strategy of avoiding battle with Hannibal and seeking to defeat him through attrition and a lack of supplies or whether to face him on the battlefield. Every attempt to do so had ended in defeat. Nevertheless, the sentiment for a decisive confrontation was strong. Hannibal's presence in Italy and his ability to move about almost at will was a demonstration to its allies of Rome's weakness. No allies had as yet joined Hannibal, but the longer he remained in the field the more likely the possibility became. Fabius' strategy was also alien to the Roman method of making war, which sought to grind down the enemy on the battlefield.

New soldiers were enrolled and, though the sources differ on numbers, they probably amounted to four legions of increased strength, consisting of 5,000 infantry and 300 cavalry. In addition four legions were now in southern Italy at Gerunium. This would bring the number of legions to eight, which along with an equal number of allies would total 80,000 infantry and 6,000 cavalry, of which probably 2,400 were Roman. The unusually high proportion of senators and *equites* serving with the army is an indicator of the popularity of the decision to fight and supports the view that the Romans were determined that the coming battle would be decisive. This sense of determination is echoed in Livy's report that the soldiers on their own initiative swore an oath not to flee the field (see **97**). Despite the high level of determination the recruits received insufficient training; though the consuls did what they could, the absence of battlefield experience and the lack of prior service together meant that the army would enter the battle at a disadvantage in comparison with the veteran troops of Hannibal's army.

Probably in June, Hannibal, who had camped opposite the Roman army at Gerunium, broke contact and moved south to the Roman's supply base at Cannae in Apulia, approximately a sixty-mile march. Polybius claims that he did so hoping to compel the Romans to fight. Other sources add that he was bothered by his lack of supplies and this may in part be true, given the fact that he had remained stationary during the winter months, a time when food supplies were at their lowest. Cannae is the modern Monte di Canne. The town was situated on the right bank of the Aufidus River on a hill about five miles from its mouth. At the time of Hannibal's arrival the town had already been razed, but supplies were still stored there and the town commanded the surrounding countryside. On the south side of the river where the town stood there was a chain of hills, but north of the river the land was relatively flat and suitable for cavalry.

The size of Hannibal's army has also been the subject of a great deal of debate. Polybius and Livy both state that Hannibal had 40,000 infantry and 10,000 cavalry, but this figure probably includes light-armed troops. A reasonable estimate would put his heavy infantry at somewhere between 28,000 and 30,000 men, with 10,000 cavalry. The major contingents consisted of Gauls, Spaniards, and the Libyans who formed his most experienced and steadiest troops. They were armed in Roman fashion from the spoils of earlier victories, and this may have caused some confusion during the battle.

The consuls with the newly raised legions joined the troops near Gerunium. The combined army then marched south to the vicinity of Cannae in late July. All of the ancient accounts of the battle fix the responsibility for the disaster on Varro, a new man, with no prior military experience. Paullus, the other consul, seems to have had no previous experience of large-scale battle either. In fact, no earlier Roman general had commanded forces on this scale. There were clearly tactical differences between the consuls; however, it is clear that the Romans had from the outset determined to engage Hannibal and that much of the negative comment on Varro is the result of an attempt by Aemilius' supporters to shift the blame on to him.

Hannibal had originally encamped on the south bank of the river and appears to have waited several weeks for the arrival of the Romans. On the second day of their march the Roman army came in sight of the enemy, whose camp lay about three miles away.

Paullus' refusal to immediately engage the Carthaginians clearly makes sense. He was unsatisfied with the ground, and supplies were also a problem. While Hannibal had access to supplies from Cannae, it is not clear how the Roman forces were provisioned.

Paullus' decision to divide his forces in the face of the enemy is extremely unusual and goes against standard military practice, and may have been an attempt to deprive Hannibal of the use of the supplies stored at Cannae. It must be assumed that, given the size of his forces, he felt able to do so. It undermines the view that Paullus was reluctant to fight, as such a move if successful would have compelled Hannibal either to move or to fight and the first alternative seems unlikely. In response Hannibal moved his camp to the north bank of the river opposite the larger Roman camp. Polybius claims that this was done because his men were disheartened. This explanation does not seem plausible. In the ensuing battle there is no trace of a decline in morale. More likely Hannibal was anxious to bring about a battle and concentrated on coaxing out the main Roman force. In addition the ground on the north bank was excellent cavalry country, as Paullus had realized.

The date of the battle, August 2, is secure, but the location of the battlefield has been a longstanding problem. Many scholars have argued that the battle was fought on the right or northwestern bank of the river. But the accounts of battle mention that both sides crossed the river before the final encounter and that the battle was fought on the bank of the river opposite to their main camps. This could only be the right or southeastern bank. The further question remains as to where on the right bank the battle was fought. Some have argued that the battle was fought east of the smaller Roman camp, since the terrain to the west of it is hillier. Recently it has been pointed out that the river has changed its course many times and that locating the battle to the west of the Roman smaller camp is feasible. Given the state of our sources a final decision is impossible.

The Roman battle line appears to be the normal three-line formation. But, as Polybius states, the maniples were formed up to a greater depth than usual and the gaps between them narrowed. This was an atypical formation to adopt. The great Roman advantage in the field was the ability for the individual maniples to maneuver, and this formation would have hindered such movements. However, a number of considerations seem to lie behind Varro's decision. First, his army was relatively untrained and he was combining troops from two different armies who had had no experience in fighting alongside one another. These factors would to some degree have nullified the advantage of maneuver, and he may have wanted to deliver a massive blow to the enemy infantry in the hope of rapidly breaking before the enemy's superior cavalry had the chance to drive off the Roman cavalry and expose the infantry's flanks and rear. At the Trebia a large body of Roman infantry had managed to break through the Carthaginian front despite being surrounded and this may have further influenced Varro's decision. Paullus was stationed with the 2,400 Roman cavalry on the right wing near the river, while Varro commanded the 3,600 allied cavalry on the left, and the proconsul Servilius commanded the infantry in the center, which numbered perhaps 50,000–55,000 men. This command arrangement recognized the need for the cavalry to hold its position while the center delivered the decisive assault.

It is clear that Hannibal, on the basis of his past experience and perhaps good intelligence, had anticipated the Roman plan of battle and arranged his army to meet it. He placed his Numidian cavalry, numbering perhaps 3,000–4,000, on his right opposite the allied cavalry, and on his left wing he stationed his Gallic and Spanish horse, totaling about 6,000–7,000, more than double the number of Roman cavalry facing them. His greatest tactical innovation was in the arrangement of his infantry. His 10,000 Africans were placed in two equal columns at each end of his infantry line. The 22,000 Gallic and Spanish infantry were deployed in the center. Hannibal moved his infantry center forwards to create a convex bulge facing the Roman line. Some have thought this bulge consisted of echeloned companies, but it is more likely on the basis of Polybius' description that they were arranged in a semicircle. He had designed his formation to channel and slow the advance of the Roman infantry while his cavalry drove off the Roman and allied cavalry and could then attack the exposed Roman rear, while the African infantry on the flanks turned in against the flanks of the Roman formation, which would be exposed as it pushed the Gallic and Spanish infantry back. The end result would be and indeed was that the Roman army found itself completely encircled.

The number of Roman casualties is a problem. Polybius' figures seem too high. If one adds the 10,000 captured after the battle along with the 10,000 infantry and 370 cavalry who escaped the resulting figure is too high for Polybius's total of Roman forces engaged. Livy gives a figure of 45,000 infantry and 2,700 cavalry killed, with 3,000 infantry and 1,500 cavalry captured, while 14,550 escaped. These numbers seem more acceptable, especially as we know that two legions were formed from the survivors. Senatorial and equestrian casualty figure were extremely high. Eighty senators or men of senatorial rank and twenty-nine of forty-eight *tribuni militum* present at the battle were killed. Hannibal's casualties seem high for a victorious army in this period, but the fighting was protracted and Hannibal's center must have suffered heavily as the Romans drove it back.

117 POLYBIUS, *HISTORIES* 3.107.2–116.13 (WITH OMISSIONS)

Judging that it would be completely in his interest to compel the enemy to fight, Hannibal seized the hill where Cannae was located. The Romans stored grain and other supplies there which they had collected from the area around Canusium and used it to supply their camp as necessary. Although the town had been razed, Hannibal's capture of the supplies stored there and the hill on which it sat caused great consternation among the Roman forces. They were upset at the loss both of supplies and of a point that dominated the surrounding area. The [commanders] constantly sent messengers to Rome asking for orders, saying that, if they approached the enemy, battle would be unavoidable since the country around was being pillaged and the temper of the allies was uncertain.... The Senate decided to fight, and ordered the consuls forward.

The Senate decided to field a force of eight legions, which the Romans had never done before; each legion was 5,000 men strong apart from the allies.

On the next day [after Aemilius had reached the camp at Gerunium and made a speech to the troops] the consuls broke camp and advanced to where they had heard the enemy was. On the second day after spotting them, they had encamped about six miles from the Carthaginians. Lucius, after looking over the ground and noting its flat and treeless character, said that they should not attack, given the enemy's superiority in cavalry, but lure the enemy on by advancing into country where the infantry could be decisive. Gaius, owing to his ignorance, was of the opposite opinion; and so the generals were divided by this dispute and hardened in their feelings towards each other, a situation that is the most dangerous possible [in warfare]. On the following day the command passed to Gaius through the usual custom of the consuls commanding on alternate days; he broke camp and moved closer to the enemy despite Lucius' forceful objections and efforts to hinder him. Hannibal, taking his light-armed troops and cavalry, surprised them on the march, throwing them into great confusion.... Then the two sides separated at nightfall; the attack was not as successful as the Carthaginians had hoped.

The next day Lucius, judging that he could neither attack nor withdraw, safely encamped with two-thirds of his army by the Aufidus.... He fortified a position for the remaining third of his army across the river east of the ford and over a mile from his first camp and a little more than that from the enemy camp, hoping in this way to cover his foraging parties from the camp across the river and to harass those of the Carthaginians.

Hannibal drew up his army along the river, with the clear intention of giving battle, but Lucius, distrusting the ground and seeing that the Carthaginians would soon have to move camp because of their lack of supplies, kept quiet, while strengthening both his camps with covering forces. Hannibal, after waiting for some time for a battle, returned to camp and sent out his Numidians to harass the water carriers from the smaller camp.

On the following day it was Gaius' turn to take command, and just after sunrise he marched out his troops simultaneously from both camps. Fording the river with those from the larger camp he drew up his battle line, placing those from the smaller camp next to them in the same line, with the whole army facing south. He stationed the Roman cavalry next to the river on his right wing. He placed the infantry next to them in the same line, placing the maniples closer to each other than usual and deploying them much deeper than usual, making their depth many times their frontage. He stationed the allied horse on his left wing and placed his light-armed troops some distance in front of his whole line. The army consisted of 80,000 infantry including the allies and a little more than 6,000 cavalry.

At the same time Hannibal sent his Balearic slingers and pikemen over the river and placed them in front; he then led the rest of his forces from their fortifications and, after crossing the river in two places, he deployed them opposite the enemy. He positioned the Spanish and Celtic cavalry on his left towards the river and opposite the Roman cavalry. Next to them he placed one-half of his heavily armed Libyans and immediately next to them Spanish and Celtic infantry. Adjacent to them he deployed the other half of the Libyans, and on his right wing he positioned the Numidian horse. When these had all formed into line, he brought forward the units of the Spanish and Celtic infantry from the middle of his line and deployed them, maintaining contact among these companies and so forming a crescent-shaped bulge. As the line moved forward the companies gradually thinned. His aim was to keep the Libyans as a reserve force and to begin the fighting with his Spanish and Celtic troops.

The Libyans were armed in the Roman manner, as Hannibal had equipped them with selected weapons taken as spoils in previous battles....

The Carthaginian cavalry numbered about 10,000 and the infantry not much more than 40,000 including the Celts.

On the Roman side Aemilius was in charge of the right and Gaius the left, and Marcus and Gnaeus, the consuls of the previous year, commanded the center. On the Carthaginian side Hasdrubal controlled the left and Hanno the right. Hannibal and his brother Mago were stationed in the center. As I mentioned earlier, the Roman line faced south and the Carthaginian north so that the rising sun presented no problem for either army.

The first contact was made by those stationed in front, and as long as only the light-armed were engaged the contest was equal; at the same time the Spanish and Celtic cavalry from the Carthaginian left wing met the Roman cavalry and they began a truly barbaric struggle. The contest was not the normal one of wheeling about and turning, but once they met they dismounted and fought man to man. After the Carthaginians prevailed and had killed most of their opponents in the melee, although the Romans struggled with desperate bravery, they began to drive the survivors along the river, slaughtering them and cutting them down without mercy. Now the heavy infantry following on the light-armed fell to fighting each other. The Spanish and Celtic infantry held their line for a short time and fought well against the Romans, but soon were hard pressed by the weight of the Romans' line and fell back, breaking up the crescent formation. The Roman maniples pursued them furiously, cutting apart their formation. As the Celts were deployed in a thin line, the Romans pressed in from the wings to the center where the fighting was going on. The fighting on the wings and center were not simultaneous; the middle came into action first, as the Celts were arranged in a crescent formation far in advance of the infantry on the wings, with the curve projecting towards the enemy. The Romans pressed on these troops, massing in the middle, and the enemy center was pressed back so far that the Romans now had the heavy-armed Libyans on both flanks. The Libyans on the right wing faced to the left and starting from the right charged the enemy's flank, while those on the left faced right and extending from the left did the same thing. The situation made clear what needed to be done. The result was according to Hannibal's plan; the Romans in their action against the Celts were caught between the Libyan wings. So they no longer kept their compact formation but both individual soldiers and maniples turned towards those attacking their flanks to fight them.

Lucius, who had been on the right wing and taken part in the cavalry action, was still safe ... [and] seeing that the decision lay with the infantry rode to the center of the whole line and joined the fight, coming to grips with the enemy, and at the same time he encouraged his men and the troops next to him. Hannibal, who had been in this part of his line from the onset, did the same.

The Numidians on the right wing attacked the cavalry of the Roman left, neither inflicting much damage nor suffering greatly, owing to their characteristic mode of fighting. Nevertheless, they kept the enemy's cavalry out of the battle, drawing them off and falling upon them from all sides at once. Hasdrubal's men after they had killed almost all the Roman cavalry by the river moved to the left to aid the Numidians; at that point the Roman allied cavalry, seeing their impending charge, turned and fled. In this situation Hasdrubal acted effectively and cleverly. Perceiving that the Numidians were much superior in numbers and very effective and frightening in the pursuit of a fleeing enemy, he turned over the pursuit to them and led his men to where the infantry were engaged to bring help to the Libyans. He fell upon the backs of the Romans, delivering successive attacks in many places, thus heartening the Libyans and discouraging and terrifying the Romans....

For as long as possible the Romans withstood the enemy, turning and presenting a front to the attacks of the enemy who had encircled them. But the outer ranks were constantly being killed, and the rest were being forced into a tighter space. Finally they all fell, including Gaius and

Marcus, consuls of the year before and courageous men who proved themselves worthy of Rome in the battle. During the struggle and the slaughter of these men the Numidians pursued the enemy's cavalry, killing some and unhorsing others. A few of them fled to Venusia to Gaius Terentius, a man shamed by his flight; his consulship had been of no benefit to his country.

Such was the result of the battle at Cannae between the Romans and the Carthaginians. Great courage was shown by both victors and the vanquished, as is clear from what happened. Seventy of the 6,000 cavalry reached Venusia with Gaius and about 300 allied cavalry made their way safety to various cities. About 10,000 infantry were captured, but not on the battlefield; perhaps only about 3,000 fled to neighboring cities. The remainder, about 70,000, died gallantly on the field. The mass of cavalry had provided the most important element in the Carthaginian victory before and in the course of the battle. It is thus clear to those who come after that it is of more advantage in war to have half the number of infantry and superiority in cavalry than to have forces equal to that of the enemy. On Hannibal's side 4,000 Celts, 1,500 Spaniards and Libyans, and 2,000 cavalry died.

The battle of the Metaurus

118 LIVY, 27.48.4–49.8

By 208 Hannibal and his army were contained in southern Italy and, though undefeated, needed reinforcements. Since his entry into Italy in 218 he had only received a draft of troops in 215. Carthaginian weakness at sea and the Roman campaign in Spain had prevented additional troops from joining him. Finally, in 208 his brother Hasdrubal, despite a defeat, managed to elude the Romans and cross the Alps into Italy.

He entered the north Italian plain earlier than expected in the spring of 207. However, he lost the advantage of surprise by fruitlessly besieging the Roman colony of Placentia. It may well be that he did this in an effort to win Gallic support, and he may have needed to wait until forage was available for his cavalry.

The news of his arrival caused consternation at Rome; Roman forces operating in the north on both sides of the Apennines attempted to block Hasdrubal's route south, but they were too weak to do more than delay him. One of the two consuls, Marcus Livius Salinator, was sent north to confront Hasdrubal, while the other consul, Gaius Claudius Nero, was dispatched to face Hannibal, each with a consular army of two legions and allies.

Hasdrubal proceeded down the east coast as far as Sena Gallica, where he was confronted by Salinator's army, which had been reinforced by two under-strength legions already in the area. Hasdrubal had sent messengers to his brother to arrange a junction with him, but they were intercepted and Claudius was informed of Carthaginian movements. One of the boldest of Roman generals, he left the majority of his troops facing Hannibal and, slipping away with a picked force of 6,000 infantry and 1,000 cavalry, he marched north to effect a junction with Salinator. Reaching his destination, Claudius secretly slipped into Salinator's camp at night to avoid detection by Hasdrubal, whose camp lay less than a half-mile away.

Claudius persuaded his colleague to join battle immediately. Hasdrubal had made the same decision and, when the Romans marched out to deploy, his line was already in formation. Hasdrubal realized that he was confronted by the two consuls and returned to camp. During the night he tried to slip away but lost his way. To rest his men Hasdrubal began constructing a camp on an elevation overlooking the Metaurus River (modern Metauro near Fano). This allowed the Romans to catch up with him and at dawn he was attacked by Roman cavalry and light-armed troops. He had no other choice but to fight.

Polybius provides a slightly different version of the battle. He omits any mention of the Ligurians in Hasdrubal's army, and this may be right. The Gauls were essentially placed in a defensive position, and Hasdrubal decided to seek a decision on his right. It has been correctly argued that the elephants were on Hasdrubal's right wing, rather than in the center where Livy places them, to add striking power to the decisive wing. The unnamed praetor in the passage is Lucius Porcius Licinus.

The location of the battle is unknown despite various hypotheses. We do not know the size of the forces involved, but it is clear that the combined Roman force outnumbered Hasdrubal's army.

Livy's casualty figures are grossly exaggerated. Polybius gives 10,000 Carthaginian dead and 2,000 Roman and allied fatalities, and this seems a reasonable approximation.

This battle was of crucial significance, as it ended any hope that Hannibal would be able to launch a major campaign in Italy. Without additional troops, he could not mount a serious challenge to the overwhelming Roman advantage in manpower.

All their troops assembled and the battle line was formed with Claudius stationed on the right wing, Livius on the left, and the praetor commanding the center. Hasdrubal abandoned his camp fortifications when he saw that battle was imminent. He placed the elephants in the front of his line before his standards; next to them on his left wing he deployed the Gauls opposite Claudius, not so much out of confidence in them as because he believed the Romans were afraid of them. He himself took command of the Spanish troops who formed his right wing, placing his highest hopes in them, and the Ligurians were placed in the center behind the elephants. His line was deep rather than extended. A looming hill protected the Gauls, and the Spaniards faced the Roman left. The Roman right wing extended beyond the enemy's battle line, and a hill to their front prevented them from launching frontal or flanking attacks.

There was a harsh, close struggle between Livius and Hasdrubal, with great slaughter on both sides. At that spot where both generals were stationed there was the greater part of the Roman infantry and cavalry, the veteran Spanish soldiers experienced in battle, with the Romans and the Ligurians, a race pitiless in war. The elephants had in their first charge thrown the front lines into confusion and forced back the standards. Then, as the struggle and shouting intensified, the elephants could no longer be controlled and wandered about as if uncertain as to which army they belonged. They were like ships drifting without their steering oars. Claudius called out to his soldiers when he attempted to march his men up the hill in front of them: "Why did we march so great a distance at such great speed?" When he saw that he could not reach the enemy at that point he took some cohorts from the right wing, where he saw that they were standing idly by rather than engaged in battle, and led them behind his battle line. To the surprise of his own men and the enemy he attacked the left flank of the Carthaginians. He moved with such speed that almost as soon as they had appeared on the Carthaginian flank they began an attack on their rear. The Spaniards and Ligurians were being cut down on every side, from the front, the flank, and the rear, and now the slaughter reached the Gauls. At that point, there was little resistance, for the majority had deserted during the night and were scattered over the fields asleep. The Gauls in the battle line were worn out by marching and lack of sleep, their bodies unable to bear the exertion; they could scarcely carry their arms on their shoulders. Now at midday thirst and heat exposed them to unlimited capture and butchery.

More of the elephants were killed by their own drivers than by the enemy.... Hasdrubal was conspicuous as leader at other times, but especially in this battle. He encouraged his men with words and by placing himself in danger; he inspired those who were exhausted and those surrendering because of their fatigue and exertion by his entreaties and reproaches. He recalled them when they fled, and at some points renewed the fight. Finally, when the enemy's victory was clear, he did not wish to outlive the army which had followed him out of personal loyalty; he spurred his horse and charged a Roman cohort. Worthy of his father, Hamilcar, and his brother, Hannibal, he died fighting.

There was in this war no battle in which more of the enemy died. It seemed a disaster equal to that of Cannae in the loss of a general and the destruction of his army. There were 57,000 of the enemy killed and 5,400 captured and, besides, great booty was taken of all types, including silver and gold. There were 4,000 Roman prisoners recovered, and that was some solace for the soldiers lost in this battle, for it was a bloody victory, with about 8,000 Romans and allies lost.

The battle of Ilipa

119 POLYBIUS, *HISTORIES* 11.20–24.9

This battle fought in 206 was the most important of the Spanish campaign. Although fighting continued, it broke Carthaginian power in Spain.

The Hasdrubal in the passage is not the same man as the brother of Hannibal who fought at the Metaurus, but Hasdrubal Gisgo, who had been commander in Spain from 214 until this battle. Mago was a brother of Hannibal and had campaigned with him in Italy until his return to Spain in 215. Publius is Publius Cornelius Scipio Africanus, the conqueror of Hannibal, who within four years (210–206) destroyed Carthaginian power in Spain.

Ilipa is near the modern city of Seville in southwestern Spain. The numbers that Polybius gives for the Carthaginians seem too high. Livy's figures seem more reasonable: 50,000 Carthaginian infantry and 4,500 cavalry.

Scipio's maneuver seems an extraordinarily complex one to execute in the middle of a battle. It shows the tremendous improvement in the Roman army's military skills after the early defeats in Italy and Spain. The same may be said in comparing early Roman commanders to Scipio. He had Hannibal's ability to use his opponent's psychology against him, in this case Hasdrubal's timing and his method of deploying his troops. The complicated and difficult maneuvers described by Polybius were made possible by the intensive training Scipio had given his soldiers after his arrival in Spain in 209 and by the long-established bonds between the general and his men. No other Roman army was to be capable of such tactics until the last century BC, when continuous service under the same commanders created similar conditions.

Polybius' description of the maneuver is not totally clear and there has been much disagreement over exactly what happened on the Roman wings. On the most reasonable interpretation Polybius is describing a movement not limited to three maniples with associated cavalry and light-armed on each wing, but a movement of all of the forces on each of the Roman wings. In the first phase the right wing turned to the right and the left wing to the left and each marched right and left respectively, parallel to the Carthaginian line, until they reached its end or extended some way beyond it. Then the right wing wheeled left and the left wing likewise wheeled to the right and both marched in column against the enemy. As they approached the enemy line they wheeled into line so that the infantry were on the inside of the line, while the cavalry and light-armed formed up on the flank. These movements must have been carried out quickly to forestall any attempt by Hasdrubal to change his deployment to meet the threat of a flank attack. Presumably the cavalry and light infantry operated as a single unit, a practice attested since the fourth century. In conjunction with this movement Scipio's center, composed of his Spanish troops, advanced to hold the enemy center, but at a deliberately slow pace. Before they met the enemy line the battle had been decided on the flanks. This maneuver allowed Scipio to make use of allies he did not totally trust. It is surprising that Polybius makes no mention of either Carthaginian cavalry or their light-armed, who are absent from his account after the initial skirmishing.

> Hasdrubal collected his troops from the various cities in which they had passed the winter. He advanced and encamped not far from a town called Ilipa. He established his camp close to the foothills in front of which there were plains suitable for a full-scale battle. He had 70,000 infantry, 4,000 cavalry, and thirty-two elephants.
>
> Publius dispatched Marcus Junius to Colichas to take command of the forces that had been prepared for him there, which consisted of 3,000 foot and 500 horse. Scipio took the remaining allies and advanced towards his objective. When he neared Castolus and the area close to Baecula he joined his troops with those from Colichas under Marcus. He was in a very difficult position, as without his allies he did not have sufficient Roman troops to risk an engagement. To seek a decisive encounter while relying on his allies seemed too hazardous and reckless. Nevertheless, after hesitation, and under the pressure of circumstances, he was forced to use the Spaniards, but only for show, while relying on his own troops to do the actual fighting. Adopting this plan he left with his whole army of 45,000 infantry and 3,000 cavalry, and when he came near the Carthaginians and in full view of them he encamped on low hills opposite their position.
>
> Mago, thinking it an opportune time to attack the Romans as they were encamping, took the greater part of his cavalry along with Masinissa and his Numidians and charged the camp, certain that he would catch Publius off his guard. But Scipio, long foreseeing what was going to happen, had placed his cavalry equal in number to the Carthaginians under a hill. Many of the Carthaginians at the start, surprised by the unexpected Roman attack, fell from their horses as they turned back, but the rest came to grips with their opponents and fought well. However, they were at a disadvantage because of the ease with which Roman cavalry dismounted, and after losing a number of men during the short time they stood their ground they turned to flight. At first, they retired in good order, but under the pressure of the attack their formation disintegrated and fled and sought safety under the walls of their camp. The result of this encounter was that the Romans were more willing to take risks and the Carthaginians less so. Nevertheless, during the following days both sides drew up their forces in the plain. Their cavalry and light-armed troops fought skirmishes, testing each other; finally they decided to fight a decisive battle.
>
> On this occasion Publius had recourse to two stratagems. Scipio noticed that Hasdrubal deployed his forces outside of his camp late in the day, placing his Africans in the middle of his line and his elephants on the wings. Scipio was accustomed to coming out even later and would station his Roman troops in the center opposite the Africans, and his Spanish troops on the wings. But on the day which he had chosen for battle he did

the opposite. This greatly contributed to the Roman victory and did not a little to weaken the enemy. At sunrise he sent a message to all of his tribunes and soldiers to breakfast, arm themselves, and move out of camp. The order was obeyed with great enthusiasm, as they suspected what was going to happen. Scipio sent his cavalry and light-armed forward, ordering them to approach the enemy camp and launch a bold missile attack. He himself moved forward with his army at sunrise and arriving in the middle of the plain he deployed his men in a manner opposite to his earlier practice, with the Spanish in the middle and the Romans on the wings.

The Carthaginians scarcely had time to arm with the Roman cavalry suddenly approaching their camp and the rest of the enemy deploying in plain sight. So Hasdrubal was forced, although he was unprepared and his men had not eaten, to send out his cavalry and light-armed against the Roman cavalry and light-armed and to deploy his infantry in battle line not far from the hills in the flat plain, as he usually did. For a while the Romans remained quiet. As the day advanced the skirmishing of the light-armed was indecisive, as those who were pressed fled back to the protection of their infantry and then returned to fight again. Then Scipio received the light-armed back into his ranks through the intervals between the maniples and placed them behind the troops arrayed on both wings, with the *velites* in front and the cavalry behind. At first he made a frontal advance on the enemy; then when he was about half a mile from the enemy he ordered the Spaniards to continue with their advance in formation, and ordered the maniples of his right wing to turn to the right and those of the left wing to turn to their left.

Scipio himself took from the right wing and Lucius Marcius and Marcus Junius took from the left the leading three squadrons of cavalry and positioned them in front of the usual number of *velites* and three maniples [the Romans called this unit of infantry a cohort] and advanced rapidly straight at the enemy. Then wheeling the units on the right to the left and the units on the left to the right and the rear units following the lead of the front ones, he advanced directly on the enemy. They pressed their attack energetically, with the following units wheeling around. When they were not far from the enemy, the Spanish, who had continued their straight-on advance, were still at some distance, as they advanced slowly; Scipio fell on both wings, with the Romans in column, according to his plan. The movements which allowed the following units to get into the line with the units in front and to fight the enemy were in reverse directions with respect to the left and right wings and for the cavalry in relation to the infantry. For the cavalry and the *velites* on the right wing wheeled to the right, attempting to outflank the enemy, while the infantry wheeled in the opposite direction. On the left the infantry wheeled right while the horse and light-armed wheeled left. The result of this was that for the cavalry and light-armed of both wings their right became their left.

Attaching little importance to these changes of direction the general focused on what was more important, the outflanking maneuver, and he was correct, for a commander should know what is happening and execute movements adapted to circumstances.

In the struggle the elephants, because of their bombardment of missiles by the cavalry and light-armed, were thrown into confusion everywhere and suffered terribly. They did as much damage to their own side as to the enemy, and rushing wildly about they destroyed both sides alike by their movements. The infantry on the Carthaginian wings were broken, and the Africans in the center, who were the elite of the army, were unable to act. They were not able to bring help to the wings because of the approach of the Spanish, nor remaining in place were they able to do what was necessary, as the enemy to their front did not come into contact. For a while, the wings fought courageously, as both sides knew that the whole matter rested with them. But when the heat of the day was at its most intense the Carthaginians found themselves exhausted, as they had not marched out at their own initiative and had been prevented from making the necessary preparations, while the Romans showed themselves physically and emotionally superior, especially because their best soldiers fought with the enemy's weakest as a result of their general's planning. At first, Hasdrubal's troops retreated step by step under pressure, and then giving way en masse they withdrew back to the heights. When the Romans pressed their attack more violently they were routed and fled back to their camp. If a god had not intervened to save them they would have been immediately chased from their camp, but an exceptionally powerful storm developed with such a fierce and continuous rain that the Romans only returned to their camp with difficulty.

The battle of the Great Plains

120 POLYBIUS, *HISTORIES* 14.8.2–14

Scipio and his army landed to the west of Carthage near Utica in the late spring or early summer of 204. After several minor victories against the Carthaginians, needing a secure base with adequate port facilities, he began a siege of Utica. After attempting and failing to detach the Numidian king, Syphax, from his Carthaginian alliance, Scipio once again resumed the siege of Utica. The Carthaginians collected a large army under Hasdrubal in alliance with Syphax and moved to face the Romans to relieve Utica. A well-planned night attack on the separate Numidian and Carthaginian camps by Scipio and his Numidian ally Masinissa virtually destroyed the enemy force.

Despite the disaster the Carthaginians resolved to continue their resistance. A combined force of approximately 30,000 was raised, including a newly arrived contingent of Celtiberian mercenaries. The Carthaginians encamped on the Great

Plains, probably the modern Souk el Kremis, which lies about sixty-five miles southwest of Utica. Leaving part of his army and his fleet to continue the siege, Scipio marched to confront them.

He may have had 20,000 men, consisting of two legions and allies plus cavalry, to face the superior enemy force.

The course of the battle makes clear the vastly improved performance of Italian cavalry since the early days of the war (see pp. 146f.). It is a little surprising that, in the battle, light cavalry was pitted against heavy on both sides. The presence of Carthaginian cavalry was the result of Carthage's desperate situation. In this period Carthaginian citizens did not normally perform military service.

The Celtiberians, who were to be among Rome's most difficult enemies in Spain, lived in and around the middle Ebro valley. The reference to their treachery must be to some sort of surrender to Scipio during his last Spanish campaign in 206.

The battle represents a further development of the flank attack seen at the battle of Ilipa three years before. Presumably, the *hastati* held the Celtiberian front, while the two rear lines advanced in column to attack the enemy's flanks.

On the fifth day Scipio arrived at the Great Plains and, nearing the enemy on the first day, he encamped on a hill about three and one-half miles from them. On the following day he descended into the plain and placing his cavalry in front he deployed his army at a point about three-quarters of a mile from the Carthaginians. For the next two days both armies remained in place and tested each other by minor skirmishing. On the fourth day both sides deliberately led their armies out and drew up their forces. Scipio simply used the normal Roman formation; his first line was formed by the maniples of the *hastati*, behind them were those of the *principes*, and in the rear were those of the *triarii*. He placed his Italian cavalry on his right wing and Masinissa and his Numidians on his left. Syphax and Hasdrubal deployed the Celtiberians in the center opposite the Roman maniples, the Numidians stationed on the left and the Carthaginian cavalry on the right.

At first contact the Numidian horse fled before the Italian cavalry and the Carthaginians before Masinissa, since they had lost heart at their many previous defeats. The Celtiberians fought courageously and bore up against the Romans, for they had no hope of safety as they were ignorant of the country and no hope of being ransomed if they were taken prisoner because of their betrayal of Scipio. Scipio had committed no hostile act towards them during his Spanish campaigns and they had come treacherously to fight against the Romans in alliance with the Carthaginians. When the wings gave way they were quickly surrounded by the *principes* and *triarii* and finally almost all were killed. So the Celtiberians perished in this way, having rendered great service to the Carthaginians not only in the battle but also during the Carthaginian flight. For if they had not resisted and had quickly followed the fleeing army very few of the

Carthaginians would have escaped. Owing to this delay Syphax and his cavalry returned home safely, as did Hasdrubal with the survivors, to Carthage.

The battle of Zama

After the battle of the Great Plains the Carthaginians suffered another major disaster when their main ally, the Numidian king, Syphax, was defeated and captured by Scipio. The seriousness of the situation led to a discussion of peace terms, and the Carthaginian government concluded a truce despite having earlier recalled Hannibal from Italy. Probably at the beginning of the spring of 202, the truce broke down and Scipio began a brutal campaign against the towns of the African interior.

Hannibal, who had now returned and gathered an army, selected Hadrumentum, a seaport about eighty miles south of Carthage, as his base. He was now bombarded by demands to move against the Romans. Hannibal moved to Zama, a town five days' march southwest of Carthage. The site is uncertain, as there are several sites that bear this name. It may be that Hannibal was attempting to place his army between Scipio and his Numidian allies. Scipio moved to meet Hannibal and camped at a place called Magaron. The battle itself was not fought at Zama, but near a site called Magaron by Polybius and Naragarra by Livy. It is probable that the battle was fought somewhere near the modern town of El Kef.

Hannibal's attempt to prevent Numidian reinforcements from arriving was unsuccessful: Masinissa brought 4,000 cavalry and 6,000 infantry with him. The exact size of the opposing forces is unclear. Hannibal's perhaps numbered 36,000 infantry and 4,000 cavalry, while Scipio may have had 23,000 foot and 5,500 horse. The Roman superiority in cavalry was to have a decisive effect on the course of the battle.

Hannibal seems to have adopted the Roman practice of forming his army in three lines, hoping to wear down the Romans before his best troops were engaged. It is clear from Polybius' account that his strategy might have succeeded if his elephants had been more effective. It has been suggested that the large number of elephants employed was an attempt to counter the Roman superiority in cavalry, and the suggestion is plausible. The perennial problem of controlling elephants on the battlefield and Scipio's innovative use of lanes to counter the shock of the animals' charge negated their value.

Scipio's marshaling his troops into a single line before the confrontation with the elite troops that Hannibal had brought from Italy is something of a puzzle. It may have been an attempt to use more experienced troops on the flanks of the enemy. In his earlier battles Scipio had consistently attempted to mount flank attacks.

121 POLYBIUS, *HISTORIES* 15.9.1–14.9

After they had spoken Hannibal and Scipio parted with no hope of reconciliation. The next day at dawn both sides led out their forces and began the battle, the Carthaginians fighting for their own survival and their dominion in Africa, the Romans for world empire. Is there any who can read such a narrative and not be moved? For where could one find more warlike soldiers or more fortunate generals than these men or any more practiced in the art of war? Nor did fortune ever offer the chance for a greater prize to those involved in the struggle. The victors would control not only Europe or Africa but also the other parts of the inhabited world, as many as are now known, and this soon came about.

Scipio deployed his army in the following fashion: first, he placed the *hastati* with intervals between their maniples, and behind them the *principes*. But he did not arrange them behind the intervals of the first line as the Romans usually do. On account of the enemy's elephants he placed them directly behind the maniples of the first line and at a certain distance. He then placed the *triarii* in the rear. On his left wing he positioned the Italian cavalry under Gaius Laelius and on the right Masinissa with all the Numidians.

Scipio filled the intervals of the first line with the companies of *velites*, ordering them to begin the battle, and if they were overwhelmed by the onset of the elephants to retreat. Those who evaded them were to retreat down the lanes between the maniples to the rear of the army, and those who were overtaken were to make their way into the gaps between the lines of maniples and to move to the wings....

Hannibal placed his elephants, which numbered more than eighty, in front of his entire line. Behind them he positioned the approximately 12,000 mercenaries. These men were Ligurians, Celts, Balearic Islanders, and Moors. At the back of them he placed the native Africans and the Carthaginians. Last of all he deployed the troops whom he had brought from Italy, positioning them more than 600 feet behind the front line. He defended his wings with cavalry, the Numidians on the left and the Carthaginians on the right....

When both sides were ready for battle and after the Numidian horse had been skirmishing with each other, Hannibal ordered the elephants' drivers to charge. With the trumpets and bugles sounding on all sides some of the animals were panicked and rushed back upon the Carthaginians who had arrived to help the Numidians.... Masinissa quickly attacked and exposed the left wing of the Carthaginians.

The remaining elephants, falling on the *velites* in the space between the armies, both inflicted and suffered much damage until some in their fear escaped through the gaps in the Roman line. The Romans received them without harm, owing to their general's foresight. Others fled to the right through the cavalry and were showered with javelins until they finally passed beyond the army. It was at this point, in the midst of the disturbance caused by the elephants, that Laelius attacked and routed the Carthaginian cavalry. He pursued the fleeing Carthaginians energetically, and Masinissa did the same.

At the same time the heavy infantry on both sides advanced against each other at a slow and impressive pace, except for the troops from Italy with Hannibal. These remained in position. When the lines were close to each other the Romans raised their war cry and clashed their swords on their shields and fell upon the enemy, while the Carthaginian mercenaries raised their cry in a confusion of sounds, for their voice was not one. As the poet [Homer] says: "There was not one sound, but their voices differed, for the men were called from many lands," as I specified in my list earlier.

It was a hand-to-hand struggle. At first, the mercenaries prevailed because of their daring and courage, wounding many Romans. But the Romans, trusting in the order of their formation and in the superiority of their equipment, continued forward. Their rear ranks followed closely those in front and cheered them on from behind, while the Carthaginians behaved like cowards and did not move up behind the mercenaries or provide support. Finally the barbarians gave way and, thinking that they had been clearly let down by their own side, attacked those Carthaginians they met and cut them down. This compelled many of the Carthaginians to die courageously; being slaughtered by their own mercenaries, they fought against their will with both their own men and the Romans. Fighting with a mad, strange courage they killed many of their own men as well as Romans. In this way they threw the maniples of the *hastati* into confusion. The officers of the *principes*, seeing what was happening, kept their ranks in check. The majority of the mercenaries and the Carthaginians were cut down either by them or by the *hastati*. Hannibal did not allow the fleeing survivors to mix with his own men, but ordered the troops to level their spears, which prevented their being received within his ranks. As a result they were forced to turn to the wings and the flat ground there.

The space between the two armies still left on the field was covered with blood, slaughter, and corpses, and the rout of the enemy proved a serious difficulty for the Roman commander, for he saw that it would be difficult for men advancing in rank to make their way through the piles of corpses slippery with blood and the equipment haphazardly discarded. After moving the wounded to the rear of the formation and recalling the *hastati* from their pursuit by trumpet calls, he placed them opposite the center of the enemy. He then ordered the *principes* and *triarii* to close up on both wings and commanded them to advance through the piles of corpses. When they had passed over these obstacles and were in line with the *hastati* the two armies closed with one another with great speed and eagerness. Both sides were equal in numbers, resolution, and bravery, as well as in equipment. For a long while the battle remained undecided, with men falling where they stood out of their desire for distinction until Masinissa and Laelius almost providentially returned from their pursuit at the crucial time and fell upon the rear of Hannibal's men. The majority were cut down while they were still in formation, while of those who fled only a few were successful, since the cavalry pursued them closely over ground suited to horsemen. Over 1,500 Romans and more than 20,000 Carthaginians fell. No fewer were taken prisoner.

A contrast: Livy on Zama

122 LIVY, 30.29.11–35.3

Polybius was Livy's major source for this battle though he seems to have added extra information from other sources, most frequently the Roman annalists, such as the references to Laelius' quaestorship and the Macedonian legion, which finds no place in Polybius and is undoubtedly a fiction which grew out of Philip V's support for Hannibal and perhaps as part of a justification for Rome's later war against him.

As opposed to Polybius, who concentrates on a factual narrative, Livy focuses on the psychological state of the troops involved, particularly on the Carthaginian side, with reference to Ligurian covetousness and the traditional enmity of the Gauls for Romans. His presentation of the Carthaginians stresses their passivity. While Polybius mentioned that the first line of both sides advanced to meet each other, Livy has the Carthaginians await the Roman advance. He emphasizes this by omitting Polybius' description of the prolonged struggle with the mercenaries. The same difference of emphasis also appears in Livy's account of battle with the second Carthaginian line, where Polybius describes the initial effectiveness of the Carthaginians and Livy stresses their fear and disorder. Polybius' narrative has been altered to produce a picture of an inexorable Roman advance in place of the hard struggle that Polybius describes.

There are factual errors in Livy's account, as well as errors in understanding and translation. The presence of the Macedonian legion has already been mentioned. To this must be added the identification of the first Carthaginian line as auxiliaries rather than mercenaries, and the more serious misidentification of the third line as unwilling Bruttian troops, when in fact they were the remnants of Hannibal's Italian army and were his most reliable and experienced troops.

The comparison highlights the need to exercise caution in assessing Livy's battle descriptions. The historian tends to concentrate far too much on states of mind at the expense of factual detail. His own lack of military experience must have contributed to his misunderstandings and mistranslations. Nonetheless, the main outlines of Livy's description are accurate, and he is of use when superior sources fail us.

Scipio arranged the line of the *hastati* in front and then the *principes* behind them and finally the *triarii* last of all. However, he did not deploy the cohorts in dense ranks, each before their standard. The maniples were set some distance apart from each other so that there would be a space for the enemy's elephants to be driven down without throwing his ranks into confusion. He placed Laelius, who had been his legate previously and who was now serving as quaestor by a special decree of the Senate, with the Italian cavalry on his left wing and Masinissa and his Numidians on his right. He filled the open lanes between the maniples of the *hastati* with *velites*, the light infantry of that period, and gave the order that when the elephants attacked they should take cover behind the line of the maniples or by running to the left to right behind the maniples open a way by which the elephants might rush upon weapons thrown from either side.

Hannibal deployed his elephants in front to inspire terror [in the enemy]. There were eighty of them more than he had ever employed before. Behind them were the auxiliary troops, Ligurians and Gauls inter-mixed with Balearics and Moors. In his second line were the Carthaginians, Africans, and the Macedonian legion; then at a moderate distance the third line was positioned as a reserve, consisting of Italian troops of whom the majority were Bruttians who had followed him when he left Italy, more because of necessity than inclination. He placed his cavalry on his wings, the Carthaginian on the right and the Numidian on the left.

Differing words of encouragement were needed in an army composed of so many men who had neither language, nor costumes, dress or appear-ance, nor the same reasons for serving. The auxiliaries served for pay and in hope of more profit from booty, and the Gauls on account of their pecu-liar and inborn hate towards the Romans. For the Ligurians, who had been brought down from their harsh mountain fastness, the rich plains of Italy served as a lure. Fear of the unchecked domination of Masinissa terrified the Moors and Numidians. Various hopes and fears impelled the others: for the Carthaginians the walls of their fatherland, their traditional gods and the tombs of their ancestors, their children, parents, and fearful wives, destruction or world rule. Their hopes and fears had nothing moderate about them.

At the very moment when their commander was encouraging the Carthaginians and his generals were conveying his words to their native troops and through interpreters to the foreigners mixed in with them, the Roman trumpets and horns sounded and such a clamor arose that the ele-phants turned on the Moors and Numidians who were behind them. Masinissa easily added to the fear of men already terrified by driving off the enemy cavalry on the Carthaginian left. Nevertheless, a few of the more courageous elephants, driven against the enemy line, surrounded by units of *velites*, and despite their many wounds, caused great slaughter. The *velites* sprang back upon the maniples to open a path for the animals so that they would not be trampled and hurled their javelins at the ele-phants, which were exposed to blows from both sides. The *hastati* kept up their volleys of *pila* until the animals were driven from the Roman lines by the hail of missiles from all directions and turned against their own right wing and put the Carthaginian cavalry to flight. Seeing the disorder of the enemy, Laelius added to their terror.

The Punic line with the loss of its cavalry had both its flanks exposed and began the infantry engagement inferior in strength and confidence. In addition, there were factors that seemed unimportant but were of great moment in the course of the conflict. The Roman war cry was delivered in unison and so was louder and more frightening; the Carthaginian was dissonant because shouted in many languages. The Roman attack was given solidity by the weight of the troops and their equipment; their opponents' was marked more by agility and speed than force. At first onset the Romans pushed back the enemy line. Striking them with their shoulders and the boss of their shields, the Romans advanced to the positions from which they had forced the enemy back. They moved forwards for some distance as if there was no resistance, with the men in the rear pushing forward as soon as they sensed the battle line had moved forward, and this added considerable pressure, which helped in forcing the enemy back. The Africans and Carthaginians of the second line gave so little support but fell back in fear that the enemy, after overwhelming the fiercely resisting front line, should reach them. So the auxiliaries quickly fled, some taking refuge in the second line, while others who were not allowed in began to cut down the men of the second line who had not helped them and had shut them out. Now there were two battles going on, since the Carthaginians were forced to fight both the enemy and their own men. They kept on refusing refuge in their own formation to the disheartened and angry fugitives; closing up, they forced them to the wings and to the ground beyond the battle to avoid mixing their intact and unharmed line with troops afflicted by flight, wounds, and fear.

But such piles of corpses and heaps of arms filled the space that the auxiliaries had just vacated that crossing it was almost more difficult than forcing one's way through the masses of the enemy. So the *hastati* who formed the first line lost cohesion because of the piles of bodies and weapons and the slipperiness caused by the pools of blood. The standards of the *principes* also began to waver when they saw what was happening to the first line. Scipio ordered the signal for the retreat of the *hastati* to be sounded when he saw what had happened. After he had the wounded removed to the rear of the battle line he brought up the *principes* and *triarii* on the wings in order to protect and strengthen the *hastati* in the center. The battle started again; now the Romans faced the real enemy, their equals in equipment, military experience, reputation, and the magnitude of their hopes or dangers. But the Romans were now superior in numbers and spirit because they had put to flight the Carthaginian cavalry and elephants and had broken their first formation and were now engaging their second.

At the opportune moment Laelius and Masinissa, who had returned from their pursuit of the Carthaginian cavalry they had driven off, attacked the enemy's rear. It was not until this cavalry attack that the enemy was routed. Many were surrounded and killed where they stood, and many others who had scattered in flight about the open country were slain everywhere by the cavalry, who were masters of the field. More than 20,000 of the Carthaginians and their allies were killed that day. There were an approximately equal number of captives, and 132 military standards were taken along with eleven elephants. The victors lost 1,500 men.

Legion against phalanx

Cynoscephalae

The conclusion of the Second Punic War allowed Rome to turn its attention elsewhere. Philip V of Macedonia had been pursuing an aggressive policy in the Aegean and, to contain the threat he presented, Pergamum and Rhodes attempted to bring Rome in against him. They provided the Romans with an excuse for an action that had already been decided on. The Romans had not forgiven Philip for his alliance with Hannibal in 215 and were determined to stabilize the situation in Greece by converting Philip into a Roman client.

They undertook a sustained and largely successful propaganda campaign among the Greek states in preparation for their war against Philip. In 200, war was declared and a Roman army crossed the Adriatic to open the campaign.

The first two years of the war were marked by maneuvers by both sides but did not produce a significant battle. The arrival in 198 of a new commander, T. Quinctius Flamininus, changed the situation dramatically. He drove Philip out of Thessaly and back to the borders of Macedonia. Flamininus' command was extended as proconsul for 197, and he now moved to bring about a decisive battle with the king.

Two courses were essentially open to Philip. He could either defend the passes from Thessaly into Macedonia or go on to the offensive. The first option was impractical, as there were too many passes to defend. If he failed to mount an adequate defense he would expose himself to the same gradual loss of territory he had experienced in Greece. The other course was more attractive. If he met the Romans in battle and defeated them he might change the course of the war. A victory might make recent converts to the Roman cause waver and rethink their alliances or at least stay neutral. It also might open the possibility of serious negotiations with the Romans in which he might salvage both his kingdom and his influence in Greece. Given the disparity of resources and the relentless character of Roman war-making, this was not a promising course, but at this point the king had little choice.

In late March Philip marched south to Dium in southern Macedonia, where he began training his new recruits for the coming battle. At the same time Flamininus was able to resume his policy of gradual conquest and to move north into Thessaly, where he received substantial aid from his Greek allies, including 6,000 foot and 400 horse from the Aetolians and a further 2,000 from other Greek states. His army now totaled 26,000 men, including his two legions with allies and 8,000 Greek infantry and 2,400 cavalry. Perhaps 4,500 of the Greeks were posted to garrison duty so that his field force amounted to approximately 21,500 infantry and 2,400 cavalry.

Flamininus marched north with the object of isolating the Macedonian strong-point at Demetrias. He had hoped to take the important town of Phthiotic Thebes by treachery, but had been forced to besiege it. He was in the midst of the siege when news arrived that Philip had entered Thessaly. Flamininus advanced north towards Pherae and encamped about six miles south of the town. Meanwhile Philip, having learned that Flamininus was at Phthiotic Thebes, marched south and then east along the Thessalian plain and encamped about three and one-half miles to the north of Pherae. He had with him an army about equal in size to Flamininus'. His most reliable troops were the 16,000 Macedonians who formed his phalanx. In addition, he had 2,000 light-armed peltasts, 2,000 Thracians, and 2,000 Illyrians, as well as a mixed force of 1,500 mercenaries and 2,000 cavalry.

The following day advance forces of both armies came into contact at a pass between Thebes and Pherae. A skirmish involving cavalry and light-armed developed, and Philip's forces were driven back. No major engagement took place, as both sides decided that the area around Pherae had too many obstructions for them to deploy easily. The next day the king marched west to his base at Scotussa to resupply and to find suitable ground for the battle. Flamininus, knowing of Philip's move, also moved towards Scotussa, hoping to destroy the local grain supplies before Philip's men could forage. Three days of parallel marching ensued, with the two armies separated by the hills of Cynoscephalae and unaware of each other.

A thick fog also hindered visibility early on the day of the battle. Unusually the battle started by accident. Normally in ancient battles both sides fought on the basis of mutual agreement. Typically, the phalanx needed level ground to operate effectively and it is rather surprising that Philip chose to engage on the broken ground Cynoscephalae offered. It appears that the rush of events propelled him forward as he brought support to his beleaguered vanguard. He may also have thought that the advantage of attacking from higher ground would balance the absence of level ground. Yet it is hard to understand his decision to advance with only his right wing fully deployed. The battle illustrates a common occurrence in ancient set-piece battles, the victory of one wing and the failure of the other. In this case both the Roman and Macedonian right wings were successful while their left wings were forced back.

The elephants that Flamininus deployed in this battle had been surrendered by the Carthaginians at the end of the Second Punic War. For the role of the military tribune, see pp. 92f. This is one of the few known instances where a military tribune acts independently. The battle illustrates the much greater flexibility of the Roman formation in comparison with the rigidity of the phalanx.

Polybius states that the Roman dead totaled 700, while the Macedonians had 8,000 killed and about 5,000 captured. Livy notes that other authors gave different totals, but he rightly relies on Polybius here. Such high figures are matched in other Roman battles, where often half the enemy army was killed in the course of the fighting.

123 POLYBIUS, *HISTORIES* 18.21–26.12 (WITH OMISSIONS)

The general area where the battle was fought is not in doubt but various arguments have been put forward about its exact location. The *turma* (plural *turmae*) is the standard Roman cavalry formation of thirty men (see p. 127). Peltasts are Greek light infantry armed with javelins and protected by a light shield, sometimes of crescent shape, with little other protective equipment. They were at their most effective when operating with cavalry or heavy infantry. The normal depth of an infantry phalanx before the Macedonian period was eight, and it is a reasonable assumption that the doubling resulted in a formation sixteen men deep. The Thetideion was a temple dedicated to Thetis, the mother of Achilles.

Flamininus, encamped near the Thetideion and uncertain where the enemy was, sent ten *turmae* of cavalry and about a thousand light-armed troops, ordering them to search the area carefully. Making their way towards the mountain pass, they unexpectedly came upon the Macedonian observation post there, as they were hindered by the poor visibility. At first there was confusion on both sides because of their surprise. Each went on the offensive and sent messengers to their commanders to report what had happened. The Romans, in danger of being overwhelmed, sent messengers to their camp asking for help. Flamininus called up the Aetolians, who were commanded by Eupolemus and Archedamus as well as by two military tribunes, and sent out with 500 cavalry and 2,000 infantry. When these joined the light-armed troops already engaged, the struggle immediately changed character. The Romans, encouraged by the arrival of aid, fought with redoubled strength, and the Macedonians, though defending themselves bravely, were now hard pressed and finally overwhelmed; they fled to the heights and sent to the king for support.

Philip did not suspect that a full-scale battle would develop that day so he had sent ahead a number of men from the camp to forage. Learning the news from the messengers and with the mist clearing, he summoned Heraclides, who commanded the Thessalian horse, and Leo, who was in charge of the Macedonian cavalry, together with all of the mercenaries apart from the Thracians under the command of Athenagoras and sent them to support his hard-pressed troops. Joining the Macedonians already fighting, the greatly strengthened force pressed the enemy hard, forcing the Romans down from the heights. The greatest obstacle to a complete Roman rout was the valor of the Aetolian horse, which fought with reckless courage. For as inferior as they are in equipment and organization in set-piece infantry engagements, so they are superior to all of the other

Greeks in individual cavalry fighting. For this reason they checked the enemy's attack, and the Romans were no longer being driven back to level ground, but close to it they turned and stabilized their position. Flamininus, seeing that not only were his light-armed and cavalry giving way but that his whole force was losing heart, led out his entire army and drew them up near the hills. At the same time a series of messengers kept giving Philip the following message: "O King, the enemy is in flight. Do not miss the opportunity. The barbarians cannot check us. This day is yours." Philip, although not satisfied with the ground, nevertheless decided to fight. The hills I mentioned previously called Cynoscephalae are rough and broken and extend to a considerable height. Foreseeing the unsuitability of the ground, Philip was not predisposed to fight, but urged on by the overenthusiastic reports of the messenger ordered his army out from its fortifications.

Flamininus formed up his whole force in line and at the same time he took measures to cover the retreat of the units engaged with the Macedonians. Making his way down the line he addressed his troops. At the same time, when the king saw that the majority of his men were drawn up outside the camp, taking the peltasts and the right wing of his phalanx he energetically led them forward to climb the hills. He ordered Nicanor, nicknamed the Elephant, and his officers to see to it that the rest of the force followed as soon as possible. As soon as the leading elements of his force reached the summits he wheeled them to the left and occupied the heights. Since his advance forces had forced the Romans back for a considerable distance to the other side of the hill, he occupied the now empty heights. As he was deploying the right wing of his army, the mercenaries appeared, hard pressed by the enemy. As I just mentioned, the Roman heavy infantry had joined their light-armed in the fighting and, taking advantage of this additional weight thrown into the scales, they pressed the enemy hard, killing a number of them. When he arrived, the king, seeing the light-armed troops making their stand not far from the enemy camp, was delighted. But when he saw his own men in turn giving ground and requesting help he had to support them and to make his decision about everything on the spot, although the greater part of the phalanx was still en route and moving up to the hills. After he had received those engaged with the enemy back into his ranks and had placed all of them on the right wing, both infantry and cavalry, he ordered the peltasts and the heavy infantry to double their depth and close up to the right. After this was done and with the enemy close by, Philip ordered the phalanx to lower its spears and charge, while the light-armed were ordered to move to the flank. At the same moment, Flamininus, after admitting his advance troops into the gaps between the maniples, closed with the Macedonians.

The encounter of the two armies was forceful and accompanied by deafening shouts from both sides as they sounded their war cries, and the noise was intensified by the shouts of encouragement by those not engaged. The furious clash was awe inspiring. Philip's right wing performed brilliantly in the battle since it was attacking from higher ground and had the greater weight and in the present situation the advantage in equipment. But, of his remaining units, the one next to the wing that was now fighting was still at a distance from the enemy and his left wing had only just crested the ridge and come into view on the heights. Flamininus, given that his line could not sustain the charge of the phalanx, that his left was being forced back, that some of his men had already been killed, and that the rest were retreating slowly, saw that his hope of safety lay in his right wing. He quickly made his way to it, noticing that the enemy formation next to the unit engaged was not fighting, that other units were still making their way down from the heights, and that still others had halted on them. He placed his elephants in the van and led the maniples forward. The Macedonians, in the absence of orders and unable to form a proper phalanx because of the difficulty of the ground and because they were coming up to those engaged in fighting and so were in marching formation and not in a battle order, did not wait to receive the Romans in close combat, but being thrown into confusion and dispersed they gave ground.

The majority of the Romans pursued them and cut them down. One of the accompanying military tribunes, with not more than twenty maniples, perceiving on the spur of the moment what needed to be done, contributed greatly to the overall victory. Seeing that the men with Philip were far in front of the others and were forcing back the Roman left with their weight, moving from the Roman right which was now clearly victorious, he wheeled his men towards the fighting, moved behind the Macedonian line, and fell on them from the rear. It is impossible for a phalanx to wheel or fight man to man. The tribune pressed his attack, cutting down those near him who were not able to protect themselves until all of the Macedonians, throwing away their arms, were forced to flee. Those Romans who had retreated before when they were face to face now turned and attacked them.

Philip in the beginning, as I mentioned, judged from the fighting in his immediate vicinity that he had achieved total victory. Then, seeing that the Macedonians were throwing away their arms and that the enemy had attacked them from behind, he withdrew a short distance from the battle and took in the whole scene. When he noticed that Romans pursuing the fleeing Macedonian left wing were now nearing the heights, he assembled as many as he could of the Thracians and Macedonians in such circumstances and fled. Flamininus, when he reached the crest of the ridge in pursuit of the fleeing Macedonians and found that the Macedonian left had just reached the summits, at first halted. The enemy had raised their sarissas, which the Macedonians customarily do whenever they surrender themselves or join the enemy. Learning the reason for what had happened, he restrained his troops, intending to spare the beaten enemy. While he was making up his mind, some of his leading troops fell on the Macedonians from above and cut many of them down; a few fled after throwing away their equipment.

The battle of Magnesia

When Antiochus came to the Seleucid throne in 222/221 he was faced with a disintegrating empire. In a series of campaigns stretching over twenty-five years he restored Seleucid control in the East, and in the following years down to 198 he regained control of Seleucid possessions in southern Syria, Phoenicia, and Palestine. Finally, in that year he moved into Asia Minor and there came into conflict with Eumenes of Pergamum, who was a close ally of Rome. The Romans politely requested that he withdraw from Eumenes' territory and the king complied, but Antiochus' expansion made the Romans uneasy. His was now the strongest state bordering Rome's sphere of interest and therefore a cause for concern, a concern that was only intensified by the Roman decision in 196 to withdraw all troops from east of the Adriatic and to control the Balkans indirectly. Not only did the lack of a garrison open up the possibility of invasion, but also Antiochus' presence provided a possible alternative focus of loyalty for Greeks who were dissatisfied with Rome.

In the spring of 196 the king crossed to Europe and began to reassert Seleucid control of what he considered to be his ancestral possessions. In response he was visited by a series of Roman embassies, but negotiations only showed that a compromise satisfactory to both sides was impossible. This inability to reach an agreement was the result of each side's different views of their self-interest. The Romans wanted to prevent the king from gaining control of the Greek cities on the Aegean coast and to keep him away from the Balkans, while in Antiochus' view the western littoral of Asia Minor and coastal Thrace were rightfully his. The arrival of Hannibal at Antiochus' court only intensified Roman suspicions.

The war against Philip had left the Aetolian League dissatisfied. It felt that the Romans had not given them adequate compensation for their support against Philip. Seeking an ally to redress their grievances against Rome, in 192 the Aetolians passed a decree inviting Antiochus to free the Greeks and to arbitrate between them and the Romans. The Aetolians seem to have misled the king as to anti-Roman feeling in Greece by claiming that if he invaded he would be met with widespread support. Antiochus accepted the invitation. He may have decided that his relations with Rome would deteriorate no matter what he did and that by fighting in Greece he would spare his own possessions. The Romans had misperceived Antiochus' intentions in Europe and imagined a threat where one did not exist. It was a war that neither side wanted.

In the fall of 192 the king began to bring his army across. It was a small expedition consisting of 10,000 infantry, 500 cavalry, and six elephants. Clearly the king expected to receive substantial support in Greece, but it never materialized. By the end of 192 the king must have realized that he could only command minimal support. In early 191 a force of two legions with their allied contingents under the command of M'. Acilius Glabrio, consul in 191, crossed over to Greece and in a series of campaigns culminating in a decisive defeat at Thermopylae in 190 forced Antiochus to evacuate Greece and retreat to Asia. The command in the Balkans was given to one of the consuls of 190, Lucius Cornelius Scipio, with his brother Publius, the conqueror of Hannibal, as his legate. Most of the year was spent in subduing the Aetolians and in settling affairs in Greece. It was not until October that the Roman army crossed over into Asia Minor to confront the king. At first Antiochus attempted to buy the Romans off through negotiation, but Roman demands were so extreme that the king had no alternative other than to continue the war.

To meet the Roman invasion, Antiochus, using Sardis as his base, had mobilized an army consisting of 60,000 infantry, 12,000 cavalry, and fifty-four elephants. The Silver Shields mentioned by Livy were an elite unit armed in the same fashion as the phalanx which served as the royal infantry guard. The Dahae were a Scythian people whose home was located southeast of the Caspian Sea. Cataphracts were heavily armored cavalry whose equipment was of central Asian origin. The cataphract was protected by a heavy coat of mail that reached to the thigh. His horse was often armored with a metal breastplate and might be clothed in mail. His main offensive weapon was a long lance, but bow and arrow were often carried as well. The Tarentines were a type of light cavalry.

Antiochus then marched northwest to meet the Romans, who were advancing southeast from Pergamum. The army under Lucius' command consisted of about 30,000 troops including two legions with allied units and Greek allies, of whom the most important was Eumenes of Pergamum, whose role in the battle is minimized by Livy.

The two armies encamped opposite each other in a plain bounded by the Phrygios (modern Kum) and Hermos (modern Gedis) rivers to the northeast of Magnesia ad Sipylum. The Hyrcanian plain is probably the area between Magnesia and Thyateira. The area was of horseshoe shape, with its narrowest point in its western part. The Romans encamped west of the Phrygios and then crossed over to offer battle in the narrowest part of the horseshoe to try to protect their flanks and minimize the effect of Antiochus' superiority in cavalry. The battle was fought unusually late in the year, and this may have been the result of Scipio's desire to gain a victory before being replaced. There are two fairly detailed accounts of the battle in Livy and Appian. Usually preference is given to Livy's as the more accurate, but some doubts have been raised.

The Roman battle order is unconventional and seems to have been drawn up on the assumption that the very weak cavalry force on its left would be protected by the Phrygios with its steep banks. The majority of cavalry and various Greek contingents appear to have been posted on the right to guard against the Roman line being outflanked by Antiochus.

Antiochus' dispositions seem to have been influenced by the defeat of Philip at Cynoscephalae and the realization that the phalanx was vulnerable to a flank attack from the more mobile legion. He placed his phalanx in the middle of his line drawn up unusually deeply (thirty-two deep) and posted mercenary infantry contingents to its left and right to guard against a flank attack. It appears that this unusual depth was to avoid the possibility of a Roman breakthrough in the center. It can be inferred that he intended to hold the legions frontally while the battle would be won on the flanks by his cavalry and light infantry. It was the sudden attack by Eumenes on the scythed chariots that disordered his line and his overenthusiastic pursuit of the Roman left that thwarted his plans.

The numbers given by Livy for various contingents in Antiochus' army amount to 45,200 infantry, but the discrepancy with the total of 60,000 can be accounted for by adding the 10,000 Silver Shields and assuming that other troops were detached to guard his camp. The figures for the Seleucid troops who were killed in the battle in Livy and Appian seem highly exaggerated. Antiochus' left was hardly engaged, and his right was victorious for most of the battle. It was his center where the greatest number of casualties occurred. The figures for Roman dead appear far too small given the temporary rout of the Roman left.

Livy gives various versions of the capture of Scipio Africanus' son, Lucius Cornelius Scipio, without vouching for any of them. The son went on to hold the praetorship in 174 but was expelled from the Senate in the same year.

124 LIVY, 37.37.1–44.1

> After the consul had completed his preparations for carrying out his plans he left his winter quarters and came first to Dardanus and then Rhoeteum and at both cities the population poured out to welcome him. He then moved on to Ilium and pitched camp in the field below the walls. After he had gone up into the city and the citadel he sacrificed to Minerva, the guardian of the citadel. The people of Ilium acknowledged the Romans as their descendents, according them every honor in both word and deed, while the Romans were proud of their descent. The army set out from there and on the sixth day arrived at the source of the Caicus River. There King Eumenes, who had attempted to bring his fleet back from the Hellespont to winter quarters at Elaea and being unable to round the promontory of Lecton for some days because of adverse winds, had disembarked and made his way to the Roman camp on foot, with a small party, by the shortest route so as not to miss the beginning of operations. He was sent back from the camp to Pergamum to oversee the transport of supplies, and after he had handed over the grain to those specified by the consul he had returned to the Roman camp. Once rations had been prepared for several days the decision was made to move against the enemy before winter put a halt to operations.
>
> The king's camp was near Thyateira. When Antiochus heard that Scipio was ill and had been taken to Elaea he sent the emissaries to return his son, and not only was this an act that was welcome to a father but the

joy that he felt acted as a restorative to his body. After Scipio had embraced his son to his own satisfaction he said to the envoys: "Carry back my gratitude to the king. The only favor I can do him is to advise him not to deploy for battle before he has heard that I have returned to camp." Although the fact that Antiochus had 60,000 infantry and more than 12,000 cavalry gave him a wavering sense of confidence about the coming battle, he was so moved by the authority of such a great man in whom he had placed his hopes for support for his future in the face of the uncertainties of war that he retreated, and after crossing the River Phrygios encamped near Magnesia ad Sipylum. To dissuade the Romans from attacking his fortification if he should decide to draw the matter out he had dug a ditch nine feet deep and eighteen feet wide, and beyond the ditch he erected a double rampart with many towers on its inner side from which it would be easy to prevent the enemy from crossing the ditch.

The consul thought that the king was near Thyatira and so by continuous marches descended into the Hyrcanian plain on the fifth day. As he heard that the king had left, he followed his trail along the near side to the Phrygios and set up his camp about four miles from the enemy. A force of about a thousand cavalry [mostly Galatians], Dahae, and other horse archers crossed the river in a rush and attacked the guard posts. At first, they threw the defenders into confusion, as they were not in formation; then, when the struggle lasted for some time, the Roman troops were easily reinforced from the neighboring camp, but the king's men were now worn out and gave way before the superior numbers of the enemy. Some were killed by the river bank before they entered the water by their pursuers, who closely pressed upon them.

For two days there was no activity since neither side crossed the river. On the third day all of the Romans crossed at the same time and encamped about two and one-half miles from the king. As they were measuring and fortifying their camp, 3,000 elite royal cavalry and infantry came up, causing great terror and confusion. There were somewhat fewer Romans mounting guard; nevertheless, without summoning help from the camp they at first maintained the struggle and then as the battle intensified repelled the enemy, killing a hundred and capturing about the same number.

During the next four days both armies deployed in front of their fortifications. On the fifth day the Romans moved forward to the middle of the plain, but Antiochus remained stationary, so that he was less than 1,000 feet from his ramparts.

After the consul had seen that the enemy refused to fight he called a war council. He asked what was to be done if Antiochus would not join battle, addressing them in the following manner: "Winter is upon us, and either the troops must be kept under canvas or the choice must be made to move into winter quarters"; the war would have to be postponed until the coming summer. Rome had never held an enemy in such contempt, and a cry went up on every side that he should immediately lead out the army and make use of the soldiers' enthusiasm, who thought that they would not be fighting with so many thousands of the enemy but rather that the enemy was so many cattle to be slaughtered. They were prepared to break into the enemy's camp, to make their way through the ditches and palisade, if the enemy did not come out to fight. Gnaeus Domitius was sent to reconnoiter the route by which one could approach the enemy rampart. After he had made his report on the next day, it was decided to move the Roman camp closer. At the third hour the standards were moved forward to the middle of the plain and the army began to form up. Antiochus decided not to delay any longer, to avoid dampening the enthusiasm of his own men and increasing the expectations of the enemy by delaying battle. His exit from camp made it clear that he would fight.

The Roman battle line was virtually of uniform appearance because of its men and equipment. There were two Roman legions and two *alae* of the allies and those of Latin status, each with a complement of 5,400 men. The Romans stood in the center of the line, with the allies holding the wings. First, there were the *hastati* and then the *principes*, and the rear was closed by the *triarii*. Beyond this so-called regular line the consul deployed Eumenes' auxiliaries mixed in with Achaean peltasts on the same line and beyond them a force of a little less than 3,000 cavalry, of whom 800 were Eumenes' and the rest were Roman. At the end of the line he placed the men of Tralles and the Cretans, each of whom numbered 500. The left wing did not seem to need forces of this magnitude, as it was closed off there by the river with its steep banks. So four *turmae* of cavalry were stationed there. This was the total Roman force. Two thousand mixed Thracian and Macedonian units who had gone along as volunteers were left to guard the camp. Sixteen elephants were placed behind the *triarii* to act as a reserve because they were considered incapable of standing up to the horde of the king's elephants [these numbered fifty-four], for African elephants are not the equals of the Indian ones because of the difference in size, Indian elephants being much larger, or because of the difference in their aggressiveness.

The royal battle line was varied with its many different peoples, equipment, and auxiliary troops. There were 16,000 soldiers armed in the Macedonian fashion, who are called phalangites, in the middle of the battle line, divided into ten companies. Antiochus separated the companies by positioning two elephants between each of them, and from front to rear it was thirty-two men deep. This formation was the basis of the king's strength and caused great terror not only by their appearance but as a result of the elephants, whose appearance was striking among so many armed men. The animals themselves were immense, but their head gear and crests, the towers placed on their backs, and the four armed men and driver riding them added to the terror they inspired. To the right of the phalangites Antiochus stationed 1,500 Galatian infantry and added to them 3,000 heavily armored cavalry that they call cataphracts. In addition, there were posted next to them 1,000 cavalry, which they call the *agema*, made up of Medes, specially selected troopers with a mixed cavalry force from many nations from the same region. Right next to them was a herd of sixteen elephants placed as a reserve. In the same part of the line the wing was extended a little farther by the royal cohort who are called Silver Shields from their weapons, then 1,200 Dahae horse archers, and next 3,000 light-armed, made up in almost equal numbers of Cretans and Trallians. Added to these were 2,500 Mysian archers. Finally, a unit of 4,000 men made up of Cretan slingers and Elymaean archers was posted on the extreme right.

On the left wing next to the phalangites were 1,500 Galatian infantry and 2,000 Cappadocians with a similar equipment [they had been sent by their king, Ariarathes] and then 2,700 auxiliaries of mixed origins, 3,000 cataphract cavalry, with 1,000 cavalry of other types, a royal cavalry regiment in which men and horses were more lightly armored, but similarly dressed [they were mostly a mixture of Phrygians and Lydians]. In front of the cavalry there were scythed chariots and the camels that are called dromedaries. They were ridden by Arab archers with slender swords, four cubits long, so that they could reach the enemy from such a great height. Beyond them was another multitude equal in size to the right wing. First there were 500 Tarentines, then 2,500 Galatians, 1,000 Neocretans, and 1,500 Carians and Cilicians similarly equipped, and the same number of Trallians, 30,000 peltasts [they were Pisidians, Pamphylians, and Lycians], then Cyrtian and Elymaean auxiliaries equal in numbers to those on the right, and sixteen elephants posted at a moderate interval.

The king himself was on the right wing; his son Seleucus and his nephew Antipater commanded the left. In the centre were Minnio, Zeuxis, and Philippus, who was in charge of the elephants.

A morning mist, which as the day progressed rose into the clouds, obscured the scene, and the drizzle that blew from the south permeated everything, which offered no problems to the Romans but seriously inconvenienced the king. For arrayed in a line of moderate length the poor visibility did not deprive the Romans of a view in every direction. Their whole line was heavily equipped, and the moisture did not blunt sword or spear.

Given the broadness of the king's line, it was impossible to see either wing from the center, nor could the wings see each other, and the moisture softened their bow strings, slings, and javelin thongs. Then the scythed chariots which Antiochus believed he could use to throw the enemy battle line into confusion turned and spread terror among their own men. Their equipment was as follows. On each side of the pole there were spikes extending out three feet from the yoke like horns, with which they could pierce anything that got in their way. And from the end of the pole two

181

scythes protruded. One was as high as the pole; the other sloped downwards to cut away any obstacle to the side, and the second was to reach enemies who had fallen forward near the chariots. Also two scythes were attached to the wheel hubs, projecting in opposite directions on each side. The king deployed these armored chariots in the front line because if they had been on the flanks or in the center they would have had to be driven through their own lines.

When Eumenes, a man not unskilled in war, was aware of how uncertain auxiliary arms of this type were, if one could create panic among the horses, rather than attacking in standard battle formation. He ordered the Cretan archers, slingers, and javelineers to run out with the support of the cavalry, not in a dense mass but in as dispersed an order as possible, and to bombard the chariots with missiles from all sides. This storm of missiles so to speak thoroughly terrorized the horses, in part because of the wounds caused by the missiles thrown from all sides and partly by means of the dissonant shouts. Suddenly, as if they had slipped their reins, they rushed about randomly. The Roman light-armed, unencumbered slingers, and the nimble Cretans avoided their onrush. The cavalry by their pressure increased the disorder and fear of the horses, as well as the camels, which were panicked at the same time, and additional discordant shouts came from the surrounding crowd. In this way the chariots were forced off the field between the two armies. After the elimination of this empty mockery the signal was given on both sides for a real battle.

However, this empty affair became the cause of a real disaster. The supporting auxiliaries who were positioned closest, terrified at the panic and alarm of the chariots, turned to flight. In doing so they exposed the whole line as far as the cataphracts, who without their support did not sustain even the first charge of the Roman cavalry; some were routed, while others were pressed down by the weight of their weapons and armor. Next, the whole of Antiochus' left wing began to give way; once the auxiliaries who were positioned between the cavalry and the phalangites were thrown into disorder, panic penetrated as far as the middle of the battle line. They were thrown into confusion and their use of their very long thrusting spears was impeded and blocked by their own troops. The Romans advanced and discharged their *pila* at the disordered ranks. Not even the elephants who stood in the way deterred the Romans, for they had become accustomed as a result of the wars in Africa to avoid the charge of the beasts and to either discharge missiles at them from the flank or if they could approach closer to cut their tendons with their swords.

At this point the middle of the battle line was almost completely defeated, and the auxiliaries had been surrounded and were being cut down from the rear when the Romans learned of the flight of their men in another part of the line and they heard the fearful cries of their troops very near their camp. For on the right wing, when Antiochus saw that there were only four squadrons of cavalry because of the Romans' trust in the aid provided by the river and that these units by keeping contact with the other units had become separated from the river bank, he charged with his cataphracts. He exerted pressure not only in front, but encircling them on the side next to the river kept up pressure on their flank until first the cavalry were scattered and then the infantry posted next to them were forced back to their camp in headlong flight.

The tribune of the soldiers, M. Aemilius, the son of Marcus Lepidus, who a few years later became pontifex maximus, was in charge of the camp. When he saw the flight of the Roman troops he rushed up with all of the camp garrison and first ordered them to halt and then to return to the fight, castigating their fear and shameful flight, and then followed these orders with threats, adding that they were blindly rushing to their own destruction. Finally, he gave the signal to cut down the front ranks of the fugitives in order to force back those behind to face the enemy by inflicting wounds upon them. This greater fear conquered their fear of the enemy. Pressured by fears on both sides, they halted and then returned to the fight. Aemilius and the garrison, about 2,000 of these brave men, fiercely resisted the disordered onrush of the king. Attalus, the brother of Eumenes, arrived in time with 200 cavalry from the right wing, where the left wing of the enemy had been put to flight as soon as contact had been made.

When Antiochus saw that those who had just shown their backs were returning to the fight and another crowd issuing from the camp and the troops from the battle line were coming towards him, he turned his horse to flee. So on both wings the Romans moved forward over the heaps of bodies which had piled up in the center of the battle, where the high morale of the enemy and heaviness of their arms impeded their flight. First the cavalry, above all those of Eumenes, and then the rest of the horse pursued the enemy everywhere and cut down those in the rear as they overtook them. A great curse to the fugitives was their own lack of order. Chariots, elephants, and camels were intermixed with them, so that losing all order, like blind men, they fell over one another and were trampled by the onrush of the beasts. There was another slaughter almost greater than that in the field, for the flight of those in front was towards the camp, and trusting in numbers the camp garrison stubbornly fought in front of the rampart. The Romans were held back at the gates by the rampart, which they had thought to capture in their first rush. Finally, they broke through and in their rage made a greater slaughter.

It is said that about 50,000 infantry and 3,000 cavalry died on that day, and 1,400 men and fifteen elephants with their drivers were captured. On the Roman side a number were wounded, but not more than 300 infantry and twenty-four cavalry fell, while Eumenes lost a total of twenty-five men.

The legion and the phalanx

125 POLYBIUS, *HISTORIES* 18.28.1–32.5

This passage follows Polybius' description of the Cynoscephalae and offers a partial explanation of why the Macedonians were defeated. The sarissa assumed by Polybius is twenty-one feet long. It appears to have been a figure settled on after some experimentation. Each rank was separated by three feet, so that only the points of the first five ranks projected beyond the front of the phalanx. There is no evidence, as was once thought, for various ranks having sarissas of different lengths. The three feet between the men were measured from the right shoulder of one infantryman to the right shoulder of the soldier to his right. Polybius exaggerates the immobility of the phalanx to make his point.

The Roman subdivision into maniples, that is a set of miniature phalanxes, allowed units to operate independently, and Roman equipment was serviceable outside group formations while that of the phalanx was not. Greeks used reserves by Alexander's time, so the contrast was overdrawn. In fact the *triarii* were armed in the same way as the members of the phalanx were when Polybius wrote. The movement of the military tribune and his twenty maniples at Cynoscephalae lies behind Polybius' contrast.

In my sixth book I made a promise that on a suitable occasion I would compare Roman and Macedonian equipment and the formations of each along with the advantages and disadvantages that each formation entails.... I shall now make an attempt to fulfill that promise. It is easy to see that when the phalanx is able to manifest its particular characteristics nothing can withstand its frontal attack or charge. When it is closed up in battle formation each man occupies a space of three feet wide and the length of a sarissa is according to its earlier design sixteen feet long, but the one in current use is twenty-one feet. Since one must subtract the distance between the wielder's hands and the length of the counterweight behind from the part that projects, it is evident that the sarissa must project fifteen feet in front of the body of each hoplite when he holds it in both hands as he charges the enemy. The result is that the sarissas of the second, third, and fourth rank extend farther than those of the fifth rank. The sarissas of the latter extend three feet in front of the men in the front rank whenever the phalanx is properly closed up.... [Then] it is clear that five sarissas extend in front of each man in the front rank, each separated by a distance of three feet from the other.

From this information one can easily conjecture the form of the assault of the phalanx with its projecting weapons, both as to its appearance and as to its force when it is sixteen men deep. Those troops behind the fifth row are unable to bring their weapons to bear in the attack. As a result each soldier does not level his sarissa, man against man, but holds it slantwise over the shoulders of the men in front of him, and so these men provide shelter for the formation by deflecting with the dense mass of their sarissas missiles that pass over the front ranks and might fall on those in the rear. Also, by the weight of their bodies they exert pressure on the men to their front and add force to the assault. Further, because of the denseness of the formation those in front cannot turn about.

What is the reason then for the success of the Romans and the defeat of those armies that use the phalanx formation? In war both the times and the places for action are unlimited, but the phalanx is suitable in only one type of situation as far as time and place are concerned .... It is generally acknowledged that the phalanx needs level and bare ground without obstacles such as ditches, ravines, depressions, embankments, and river beds. All of these obstacles can hamper and break up the formation. Given this, one can hardly find within an area of three miles or even more places without such hindrances, as all would admit. And if our enemies refuse to encounter us, but go around and sack the land and cities of our allies, how can such a formation help us? Remaining in a place where it can be effective, it cannot help its allies or even preserve itself, since the flow of supplies is easily hindered by the enemy while they control the open country. But if the phalanx leaves favorable ground to meet the enemy, it will be easily defeated. Even in those cases where the phalanx moves down to favorable ground, if the whole of it is not used when it should be and a favorable opportunity not taken, it is easy to see from what the Romans do at present what will happen if even a small portion of the phalanx is held back at the decisive moment from the charge. This is not a matter for argument but can easily be proved by past events. The Romans do not extend their line equally to face the attacking phalanx frontally, but retain some men in reserve, while the rest are thrown into the battle. If the phalangites should drive back those troops that they are attacking, they are in turn repulsed by the reserve and their formation broken up. In attack or defense the phalanx leaves behind parts of its own army, and when this happens the spaces provide an opportunity for the enemy's reserve, in the space that the phalanx had occupied, not to attack it frontally but to outflank it and attack its sides and rear....

The Macedonian phalanx is at times either of little use or of no use at all, since the hoplite is useless fighting in detachments or man against man, but the Roman formation is useful in such situations. Every Roman, once he is armed and sets about his business, can adapt to fighting at any place or time and can face any attack. He is prepared when it is necessary to fight in formation, in detachments, and man to man.

The Third Macedonian War

When Perseus succeeded his father, Philip V, on the Macedonian throne in 179 his relations with the Roman Senate were already fragile. The Romans were suspicious of his role in the death of his brother Demetrius, who had had strong senatorial support, and of his closeness to his father, who had long been an object of suspicion at Rome. In the following years his marriage with the Seleucid royal house and his actions in Greece, where he was popular, deepened Roman distrust and appeared to threaten Rome's position as friend and patron of the Greek cities. It also aroused the enmity of Eumenes of Pergamum, who also competed for Greek support. He was the most important ally that Rome had in the East, and while in Rome spoke before the Senate of Perseus' plans to wage the war against the Romans that his father had not lived to launch.

By late summer 172 the Senate had decided to open hostilities, although a formal declaration of war was not made until the following year. An embassy was dispatched to win Greek support, and it was decided to send an advance force to prevent Perseus from closing the passes across the Pindus Mountains into Thessaly and Macedonia. The disparity in resources meant that an eventual Roman victory was all but certain.

Finally in 171 a standard consular army under P. Licinius Crassus was dispatched to the Balkans. In response, Perseus assembled his forces and marched into Thessaly. There his cavalry met Crassus' at Callinicus and won a clear victory. In its immediate aftermath Perseus asked for peace and was presented with a demand for unconditional surrender. The Roman attitude to war-making, which had been clear in the war against Hannibal, was still not understood in the Hellenistic East.

The consul of 170, A. Hostilius Mancinus, achieved little. The consul of 169, Q. Marcius Philippus, was more successful. Combining effective diplomacy with an offensive against Perseus that broke into Macedonia, his year in office ended with the Roman army now encamped on the banks of the Elpeus River, which flowed into the Thermaic Gulf, and with southern Macedonia now open to attack.

For 168, Macedonia was assigned to Lucius Aemilius Paullus, who had been consul in 182 and had prior military experience fighting in Liguria and Spain. Extensive reinforcements and a strengthened fleet were provided for further operations against Perseus. The arrival of the consul with the praetor Cn. Octavius in the early spring led to further preparations by Perseus. Troops were dispatched to strengthen coastal defenses, and garrisons were sent north to protect the pass through Pythium and Petra to stop any Roman attempt to turn his position. In addition, he fortified the banks of the Elpeus, which at this season was dry, and with Dium at his back he had a suitable base of supply. Given the inequality of Macedonian and Roman resources it appears that Perseus hoped to pursue a defensive strategy by prolonging the war in hopes that the Romans would tire of it.

Paullus in his position south of the Elpeus decided that Perseus' position was too strong to take by direct assault. The consul determined on a turning movement to force Perseus out of his position. A force of 8,200 troops, including both infantry and cavalry, was entrusted to Scipio Nasica Corculum, who was serving as military tribune. The exact route that Scipio took is unknown. He successfully surprised the garrison that blocked his route, though the inflated figures for it found in Plutarch and Livy may be the result of Nasica's own exaggeration, as they both relied on his report. The presence of Nasica's force in his rear turned Perseus' position on the Elpeus, and he retired farther north. The exact site where Perseus chose to deploy is a subject of dispute. It most likely lay to the south of the city of Pydna, where there is a combination of a plain and ridges that fits Plutarch's description and through which the two rivers mentioned in Livy and Plutarch ran which could act as minor barriers mentioned in these accounts.

Both Livy's and Plutarch's narratives of the battle depend on a combination of Polybius, whose account has survived only in fragments, and Nasica's letter as their main sources. It is likely that Polybius' account relied on eyewitnesses for Pydna. The Posidonius mentioned by Plutarch may perhaps be identical with the author of works on the Dniester region of southern Russia. There is additional information of varying quality in later sources such as Frontinus' *Stratagems*. There are a number of gaps in Livy's text, but given his dependence on the same sources as Plutarch these can be filled in from the latter's narrative.

The date of the battle is fixed by the lunar eclipse mentioned by both Plutarch and Livy that occurred on June 21, 168, so that the three days of skirmishing prior to the final battle should be June 18–20.

We do not have exact numbers of the relative strengths of the forces engaged. Plutarch gives a figure of 40,000 infantry and 4,000 cavalry for Perseus' army. Livy claims that 20,000 Macedonians were killed in battle, with 11,000 captured. Plutarch gives a higher figure of 25,000 killed. Both are compatible with the figure that Plutarch gives for Perseus' troops, assuming a number guarding his camp with some troops detached on garrison and other duties. Perhaps 21,000 belonged to the phalanx, with another 16,000 or 17,000 troops of various types deployed on the wings of the phalanx. Paullus' army was the normal consular army of two legions and a roughly equivalent number of allied troops, perhaps more than the normal 20,000 in total, as Livy mentions that his force received sizeable reinforcements. To these must be added Greek allied units such as Attalus'. There is no mention of a disparity of forces or fear of outflanking and so probably the Roman force plus its allies were roughly equal in size to Perseus' army.

The battle lines of both sides can be reconstructed. The Macedonian line was facing to the southwest and the Roman to the northeast, with the Leucus River between them. The Macedonian left consisted of approximately 10,000 Thracians, mercenaries, and Paeonians, along with the *agema* (royal guard). In the center was the phalanx consisting of two divisions, the Silver Shields and the Bronze Shields, with the Bronze Shields on the left and the Silver Shields on the right. Finally, the Macedonian right was formed by mixed troops numbering about 10,000, as well as 3,000 cavalry under the command of Perseus. The cavalry was placed on the left, since that wing simply extended into the plain with no natural protection. The Roman disposition for the most part appears to have been the normal one, with allies on the wings and the legions in the center opposite the phalanx, with the elephants of unknown number stationed on the right. There must also have been cavalry positioned on the wings, though they play little role in the battle and seem to have operated to little effect, as the sources mention that all of Perseus' cavalry escaped after the battle. It was only in the pursuit that they seem to have been of value.

Despite claims of a stratagem by Paullus it is probable that the battle developed accidentally. In the course of the battle it seems only the Macedonian left and center were engaged. The initial success of the phalanx in forcing the Roman line back proved fatal to it. Once it began to operate on uneven ground it lost cohesion, and the more flexible maniples were able to insinuate themselves into the gaps and pry the phalanx apart. (For a comparison of the phalanx versus the legions see pp. 184f.)

The battle had a decisive impact. It marked the end of the Antigonid dynasty and marked the first steps in the conversion of Macedonia into a province.

The battle of Pydna

126 PLUTARCH, *LIFE OF AEMILIUS PAULLUS* 16.3–22.1

After suffering this calamity [Scipio's descent on his rear] Perseus broke camp and retreated in fear with his hopes dashed. In spite of what had happened he had to hold his position before Pydna and risk a battle or scatter his forces among various cities. Once war had entered a country there was no way to drive it out without much bloodshed and butchery. He would have more troops in his present position and his men would be especially courageous in defending their children and wives in the presence of a king, Perseus' friends encouraged him. Accordingly, he encamped and deployed his army for battle, reconnoitering and assigning commands so that he could meet the Romans as soon as they appeared.

The place afforded a plain for his phalanx which needed firm footing and smooth ground and heights one behind the other which afforded his light-armed and skirmishers routes for both retreat and flank attacks. Through the middle of the plain there flowed the rivers Aeson and Leucus, not very deep at that season, for it was late summer, but which were likely to create difficulties for the Romans.

After Aemilius had joined with Nasica he moved down against the enemy and deployed for battle. When he saw their formation and numbers he halted in amazement, giving thought to the matter. His young officers were eager to fight; riding up, they urged him not to delay, especially Nasica, who was the most insistent of all, elated by his success near Mount Olympus. But with a smile Aemilius said "Indeed, if I was your age I would share your eagerness, but many victories have taught me the mistakes made by the defeated and keep me from engaging in battle against a phalanx already deployed and formed up, right after marching." Then he ordered his leading troops and those in sight of the enemy to form maniples and the appearance of a battle line, while he ordered the others in the rear to turn and dig trenches and encamp. After they had done so, the troops next to them wheeled off in appropriate order and he disbanded his formation and brought them into camp undisturbed and without the enemy's knowledge.

When night fell and after the soldiers had eaten dinner and were turning towards sleep and rest, the moon, which was full and high in the sky, grew dark and its light disappeared, taking on all of the colors one after the other, and then it disappeared. By clashing together bronze utensils and by holding up burning firebrands and lit torches to the sky the Romans, as is their custom, tried to recall the moon's light. In the Macedonian camp none of these things were done, but the rumor spread quietly through the camp that the portent signified the eclipse of the king. Aemilius was neither ignorant nor inexperienced in the anomalies of eclipses, which at fixed intervals carry the moon in its course into the earth's shadow and hide it from sight until it passes through the region of shadow and again reflects the sun's light. However, since he was very devout and much given to sacrifice and divination, as soon as he saw the moon begin to emerge from the shadow he sacrificed eleven heifers to it. As soon as it was daylight he sacrificed not less than twenty oxen to Hercules, hoping for a favorable omen. But at the twenty-first sacrifice favorable omens appeared, indicating victory if the Romans stood on the defensive. So vowing a hundred oxen and sacred games for the god he ordered his officers to draw up the army for battle. But he waited for the movement of the sun and its setting to avoid having the morning light shining on the faces of his troops. He spent the time sitting in his tent, which was open towards the plain and the enemy camp.

About dawn Aemilius worked out a plan, as some say, to make the enemy attack. The Romans driving out a horse without a bridle came into collision with the enemy and this provided the occasion of the battle. But there is another version that the Thracians, commanded by Alexander, attacked Roman draft animals bringing in forage and that 700 Ligurians made a strong counterattack. More men poured in from both sides to help, and the engagement became general. Aemilius, like a ship's steersman inferring from the present tossing wave the greatness of the coming storm, left his tent and moving along the front of the legions encouraged them, while Nasica, who had ridden out to the skirmishers, saw that the whole enemy force was almost upon them.

First came the Thracians, who Nasica says were especially striking in appearance, being tall with black tunics under their white, shining shields and greaves, shaking battleaxes with heavy iron heads on their right shoulders. Next to them the mercenaries marched to the attack with equipment of every type and with Paeonians mixed with them. Then came a third unit, the select Macedonian troops, men of exceptional courage and at their physical peak, flashing with gilded arms and scarlet cloaks. As these men took their place in line there issued from the camp the phalanxes of the Bronze Shields, filling the plain with the gleam of iron and the brightness of bronze as well as the hills with noise and clamor. Thus courageously and at such speed did they advance that the first to be slain fell two stades (1200 feet) from the Roman camp.

Aemilius was present as the attack began and discovered that the Macedonians in the *agema* had already planted the tips of their long spears in the Romans' shields, which prevented the latter from reaching them with their swords, and saw that the other Macedonians were swinging their shields from their shoulders round to the front and that the sarissas set at a single level were keeping off his troops with their weapons and the strength of their interlocked shields as well by the fierceness of their onset. He was struck with amazement and fear, never having seen anything more terrifying. Later he would often speak of that sight and his feelings. But then showing a cheerful and happy face to his soldiers he rode past them without helmet or breastplate. On the other hand, according to Polybius, the Macedonian king at the beginning of the battle acted in a cowardly fashion and returned to the city, pretending to make a sacrifice to Hercules, a god who does not receive sacrifices from cowards or fulfill unjust prayers.... But the god listened to the prayers of Aemilius. Brandishing his spear, the consul prayed for strength in war and victory in the war which he fought as he called upon the god as his ally.

But there is a Posidonius, who says he was a contemporary and a participant in these actions, who has written a history of Perseus in several books and he says that the king departed not because of cowardice or to make a sacrifice, but because on the day before the battle he happened to have been kicked in the leg by a horse. Further, he states that, during the battle, although in a dreadful state and hindered by his friends, the king ordered a pack horse to be brought to him and mounting it joined his phalanx without wearing a cuirass. In the midst of a hail of missiles from every side a javelin made entirely of iron struck him, though not with the point, but went obliquely along his left side and ripped through his tunic and made a dark red bruise by the force of its passage which lasted a long time. This is Posidonius' defense of Perseus.

When the Romans attacked the phalanx they were not able to force a passage through, and Salvius, the commander of the Paeligni, snatched up a standard of his unit and hurled it among the enemy. The Paeligni, since it is not acceptable or permitted to Italians to abandon a standard, rushed towards the spot and both sides suffered terrible losses. The Romans attempted to turn aside the sarissas with their swords and to force them back with their shields or push them aside with their hands, while the Macedonians held them firmly in both hands, driving them through those who fell upon them, since neither shield nor cuirass could resist the force of the sarissa. They hurled back headlong the Paeligni, and Marrucini thoughtlessly and with animal fury rushed forward against the blows to a certain death. After the front ranks had fallen they pushed back the ranks behind them. There was no flight but a movement back towards Mount

Olocrus. At the sight of this, Posidonius says, Aemilius tore his tunic, because these men were in retreat and the rest of the army was turning aside from the phalanx which faced them with a dense wall of spears which gave no point of attack.

But at those points where the ground was uneven and because of the length of the battle line the shields could not be kept locked together Aemilius saw that the Macedonian phalanx had many gaps and openings as normally happens in large armies, as the efforts of the fighters vary greatly, and that parts of it were under pressure and others pushing forward. Moving quickly and dividing up his units he ordered them to charge into the gaps and empty spaces in the enemy line. He instructed them to come at close quarters with the enemy and not to fight a single battle of all against all but many separate and successive encounters. Aemilius gave these orders to his officers and they in turn passed them on to the troops, and as soon as the troops got between the ranks of the enemy and separated them they attacked some from the flank on their unshielded side and attacked others by running around them and attacking them from the rear. The phalanx lost its force and general effectiveness as it was broken open. Singly and in small groups, the Macedonians used their small daggers against the stiff and long Roman shields and defended themselves with light wicker shields against swords which on account of their weight and force penetrated their armor and pierced their bodies. Therefore, after putting up a weak defense they turned to flight.

... In the end 3,000 of the picked Macedonians who remained in formation and continued fighting were all killed. There was a great slaughter of the rest in their flight, with the result that the plain and the lower slopes of the hills were filled with corpses and the waters of the Leucus River were still mixed with blood when the Romans crossed it on the day after the battle. It is said that more than 25,000 of the Macedonians died, while the Romans lost either one hundred, if one follows Posidonius, or eighty according to Nasica.

And this greatest of battles was decided swiftly. The fight began at 3 p.m. and victory came within the hour. The Romans used the rest of the day for pursuit, which they continued for 120 stades, so that it was already late in the evening when they returned.

Battle in western Europe

The Battle of Emporiae

127 LIVY, 34.14–15

Directly after the defeat at Ilipa in 206 (see **119**) the Romans began to expand their area of control in Spain. By the next year they had already decided to appoint regular magistrates to govern it and had divided the Iberian peninsula into two provinces, Nearer and Further Spain, under two praetors, though the exact boundaries of these provinces may not have been fixed until 197. Nearer Spain essentially ran along the east coast and extended a short distance into the interior, while Further Spain consisted of the southeast coast and the valley of the ancient Baetis River (modern Guadalquivir).

Aside from some coastal towns there were few large centers and there was extensive political fragmentation, with the peninsula divided among a number of tribes. Despite a formidable array of weapons and extensive experience in serving as mercenaries or auxiliaries in both the Carthaginian and Roman armies the tribes could match neither the organization nor manpower available to the Romans.

Rebellion had already broken out after 205, but by 199 most of the fighting had ended. In 197 the two legions that had formed the Spanish garrison were withdrawn, leaving only a token force of Latin, Italian, and Spanish troops. This seems to have formed the background for another rebellion that started in 197. The extent of the rebellion is unclear, owing to our inadequate sources. Despite a string of Roman victories the situation was serious enough in 196 for the unusual step to be taken of sending one of the two consuls to Spain in the next year. As a result of a drawing of lots, M. Porcius Cato was given Nearer Spain, with extra legions, allied forces, a total of over 25,000 troops.

Cato and his troops set sail probably in late March or early April and after some minor actions reached Emporiae probably in the middle of May. Emporiae lies to the northeast of Barcelona in the modern Spanish province of Catalonia. It was a major port that the Romans had several times used during the Second Punic War. The city itself consisted of a double town, both Greek and native. Cato was able to use the town as a temporary base, but the native section seems to have been disaffected.

The account of the battle found in Livy and our other major source, Appian, probably stems at least in part from Cato's published account of his consulate, as Livy makes clear in his reference at the end of his account to Cato's omission of detailed enemy casualty figures. There is no reason to doubt the general accuracy of the narrative, though there is clearly some exaggeration of Cato's effectiveness as a commander.

The night march by which Cato positioned his army west of the enemy's camp is extremely unusual and dangerous and implies either close prior reconnaissance or excellent local guides. It appears that Cato was convinced of his superiority and was attempting to force a battle by cutting off the enemy's line of retreat. Livy is unclear about the deployment of both sides. Apparently, from Livy's account, there was some sort of barbarian formation, as Cato launched his attack before the Spanish could fully form up, but no details are provided. The same can be said of the account of the Roman deployment. Mention is made of a second line and a reserve force. It is unlikely that this is the normal three-line formation of the manipular legion, since the second legion appears to act as a reserve and does not come into contact with the enemy until late in the battle. For the use of the cohort, see pp. 199ff. The march of the two cohorts around the Spanish right is an extremely surprising maneuver. Presumably, these must have been taken from Cato's second line that was not yet involved in the fighting. Such a march would expose the men's unshielded side to a flank attack, and the fact that the attack never materialized seems to imply either that the enemy was fully engaged or the units were screened by a hill or other feature not mentioned in Livy's account.

The iron javelin that Livy refers to is the *soliferreum*, of which we know little beyond the fact that it was made entirely of iron and as a result of its weight must have been used only at close quarters.

Livy cites Valerius Antias, a first-century BC annalist, for enemy casualty figures. Elsewhere Livy makes clear his distrust of Antias' inflated numbers.

After assembling his forces, Cato began to march inland, where he found that the Spanish rebels had already put a substantial army in the field. The figure of 40,000 given in the sources is far too large, but it must be assumed that the army was probably comparable in numbers to Cato's own force. Instead of continuing his march Cato built a substantial camp about three miles west of Emporiae and did not immediately engage the enemy. He launched a series of raids and skirmishes as well as engaged in the intensive training of his army, which implies many of the men were probably new recruits.

After having taken the auspices, the consul set out in the middle of the night to seize the position he had chosen before the enemy was aware of what he was doing. He led his troops around beyond the enemy camp and at dawn deployed his line and sent three cohorts up to their rampart.

The barbarians, amazed at the appearance of the Romans behind them, ran and armed themselves, while the consul addressed his men. "Soldiers, courage is our only hope. I have worked diligently that there would be none other. The enemy is between us and our camp and their territory is behind us. The noblest course is also the safest, to rest one's hopes in one's courage." He immediately ordered the recall of the cohorts to draw out the barbarians by simulating flight. Events turned out as he had hoped. The barbarians, thinking that the Romans were afraid and in retreat, burst forth from the gates and filled the area between their camp and the Roman line with armed men. While they were hurrying to deploy, the consul, who had seen to everything, attacked them before they had formed up. First, he sent in the cavalry on both flanks, but on the right wing they were immediately thrown back and, retreating in terror, they created panic among the infantry. When he saw what had happened, Cato ordered two select cohorts to march around the enemy's right flank and to show themselves behind the enemy before the infantry lines met. The fear this inspired in the enemy equalized the weakness displayed by the Roman cavalry. Nevertheless, the cavalry and infantry of the right wing were in such a state of panic that the consul had to restrain some of the solders with his own hands and face them towards the enemy. As long as the battle was an exchange of missiles the result remained uncertain, and on the right wing where the Romans' panic and flight had begun the troops held their ground with difficulty. On the left and in the center the barbarians were hard pressed and fearful, with their eyes on the cohorts pressing on them from behind. When they had expended their iron javelins and fire missiles, they drew their swords and the battle as it were began again. Wounds were not made by unforeseeable blind throws from a distance, but it was a battle at close quarters where hope rested in courage and strength.

The consul revived his now weary men by putting in line supporting cohorts from his second line. A new line was now formed. Fresh troops with unused weapons attacked the weary enemy and at first forced them back in a wedge-like charge, scattering them in flight. Rushing through the fields they sought their camp in a disordered flight. When Cato saw that the rout was complete he rode back to the second legion, which had been held in reserve, and ordered the standards to be moved forward and the troops to attack the enemy's camp. If any of his men broke ranks and ran forward too impatiently, the consul himself struck him with a small curved spear and ordered the tribunes and centurions to punish him. Now the camp was under siege. The Romans were being forced back by stones, stakes, and every type of missile. The Romans fought with more spirit and the enemy with more ferocity at the point where the fresh legion had been brought up. The consul scanned the whole situation to find a place where resistance was least so that a break-in could be made. He saw that there were few of the enemy at the left-hand gate and he directed the *principes* and *hastati* of the second legion there. The guard stationed opposite to the gate could not resist their attack, and the rest after seeing the enemy mount the rampart threw away their arms and standard since they had now lost their camp. They were cut down at the gates, where they were pressed together by their own numbers. The men of the second legion cut them down from behind; the other soldiers sacked the camp. Valerius Antias writes that over 40,000 of the enemy were killed on that day. Cato himself, surely never stinting in self-praise, said that many were killed but does not give a number.

The aftermath of battle

The massed close-order fighting on the Roman battlefield left a distinctive pattern of casualties, both dead and wounded. The densest mass of casualties would have been at the point of initial contact between the two armies. If one side had broken and fled, the concentration would be higher, as those in front would have been instantly exposed to their pursuers and slowed by the mass of men behind them. The loss of an army's cohesion was the point at which the greatest slaughter occurred. Numbers would decrease as the distance from the point of contact increased, but the dispersion of casualties would differ according to the circumstances of the battle.

At the Metaurus or Cynoscephalae, where a successful attack on the rear of the enemy formation was mounted, there would be additional clusters of the dead and wounded. The presence of cavalry meant that bodies might be scattered about the countryside after an extended pursuit such as occurred at the battle of Pydna, where Plutarch mentions that the Romans pursued the routed Macedonians for about fourteen miles.

The wounded who could be helped off the battlefield by their comrades had varied chances of survival. Those with flesh wounds, simple fractures, or concussions normally had a fair chance of surviving as long as infection did not set in. However, those with deep penetration wounds, often leading to infection, or severe blows to the head, especially with heavy internal bleeding, had little chance of survival given the state of contemporary medicine. While captives could be sold, ransomed, or occasionally persuaded to change sides, the enemy wounded would only be a hindrance, so they were probably either left to die or dispatched by the victors during their search for booty on the battlefield.

The ancient sources normally give casualty figures for major battles, although they often differ in the figures that they give. It has been argued that the Roman figures are of little value. For instance, the ancient sources seem to assume that army units are at full strength even in situations where it is more than likely that they were not. The sources do not distinguish between those missing who would turn up later and the dead. They seem to take no account of deaths due to disease, which killed more men in pre-modern armies than the actual fighting did. Other factors, such as the desire to exaggerate enemy strength and minimize losses, contributed to inaccurate counts. A further problem is the result of the known inclination of some authors to exaggerate such figures.

The basic question is whether there ever were any accurate figures available. Some indications point in that direction. The basis of enrollment was the census list. Censors revised it every four years, and it is hard to believe that a list on which the war tax was levied and from which conscripts were enrolled was not kept as current as possible. Since Roman soldiers encamped in small units it would not have been difficult to assemble a list of the missing. The use of the maniple, another relatively small group, would also have aided such an identification. Further, the use of supplements for under-strength legions indicates that the state must have known at least the approximate number of casualties.

There is a less evidence for knowledge of enemy casualties. Commanders did send dispatches to the Senate after major operations. It may be that these documents contained numbers of both enemy and Roman losses. Finally, the number of enemy losses was a prerequisite for the award of certain military honors for the commander, and this might have encouraged the counting of enemy losses at least on occasions where the Romans emerged as victors. None of the arguments are conclusive, but they lend support to the possibility that the figures we have are at least indicative of the magnitude of the losses suffered. Despite the accuracy of figures, the problem remains that writers could and did manipulate such figures for their own purposes.

It is only with the Second Punic War that an order of magnitude for Roman casualties can be established. In the opening years of the war, from 218 to 215, based on conservative estimates approximately 50,000 citizens died of the approximately 108,000 who had seen service. Estimates have to take into account probable legion size and so can vary, but at least this gives a general scale for losses sustained. Again, based on conservative estimates of the number of those who died this would represent about 18 percent of adult males and approximately 5 percent of the population. It was not until the First World War that casualties on this scale would again be seen in Europe. Figures for allied casualties are more uncertain, but since in this period they normally provided two-thirds of the force the inference must be that they experienced twice as many casualties from a population double that of Rome. Their casualty rate was approximately the same as the Roman. These figures do not take into account naval personnel, who perhaps averaged about 60,000 during the war years, though these figures are less reliable than they are for legions.

From 214 to the end of the war perhaps 75,000 legionaries died, resulting in a figure of 120,000 deaths for those serving in the legions in the course of the war. This would result in a decline by about 6 percent of the total population by the end of the war. It is doubtful if any other Mediterranean state could have borne losses on this scale for such an extended period.

Even after the end of the war Rome's military demands remained high. The Roman expansion into the eastern Mediterranean continued, and costly fighting in Spain and campaigns in northern Italy account for the high figures recorded. In the period down to 168, for which we have Livy, the average number of legions in the field each year was nine. This would mean that approximately 50,000 citizens in service and 73,000 allies were serving in the armed forces each year. Livy also provides figures for Roman losses down to 170. His casualty rates are lower than the extremely high rates of the Second Punic War, but there are serious problems of the reliability of the figures we do have. The figures total 64,000 in legionary fatalities over a thirty-year period, or an average annual rate of approximately 2,300 per year, or about 0.5 percent per year of those in service, which seems low and leads one to suspect that the figures are incomplete. We have no information on deaths due to other causes, and so given the omissions and the absence of figures of fatalities due to other causes than fighting little can be done with this information. All that can be said is that military service was sufficiently burdensome for it to have become a political issue and that attempts were made to limit the duration of service.

128 LIVY, 22.51.5–9

The general picture that Livy gives of carnage and the suffering of the wounded at Cannae seems realistic. However, some of the details are hardly credible and designed to invoke pathos in the reader. The reference to the soldiers who had buried their heads in the earth to commit suicide has a faintly ridiculous air. It can be seen either as a misunderstanding or more likely an invention of the author or his source. The picture of the Numidian and the Roman belongs to a long history of similar commonplaces on the aftermath of battle and is clearly designed as a hymn to Roman bravery and tenacity.

> The following day at dawn the [Carthaginians] set about collecting the spoils and surveying the carnage that even they found appalling. So many thousands of Roman corpses lay everywhere on the field [of battle] as chance had found them during the battle or flight. Some rose up from the middle of the bloody mass tortured by their wounds, which the cold of the morning had drawn tight, and were killed by the enemy. The enemy found some prone but still alive, with their thighs and knees lacerated, who bared their throats and necks demanding that their streaming blood should be drained. Others were found with their heads buried in ditches which they appeared to have dug and covering their faces with dirt had suffocated themselves. All eyes were drawn to a Numidian who was dragged still alive from over the body of a dead Roman. His nose and ears were lacerated, since the Roman, when he could no longer use his hands to hold his weapon, had in his insane rage torn his enemy with his teeth as he died.

Changes in census qualifications

The Roman military remained a militia at least in theory during the Republic, and liability for service in the legions required the possession of a minimal amount of property as specified in the census returns. Those who fell below the minimum were still liable for service, though for the most part in the fleet. Occasionally, they served in the legions as well in times of crisis. The first recorded reference to such service is in 280 in the war against Pyrrhus. An individual eligible for service in the legions and meeting the property requirements was termed an *asiduus*, while those falling below these requirements were termed *proletarii*. The sources give a traditional minimum of either 11,000 or 12,500 asses (see p. 21). However, in the mid-second century Polybius gives a figure of 4,000 asses as the minimum, while Cicero, in a dialogue whose dramatic date is 129 BC, cites a minimum of 1,500 asses. The obvious implication is that there was a reduction in the minimum census rating for military service, though there is no specific reference to such a reduction in any ancient source.

The date of these changes has caused problems. The appearance of the sextanal as of two Roman ounces as the result of recent work has been fixed to 212/211 in the midst of the Second Punic War. The as was again reduced in about 140 BC to one Roman ounce, though only notationally, as it was no longer struck. Since the earliest census figures are valued in sextanal asses it has been argued that they can have only been in use for a short time. But it seems more likely that the original source or some later writer changed the figures based on the libral as of twelve Roman ounces into ones based on the sextanal as in recording these figures. There is evidence from Livy that in 214 the Servian figures were in use for the higher census classes. A date either in 214 or 212/211 has been suggested for a lowering of the census figures either on the basis of an increase of army size or caused by the introduction of a new class of light-armed, the *velites*. Both dates are equally probable and the evidence does not allow a choice between them. The second lowering of the minimum census figure has been dated anywhere from *circa* 170 to the dramatic date of Cicero's dialogue in 129 BC.

Most scholars have connected the lowering of the minimum census requirement to the massive enlargement of the army during the Hannibalic War (see p. 196) and the continuing military demands that resulted from almost continuous campaigning after 200. The normal service requirement was for sixteen campaigns in the infantry, which could in unusual circumstances be extended to twenty, and ten years' service in the cavalry. In the earlier Republic these campaigns would have been conducted close to Rome, and the soldier, who was primarily a peasant farmer, would have been able to return home at the end of the campaigning season. During and after the Second Punic War most military service was overseas, except for the campaigns in northern Italy, where fighting had substantially ended by the 170s.

These changed conditions of service must have pressed heavily on both Roman and allied peasant farmers and led in many cases to the failure of their farms. Estimates of the decline of the Roman and Italian peasantry have often been overstated in the past, and some areas such as southern Etruria show a high density of settlement in this period. The decline of the rural population, though its extent is debatable, is an accepted fact. In addition to the loss from military service there appears to have been increased migration by peasants to urban centers, which must have decreased the free population of the countryside, although this was accompanied by a rise in the slave population that resulted from Roman military successes.

The decline of the peasantry seems to be reflected in contemporary literature and politics, though phrased in terms of the free population and not specifically directed at those qualified for legionary service. Resistance to the levy also appears in this period, though it seems that it was limited to unpopular wars, such as the two-century-long war in Spain.

On balance, it would seem that it was the need for manpower that motivated the lowering of census qualifications for legionary service. This trend would have been strengthened by contemporary developments in Roman war-making. It seems likely that by the mid-second century the state supplied weapons and that individual soldiers were liable only for replacements. In addition, this was a period of increasing homogenization of equipment within the legions, except for certain vestiges such as the requirement for men of the first class to provide a chain mail cuirass. These two developments rendered the old distinctions based on property ratings obsolete and made service possible for men whose property fell below the old requirements.

3

THE ARMY OF THE LATE REPUBLIC

The development of the cohort as a tactical unit

By the first decades of the first century the maniple had been replaced by a larger unit, the cohort. In Caesar's description of his campaigns in Gaul, the maniple has disappeared from the battlefield and has been replaced by the cohort. As is the case with so many military changes, the sources provide no evidence as to when the reform was carried out or for what reasons. This term for a new tactical unit had earlier been applied to units of allied infantry. These units appear to have varied in size, with an upper limit of about 600 men. They were generally commanded by a Roman officer, the *praefectus cohortis*, and besides being used in battle supplied men for service as camp guards and for other duties. It is not totally clear whether the Roman cohort derived its name from allied units or whether the term was applied for some other reason.

The earliest secure evidence for the Roman cohort appears during the Second Punic War in the course of the Spanish campaigns. Polybius mentions the cohort at the battle of Ilipa in 206. He describes Scipio executing a complicated maneuver to extend his battle line (see **119**). The Roman troops executed this movement grouped in cohorts, which Polybius defines as a unit of three maniples with their accompanying light-armed. Polybius' statement implies that the cohort was by his time a regular military unit. Polybius again mentions the use of cohorts by Scipio in a battle later that year fought at the Ebro River. He says that Scipio sent four cohorts to engage an enemy force of cavalry and infantry that had entered a valley at some distance from his camp. Livy mentions cohorts in Spain on a number of occasions during the course of Rome's second-century wars in Spain. Occasionally, he refers to the use of maniples and cohorts at the same time. In general, his references to cohorts occur in his narrative of campaigns in Spain and the West, while maniples figure in his accounts of eastern campaigns. For example, at the battle of Magnesia against Antiochus III in 189 Livy and Appian both describe a Roman army organized in maniples.

However, there are two serious problems with our sources in trying to understand the evolution of the cohort. The first is the problem of the imprecision of these writers' terminology, especially serious in translating the terms used by Greek writers into Latin. The second difficulty is the tendency, perhaps most often found in Livy, to use terms anachronistically. Most of our sources except for Polybius have no direct knowledge of the manipular army and have a propensity to substitute the unit they knew, the cohort, for the maniple.

Despite these difficulties the sources paint a picture of the Roman cohort as emerging in Spain. Livy has several references to cohorts very early in Republican history, but it is probable that these are anachronisms. The unit appears most often in detached operations or those requiring quick movement. Speed of movement was crucial at Ilipa and for expeditionary force at the Ebro. Cohorts also appear as reserve forces, camp guards, and sometimes advance units sent out from the main army. That such forces existed from a very early period seems likely. In general, the lines of the manipular legion were mutually supporting, and it would make no sense to dispatch troops of a single line to operate independently. Spain, with its extensive open spaces, few urban centers, and continuous guerilla warfare, would have favored the use of detachments of this type. In the eastern Mediterranean, with its greater urban density and organized political units, a set-piece battle was far more likely.

The more difficult and important question is when a unit designed for rapid movement and independent operation became the standard tactical unit in major battles. The last clear reference to the use of the maniple on the battlefield is to the army operating under the consul Metellus in the war against Jugurtha at the end of the second century. But Sallust also mentions Metellus using cohorts. It is perhaps likely that Metellus' arrangements represent a transitional stage between the use of the maniple as the basic unit and its replacement by the cohort. After this point the maniple remains only as an administrative unit.

One factor which was probably of importance was the change in equipment of the three lines of the manipular legion (see p. 65). This was probably completed by the 120s. After this change there was no longer any obstacle to combining the three lines in a single unit.

The use of the cohort structure would have simplified the exercise of command. Orders could now have to be transmitted to ten rather than thirty units. It has also been suggested that these larger units would have dealt more effectively with the irregular formations of barbarian troops. However, during Rome's encounters in Italy with Celtic forces that fought in just such a dispersed fashion, the maniple seems to have been effective. It was rather the dispersed operations that the Romans encountered in Spain and elsewhere in the West that increased reliance on the cohort as a basic tactical element. Once homogeneity of equipment developed there was little point in reforming units into maniples and discarding the advantages of a simplified command system. The change was once seen as a military innovation of Marius to be connected with his struggle with Germanic invaders in the last years of the second century. It is more likely that the change was the product of a long and continuous process.

The appearance of the cohort

129 POLYBIUS, *HISTORIES* 11.23.1–2

The following description of the cohort is part of Polybius' narrative of the battle of Ilipa (see **119**).

The use of a cohort formation during a battle indicates that the use of such units was long familiar to Roman troops. The change back to manipular formation for the battle may have been necessary given the differences in offensive weaponry of the *triarii*. Scipio's use of the cohort is simply a variant of the employment of cohorts in situations requiring rapid movement.

> [Scipio] taking the three leading *turmae* of cavalry, and placing in front of them the usual number of *velites* and three maniples – the Romans call this a cohort – from his right wing, while Marcius and Junius took the same units from the left, he advanced straight against the enemy, wheeling his men to the left while Marcius and Junius wheeled their troops to the right. The units immediately following them wheeled in turn.

130 SALLUST, *THE WAR AGAINST JUGURTHA* 49.4–6

This passage is from Sallust's narration of the battle with Jugurtha near the River Muthul, a tributary of the Bagradas River (see **107**), in 109, which ended in a major Roman victory. Sallust makes it clear that Metellus is deploying his army in traditional manipular fashion, with the addition of light-armed troops in the gaps between the legionaries. The following passage, taken from the description of the same battle, has Metellus organizing his infantry in cohorts at a later point in the battle.

Some have taken the combined use of cohort and maniple as marking a transitional phase, and they may be right. However, the terminology is unclear. The reference could be either to a tactical formation or simply to a section of a legion. Sallust's account of this war contains the last references to the use of the maniple in battle; for this reason many scholars accept that Marius introduced the cohort as a tactical unit in battle. It seems more likely that this period saw the end of a long evolution from maniple to cohort and that Marius simply extended a practice already evident in the account of Metellus' tactics.

> Meanwhile Metellus, unaware of the enemy's position, was visible descending the hill with his forces. At first, he was uncertain as to what the unaccustomed appearance of the enemy's forces signified, for the Numidian horsemen were stationed among the thickets of shrubbery, although they were not hidden because of the low height of the bushes. Nevertheless, he remained uncertain both because of the nature of the territory and because their identity was obscured by the vegetation. When Metellus quickly recognized that it was an ambush he briefly halted his

men. He changed the battle order on the right of his line, which was closest to the enemy; he deployed the battle line there with extra support. He
distributed slingers and archers among the maniples and placed all of the
cavalry on the wings. He gave a short speech to the soldiers in accordance
with the situation and then led his army down into the plain, with his front
ranks at right angles to the enemy's line.

131 SALLUST, *THE WAR AGAINST JUGURTHA* 51.3

It seems probable that these cohorts were operating as a detached force.

When the Romans were exhausted by their exertions and the day's heat,
Metellus noticed that the Numidians were attacking with less energy. He
gradually reformed his army and deployed four legionary cohorts against
the African infantry.

The structure and disposition of the cohort in the battle line

Our information on the structure and employment of the cohort is mainly imperial,
but there is no reason to think that there had been major changes in the early Empire.
There were ten cohorts to a legion, which varied in size depending on the strength
of the legion. Most often they seemed to have numbered about 500 men, which was
the approximate size of allied cohorts. As one scholar has noted, a unit of 500 men
forms the maximum possible frontage of a marching unit that can be controlled
effectively under pre-modern conditions. This is best thought of as a paper strength.
The numbers of men in a cohort could vary widely; at the battle of Pharsalus in the
late summer of 48, Pompey's cohorts were composed of 409 men while Caesar's
cohorts had a strength of 275 legionaries.

Maniples and centuries continued to be used as subdivisions of the cohort and as
administrative units. In excavations of the camp at Numantia dating from the 130s,
the layout of soldiers' quarters is based on the century and maniple and shows no
trace of any organization according to cohorts. Elements of the manipular structure
also remained in the hierarchy of centurions, who were ranked by their command
of the centuries. The continued existence of centuries and maniples at the organi-
zational level probably is the result of two factors. The first is the innate conser-
vatism of Roman military structures and the second, perhaps in the long run the
more important reason, is that cohorts were rather large units to manage and that it
remained simpler to keep the previous, smaller administrative units.

Strangely there is no attested commander for the cohort. It is probable that the
senior centurion would have exercised command, that is, the prior centurion of the
triarii (see p. 76).

The difficult question remains as to how the cohort itself was deployed. There is
no explicit evidence for the Republican period. One possibility was that it deployed
six men deep, which may have been the normal depth of the maniple. There is some

support for such an arrangement in Josephus' account of the Jewish rebellion of 66–70 AD. In his account of Vespasian's march into the Galilee he gives the order of the march, stating that the legionaries marched in six columns. If the cohort depth was also six this would have made the transition from column into line relatively easy. Such a depth would have yielded a standard cohort frontage of eighty men, which was also the standard strength of a century and would give some support to the view that in the maniple the centuries fought one behind the other. Certainty is impossible, and it is clear that depth and frontage varied according to circumstances. Julius Frontinus, the late-first-century author of a book on stratagems who had military experience, though not a writer who warrants uncritical trust, states that Pompey's cohorts at the battle of Pharsalus were arranged ten men deep. This depth may have been greater than normal and the result of Pompey's attempt to stiffen his line, which was mainly composed of new recruits and facing Caesar's veterans.

The cohorts were used on the battlefield in various formations. The most common seems to have been a formation in three lines with four in the first line, four in the second, and three in the third. The first two lines seem to have functioned as the fighting force, with the third line held back as a reserve. Occasionally, we hear of a two-line arrangement such as that of Lucius Afranius facing Caesar at Ilerda in Spain in 49. Afranius' first two lines were composed of cohorts from five legions, with his third line composed of auxiliary cohorts acting as a reserve. On a single occasion Caesar drew up his cohorts in a single line in 46 during the civil war in Africa. But this occurred in an unusual situation when Caesar was facing an enemy force composed primarily of light-armed troops and cavalry so that he felt he needed to extend his line as far as possible to avoid flank attacks.

One final problem was the disposition of cohorts within the line at the moment of contact with the enemy. Did the cohorts form a solid line as they met the enemy? As in the case of the manipular legion the answer is probably that they did not. It would have made control of individual cohorts impossible. To the objection that gaps between the maniples would have allowed enemy penetration, the most cogent answer is that any force of similar size must have been divided into smaller units to be maneuverable in battle and that the enemy probably also had gaps in his line. Presumably, as is the case with maniples, the cohorts were separated by a distance equivalent to their frontage. This is made more likely by references to the opening of maniples to admit fugitives in Caesar and also during the imperial period in Tacitus' *Histories*. Without some distance from maniples on either side it would have been impossible to perform such a maneuver.

132 CAESAR, *CIVIL WAR* 1.83

Caesar's description comes from his account of his campaign against two Pompeian generals, Lucius Afranius and Marcus Petreius, in 49. He had six legions to face their five. The encounter took place at Ilerda near a tributary of the Ebro. In the end no major battle took place; Caesar achieved his victory by cutting the enemy off from his supplies and so forcing surrender.

Notice the flexibility of these formations, with cohorts being drawn up in two or three lines. The reference to the second line acting as support for the first is reflected in other accounts. In many of these accounts the first two lines form the actual fighting force while the third line acts as a reserve. Interestingly, this mirrors the original manipular formation where the *triarii* were used only in emergencies.

> Afranius' battle line consisted of cohorts from five legions arranged in two lines; behind them were cohorts of auxiliary infantry. Caesar's formation was in three lines; four cohorts from each of the five legions were stationed in the front line, with three cohorts in the second line acting as support. The third line again consisted of three cohorts from each of these legions. The archers and slingers held the middle of the line and the cavalry guarded the flanks.

133 CAESAR, *GALLIC WAR* 2.25

In 57 Caesar was in the process of subjugating northern Gaul. After subduing a number of tribes he was ambushed by the Nervii, who were fiercely opposed to his presence in northern Gaul. It was only the timely arrival of his legate Labienus and his Tenth Legion that turned the tide.

As the passage makes clear, Caesar's cohorts had become massed together and so could not use their swords effectively. The order to open the maniples must imply room to do so and so supports the theory that the cohorts did not form a continuous front but that there were gaps between the units, most likely equivalent to the frontage of the unit.

> After encouraging the Tenth Legion, Caesar set out for his right wing, where he saw that his men were under pressure. The standards had become bunched together, as well as the soldiers themselves. The crowding hindered their ability to fight, and all of the centurions of the fourth cohort had fallen with the standard bearer. The remaining cohorts had also had almost all their centurions killed or wounded.... With the enemy continually pressing up the hill and attacking the flanks, the situation was grave; nor was there any hope for reinforcements. Caesar grabbed a shield from a soldier in the rear, since he had come without one, and moved forward to the front of the battle line. Calling on the centurions by name and encouraging the others he ordered the soldiers to advance and open ranks so that they could use their swords more easily.

The end of the velites

In the mid-second century Roman light-armed troops, the *velites*, had been drawn from the youngest and the poorest of citizens (see p. 91). During the rest of the century there are references to them in Spain and in the eastern Mediterranean. It is difficult to gauge how effective they were. Their main functions, such as screening or operating in conjunction with the cavalry, were never decisive on the battlefield. They could contribute to victory, as they did at Ilipa and in Macedonia in 199 (see p. 92 and **119**), but for the most part they seem to have played a secondary role. One measure of their lack of effectiveness may be the increased use of lightly equipped legionary troops for tasks that would normally have been assigned to the *velites*. The last firm indication of their presence in Roman armies is in Sallust's description of the war against Jugurtha. Frontinus mentions their presence in a battle at Orchomenus in Boeotia in 86, though some scholars have dismissed this as an error on Frontinus' part, as his general level of accuracy is not high.

Their disappearance is usually ascribed to Marius, since the last trustworthy reference to the *velites* is under his predecessor, Metellus, in the Jugurthine War, and the tradition ascribes a number of other military reforms to him. However, there is no explicit reference in the sources to such a reform and importantly all of the known Marian reforms deal with the legions and not light-armed troops. One explicit reference we have to a reform of the light-armed by Marius is the substitution of a rectangular shield similar to the legionary shield in place of the traditional round shield or *parma* (see p. 91). Such a reform would fit with the general standardization of equipment among legionaries in the same period.

It is more likely that the lowering of the census rating (see pp. 197f.) was the basic reason for the disappearance of the *velites*. By the time of Marius the census rating had been lowered so far that the pool of available manpower must have been extremely limited. Presumably, the pay and conditions of service as well as the higher prestige of the legions would have channeled recruits away from service as light-armed skirmishers. It might well be that there was no single measure that abolished the *velites*, but that given recruitment problems they slowly disappeared. This might explain Frontinus' reference to their presence at Orchomenus. By this date it might still have been possible to levy them when the occasion demanded. Their complete disappearance was made possible by the availability of other sources of recruitment for such troops.

The *velites* were replaced by non-Roman forces drawn from provincials and allies. Rome had a long history in Italy of using allied manpower in its armies. In doing so it followed the standard practice of this period in the Mediterranean. We have little information on the composition of Roman armies in the First Punic War, but by the Second Punic War Scipio and other commanders were making extensive use of local and allied levies, especially of Numidian horse in the later stages of the war. This policy was standard practice for the rest of the Republican period and made particularly necessary by the granting of citizenship to most of Italy south of the Po after the Social War of 90–88.

The traditional use of non-Roman troops must have accelerated the disappearance of the *velites*. The use of non-Roman forces brought advantages, as some of these troops had specialized skills in the use of the sling or in archery that Roman troops did not possess. There seems to have been a sizeable increase in the use of these contingents in the armies of the civil war period.

Whatever their skills, they were often of doubtful worth, and the Romans seem to have been unconcerned about their fate. Appian, in his account of Pharsalus in 48, notes that they were considered of small importance to the outcome of the conflict. There is little information on the organization of these troops. There are some indications that at least a portion of such units had Roman officers with titles similar to those in use in the legions. Until the end of the Republic such units were raised only for specific campaigns and were not assigned a permanent status.

The disappearance of Roman cavalry

The disappearance of Roman light-armed troops was paralleled by the disappearance of Roman and Italian allied cavalry. Both developments are equally obscure given the state of our evidence. Roman and Italian cavalry continued in use in Spain as late as 139 BC. There is some rather uncertain evidence for Roman and better evidence for Italian cavalry in action during the war against Jugurtha, and there may be evidence for Roman cavalry in action during the war against the Cimbri in 102. Attempts have been made to see references to them in the 90s, but none have been convincing. Certainly, by the time of Caesar's campaigns in Gaul, Roman and Italian cavalry have vanished from the battlefield and have been replaced by cavalry drawn from allies, subject peoples, and mercenaries.

Any explanation of this development in the absence of firm evidence is problematic and cannot be explained in the same way as the disappearance of Roman light-armed forces, as the social and political factors are strikingly different in the two cases. The character of *equites* had changed since their origin as Rome's cavalry force. There still existed *equites*, with a public horse granted by the state, who by this time were mainly senators' sons. Probably the majority of men who qualified as *equites* in the late Republic did so on the basis of their personal wealth, and within this group a smaller subset acted as *publicani* who undertook state contracts, some of them extremely lucrative. Many of these men would not have been physically fit for service. Nonetheless, there may have been as many as 18,000 who were capable of active service. Sons of senators and others who wished to pursue a political career were obligated to serve, as there was a ten-year requirement for military service prior to standing for political office. Yet despite this incentive and the prestige attached to military service the cavalry had ceased to function by approximately the end of the second century.

The practice of using non-Italian cavalry on a large scale dates from as early as the Second Punic War when Scipio Africanus employed large contingents of Spanish and Numidian cavalry in the war against Carthage. From this period it became standard practice to employ non-Roman cavalry of various types in Roman armies despite problems created by repeated instances of disloyalty and desertion. It has been argued that Roman cavalry in the Second Punic War had performed poorly and this was the decisive factor in the decision to employ foreign cavalry exclusively. Recently, an argument has been made in favor of the effectiveness of Roman cavalry, and whatever the exact merits of the case the Romans continued to employ their own cavalry for another century. It therefore seems unlikely that the question of military efficiency is the key to this problem. One other possibility has been suggested, and that is that the manpower needs of the Social War of 90–88 had diverted *equites* into the legions. There is evidence for the use of foreign cavalry, specifically Numidian, in the course of the war. Unfortunately, there is little evidence for equestrians serving in the legions, and it seems unlikely given the social differences between infantry and cavalry that *equites* would have done such service if they could have avoided it. It leaves unexplained the absence of such cavalry after the end of the Social War. What the war did bring about was the disappearance of Italian cavalry with the extension of Roman citizenship to most of Italy.

By the last century BC military service for *equites* seeking entrance into politics decreased in importance despite its continuing significance for men who had attained the highest offices. The evidence for the later decades of the first century indicates that military experience still retained some importance for those with political ambitions, but that such service was often limited to two or three years serving as a military tribune, a member of a commander's suite, or a legate, and not in the cavalry. Such positions were few in number, so only a small percentage of *equites* saw military service.

Evidently, the military prestige that resulted from cavalry service was no longer of great importance. What is difficult to explain is why this should be so. There were now alternative career paths that brought prestige and office. Cicero, consul in 63, is perhaps the best-known example of a man who achieved political success with almost no military experience. It may be that the growing professionalism of the army in the course of the later second century had something to do with this change. Professionalism in general was antithetic to the values of the Roman upper class. Another possible cause is the fact that such service was increasingly performed in this period in overseas theaters and in combination with foreign cavalry. Such service would be less visible and so perhaps less important than it had been earlier. The association of foreign troops would also have acted to diminish the status of cavalry service. The replacement of cavalry service by positions that conferred the power to command would point in the same direction. Nonetheless, it remains difficult to understand how the voters themselves, who were increasingly subject to greater demands for military service, tolerated its decline among the ruling elite. Perhaps it is best seen as part of the tendency in Rome and Italy to avoid military service except in exceptional situations such as the civil war, a trend that finally culminated in non-Italians forming the bulk of Rome's forces by the end of the first century AD. It is likely that the disappearance of the cavalry was part of this larger change and the result of official action.

134 SALLUST, *THE WAR AGAINST JUGURTHA* 95.1

Lucius Cornelius Sulla, quaestor in 107, arrived in Numidia either that year or early in 106 with the force described in the passage. There are possible references to Roman cavalry at several points in Sallust's narrative of the war, but his uncertain use of military terminology makes it impossible to be sure that they served in this war. This is the last definite reference to Italian cavalry serving in the field.

> While these events were underway Lucius Sulla, who was quaestor, arrived in camp with a great number of Latin and allied cavalry which he had been left in Rome to assemble.

135 CAESAR, *GALLIC WAR* 1.42

The events narrated in the following passage belong to the spring of 58, Caesar's first year in Gaul. Ariovistus, king of the Germanic Suebi, had crossed the Rhine and launched a series of successful attacks on Gallic tribes in eastern Gaul. The tribes' appeals to Caesar gave him the opportunity to check Ariovistus' expansion. Caesar's victory over his forces in Alsace ended any further threat from the Suebi.

The text supplies evidence that Caesar did not employ Roman cavalry. This conclusion is supported by the absence of any authoritative evidence for Roman cavalry in any of Caesar's campaigns. *Equites* still served in Caesar's army, but as officers and legates, not as cavalry.

> Caesar and Ariovistus fixed the day for their conference for the fifth day after [Ariovistus' emissaries had requested a meeting from Caesar]. In the meanwhile they often sent representatives to each other. Ariovistus asked Caesar not to bring infantry with him to the meeting, alleging that he feared an ambush; let both sides come with horsemen; otherwise he declared he would not come. Caesar did not wish the conference to be cancelled for such a reason and, since he was afraid to entrust himself to his Gallic cavalry, he judged it the most expedient course to remove all the horses from the Gallic cavalry and give them to the soldiers of the Tenth Legion, in whom he had the greatest trust, so as to have the most faithful guard if there should be need of it.

Booty

For Rome, as for other ancient states, war was an economic activity as well as a political one. One of the expected consequences of victory was the appropriation of wealth by the victors. One method of transfer was the confiscation of enemy land and its conversion into Roman public land or its distribution in the form of individual allotments or in the form of colonial settlements. In addition to land, movable wealth in the form of precious metals or other property was confiscated as booty. The booty could be kept in its original form or sold at auction by the quaestor and converted into money. The latter procedure was often necessary, as a substantial portion of the booty was in human form and profits could only be realized by selling the captives into slavery.

All booty was in theory collected by the army and became the property of the army's commander under the name of *manubiae*. The commander had the right to distribute this booty as he saw fit. In theory, the commander could retain all of it for personal use, but this was rarely the case. Usually, he kept a portion and the rest was distributed to the soldiers, and a portion was normally deposited in the state treasury. On occasion generals chose not to distribute any of it to their troops. Livy records that in 410, because of hostility between consul Valerius and his troops, Valerius ordered all of the plunder to be sold and the proceeds to be deposited in the state treasury, a step that caused great anger among his troops.

Booty was an obvious source of wealth for the commander, but it is only in the second century and only in a few instances that generals are said to have mounted expeditions for financial gain. Such a motive may have been more important in the early Republic, when the elite had relatively little personal wealth, and in the later Republic, when the costs of political competition had risen dramatically.

There were other ways that booty could be used for personal ends. Its distribution to the commander's officers and friends created personal ties and mutual obligations. Booty was also used to publicize a general's success. A number of altars and temples were built from the proceeds of successful warfare. For instance, in 146 at the successful termination of the Fourth Macedonian War, the victor, Caecilius Metellus, built two temples honoring Juno and Jupiter in the Campus Martius out of his share of the booty, and in 42 Munatius Plancus constructed the temple of Saturn to serve as a state treasury out of the booty he had won while fighting in Gaul. Booty also played an important role in the triumphal procession. Its importance to the people is illustrated by Livy in his account of Papirius Cursor's triumph as consul in 293. Livy mentions people assessing the richness of the spoils taken from the Samnites and comparing them to the booty displayed in previous triumphs.

Booty was an important incentive for the troops. Pay for the average soldier was regular but low. The distribution of booty offered the only opportunity for a substantial profit. The desire for booty occasionally harmed military discipline and the troops' safety. During the Gallic revolt of 52 Caesar warned his legates not to allow their men to advance too far in search of plunder; despite these orders the troops did so, with disastrous result. It could also act to stimulate the desire for battle. At Telamon in 225 the Romans found the appearance of the Gallic chieftains intimidating, but their enthusiasm for battle was rekindled by the sight of the gold collars and armbands worn by the Gauls. In arguing for war in Sicily in 264, the consul Appius Claudius pointed to the prospect of the booty that the war would bring.

During Rome's expansion in Italy, the distribution of land and the planting of colonies offered the most important financial incentives. After Italy had been subdued, distributions of money from the sale of booty assumed a growing importance. In the course of the second century the amount distributed to the troops after a victory rose steadily. The distribution normally included a bonus amounting to double the normal pay, which increased its worth. The value of such distributions to centurions and other lower-grade officers was multiplied by the fact they received double or triple the amounts distributed to the common soldiers. The importance of booty is clear from the fact that in the second century difficulties in recruiting were for the most part confined to campaigns in Spain and the West, where the soldiers knew there would be little booty available. The possibility of acquiring rich booty in the third war against Carthage spurred widespread volunteering, while fifteen years later Scipio Aemilianus was hard pressed to find soldiers to fight at Numantia in Spain. There were other motives at work besides the financial, such as patriotism and the attractions of adventure and fighting, and other considerations could sometimes override the attractions of profit. Crassus, despite the obvious opportunities for wealth that a campaign in the East offered, had to resort to conscription to fill his armies for the war against Parthia in 53, as did Caesar in the course of his campaigns in Gaul.

Booty also served as an incentive for the Italian allies. It gave allied cities the chance to recoup some of the expenses involved in supplying troops to Rome and offered their troops the chance for extra income. This would have been of importance, as they could not participate in the land distributions of the late Republican period, which were open to citizens only. The allies normally received a percentage of the booty, although they had no legal claim to it. There is no definite evidence of the proportion of the booty that was allocated to the allies. What evidence there is indicates that allied soldiers received the same amount as their Roman counterparts. In addition, there were always opportunities for an individual soldier to amass plunder on his own.

The pillaging of captured cities

136 POLYBIUS, *HISTORIES* 10.16.1–17.3

Polybius' description of the sack of New Carthage by Scipio Africanus' forces in 209 probably represents the standard procedure the Romans used. It is likely that the same method was followed after the capture of an enemy camp and in the aftermath of battle. It is clearly idealized, and it would have been hard to stringently enforce in the confusion that normally followed the capture of a city.

The division of the booty into equal shares and its distribution among the soldiers give a false impression on two points. First, the distribution of the booty was the prerogative of the commander, and we know of several occasions when troops received nothing. Second, the amount distributed varied according to rank. In addition, the booty was often not put up for sale but given directly to the men. The oath referred to must be the one in which soldiers swore not to steal (see **98**).

On the following day the baggage of the Carthaginian troops and all of the possessions of the citizens and craftsmen were gathered in the market place. The military tribunes then divided it among their respective legions according to the Roman custom. The following is a description of the Roman procedure after the capture of cities. Either a number of men in accordance with the size of the town are assigned to the collection of booty from each maniple or a number of maniples [from each legion] are allotted the task. They never assign more than half of the army to this duty. The rest remain on guard in formation, sometimes outside the town and at times within it at the ready. Their armies usually have two legions, as well as an equal number of allies; rarely, the armies have four Roman legions. Those assigned to gathering the booty take it to their respective legion, and after the booty has been sold the military tribunes distribute an equal share to each soldier, not only to those on guard but also those guarding the tents and to the sick and those on detached duty. I have already written in detail in my section on the Roman constitution about the fact that no one appropriates the booty for himself but keeps faith with the oath they all have sworn when they first assembled in camp at the point when they were setting out on campaign.

So, whenever half the army sets out to pillage, the remainder remain in formation, protecting those involved in the plundering. In this way the Roman force is protected against individual rapacity and no one abandons his position, as there is no mistrust about the booty, but all have confidence, both those on guard and those involved in the pillaging. The absence of such confidence often harms armies.

Since most men undergo suffering and danger for the sake of gain, it is clear that whenever the opportunity arises it is unlikely that those left on guard or in the camp will refrain [from pillaging], since the booty belongs to the one who seizes it. Even if a watchful king or general orders the booty to be brought together in common, nevertheless, certainly, each considers as his own what he can conceal. So, when the majority begin pillaging, commanders are unable to exercise control and the whole army is endangered.

Sharing booty with allies

137 THE ROMAN–AETOLIAN TREATY OF 212 OR 211, LINES 4–15

The alliance with the Aetolian League dates to the Second Punic War and was designed as a counter to the treaty Philip V of Macedonia concluded with Hannibal in 215 after the battle of Cannae. That alliance created another front, where the Romans were mostly active at sea while the Aetolians conducted the land campaign. This treaty is the oldest extant copy of a Roman treaty, as well as the earliest concluded with a Greek people. The Roman share of the movable booty is to consist of all of the booty from cities they had taken themselves and probably a 50 percent share of booty from cities captured by joint actions with the Aetolians.

The concern for booty evident in this treaty also appears in the oldest quoted treaty we have between Rome and the Latin League and is a common feature of ancient military alliances.

> If the Romans take by force any of the cities of these peoples, let these cities and their lands belong to the people of the Aetolians as far as the Roman people is concerned.
>
> What the Romans take apart from the cities and their land belongs to the Romans. Those cities which the Romans and Aetolians capture in common shall be the property of the Aetolians as far as the Roman people is concerned. Whatever is seized apart from the cities themselves shall be shared in common.

The spolia opima

The *spolia opima*, triumphal or supreme spoils, form a special class within the larger category of booty. They are the arms and equipment taken from a slain enemy commander and could only be won by the supreme Roman commander who killed him in single combat. There is some evidence that at one time other officers might have been eligible to win the *spolia opima*.

Tradition records only three men as dedicators of these spoils, Romulus, Cornelius Cossus in a mid-fifth-century war against Veii, and the consul M. Claudius Marcellus as the result of a battle with the Gauls in 222 BC. The last two dedications are historical, while the mythical dedication of Rome's first king served as an explanatory myth for the practice.

The spoils were suspended from an oak frame, a practice which has parallels elsewhere in the Mediterranean, and dedicated in the temple of Jupiter Feretrius on the Capitoline hill. The custom may have had its origin in warfare between aristocratic bands in the archaic period.

138 PLUTARCH, *MARCELLUS* 8.1–3

Marcus Claudius Marcellus had defeated and killed in single combat the king of the Insubrian Gauls, Viridomar, at Clastidium in 222. Marcellus seems to have had a penchant for single combat and fought other duels as well.

> Marcellus provided the most welcome and unusual spectacle bearing the arms of the barbarian to the god. He cut the trunk of a tall, straight, and slender oak tree and, working it, he attached and adjusted each piece, fastening the armor in order. As the procession began to move, Marcellus took up the trophy and mounted the chariot, presenting the most impressive and beautiful trophy-bearing figure of his time; he passed through the city.... Proceeding in this manner he entered the temple of Jupiter Feretrius and set up and consecrated his spoils, the third and last time this was done down to my own time.

Military rewards and honors

The Roman military system was underpinned by an elaborate system of rewards and punishments and, as Polybius states, they played a key role in maintaining discipline and promoting the values essential for military success. It is indicative of the importance of warfare in Roman political and social life that the elaborate system of rewards has no parallel in Greek armies. Though there were various forms of public recognition for military prowess among the Greeks, the only comparably developed system of reward was for athletics victories.

The system included both tangible and symbolic rewards, but it was the latter that conferred on the receiver the highest social status. The same system also characterized Greek athletic prizes. Such awards conferred social status. In a community that highly prized success in warfare, such status could be more valuable to the individual than material rewards. In the case of the elite the quest for such rewards also had tangible consequences in the form of political success, but it also must have operated at less exalted levels. Tangible rewards included gifts of money, promotion, and increased rations. For instance, promotion to the rank of centurion meant a fifteen-fold increase in pay and a larger share of booty. Military decorations and rewards offered those below the elite a chance for social mobility not normally open to them.

The awarding of Roman military decorations seems to have first developed as an *ad hoc* system during the Republic, with the type of reward given dependent on what had been done and not on the rank or position of the doer. However, by the last third of the second century an elaborate system had arisen, which attained full maturity in the first century. Awards were now dependent on both the act and the rank of the man who performed it. It has rightly been suggested that such an evolution is tied to the parallel development of a professional army, and there are analogies to such a system in the modern British army.

The decorations or *dona militaria* fall into two groups in the developed system, the crowns listed in the Gellius passage (**140**) and other lesser symbolic rewards. These were the *hasta pura*, a full-size replica of a spear, torques or collars, *phalerae* or disk-shaped metallic ornaments, the *phiale*, which may have been some sort of dish, and the *vexillum*, a miniature representation of a military standard. The primary evidence for these lesser decorations is furnished by gravestones from the Empire and indicates a variety of forms and lack of standardization.

In origin most forms of the decoration seem to have been of foreign inspiration. It has been suggested that the crown has a Greek origin. The torque or collar is found among many barbarian peoples, in particular the Gauls, with whom the Romans fought a long and costly series of wars. It may be that it began its career as a form of booty. The *hasta pura* may have owed its origin to the existence of the phalanx as Rome's first fighting force. In addition, in the imperial period there was a category of rewards given not to the individuals but to whole units, such as the grant of various honorary epithets associating the unit with the reigning emperor or imperial house.

These rewards were open only to citizens in the imperial period. In the Republic there is evidence for at least occasional grants to non-Romans. For instance, in 203 Scipio Africanus gave the Numidian king Masinissa a gold crown and dish as well as various Roman magisterial emblems. The regularization and incorporation of non-Romans as regular troops ended this procedure. However, by the first decades of the third century the Romans themselves had abandoned the practice. Rewards remained, but they were no longer symbolic but of a practical kind, such as promotion and monetary bonuses. There is no easy explanation for their disappearance. It has been suggested that it is connected with the extension of citizenship to almost all of the inhabitants of the Empire in 212, which would have made any soldier eligible and would have created an immense increase in the costs of such awards. It is perhaps more likely that the decreasing role of Rome as imperial capital and center of the Empire and the long prevalence of local recruiting deprived the older symbolic system of meaning for both the officer corps and private soldiers.

139 POLYBIUS, *HISTORIES* 6.39.1–11

Polybius' discussion of military decorations follows his description of the Roman system of military punishments. This passage provides the first reliable evidence for such awards. Polybius' javelin must be the *hasta pura*. He gives it the Gallic name of *gaison*, which other sources describe as a heavy javelin of Gallic origin. *Phalerae* were also used by cavalry as decoration for their mounts. The gold crown is the mural crown which by the early Empire was given only to senatorial commanders, equestrians, and centurions as a decoration without any connection to actual sieges. The crown given to those who saved the life of a citizen is the civic crown. It was second in prestige to the siege crown and came to be used as part of imperial symbolism.

> They also have a commendable way of encouraging the young men to brave danger. Whenever there is a battle and some of their troops have distinguished themselves, the general calls an assembly of the army and brings forward those who he thinks have distinguished themselves. He first speaks in praise of each man's courage and mentions anything else they have done that merits mention. After this he gives a *gaison* to the man who has wounded the enemy; to the soldier who has taken an enemy prisoner and stripped him he gives a *phiale* if he belongs to the infantry or *phalerae* if he is a cavalry trooper, though originally the award was a javelin. These awards are not made if the enemy is wounded or stripped in the course of a regular battle or in the storming of a city, but for actions in skirmishes or other such occasions when there is no need for single combat. The recipients must engage willingly and deliberately.
>
> They give a gold crown to those who are the first to mount the wall during the capture of a city. In the same way, the consul marks out with gifts those who have shielded and saved the lives of citizens or allies. Those

who have been saved willingly crown their preservers, and in the case of those who are unwilling the military tribunes act as judges and compel them to crown those who have saved them. They pay reverence to such a man as a father for the rest of their lives and must treat him in all ways as a parent. With such inducements they incite to rivalry and imitation in war not only their listeners but also those who remain at home, since those who obtain such gifts, apart from their fame in the army and their immediate renown at home, when they return home are especially distinguished in religious parades, as only those honored with these decorations for bravery by the consuls are entitled to wear them. They hang up the booty they have won in the most visible places in their homes, using them as signs and tokens of their bravery. With such attention and enthusiasm given to military rewards and punishments, it is no surprise that Roman wars end successfully and brilliantly.

140 AULUS GELLIUS, *ATTIC NIGHTS* 5.6–5.26

For the triumph, see pp. 218ff. The triumphal crown was originally made of laurel leaves. After the restriction of the triumph to the emperor or members of his family, triumphal ornaments or regalia were given in its place; it may be at this stage that the gold crown was substituted for the laurel.

The siege crown was one of the most prestigious awards, and a late-first-century AD source records only six recipients. Given the nature of the award it was normally given only to commanders. Gellius' reference to Q. Fabius Maximus is to an award dated to 203, the year that Hannibal left Italy, by another source.

Caecilius Statius is a mid-second-century BC playwright. Gellius' quote is from an unknown play.

Masurius Sabinus was an important lawyer and legal writer of the mid-first century.

The allusion to Cicero is to his efforts as consul in 63 BC which led to the suppression of Cataline's conspiracy. Lucius Gellius is Lucius Gellius Poplicola, one of the censors of 72 BC.

The naval crown must have originated during the First Punic War, as this was the first time Rome was engaged in major naval battles. The only certain recipient in the Republican period was Marcus Agrippa for his naval victory at Naulochos in 36 BC. It survived into the imperial period, but had lost all connection with its naval origins.

Marcus Licinius Crassus' refusal of the myrtle crown was in the aftermath of his victory over Spartacus in 70 BC.

Cato's speech was occasioned by Fulvius Nobilior's campaign as consul in 189 against the Galatians in central Asia Minor. The remarks illustrate the importance of these awards.

There are many military crowns of different types. We have learned that the most admired ones seem to be the following: the triumphal, siege, civic, mural, camp, and naval crowns. In addition there is the so-called ovation crown, and likewise the olive crown worn by those who have not engaged in battle but have obtained a triumph.

The triumphal crowns given to commanders are made of gold. This is commonly known as "triumph gold." In ancient times they were made of laurel and later began to be made of gold.

The siege crown is bestowed by those freed from a siege on the commander who liberated them. This is a grass crown, and the custom is observed that it should be made of grass which grows in that place where the besieged were shut in. The Senate and Roman people gave this grass crown to Q. Fabius Maximus in the Second Punic War because he freed the city of Rome from an enemy siege.

"The civic crown is given by a citizen to another citizen as recognition of the preservation of his life and safety. It is made from edible oak leaf because the earliest food and sustenance came from the oak." It used to be made from the evergreen oak that is most closely related to the edible species, as is clear from these lines from a certain comedy of Caecilius: "They pass by [he said] with crowns and cloaks of evergreen oaks, you gods!"

However, Masurius Sabinus in the eleventh book of his *Books of Memoranda* says that the civic crown was customarily given when the man who has saved a citizen at the same time also has killed the enemy and had maintained his place on the field of battle. He says the civic crown cannot be awarded otherwise. Nevertheless, Tiberius Caesar was asked whether a civic crown could be given to a man who saved a citizen's life in battle and had killed two of the enemy, but had not maintained his position which had then been occupied by the enemy. The emperor ruled that such an individual could receive the civic crown because it was clear that he had rescued a citizen from a position that was so dangerous that even brave fighters could not hold it. Lucius Gellius, a man who had held the censorship, recommended in the Senate that Cicero receive the crown from the state on the grounds that through his efforts that most horrible conspiracy of Cataline was uncovered and punished.

The mural crown is that crown which is given by a commander to the man who first climbs the wall and forces his way into a hostile city. For this reason it is decorated with representations of battlements. The camp crown is given by the general to the first man to enter the enemy's camp, and this crown has a representation of a palisade. The naval crown is that given to the first man to board an enemy ship under arms in a naval battle and is embellished with the prows of ships. The mural, camp, and naval crowns are made of gold.

The crown awarded for an ovation is made of myrtle leaves and is worn by commanders who enter the city while celebrating an ovation. Such an ovation is celebrated in place of a triumph when the war is not

216

declared in due form or fought with a suitable enemy, or the enemy is of low status or is not suitable, such as wars against slaves or pirates or because of a speedy surrender. Such victory is known as dustless and bloodless. They believed that the leaves sacred to Venus were appropriate in such a case, as it was a triumph of Venus and not of Mars. Marcus Crassus refused a myrtle crown on the occasion when he was celebrating an ovation after the servile war and saw to it through his influence that a decree of the Senate was passed that crowned him with laurel and not with myrtle.

Marcus Cato charged Fulvius Nobilior because he had given crowns to his solders for the most insignificant reasons in his quest for popularity. I quote Cato's very words: "Now in the first place who ever saw anyone given a crown when the town was not captured or the enemy's camp was not burnt?" But the Fulvius against whom Cato said these things had given awards to soldiers who had been involved in building a rampart or digging a well.

141 CAESAR, *CIVIL WAR* 3.56

After the outbreak of the civil war in January of 49 and Caesar's lightning invasion of Italy, Pompey had crossed to Greece to organize his forces to confront Caesar. In early 48 Caesar crossed the Adriatic to seize the coastal ports of Apollonia and Dyrrachium on its eastern shore. Successful at Apollonia he was anticipated by Pompey at Dyrrachium. In response, Caesar brought up his army and blockaded the Pompeian forces there after both sides had constructed fortifications. The blockade was not wholly successful, as Caesar could not cut off Pompey on the seaward side and began to suffer severe supply difficulties. Pompey launched a major attack to try to end Caesar's blockade on the landward side and was repulsed with heavy losses, but the action was costly for Caesar. The passage below narrates several incidents from this action. A second attack by Pompey allowed his army to break through to the east and the rich grain-growing areas of Thessaly.

M. Cassius Scaeva's name is found on a sling bullet from the siege of Perusia in 41/40 as *primipilus* of the Twelfth Legion. Scaeva's rewards were substantial. His cash bonus was fifty-six times the annual pay of a common soldier. His promotion to the leading centurion of a legion, a post which was normally held for a single year, brought him prestige and standing as well as substantial financial benefits in the form of increased pay and booty shares.

On that day the six battles took place, three at Dyrrachium and three at the fortifications. When a balance sheet is drawn up for all of them we find that approximately 2,000 Pompeian soldiers fell and many veteran volunteers and centurions [in that number was Valerius Flaccus, the son of Lucius, who had been praetor in Asia] and six standards were captured.

Not more than twenty of our men were missing in all of these engagements. But in the fort there was no soldier unwounded, and four centurions from a single cohort were permanently blinded. And when some of them wished to show proof of their efforts and the danger they had undergone, they told Caesar that about 30,000 arrows had been shot into the fort, and in the shield of the centurion Scaeva which was brought to Caesar there were 120 holes. On account of his services both to Caesar himself and for the benefit of the state Caesar presented him with 200,000 asses and after praising him declared him promoted from a centurion of the eighth cohort to the leading centurion of the legion. There was general agreement that it was mostly through his efforts that the fort had been saved. Later Caesar amply rewarded the cohorts with double pay, grain and clothing rations, and military decorations.

The greatest of all awards: the triumph

The most prestigious of all Roman awards, the triumph, may have been in origin a religious ceremony of purification connected with the blood guilt that resulted from warfare. Its origin and early development are obscure. Greek and Etruscan elements have been identified, although Etruscan influence is dominant. This is hardly surprising, as Etruscan dress and symbols frequently appear in connection with various Roman offices. Etruscan elements may have been assimilated in the period of the last kings of Rome, who had ties to Etruria (see p. 9). The dress of the triumphator has elements in common with that of the Roman kings. But there is no compelling evidence of an Etruscan origin for the ceremony and it may well have been a Latin rite which absorbed foreign elements. Some support for this view can be found in the fact that the ceremony could also be celebrated outside of Rome on the Alban Mount, the site sacred to a number of Latin communities. The rite is also closely linked to the chief god of the Roman state, Jupiter Optimus Maximus, and his temple on the Capitoline hill. Some elements such as the palm-embroidered tunic and the scepter of the triumphing general are attributes of Jupiter. The triumph is part of a set of religious ceremonies pertaining to war. It is also a secular display of the victorious general's prowess that highlights the success of the triumphing general.

The celebration consisted of three parts. The first centered on the army and its commander. In an assembly in the Campus Martius outside the religious boundary of the city, the army hailed its victorious commander and he in turn celebrated the courage and prowess of his army by singling out individuals for praise and conferred prizes and awards. The second part was a procession which wound its way from the southern end of the Campus Martius through the Porta Triumphalis (Gate of Triumph), passed through the vegetable and cattle markets to the Circus Maximus, then around the Palatine hill, through the Forum, and made its way up the Capitoline hill to the temple of Jupiter Optimus Maximus. This circuit was traditional and goes back to the origins of the ceremony.

The procession was divided into three parts: first came the booty and prisoners, then the triumphing general accompanied by magistrates and various officials, and finally the army or that portion of it which had been assembled for the parade. At the center, framed as it were by the spoils he had won and the army that had helped to win them, stood the general. Riding in a four-horse chariot, he was dressed in a purple tunic decorated with gold thread, with a purple toga similarly decorated worn over it. He carried a laurel branch in one hand and an ivory scepter crowned with an eagle in the other. His face was painted red and on his head he wore a laurel crown, also worn by the other participants. A late source claims that a slave stood behind him, holding a gold crown over his head, repeating the words, "Look behind you; remember you are a man." His younger children rode with him in the chariot and his older ones, as Domitian does in the Josephus passage (**144**), rode beside the chariot on horseback. The ceremony not only highlighted the achievements of the celebrant but also brought glory to his family. At the rear of the procession marched the victorious army, wearing its military decorations and often singing ribald songs such as that sung by the soldiers of Caesar in his triumph over the Gauls in 46 BC when his soldiers made jokes about Caesar's homosexual activities. The goal of the procession was the Capitoline temples of Jupiter, and a sacrifice of white oxen was made to the god as a thanks-offering for bringing victory. The scale of the celebration must have varied widely, and the sources single out especially magnificent triumphs such as those of the consul Manlius Vulso in 189 over the Galatians of central Asia Minor or Scipio's triumph at the end of the Second Punic War in 201. It appears that normally the triumph lasted for one day, but longer ones are recorded. For instance, in August of 29 BC Augustus celebrated a triumph over Egypt lasting for three days.

The granting of the triumph and the granting of funds for it were normally in the hands of the Senate. But the fact that generals could celebrate triumphs on the Alban Mount on their own initiative if the Senate refused to sanction them points to a ceremony that had originally been held at the discretion of the commander. In the mid-Republic the magistrate or promagistrate making application to the Senate had to fulfill very precise conditions. He had to have been fighting under his own *imperium* and auspices. The victory must have been won in the course of a formally declared war against a suitable enemy. Commanders in wars fought against slaves or pirates were not eligible for this honor, so Crassus was granted only an ovation for his victory over Spartacus. The sources note that 5,000 of the enemy had to be killed in a single battle as a further qualification. The stress on direct confrontation and defeat of the enemy also appears in the requirement that fighting must have taken place; a bloodless conquest earned only a lesser award.

The fame and prestige that accompanied a triumph supplied strong incentives to undertake campaigning, as Polybius notes. There are occasional references to commanders, especially in Spain and Liguria, deliberately starting a war in order to earn a triumph. Cicero's labored efforts to gain a triumph for minor actions while governor of Cilicia in 51–50 are evidence of the importance of the prestige that a triumph could bring.

Nothing is more indicative of the prestige and propaganda value of the triumph than its gradual monopolization in the imperial period by the emperor. The last triumph celebrated by a senator who was not a member of the imperial house was that of L. Cornelius Balbus, proconsul of Africa in 19 BC. From this point until 71 AD triumphs could only be celebrated by the emperor and members of the imperial house. After the triumph of Vespasian and Titus in that year the circle became even more restricted, with only the reigning emperor able to celebrate a triumph.

Some compensation for the loss of the right to the triumph existed in the form of a lesser triumph, the ovation, which lacked much of the magnificence of the full ceremony. The celebrant walked instead of riding in a chariot, wore a crown of myrtle instead of laurel, and wore a differently decorated toga. However, the last ovation granted to a senator outside the imperial family was in 47 AD, awarded to Aulus Plautius for his part in the Emperor Claudius' British campaign. One other substitute award that developed during the early imperial period was the presentation of triumphal ornaments. The recipient received the tokens of a general, celebrating the triumph without actually holding the ceremony. But this too disappeared after the middle of the second century AD. The last recorded triumph was that of the Emperor Diocletian celebrating a victory over the Persians on December 17, 303. The traditional ceremony was too closely tied to pagan religious ceremonies and to the city of Rome to survive the rise of Christianity and the removal of power to Constantinople. Celebrations of victory survived that bore some relation to the earlier triumph but had shed many of the traditional elements. Homage was now paid to Christ and not Jupiter, and new elements were introduced such as the performance of public panegyrics and the holding of circus games and were held elsewhere than at Rome.

142 POLYBIUS, *HISTORIES* 6.15.8

Polybius' generalization is too broad even for his own time. There were triumphs such as that of Appius Claudius Pulcher in 146 that were held despite senatorial disapproval and were recorded in official triumphal records. In addition, in the middle Republic such triumphs could be held on the Alban Mount at the personal expense of the triumphator. However, the Senate's approval was needed in the case of a proconsul whose *imperium* would normally lapse when he entered the city.

> The ceremony which the Romans call the triumph by means of which the evidence of the exploits of Rome's generals passes under the inspection of its citizens cannot be undertaken as it should be or even celebrated at all unless the Senate permits it and provides funds for it.

Ioannes Zonaras, a Byzantine epitomater, wrote a universal history to AD 1118 which relied heavily on the third-century history of Cassius Dio for events down to AD 235. His work is a compilation whose value is dependent on the quality of his sources.

The passage offers a general description of the triumph, but there are a few errors. The assertion that the people as well as the Senate granted a triumph is inaccurate (see p. 219). In addition, his attempt to standardize the form of various crowns does not fit the archaeological evidence, which shows a basic pattern with numerous variations. In terms of prestige the siege crown outranked the civic, despite Zonaras' assertion to the contrary.

The wording of the public slave's declaration to the triumphator is given incompletely. The slave added "Remember you are mortal." It was less a prophylactic against excessive pride than an attempt to turn aside any jealousy the gods might feel and so protect the general and the state. It was not a bell or a whip but rather a phallus that was suspended from the chariot, (another magical protective measure). In the imperial period the length of the celebration increased, culminating in the unprecedented triumph of Trajan after the Second Dacian War of 105–106, which lasted for 123 days.

> Their processions to celebrate their victories which they call a triumph have the following form. When a great victory worthy of triumphal celebration took place, the general was immediately proclaimed imperator by his troops and he would wreathe his fasces with branches of laurel and would send runners with them to Rome to announce his victory. He then returned to Rome and summoned the Senate to request that a triumph be voted to him. If the vote of the Senate and the people was in his favor his title as imperator was confirmed. If he held a magisterial office when he achieved his victory he retained it for the celebration; but if his time in office had lapsed, he obtained a suitable title, since triumphs could not be celebrated by private individuals.
>
> Dressed in triumphal garb and putting on armlets, he tied a laurel wreath about his head; with a branch in his right hand, he summoned the people. After praising those who had served with him both as a group and individually, he distributed money to them and also conferred honors on them by the award of various decorations. He gave armlets and spears without points to some; on others he conferred gold or silver crowns. He also bestowed models representing the various feats of bravery. So if someone was the first to scale a wall, his crown carried the representation of a wall, or if someone had forced a besieged town to surrender that was also represented. For a naval victory the crown was decorated with ships; a cavalry victory produced a crown modeled with ornaments pertaining to the cavalry. The individual who preserved a fellow citizen from danger in battle or from a siege or from some other threat received the highest

award, being given a wooden crown that was valued as the most honorable of decorations, even above those made of gold and silver. The decorations were given not only to individuals but also to maniples and whole legions. Much of the booty was distributed to the troops; some triumphators even distributed money to the whole populace in addition to paying for the celebration and depositing money in the public treasury. If there was a surplus remaining, they spent it for temples, porticoes, or some other public building.

After doing these things the triumphator mounted his chariot. This chariot was not like those used for sport or war but was rounded in the shape of a tower. He was not alone in the chariot, but would have his daughters and infant male children with him. He placed the older ones on the horses yoked to his chariot and on the trace-horses. If there were more of them, they accompanied the procession on horseback. None of the other participants rode, but walked in the procession wreathed in laurel. A public slave also rode on the chariot beside the victor holding a crown of gems set in gold above the triumphator's head and saying to him: "Look behind you." The past was clearly visible and the future of the triumphator's life foreseen by him so that he would not be swollen with pride or overbearing because of the present. A bell and a whip were suspended from the chariot to symbolize that he could meet with misfortune, even to being whipped or condemned to death. For those who are condemned to death for some misdeed died carrying a bell so that no one would accompany them and so be affected by the same religious pollution. In this fashion they entered the city with the head of the procession formed by the booty and trophies on which were represented captured forts, cities, mountains, rivers, lakes, and seas, everything that had been taken. At times, a single day might be sufficient for the triumph; if it was not, it continued into a second and third day. After the procession had been completed and the triumphator conveyed to the Forum, certain captives who had been chosen for execution were led off to the public prison. The general mounted the Capitol and performed certain religious rites there. He then made dedications and took a meal by the porticoes there. Towards evening he returned home accompanied by flutes and horns. This was the ancient form of the triumph. Many changes were later made to this celebration by various parties and dynasties.

The triumph of Vespasian and Titus, 71 AD

144 JOSEPHUS, *THE JEWISH WAR* 7.3–6

Josephus' account of the triumph of Vespasian and Titus over the Jews in 71 is the only extant narrative of a triumph by an eyewitness. This was the last triumph which was celebrated by someone other than the reigning emperor; Titus did not come to the throne until 79. In his account Josephus omits the speeches and military awards to the army on the morning of the procession. The magistrates and other officials who participated in the triumph are also passed over in silence.

The gate referred to at the start of the procession is the Porta Triumphalis. The description of the gold booty refers to the spoils taken from the temple in Jerusalem. The lamp described is the seven-branched candlestick or menorah. The culmination of the procession was the sacrifice of white oxen at the temple of Jupiter Optimus Maximus on the Capitoline hill.

> Before many days had passed they decided to celebrate their achievements by a single triumph, although the Senate had voted a separate triumph for each of them. As previous notice had been given of the day on which they were to celebrate the triumph, no one of the numberless population of the city stayed home. Everyone came out and occupied any place where one could stand, leaving only a passage for those whom they had come to look at.
>
> The whole of the army had been led out by their officers during the night in ranks and companies and were stationed around the gates not of the upper palace but near the temple of Isis. The emperors spent that night there and at sunrise Vespasian and Titus came out crowned with laurel, wearing the ancestral purple robes, and went to the portico of Octavia. There the Senate and the magistrates along with those of equestrian rank awaited their arrival. A tribunal had been built in front of the porticoes, with ivory chairs placed upon it. The emperors sat in these chairs when they arrived. Straight away, the troops acclaimed them, giving full witness to their virtue. The soldiers were without their arms, dressed in silk clothing and crowned with bay leaves. After receiving these acclamations Vespasian gave a sign for them to be silent, although they wished to speak. When a deep silence prevailed, Vespasian stood up and, covering most of his head with his mantle, said the customary prayers, and Titus did likewise. After the prayers, Vespasian briefly spoke to the assembled crowd and dismissed the soldiers to their traditional breakfast provided by the emperors. He moved to the gate which has taken its name from the triumphal processions which always pass through it. There the emperors, after they had eaten, put on the triumphal clothes and sacrificed to the gods, whose statues stood beside the gate, and set in motion the triumphal procession, driving off through the theater to give the crowds an easy view.
>
> It is impossible to adequately describe the multitude of sights and the magnificence of the works of art or types of riches on display or their rarity. For almost all of the things wonderful and precious which have been acquired one after another from other peoples by these men blessed by good fortune were on display. One could see all types of wrought objects of silver, gold, and ivory; they appeared not as a mass of objects carried in

procession, but one could say it was like a flowing river. Here, there were the rarest tapestries, some made of purple, and, there, others embroidered with Babylonian art with portraits true to life. Some transparent jewels were set in golden crowns, others placed in different settings. So many were carried by that one realized it was wrong to consider them rare. Images of the gods of the conquered were carried by of amazing size, made with no little skill and all of rich materials. Animals of many species were led by covered in fitting trappings. The great numbers of servants accompanying them were dressed in purple clothes interwoven with gold, and those who had been chosen for this procession wore garments of striking richness. In addition, all of the captives were adorned. The variety and beauty of their clothing hid any bodily defects.

The most striking sight was the moving stages, the massiveness of which might make one distrust in their stability; many were three or four stories tall, and their rich decoration struck the bystanders with amazement. They were covered in tapestries woven with gold and their structure was of ivory and gold. The war was displayed in many representations which provided a vivid sense of it. One could see a rich land being ravaged, whole formations of the enemy being cut down and those in flight and others being led away to captivity, walls of immense size being destroyed by engines of war, powerful fortresses being taken, cities with well-manned defenses being captured, an army rushing inside the walls with every place filled with slaughter, those unable to resist raising their arms in supplication, fire thrown onto temples, houses pulled down over their owners' heads, general ruin and destruction, and rivers flowing not over land under cultivation nor giving drink to men or cattle but running through a land filled with fire, for the Jews suffered these things when they undertook the war. The workmanship and magnificence of these structures showed these things to those who had not seen them as if they had been present. On each of the stages was placed the commander of the city that had been taken in the position in which he had been captured. Many ships also followed.

Spoils were carried by in mixed piles, but the most striking of all by far were those taken in Jerusalem: a gold table weighing many talents; a lamp stand also made of gold, but constructed differently from those used in daily life. A central shaft was fixed to a column from which slender branches extended arranged like a trident, with a decorated lamp attached to the end of each branch. There were seven in number, making clear the honor paid by the Jews to this number. Finally, the law of the Jews was carried by. In addition, they passed by carrying many images of Victory fashioned from gold and ivory. After these things had passed, Vespasian rode first, followed by Titus, while Domitian rode beside them, magnificently dressed and mounted on a horse that was itself a sight.

The goal of the procession was the temple of Capitoline Jupiter, and reaching it they halted. It was the ancestral custom to wait there until an announcement was made of the execution of the enemy general. On this occasion it was Simon, son of Giora, who had taken part in the procession among the prisoners. He was dragged along by his guards with a halter around his neck while being whipped to a spot near the Forum. It is the Roman practice to execute at that place those condemned for their crimes. When his death was announced and all had shouted their approval, they sacrificed, uttering the customary prayers, and departed to the palace. They entertained some with a feast at their table; for the rest, preparations for banquets had been made at their homes. For the remainder of the day the city of Rome celebrated the victory of its army over its enemies, and an end to civil strife and beginning of hopes for its future happiness.

Punishments

The ancient sources project a harsh image of Roman military discipline, with exemplary stories of consuls executing their own sons for breaches of discipline or deserters being crucified in the aftermath of the fall of Carthage in 149. They claim that it was crucial to Rome's military triumphs, and one of the standard themes in the portrait of a successful commander is his harsh restoration of discipline as a prelude to victory over the enemy. The examples of disciplinary action in the sources appear to confirm this general judgment. However, some caution is necessary in evaluating them. The examples focus on the dramatic and exceptional and therefore offer little information on the day-to-day administration of military justice. In addition, the commonplace of the effective general presupposes lax discipline prior to his arrival and so calls into question whether the maintenance of discipline and administration of punishment were really as relentless as some of the sources would have us believe. In particular, in the imperial period there is a constant theme of laxity among the eastern legions that should caution us against taking the picture of a rigidly maintained discipline as the norm.

In the Republic ultimate disciplinary power was vested in the commanding general and derived from his *imperium*. In essence, the army was an extension of the citizen body, and the same basic power that formed the basis of jurisdiction in civilian life also underpinned military justice. The difference between the civilian and military administration of justice lay in the far more untrammeled powers of the magistrate while on campaign. The normal right of appeal and intervention by other magistrates, such as the tribunes, to halt proceedings were not allowed. One further distinction can be observed, and that is that the punishment of groups such as whole units was permitted, which was not a feature of Roman criminal procedure in civilian life.

The general was not bound by specific rules but was in theory able to investigate and punish as he saw fit. Nevertheless, a set of norms evolved that established a set of customary penalties for specific acts, but despite this there are examples of commanders disregarding such norms and using their own discretion as to which penalties to inflict. In normal circumstances, as Polybius remarks, the military tribunes tried malefactors and decided on the appropriate punishment, while prefects of the allies did so for auxiliary troops. The punishment of officers was left to the commanding general. Below the level of the tribunes, centurions and their junior officers seem to have exercised only disciplinary but not judicial authority.

There was not a simple one-to-one correspondence between offense and punishment. Mitigating factors could be and were taken into account. Length of service, prior record, and personal character as well as the type of offense were factors that influenced the severity of punishment.

In general, offenses and penalties can be divided into broad categories. The overriding division was between offenses committed by the individual and those committed by a unit or group. The latter rested on the notion of collective responsibility. The infliction of decimation and the disbandment of the unit are obvious examples of such punishments. The actions by individuals worthy of punishment were of two kinds: those classified as crimes by law and those which violated customary but not legal norms. It is not clear that Romans in practice drew any definite boundary between them.

This system of punishments seems to have endured for as long as the Roman army did, but there are certain changes of emphasis over time. The most important modification resulted from the professionalization of the army. Demotion now became a possibility and loss of the retirement bonus a serious penalty. Decimation almost disappears. Given the expense involved in training and equipping professional soldiers the government was reluctant to lose its investment.

145 POLYBIUS, *HISTORIES* 6.36.9–38.4

Polybius saw reward and punishment as part of a single system that had produced the most effective military force he knew. The following passage occurs in his discussion of the Roman camp.

The Latin term for beating with the club is *fustuarium*. It appears to have consisted of the convicted man running a gauntlet of his fellow soldiers. Polybius mentions that some men managed to survive the punishment. It was designed to ensure that as large a number of soldiers as possible participated in inflicting the penalty so as to make it an assertion of group norms. It must have made it more bearable for the common soldier that his officers were also liable to suffer the same fate. The *optio* was an adjutant to a more senior officer, usually a centurion. The prefects of the cavalry squadron bore the title of *decurio* and stood in the same position as the *optio* in the infantry.

> If the mistake has been made by a member of the guard, the man in charge of the guard can immediately clear matters up by calling upon his fellows as witnesses, and he is obligated to do this. If nothing of the kind has taken place the blame comes back upon him. Immediately, a tribunal composed

of all the military tribunes is set up. It tries him and if he is found guilty he is beaten with a wooden club. A tribune picks up the club and only touches the condemned with it; then all the soldiers in the camp attack him with clubs and stones. They kill the majority of the condemned in the camp itself, but there is no safety for those who manage to escape. How could there be? They cannot return to their homeland. Would any of their relations dare to take them into their homes? As a result those who have once fallen victim to such misfortune are completely destroyed. The *optio* and the prefect of the cavalry squadron suffer the same punishment if they do not transmit the necessary orders at the specified time to the guard and to the commander of the next cavalry squadron. It is because the Romans punish so harshly and implacably that their night guard posts execute their duty without fault.

Common soldiers must obey the tribunes and they in turn the consuls. The tribune is also in charge of fines, holding goods as pledges and inflicting beatings, while the prefects do the same for the allies. Beating with clubs is also inflicted on those who steal from the camp, those who give false witness, and young men who are discovered abusing themselves. In addition, those who are convicted of a third offense on the same charge are punished in this way. These offenses are punished as crimes. But the following are held to be cowardly acts and shameful conduct in a soldier: if someone makes a false report to the tribunes of his courage in battle for the sake of obtaining reward; likewise if someone assigned to a reserve unit leaves his post for reasons of cowardice; also if someone throws away any of his equipment in fear. These are the reasons that men in reserve units often face certain death, refusing to leave their post though facing many times their number. Some who have discarded their shields or dagger or some other piece of equipment throw themselves upon the enemy without thought, hoping either to regain what they had thrown away or by dying to escape public shame and the mockery of their relatives.

If the same thing happens to large groups and if maniples being hard pressed shamefully leave their positions, they refrain from subjecting them to beatings or execution. They have discovered a solution both advantageous and frightening. The tribune, after assembling the army and bringing forward those accused of leaving their posts, upbraids them harshly. Finally, he chooses by lot sometimes five, sometimes eight, sometimes twenty, with the number proportionate to the whole so that the total is one-tenth of those who have displayed cowardice. Those selected by lot are clubbed without mercy in the manner mentioned above. They are given rations of barley in place of wheat, and the men are ordered to camp outside the camp defenses in an unprotected spot. Given that the danger and fear from the lot affect all, as it is uncertain on whom it will fall, and the public dishonor of being fed barley rations likewise falls on all equally, the best possible practice has been adopted both to inspire fear and to repair the harm done.

The restoration of discipline

146 SALLUST, *THE WAR AGAINST JUGURTHA* 45.1–3

The Romans saw the maintenance of discipline as an essential part of the commander's responsibilities. A standard theme in accounts of successful generals is their restoration of discipline through punishments and also through rigorous training.

The following passage describes the methods used by Caecilius Metellus on his arrival in Africa in 109. There is a noticeable stress in the passage on imposing discipline without harsh punishments.

> My view is that both in this difficult situation and in waging war Metellus showed himself both great and wise. He was able to steer a course between the extremes of indulgence and harshness.
>
> In the first place he removed the incentives for laziness by forbidding the sale of bread or other cooked foods within the camp. He also banned merchants from following the army and common soldiers from having servants or pack animals in camp or on the march and did away with other such practices.
>
> Every day he held cross-country marches and had the marching camps fortified with a palisade and ditch just as if the enemy was present, and posted guards at short intervals and went round the posts with his legates. On the march, he placed himself sometimes at the head of the column, sometimes in the rear, and often in the middle, to prevent men leaving the ranks so that they would advance in a body with the standards, and had the soldiers carry their own food and arms. In this way, by keeping them from committing acts of indiscipline rather than by punishment, he restored the morale of the army in a short time.

Decimation

147 LIVY, *HISTORY OF ROME* 2.59.9–11

This incident is part of Livy's narration of the events of 471 and the wars against the Volsci (see p. 45). The consul Appius Claudius Inregillensis had been a harsh opponent of the plebeians' struggle against the patricians, which caused the deliberate insubordination of the army that led to Appius' action. These events are probably fictitious, but nevertheless the passage offers a good summary of normal Roman practice in such cases.

Livy seems to draw a distinction between the first group of soldiers, who had thrown their arms away, and the other troops and their officers. The first group seem to have been treated as deserters and were individually subject to the death penalty, while the remainder suffered collective punishment. The double-pay men were those who received double pay or rations and often occupied the position of junior officers below the rank of centurion. Probably the term is used here anachronistically. In his discussion of punishments (145), Polybius calls attention to the disgrace that accompanied the loss of arms.

> [Appius] the consul finally collected together his troops who had been scattered in flight after having fruitlessly attempted to pursue the enemy by rallying his men. He established his camp in an area untouched by the war. After he had assembled his troops, he spoke harshly and quite rightly to an army that had betrayed military discipline and deserted its standards. He questioned individual soldiers, asking them where their arms were, and also questioned the standard bearers as to where their standards were. He ordered scourging with rods and beheading for all soldiers found without their arms and for all standard bearers without their standards. He did the same for the centurions and double-pay men who had left the ranks. As for the rest, every tenth man was selected by lot and executed.

Military training

Roman writers regarded proper and constant training as an essential element in military success. It instilled the discipline which the Roman regarded as the key to victory. It was also seen as giving the Roman soldier the advantage over the enemies he faced, particularly the barbarian peoples of Europe. Behind this practice lay the idea that military success was based on a series of technical skills that could be learned by both commanders and common soldiers. Writers compared military training to athletic training and training in the gladiatorial schools. Roman tactics were based on sword fighting and the use of small independent units that placed a premium on mobility. The lack of it could seriously hamper military operations, as the absence of soldiers trained to operate with each other hindered the Roman deployment at Cannae in 216 (see p. 152).

There is no evidence of a set scheme for training before the first century BC. The use of a militia and the yearly change in units did not make for consistent, long-term practice. Much of the training seems to have depended on the initiative of the commander, as the passage from Polybius on Scipio Africanus (149) and the training imposed by Metellus Numidicus in Africa indicate. It is indicative that we do not hear of any standard method of training in Caesar's army, though some of the units served with him for the full ten years of his Gallic command. With the development of a professional, long-service army under Augustus, a more standard regimen was developed. It may even have been codified in some manner, as the Jewish historian Josephus states at the end of the first century AD. Vegetius makes reference to the rules of Augustus and Hadrian. The presence of amphitheaters and training grounds outside of Roman camps as well as the presence of officers whose specific duties were directed to training indicates some form of standard practice.

Our best guide to training methods is the late writer Vegetius (see **52**). The standard course of training was divided into three parts: The first part consisted of various exercises devoted to improving physical conditioning such as gymnastics, route marches, swimming, and jumping. The second part was directed to developing proficiency in the use of weapons by employing practice weapons. It included exercises designed to develop swordsmanship, especially prolonged training in fencing against a *palus* or wooden pole with wooden swords and special shields heavier than those employed in combat. Training was also given in the use of missile weapons, including the *pilum*, bow, and sling. The third section consisted of activities that focused on collective activities such as marching, forming up in various tactical formations, and civil engineering projects. This fostered the ability of the men to work together on and off the battlefield, as well as heightening *esprit de corps*. Such training was fairly constant and repeated throughout the soldier's career.

In the imperial period the army employed specialists to train its troops. The careers of such men were only possible in a professional army, which did not exist under the Republic. Probably men of long military experience were chosen to perform these duties. Centurions inspected their centuries, and military tribunes supervised the training. Even under the Republic the thoroughness of Roman training was unmatched in most other ancient armies.

148 VEGETIUS, *HANDBOOK OF MILITARY AFFAIRS* 1.9

The following passage serves as a preface to Vegetius' military handbook, which covers most aspects of military affairs. Much of it is, as the author notes, drawn from earlier military manuals and not directly relevant to his own time. The reference to the stature of the Germans in comparison to the small size of the Romans is a commonplace that was also applied to the Gauls. Caesar in his *Gallic War* mentions the nervousness of his troops when they first encountered the Germans. The list of various peoples compared to the Romans is based on a series of ethnographic stereotypes widespread in ancient Greek and Roman literature.

> We see that the Roman people conquered the world in no other way than by training in arms, through the discipline of the camp and by the practice of the military arts. By what other means could the small number of Romans have prevailed against the multitude of Gauls? What could men of small stature have dared [to do] against the size of the Germans? It is clear that the Spanish surpassed us not only in numbers but also in physical strength. We were not the equals of the Africans in cunning or resources. There is no doubt that we were overcome by the skills and prudence of the Greeks.

But to all of these advantages the Romans opposed unusual care in the choice of their levies and in their military training. They thoroughly understood the importance of toughening them by continual practice, and of training them to every maneuver that might happen on the march and in action. They were just as strict in punishing idleness and laziness. The courage of a soldier is heightened by his knowledge of his craft, and he desires an opportunity to do what he is convinced he has been perfectly taught. A handful of men, accustomed to war, proceed to certain victory, while on the contrary numerous armies of raw and undisciplined troops are but mobs dragged off to slaughter.

Scipio Africanus' training program

149 POLYBIUS, *HISTORIES* 10.20.1–7

Scipio had arrived in Spain in 210 to take over the defeated Roman forces. In 209 he was able to capture the main Carthaginian base on Spain's east coast, New Carthage, by a speedy and efficient assault. Instead of following up his initial success by further campaigning he turned to training his army, as Polybius describes. The training was designed to toughen his troops and to rebuild their morale after their double defeat in 211. The similarity to imperial methods of training is clear. The craftsmen to whom Polybius refers were citizens of New Carthage drafted as public slaves for the duration of the war in Spain.

The quotation from Xenophon cited in the passage is from his life of the Spartan king Agesilaus.

Remaining for some time at New Carthage [Scipio] constantly exercised his naval forces and gave the following instruction to the tribunes about the training of the army. On the first day, he ordered the soldiers to march three and one-half miles at the double carrying their arms. On the second day, he ordered them to polish, repair, and examine their equipment in public. Then, on the following day, they were to stop working and rest. On the next day, some were to practice sword fighting with swords made of wood, covered in leather and with a button over the point, while others were to practice javelin-throwing with javelins which also had a button covering their points. On the fifth day they were to repeat the same set of exercises.

Scipio paid special attention to the equipment makers so that his men would have no lack of weapons for practice and for real warfare. He appointed supervisors for each section of workers, as I mentioned earlier. He would visit the various shops and furnish them with supplies for their work. So, with the infantry exercising in drilling on the grounds before the city, the navy practicing maneuvers and rowing, those in the city sharpening weapons, forging bronze, and working as carpenters, and all of them industriously making arms, no one could avoid saying in the words of Xenophon that "the city was a workshop of war."

A reform in weapons training

150 VALERIUS MAXIMUS, *MEMORABLE SAYINGS AND DEEDS* 2.3.2

During the reign of the emperor Tiberias (14–37 AD), Valerius composed a handbook of illustrative examples for rhetoricians drawn from Greek and Roman history.

P. Rutilius Rufus was consul in 105 BC.

> Practice in the use of weapons was given to the soldiers by the consul P. Rutilius, the colleague of C. Mallius. Doing what no general before him had done, he summoned weapons instructors from the gladiatorial school of C. Aurelius Scaurus and he trained the legionaries in a more flexible method of giving and avoiding blows. Blending skill with courage and courage with skill, he made skill more effective by combining it with courage and courage more courageous by the use of knowledge.

151 [CAESAR], *THE AFRICAN WAR* 71

The African War survives under Caesar's name, but its author is unknown. It was written by one of his officers, as are the existing accounts of the civil war in Egypt and Spain.

Caesar began his campaign against the surviving supporters of Pompey in Africa in the course of the winter of 47/46 BC. He brought over a force of eight legions, and at Thapsus on the coast southeast of Carthage he defeated Metellus Scipio and his own former legate Titus Labienus. The Numidians fought as both light cavalry and infantry, though they were especially known for their cavalry forces. On this occasion it was a mixed force of Numidian cavalry and light infantry fighting together and harassing Caesar's troops on the march that led to the training described in the passage. Light troops were especially effective in this role, and Caesar does not appear to have had light-armed troops of his own to counter the enemy.

> Caesar, to counter an enemy of this type, trained his troops not as a successful general instructing a veteran and victorious army with great achievements to its credit, but as a trainer of untried gladiators. He taught the men how many feet to step back from the enemy and how they should turn around to face them and that they should engage them at close quarters. He told them that sometimes they should charge and sometimes retreat and sometimes simply threaten an attack. Also, he taught them from what position and in what manner they should throw their missile weapons. The enemy's light-armed troops had distressed and worried our

army to a remarkable degree, for they deterred our cavalry by killing their mounts with javelins, and they wore down our infantry with their speed. Whenever our heavily armed soldiers, harassed by them, formed and launched an attack, the Numidians easily avoided the danger by their swift movements.

Physical training

152 VEGETIUS, *HANDBOOK OF MILITARY AFFAIRS* 1.9

The figures for the distance of the march are given in Roman miles. The Roman mile was approximately 0.9 current international mile. The Roman divided the day into twenty-four hours, reckoning from sunrise and sunset. Since the amount of light and darkness varied in the course of the year the hours of daylight were longer in the summer. It is to these longer hours that Vegetius refers in this passage. The normal marching pace in modern armies is three miles an hour, including a ten-minute rest period. Normally, an ancient army on the march could cover between ten and fifteen miles a day, although the distance covered depended on the terrain, army size, and other conditions. The normal march-rate specified here by Vegetius matches modern rates. The reference to the exercises of Pompeius in Sallust presumably comes from a lost section of Sallust's *Histories*. Plutarch describes Pompey's military exercises in his biography.

Recruits must be taught the military pace as a first step in their training. There is nothing more important on the march or in battle than that all soldiers preserve their order. They cannot learn to march quickly and in step unless they constantly practice. A divided and disordered army is most in danger from the enemy.

Twenty miles should be covered at the military pace in five hours during the campaigning season. Twenty-four miles should be covered by using the "full pace," which is more rapid than the military. If that pace is increased, the result is a run whose distance cannot be measured. However, young soldiers should be accustomed to running so that their attack on the enemy is more forceful and so that they can occupy advantageous ground more quickly when they have the opportunity to do so or to occupy a position before the enemy does. It will allow them to quickly set out and return from scouting missions as well as permit them to overtake the enemy in flight. These exercises should also include jumping across ditches and climbing over any high obstacles in their path, since practice in this will allow them to easily overcome any obstacles of this sort. In addition, both in battle and during an exchange of missiles a soldier who approaches on the run and with a jump will blind the enemy and strike fear into his heart and so prepares himself to avoid or deflect the enemy's blow before he delivers it. Sallust mentions that Gnaeus Pompeius Magnus competed with the quickest men in jumping, with the fastest in running, and with the strongest in carrying loads. He could not have matched Sertorius in battle unless he had prepared both himself and his army through frequent exercises.

Conditions of service

The burdens of service

The nature of military service had begun to change by the start of the second century. The most important development was the creation of provinces outside of Italy, starting with the two Spanish provinces in 197. Wars in Italy had been marked by a seasonal rhythm, with the army returning home at the end of each campaigning season. The Punic Wars had temporarily altered this pattern, as armies remained in Sicily, Spain, and Africa for extended periods. However, a permanent change came with the gradual expansion of the provincial system and the need to garrison Rome's new conquests.

Many of the small farmers who formed the majority of conscripts were now faced with the prospect of separation from their farms and families for long periods. How long is not clear, but there is some evidence that the average length of service was six years in the mid-second century at a time when there was an average of about 75,000 men under arms in any one year. It has been estimated that perhaps half of all males would see at least some military service.

The response to this heavy military commitment varied in accordance with individual preferences and the opportunities that military service brought. The prolonged and bitter wars of conquest in Spain, an area that presented few opportunities to obtain booty, seem to have generated the most resistance to the draft. In 151, reports of constant fighting and high casualty rates led to attempts to evade the levy. Further difficulties followed. In 145, again resistance to the levy was so strong that only new recruits were drafted for service, with an exemption for those who had just finished their service in the last war against Carthage. But other campaigns such as the last war against Carthage or some of the eastern campaigns had little trouble in attracting recruits because of the prospects of booty and plunder those wars offered.

The burden of service was exacerbated by changing economic conditions. The decline in the minimum census requirement in an army that depended for its recruitment on a substantial body of small farmers meant that for many of them several years' service overseas could result in economic disaster because of the loss of their labor. This situation must have been made significantly worse by the fact that the wars, especially in the eastern Mediterranean, generated immense amounts of booty that flowed predominantly into the hands of the upper class. The latter in turn tended to invest in land as the safest and most prestigious investment. The landholdings of the elite appear to have expanded at least in part at the expense of smallholders whose absence on military service made their farms unproductive. A further aggravating factor was the importation of slave labor to replace free labor on the lands of the wealthy. It is clear that a substantial body of free, occasional labor and seasonal workers remained in the countryside, but the emigration to the cities, especially to Rome, in this period is evidence for deteriorating rural conditions. The evidence for dense rural settlement in parts of Italy that comes from this period provides little indication of the conditions under which the rural population lived. Certainly, the literature of the period is full of concern for deteriorating conditions among the peasants who formed the backbone of the army.

The demands of empire and worsening economic conditions seem to have created resistance to the levy at the same time as they made military service more attractive in certain ways. Military service was poorly paid, but booty and rewards, though uncertain, would be much more attractive for those with few economic prospects. In addition, prolonged fighting increased the need for men with military experience who could help to train new recruits. These factors led to the creation of a group that can be called quasi-professionals. Their length of service and military experience qualified them as professionals, but they were not yet professional in the sense that they either saw themselves or were seen by others as career soldiers.

The strains of military service

153 LIVY, 32.3.1–6

In 199 the consul P. Villius Tappulus was assigned Macedonia to carry on the war against Philip V (see pp. 171ff.) begun the year before. The passage must be read in the context of an initial refusal of the centuriate assembly to cast a vote in favor of war because of the weariness caused by the Second Punic War. In 200, the consuls enrolling troops for Macedonia had been given the authority to enroll as volunteers men who had served with Scipio Africanus. These men, part of the army defeated at Cannae, served in Scipio's expedition to Africa in the spring of 204. By 199 they would have had sixteen years of almost continuous service, which is extraordinary. The sixteen-year liability to service in the infantry was not normally fulfilled by continuous service.

The troops' grievances also focused on their claim that they had been falsely enrolled as volunteers. There is much evidence that commanders often took steps to stiffen recruits with experienced veterans. The incident provides an illustration of the tension between the needs of empire and a militia system.

> When P. Villius arrived in Macedonia he encountered a serious mutiny which had been stirred up some time before and not sufficiently suppressed at the start. There were 2,000 soldiers who after the defeat of Hannibal had been moved from Africa to Sicily and then, about a year later, had been posted to Macedonia as volunteers. They denied that they had volunteered and said they had been embarked despite their protests. But whatever the case might be, whether they served under compulsion

THE REPUBLICAN ROMAN ARMY

or at their own free will, they said that their term of service had been fulfilled and that it was right that there should be some limit to their military service. It had been many years since they had seen Italy; they had grown old in service in Sicily, Africa, and Macedonia. They were worn out by the effort and labor and were drained of blood by their many wounds.

154 POLYBIUS, *HISTORIES* 35.4.1–6

Nobilior had been consul in 153 and had sustained serious defeats at the hands of the Celtiberians in Nearer Spain. Marcellus is M. Claudius Marcellus, consul in 152, operating as a proconsul. The fear that Polybius describes may have been exaggerated as a device to heighten the appearance of his hero Scipio Aemilianus; nevertheless, the wars in Spain created serious difficulties for the Romans. It took almost two centuries of difficult fighting for the Romans to pacify the Iberian peninsula. Campaigns in Spain were often fought as a series of guerilla actions punctuated by large-scale battles. The prospects for booty were negligible and the physical conditions harsh. The sources record more trouble with the levy for Spain than for any other theater of war. The problems with the levy in 151 led to the temporary imprisonment of the consuls by the tribunes of the plebs, an act that was repeated in 138. At least temporarily, in 150, the levy was held by lot because of accusations of unjust treatment by the consuls and complaints that some draftees had been given easier service.

> The more intensely the Senate prosecuted the war the more things turned out contrary to their expectations. Since Quintus Fulvius Nobilior, the commander in Spain in the previous year, and his army had made known at Rome the constant succession of pitched battles, the number of the Roman dead, and the courage of the Celtiberians, and Marcellus was clearly afraid of fighting, an extraordinary terror had seized the young men, which their elders claimed had no earlier parallel. This cowardice went so far that suitable men did not stand for office as military tribunes, though earlier it was usual for many more men to come forward for the position than was required. The legates nominated by the consuls, who should have accompanied them, were unwilling to serve. Worst of all was the fact that the young avoided enrollment and presented excuses that were shameful to say, unseemly to investigate, and impossible to verify.

155 SALLUST, *THE WAR AGAINST JUGURTHA* 41.3

The following passage comes from Sallust's account of the growth of factions at Rome and the disintegration of the Roman state as a result of the end of fear of external aggression after the destruction of Carthage in 146. He links the demands for military service to the growth of poverty among the rural population. This theme also occurs in other writers dealing with this period, such as Plutarch and Appian. None of these sources specifies the nature of the connection between rural poverty and military service. The extended absence of soldiers from their small farms combined with the influx of wealth into the hands of the upper class who normally invested in land as the safest and most prestigious place to put their money brought pressure to bear on these small proprietors.

Added to this was the influx of slave labor into the countryside, which constricted the available opportunities for tenancy and seasonal work. Slaves were attractive, as the sources make clear, since they were not liable to be called up.

Sallust does exaggerate, but there is evidence for difficulty with the levy in this period. Gaius Gracchus, tribune of the plebs in 123 or 122, proposed legislation forbidding the call-up of those under the age of seventeen and an end to deductions for clothing from soldiers' pay. We also learn that in 109 one of the consuls, M. Junius Silanus, abrogated a number of laws that in some way limited military service.

> Power rested with a small group of nobles who controlled everything in both war and peace, the treasury, the provinces, magistracies, and all distinctions and triumphs. The people were oppressed by military service and poverty. The commanders along with a few friends plundered the spoils of war. Meanwhile the soldiers' parents and young children whose property was near that of powerful neighbors were being driven from their land.

Marius and changes in the levy: volunteering

156 APPIAN, *THE SPANISH WARS* 84

P. Cornelius Scipio Aemilianus was a son of Aemilius Paullus (see pp. 185ff.) and was adopted into the family of Scipio Africanus. He had seen service previously as military tribune in Spain in 151. In 147 he had been elected consul for the first time and took Carthage in the following year. In 134, the date of this passage, he was elected consul to carry on the campaign against Numantia although he was only thirty-seven or thirty-eight, below the legal minimum age of forty-two.

Numantia was the capital of the Celtiberians, who lived on the upper Durius (modern Douro) River in central Spain. It had resisted a number of attempts at conquest by the Romans dating back to the beginning of the second century. By 134 it was the last center of resistance in a war that had lasted almost a decade.

The Senate was less supportive of Scipio than Appian implies. It withheld an immediate grant of funds for the expedition and did not allow Scipio to hold a levy; however, this may have been the result of a shortage of available manpower. In this situation Scipio had no alternative but to call for volunteers. Volunteering for military service is sporadically attested from the late third century. Scipio Africanus had used volunteers in Africa. The use of clients as soldiers was to become more frequent in the next century. Buteo is most likely Quintus Fabius Maximus Allobrogicus, consul in 121, and he probably served as Scipio's quaestor in Spain.

Since the war against the Numantines was long and drawn out, contrary to their expectations, the Roman people elected Cornelius Scipio, the conqueror of Carthage, as consul again, in the belief that he was the only commander who could defeat the Numantines. As he was then below the legal age for the consulate, the Senate, as it had done when Scipio was elected to command against the Carthaginians, instructed the tribunes to repeal the law on age requirements and to reinstate it for the following year. So Scipio was elected consul and hurried to Numantia. He did not hold a levy, as there were a number of wars in progress and many troops in Spain. However, with the Senate's consent he brought from Rome some volunteers sent by cities or kings out of personal friendship and 500 friends and clients whom he formed into a single unit he called the "troop of friends," and all of these troops numbering about 4,000 he turned over to his nephew Buteo to command.

The reform of Marius

157 SALLUST, *THE WAR AGAINST JUGURTHA* 86.1–4

Elected consul in 107, despite aristocratic opposition, with a combination of plebeian and equestrian support, Marius received the command of the war against Jugurtha which the Romans had been waging since 111 with indifferent success. The Senate allowed him to levy a supplement to the existing consular army of two legions already in Africa. Such supplements are attested as early as the Second Punic War and were frequently used in Spain.

Marius' use of volunteers also had earlier precedents, such as Scipio Aemilianus (see **156**) for the campaign in Spain in 134. The innovation he introduced was to allow men to serve in the legions who fell below the minimum property rating. Such men had served before but only in emergencies (see p. 197). This change seems to have become standard practice from this point on. Marius' action marked the end of a long evolution marked by the continued fall in the property rating necessary to qualify for legionary service. At the point that Marius held his levy there would have been little difference in wealth between the poorest of those liable to serve and those even worse off. The importance of the step was that it now opened up the possibility of new employment for those who had few other prospects. It also, at least in part, created the possibility for the development of a semi-professional army, given the meager prospects for other employment for many of the poor. The long-term service that Rome's expanding empire required could now be provided by such an army.

Nevertheless, the older form of levy according to census classes continued, though our evidence for them is not very full. Certainly, down to the 40s when large numbers of troops were needed the traditional draft was used. This was especially true in periods of civil war and unrest. For instance, in the war between Rome and its Italian allies 150,000 were called up, and during the civil wars between 49 and 31 about 420,000 men were enlisted.

In considering the effects of long-term service it is important to keep in mind that such volunteers might often be in a position to influence the conduct of the rest of the troops. Generals such as Caesar were conscious of the value of experienced troops. It appears from Sallust's account that in Marius' levy many of the conscripts were plebeians from the city of Rome, though normally volunteers and conscripts both came from the same rural background. Given the pressure on the rural poor, this is hardly surprising, though the level of pay and its irregularity during the last century of the Republic would not by themselves have been strong attractions. But the prospect of booty, as the following passage makes clear, as well as donatives or money gifts to the troops, and the regularity of employment would have been attractive. Evidence for the changes in the orientation of the army is provided by the regularity of demands for land for demobilized veterans. Distributions of land had been made since the early Republic, but the intensity of demand after Marius' reform points to a change in the economic position of many of the troops.

Roman writers saw Marius' action as marking a break with earlier practice, though they may have exaggerated its immediate effects. They were correct in perceiving that, by enrolling those whose present and future economic security depended on their military service, Marius had begun a process of slowly widening the gap between the state and its armed forces.

> Meanwhile, he considered preparations for war the first priority. He demanded a supplement for the legions, summoned help from peoples and kings, as well as the bravest soldiers from the Latins and the allies, many of whom were known to him either because they had served with him or by reputation, and going around encouraged veterans to join his expedition. The Senate, though opposed to him, did not dare to hinder any of his actions. It happily decreed his supplement because it thought that none of the plebs wanted to fight and Marius would lose either their service or his popularity with them. But the Senate's hope was in vain, since most of them were eager to serve with Marius, thinking that the booty would make them rich and that they would return home in triumph. Other similar considerations also induced them to serve....
>
> After Marius saw that he had kindled the enthusiasm of the plebs, he quickly loaded his ships with food, pay, arms, and other things useful in war and he ordered his legate Aulus Manlius to set out [for Africa]. Meanwhile, he began to enroll soldiers neither in the traditional manner nor according to property distinctions, but accepted volunteers, of whom many were below the minimum property requirement. Some said that he did this because of the lack of men of the better kind, while others claimed that he wanted to ingratiate himself because he owed to the poor his fame and advancement and, for a man seeking power, the needy, to whom their possessions are unimportant since they have none and for whom all good qualities have a price, are the best supporters.

Long-term service: an extreme case – the Fimbrians

158 PLUTARCH, *LIFE OF LUCULLUS* 7.2.1

The Fimbrians or Valerians were members of the two legions that accompanied L. Valerius Flaccus, consul in 86, to the East to continue the war against Mithridates VI of Pontus. Flaccus' lack of military experience and his avarice led to the alienation of men and resulted in a mutiny led by his legate C. Flavius Fimbria in which Flaccus was killed and his army taken over by Fimbria, who enjoyed some success against Mithridates. In 85 he was besieged by a rival commander, Sulla, at Thyateira near Pergamum; abandoned by his troops, he committed suicide. His men then served under Sulla and his successor, and then although discharged they remained in the East. In 74, L. Licinius Lucullus, who had arrived in Asia to take up the command in the third war against Mithridates, incorporated them into his army with some difficulty, as the following passage shows. They served under Lucullus, but in the campaigning season of 68/67 they mutinied and then learning they had been discharged at Rome simply left the army. With the arrival of Pompey in the East in 66 they once again joined the army and seem to have remained in service until the end of Pompey's eastern campaigns in 63.

Despite their two discharges the twenty or more years of service that this unit saw is extraordinary by Republican standards. It is considerably more than the presumed maximum of sixteen years and the perhaps eight to ten years' service which may have been the norm in this period. Unlike soldiers serving in earlier periods these troops were away from Italy for the entire period. Perhaps the most striking aspect of their service was the ability of these troops to maintain their identity as a group throughout the period.

In all but name they had become professionals. The Fimbrians illustrate the effects of both civil war and long-term service in producing a quasi-professional army.

> Lucullus crossed over into Asia with the one legion he had recruited and there took over the command of the rest of the army. All of these troops had for a long time been corrupted by luxury and greed. The group called the Fimbrians were the most unmanageable to deal with, as they had become accustomed to disorder. They had in company with Fimbria murdered the consul Flaccus and then had handed over Fimbria to Sulla. They were arrogant and lawless, but they were warlike, courageous, and experienced in warfare.

After military service: the problem of land

A central theme in the period after the elimination of a minimum census rating for legionary service is the demand for land by soldiers at the termination of their military service. In fact, land in the form of individual allotments or the foundation of colonies outside of and within Italy had been given at the end of major conflicts in the late third century and first half of the second century BC. At the termination of his campaign in Spain against Carthage, Scipio Africanus had founded the Roman colony of Italica in 206, as well as Latin colonies such as Cordoba. Scipio's veterans had also received land in Apulia and Samnium. Extensive colonization and individual allotments had also marked Rome's expansion in Cisalpine Gaul. However, after 150 such allotments ceased, at the very time when declining census figures showed the peasantry in increasing difficulties. The pressure on the small farmer through increased debt, often resulting in the loss of his land, the importation of slaves, and the resultant fall in the opportunities available for free rural labor, were to continue until the end of the Republic.

Starting in the 130s a reflection of the increasing difficulties faced by the peasantry can be seen in agitation for the distribution of public or state lands. However, under Sulla at the end of the 80s and again in the last phase of the civil war after 43 distributions of private land confiscated in the course of civil strife were also made.

The tribunate of Tiberius Gracchus in 133 marks the beginning of a new period of agitation for the distribution of public land, and it now became a frequent demand of soldiers who had finished their service. This is hardly surprising in an army that was recruited for the most part from the countryside.

Certainly for some of the soldiers land grants would have been the most attractive benefit of service. But the provision of land for veterans was never automatic and often came up against strongly entrenched and effective opposition. The opposition was mounted by members of the elite whose own economic and political interests would have been under threat and also by the urban plebs. Most of them appear to have had little interest in military service and were infrequently called up. Jealous of their privileges they were especially sensitive to any concessions granted to the Italian allies which implied sharing the profits of empire. This attitude persisted even after the Social War of 91–89, when Roman citizenship was extended to all of Italy south of the Po.

Only major political figures such as Marius, Sulla, Pompey, and Caesar were able to secure land for their veterans. Even as important a figure as Pompey experienced severe difficulties, and it was only in alliance with Caesar and Crassus in 59 that he was able to obtain land for the veterans of his eastern campaigns. His earlier attempt to secure land for soldiers who had served with him and Metellus Pius in Spain in the 70s seems to have ended in failure.

The continuous service overseas that expansion necessitated, as well as the fact that the rewards of service including donatives, promotions, and booty depended on the general, fostered the development of loyalty to the commander rather than to the state. This was especially true in the case of land distributions. Since there was no automatic provision, the commander often had to forge a political coalition to pass the necessary legislation in the assembly.

These factors tended to cement a bond between soldiers and their general, which the general could use for his own political purposes. For instance, when Caesar brought forward his land bill in 59 the armed veterans of Pompey played a leading role in getting the measure successfully through the assembly. The commander could use military service as a means to create a mutual relationship with his army and later his veterans that had some of the elements of a patron–client relationship. So Sulla's settlement of his veterans after the first civil war was a way of creating a loyal following that would have an interest in maintaining Sulla's political reforms. It was hardly an automatic relationship, and much depended on the less tangible bonds of mutual trust and familiarity. Part of the reason why Marius was able to replace Metellus Numidicus in the command of the war against Jugurtha was that Metellus' aristocratic disdain alienated his troops. Perhaps the clearest illustration of the importance of the personal bond is the relationship between Caesar and his troops, forged by prolonged campaigning in Gaul and then through the civil war. In 47, veterans awaiting discharge in Italy, upset at the fact that promises made to them after the battle of Pharsalus had remained unfulfilled, mutinied and marched on Rome. By a subtle mixture of renewed promises and hints that if dismissed these soldiers would miss the profits of a successful campaign in Africa, Caesar was able to control them simply by addressing them as citizens rather than as fellow soldiers, thereby implying their dismissal from service.

The devastation resulting first from the Social War and then from the civil wars and other problems such a piracy in the last century BC intensified rural poverty and raised the issue of land distributions in starker terms. Sulla, after the first round of civil wars and with a large number of legions to demobilize, confiscated land for his soldiers and perhaps settled 80,000–100,000 veterans. In the period from Sulla to the Second Triumvirate public land was again the main source for land distributions to veterans. Caesar planted various types of settlements. Veterans were settled overseas in colonies such as Curubis and Carpis on the North African coast, in southern France, and perhaps in Spain. One estimate is that as many as 100,000 veterans were compensated in this way. Veterans were also settled in Italy, often on individual grants, especially in Campania.

In the period after Caesar's death to the end of the civil wars in 31, once again there was recourse to large-scale land confiscation due in part to the enormous number of men under arms, probably not less than 150,000, and the lack of any public land to distribute. These distributions were spread throughout Italy, mostly in colonies for perhaps 50,000 ex-soldiers. After 30, perhaps another 60,000 were settled. The situation was finally regularized under Augustus when he instituted a system of land distribution or a cash bonus at the end of service.

Despite a century of legislation, no fundamental changes in the pattern of landholding in Italy resulted. Individuals may have bettered themselves through military service but rural poverty remained. It appears to have been alleviated only by the massive resettlement of Italian peasants overseas by both Caesar and Augustus.

Empire had created conditions that demanded long-term service and had created stresses that intensified the poverty of small and middling farmers. Military service had offered a possible way out for them in the form of land distributions at the end of their service. As long as the state left it to private initiative to satisfy this land hunger, the danger remained that the state might lose control of the armed forces. In fact, that is what happened. The system instituted by Augustus allowed the state to regain control of its military forces.

The demobilization of Marius' veterans and the land law of
L. Appuleius Saturninus

Lucius Appuleius Saturninus was elected tribune for 103 with Marius' help. Theirs was a marriage of convenience. Marius had made promises to his troops when they were demobilized after the end of the war in Africa, and his alliance with Saturninus was concluded to fulfill those promises. Our only evidence for the proposal is a late antique series of short biographies of important Republican political figures. Overseas settlement already had a precedent in the legislation Gaius Gracchus had passed over twenty years before. The grants were to be in the form of individual allotments, although their size is unusually large. The norm seems to have been between fifteen and thirty acres. There is inscriptional evidence for the settlements in the province of Africa and off the coast on the island of Cercina. Unlike other legislation passed to reward veterans, the law was put into effect. The tribune Baebius is otherwise unknown.

159 ON ILLUSTRIOUS MEN 73.1

> In order to win the gratitude of Marius' veterans L Appuleius Saturninus, a rebellious tribune of the plebs, carried a law that land in Africa should be divided into sixty acre plots for these veterans and removed his colleague Baebius who was vetoing the measure by having the people stone him.

The sources record another land law proposed by Saturninus in his second tribunate in 100. The bill proposed to distribute land in Cisalpine Gaul held by the Cimbri after their defeat by Marius. In itself such a distribution has precedents as early as the third century BC. There is no definite evidence that the land distribution was intended for veterans alone, but Marius was, according to Plutarch, able to rouse his veterans in support of the law. These are probably the rural supporters mentioned by Appian (**160**), and such evidence implies that they saw themselves as beneficiaries. We have no information on the methods that were to be used for distributions, though there is evidence for a commission of ten men who were to oversee the assignment of lands, one of whom was the father of Julius Caesar.

The oath to observe the law also has earlier precedents and in this case seems to have been specifically directed at Marius' political enemy Metellus Numidicus, whom Marius had replaced in Africa. The resistance of the plebs at Rome to providing land for allied veterans (see p. 243) may also have been exacerbated by the fact that in this period they seem to have rarely served in the army and so had few shared interests with the peasantry who made up the bulk of the armed forces.

The sources also mention a plan for the creation of overseas colonies in Sicily, Achaea, and Macedonia which may be part of the same plan. Cicero informs us that the provisions of this land bill and the overseas colonies were never put into effect, though the majority of his other laws remained in effect.

L. Appuleius Saturninus proposed a law to divide the land in the area now called Gaul by the Romans, which the Cimbri, a branch of the Celts, had held and from which Marius had recently expelled them, and it was considered no longer Celtic land, as it now belonged to the Romans. It was also specified that, if the people should enact the law, senators had to swear to observe the law within five days of its passage and that any senator who did not swear would cease to be a senator and be subject to a public fine of twenty talents.... This was the content of the law, and Appuleius appointed the day for its passing and sent around messengers to announce it to the country people, especially those who had served under Marius and in whom they had the most confidence. The plebs were unhappy with the law, as it was too favorable to the Italians.

Sulla's settlement of his veterans

After defeating Mithridates VI of Pontus and concluding the treaty of Dardanus with him in 85, Sulla prepared to return to Italy to face his opponents, who were in control of the home government. Landing in Italy in 83, he defeated adversaries in a bloody civil war that ended the following year. Sulla followed up his victory by proscribing his enemies and confiscating their lands. Appointed dictator, he embarked on an extensive program of legislation designed to refashion Roman politics.

One of his most pressing problems was to provide land for his demobilized soldiers. In doing so not only would he redeem the promises he had made to his troops, but he would also provide himself with concentrations of ex-soldiers whom he could call upon to guarantee that his settlement would be permanent.

It appears that the number of veterans provided for was less than Appian's figure of 120,000. It has been plausibly argued that Appian's figure was arrived at simply by multiplying the number of legions by their normal establishment. Many of these units had seen long service or had been hastily raised during the civil war and were probably under strength. A figure of 80,000 seems closer to the truth. It appears that the majority of veterans were settled as colonists, though a number of individual allotments may also have been granted. For the most part they were settled on expropriated land. It has been suggested that the majority of it came from large estates, but peasant land was also expropriated, and the sources give the impression that many of the large estates were distributed to important supporters of the dictator and not distributed to veterans. The colonies were concentrated in areas that had opposed Sulla during the civil war, with the greatest number in Etruria, Latium, and Umbria.

[Sulla] thinking to create the same safeguard for himself distributed much land in different communities, some of it public and some confiscated as a punishment, to the men of the twenty-three legions which had served under him.

A Sullan colony

162 ILS 5671 = ILLRP 617

The following inscription comes from Interamnia (modern Teramo) in the southern Picenum and dates to soon after Sulla. The Poppaeus mentioned in the inscription also appears in one other from the same town which also honors him as patron of both the colony and the municipium. Interamnia is mentioned by a second-century source as one of a number of municipia whose land was confiscated by Sulla.

Sulla appears to have employed three methods of settling his veterans: individual allotments in existing municipia and colonies; founding a colony within the territory of an existing municipium but leaving the municipium intact; and replacing an existing municipium with a colony and downgrading the status of the former inhabitants. The arrangement at Interamnia obviously belongs to the second method and has a parallel at Arretium in Etruria.

Q. C. Poppaeus, son of Quintus, patron of the municipium and colony, granted money in perpetuity for a bath for the members of the municipium, the colonists, inhabitants, guests, and visitors.

The fate of the Sullan colonists

163 CICERO, *AGAINST CATALINE* 2.20

The following passage comes from a speech delivered by Cicero to the people. It lists the various groups supporting Cataline's conspiracy of 63, which to a large extent was fueled at a popular level by rural distress and indebtedness. Gaius Manlius had been sent to Faesulae in Etruria, an area that had suffered heavily from Sulla's colonization, to gather an army. Manlius was himself an ex-Sullan centurion. It is significant that he found a ready response from the local population.

The general modern view is that many of the Sullan colonists were unsuccessful at farming. This was due not to the extravagance cited in the sources but to the marginal land many of the colonists received and the generally difficult economic climate of the 70s and 60s. Unlike earlier colonists, the Sullan veterans remained an identifiable group for several decades. In part, this may have been due to resentment by the locals. We occasionally hear of fighting breaking out between the two groups.

The third group is at this point marked by old age but is strong in body because of exercise. Manlius, who had now replaced Cataline, belongs to this group. These are the men from the Sullan colonies, all of which contain the best and bravest citizens, but these men are the colonists who with their sudden and unlooked-for wealth behave with extravagance and insolence. While they build as though they were wealthy and take delight in their estates, litters, hordes of slaves, dinner parties, and furnishings, they fall into such debt that Sulla would need to be summoned back from the grave to save them. They also entice the poor and needy men of the countryside into that same hope for plunder as themselves. I place both groups in the same category of robbers and bandits.

Veteran settlement during the civil wars

The civil war period saw the last extensive land distributions in Italy. Despite Caesar's doubling of military pay in 49 and substantial distributions of cash, the prospect of an allotment of land at the termination of service remained as important as ever. Though such allotments had never been automatic benefits, they seemed to have been major inducements for those in service. It is revealing that, in the struggles in the aftermath of Caesar's assassination, both Antony and his senatorial opponents promised land to attract recruits.

Caesar began settling his veterans in 47 after his victory over Pompey at Pharsalus, and the process continued until his death in 44 BC. In all, he probably found land for 20,000 men, three-quarters of whom were settled in Italy. Colonies were also established overseas in Africa, Spain, Illyricum, Macedonia, and the East. Although veterans were included, the majority of colonists were civilians, numbering approximately 80,000.

Caesar's allotments in Italy, which seemed to have been concentrated in the rich farming land of Campania, were designed to minimize the disruption of existing economic and social arrangements. The same aim is clear in other economic measures that Caesar took in these years. Caesar also used land from his own estates. Apparently no new colonies were established, but the ex-soldiers, maintaining ties among themselves developed during their service, tended to form close-knit groups within existing towns.

164 APPIAN, *THE CIVIL WARS* 2.94

Though Caesar's speech is Appian's own composition, its main points are supported by other sources dealing with Caesar's allotments of land. It was delivered in the context of a mutiny by veterans in Italy awaiting discharge in 47 and was supposedly quelled by Caesar's addressing them as citizens rather than fellow soldiers.

The settlement of these soldiers seems to have begun on a large scale in the following year on the principles outlined in this speech. Caesar's measures appear to have been less disruptive than earlier or later schemes of this type.

They could bear it no longer, but shouted out that he [Caesar] should change his mind and pleaded to remain in service. As Caesar was turning

246

away and leaving the speaker's platform, they cried out with greater urgency, pressing him to remain and to punish the guilty among them. He hesitated for a while, not leaving or returning, pretending to be undecided. However, he returned and said that he would punish no one, but he said he was upset that the Tenth Legion, which he had always honored, had joined this disturbance. He said that he would discharge that legion alone, but that he would give it all he had promised upon his return from Africa. He would give land to all after the wars had ended, not the way Sulla did by confiscating others' land, making those deprived of their land and those who had taken it into a single colony, and so making them eternal enemies. He would use public land and his own estates and buy the rest.

The Second Triumvirate and Augustus

The formation of a political compact between Antony, Octavian, and Lepidus at Bononia in November 43 to prosecute the war against Republican forces and to further the participants' own interests was formalized by the passage of the Lex Titia. Among the arrangements arrived at was a decision that the principal reward for service would be the distribution of land. After their victory over Brutus and Cassius at Philippi in 42, land had to be found for approximately 45,000. Almost all of these settlements were in Italy. Only one colony was established overseas, at the site of the triumvirs' victory in Macedonia. Eighteen cities were selected, though it is impossible to identify them because of lack of evidence. They were deliberately chosen for their wealth and fertility and, where the city's territory was insufficient, land was added from the territory of adjacent cities. As a result of the distribution of powers among the triumvirs, Octavian was given almost total control over the process. Expropriation began in 41, and the resulting suffering of those who lost their land and possessions was immense. It is reflected in contemporary poetry and contributed to an uprising against the triumvirs at Perusia in Etruria in the winter of 41/40. The settlement bears a strong resemblance to that of Sulla. It also provided a core of supporters whom the triumvirs could call upon and who had a vested interest in the maintenance of their power.

After his victory over Sextus Pompeius at Naulochus in 36, Octavian initiated another round of colonization in response to agitation by his troops to be demobilized. Octavian distributed a substantial cash bonus and demobilized a large number of veteran troops, somewhere between 20,000 and 40,000 men. Octavian seems to have made a deliberate attempt, in contrast to the expropriations after Philippi, to mitigate the impact on existing landholders. In Italy, where perhaps 15,000 veterans were settled, public land was used where available and additional land was purchased. There were additional settlements in Gaul and Sicily.

A further land distribution was made after Antony's defeat at Actium in September 31. This was perhaps the largest of all of Octavian's settlements. Octavian claims that he settled 120,000 veterans, though this figure is often thought to be too high, and it is not entirely clear who was included in this total. Suetonius mentions twenty-eight colonies founded in Italy by Augustus but does not mention when they were founded, and there were certainly land distributions after 30/29. If they belong after Actium, 120,000 would not be an impossible figure, especially as Octavian distributed cash to, at least, some of the veterans in place of land. The resulting disruption was in part dealt with by resettling some of the displaced in overseas colonies in Dyrrachium, Philippi, and other places.

The end of the civil wars did not mark the end of the Augustan settlement program. Between 26 and 15, veterans were settled in a number of overseas colonies in Africa, Gaul, the East, and Spain where the majority of colonies were established.

After 14, land was no longer regularly granted to retired soldiers. In parallel with the development of a professional long-service army, cash grants at the end of service replaced land distributions. The difficulty in finding land as well as the laborious process of founding new colonies made a cash grant an attractive and efficient alternative. Much of the money was paid out of Augustus' own pocket until in 6 AD a military treasury was created with a massive grant of the emperor's own money. Regular funding was to be provided by a 1 percent auction tax as well as a 5 percent tax on certain types of inheritances. The private soldier received 12,000 sesterces upon retirement, which was equal to approximately thirteen years' pay. This became the normal system under the Empire, though there were some exceptions. It was another fifty years before any further military colonization took place in Italy, and it was not a success.

The Second Triumvirate, the army, and the land

165 APPIAN, *THE CIVIL WARS* 4.3

The impending struggle with the Republican forces under Brutus and Cassius impelled the triumvirs to make the prizes of victory as attractive as possible. Appian's list of towns is not complete. Those listed are located in southern Italy; Arminium just north of the Apennines on the east coast is the exception.

> To encourage the army with the prizes of victory, they promised along with other gifts to establish colonies for the soldiers in eighteen Italian towns conspicuous for their wealth, lands, and buildings. They would divide the wealth, lands, and dwellings among them just as if they were the booty of war. The best known of these towns were Capua, Rhegium, Venusia, Beneventum, Nuceria, Arminium, and Vibo. So they marked out the most parts of Italy for their army.

166 VERGIL, *ECLOGUES* 1.64–72

The first of Vergil's pastoral poems was probably published in 42 or a little later, under the threat of the confiscations agreed upon by the Second Triumvirate. There is a tradition that Vergil's father's land was among the confiscated estates, but it is difficult to be sure whether this is an extrapolation from the poems. The shepherd Meliboeus' complaints offer some insight into the reactions of those who suffered during veteran settlement.

The opening lines are a poetical equivalent of the ends of the earth. There is some problem with identifying the Oaxes, which may have flowed through the Caucasus to the Caspian Sea.

> "But we must depart, some for the thirsty Africans; some will come to Scythia and to the Oaxes, snatching up clay as it flows, and to the Britons separated from the whole world.
>
> Will I ever far in the future look again at my kingdom, my native land, the turf roof of my poor hut, and afterwards at my few ears of grain? Or will some impious soldier own this well-tended land and a barbarian these crops?
>
> See, Meliboeus, to what a pass civil strife has brought us. I sow my fields for men such as those."

167 AUGUSTUS, *THE ACHIEVEMENTS OF THE DIVINE AUGUSTUS*

The 500,000 must have included those serving in the armies of Lepidus and Antony, as they were either given land by Augustus after Philippi or incorporated in Octavian's army. The figure of 300,000, given ancient mortality rates, must have excluded serving soldiers.

The document omits the expropriations after Philippi, as well as settlements made between 29 and 14 on land taken from conquered areas. Augustus also mentions money given, presumably in place of land, in 7–6 and 4–2 BC. These last distributions are part of the gradual substitution of a cash bonus for land. The use of cash was administratively easier, and it may have become increasingly difficult to find available land, as was certainly the case in Italy. In addition, the growing professionalism of the army meant that many of the veterans would have had little experience in or taste for farming.

> 3.3 Approximately 500,000 Roman citizens took the soldier's oath to me. I settled in colonies or sent back to their own towns, after the completion of their service, rather more than 300,000. I gave land or money to all of them as a reward for the military service.

The army in politics in the first century BC

The sources date the start of the involvement of the army in politics to the beginning of the fifth century. Its earliest involvement took the form of military strikes as a method of enforcing plebeian demands for political equality and debt relief. The exact details may be fictional, but most scholars accept the fact that the refusal of military service was an important plebeian tactic in their struggle with the patricians. The tactic of refusing military service continued until the end of the plebeian–patrician struggle at the beginning of the third century. In the course of the second century, especially during the wars in Spain, problems with military service surfaced again. The earlier problems connected with military service were social and economic struggles within the citizen body. The refusal of military service was simply the most effective tactic available to the less wealthy and powerful.

There is no evidence that soldiers who acted as citizens fulfilling their military obligation were conscious of themselves as a separate group within Roman society. The narratives of mutinies and other acts of insubordination that occur throughout this period either are related to broad social or economic issues or are reflections of specific problems and grievances linked directly to the troops' conditions of service.

The first century BC is marked by the increasing prominence of the army in politics. The reasons for the increasing prominence of the military lay in the intersection of three separate developments. First visible from the last third of the second century was an agrarian crisis that led to a deterioration in the situation of the poor and of small farmers. Factors in this development were the expansion of estates belonging to the elite, their increasing use of slave in place of free labor, and the prolonged separation of soldiers from their farms due to service overseas. These factors led to increasing rural impoverishment and immigration to various urban centers. The effects of the loss of land and increasing debt are most visible in the events of the Cataline conspiracy of 63, where the rural dispossessed provided a significant proportion of those who joined Cataline.

The changes in the nature of military service had more than simply economic consequences. Prolonged service far from home must have developed a sense of separation among those serving in the army from the civilian population as well as a feeling of group solidarity of soldiers from the same background and faced by similar problems. These factors were probably intensified after the Social War of 90–88 when thousands of new citizens were added who had little in common beyond their finding themselves in the army at the same time. This is not to imply that soldiers developed a sort of collective consciousness of themselves as a separate group from other citizens. There is no evidence of that until the imperial period. Rather, they were individuals who found themselves in a similar predicament, and that created the opportunity for collective action.

The increase in the number and duration of extraordinary commands also played a role in determining the direction of political activity by the army. There had been prolonged commands before. During the difficult struggles with the Samnites in the third century, men had held repeated consulships and had often been prorogued in command. During the Second Punic War, Scipio Africanus held commands continually in a number of theaters for almost a decade. However, during the first century the number of such commands multiplied with the needs of an expanding empire. The commands of Lucullus, Pompey, and Caesar in Gaul are obvious examples. These commands provided the opportunity for the commander and his men to form ties of mutual self-interest and personal affection. This was not an invariable accompaniment of such commands. The conflicts between Lucullus and his men are evidence that the opposite could happen. Perhaps the best example of what was possible was the bonds that formed between Caesar and his men in Gaul. Their loyalty to his memory and the hope of keeping the benefits he gave them were to provide a basis for his heir's rise to power.

Another factor was a change in the rules of political competition among the elite. Successful warfare and the expansion of empire led to an enormous influx of wealth into the hands of the elite, particularly those who had been successful commanders. Some of this wealth went into the expansion of estates. It also raised the level of the cost of an aristocratic lifestyle, as well as the expense of running for office. These factors made prolonged military command even more attractive. On his return from his commands in the East, Pompey possessed 200,000,000 sesterces in land alone. War brought not only prestige but immense wealth. With the stakes so high, competition for office and power became more intense than ever. This intensification led to a breakdown in the agreed rules of competition that had governed the aristocracy's quest for office and power. This competition began to tear the state apart. With the breakdown of the normal rules of competition the locus of legitimacy became unclear. Competing interests could all claim to be the true representatives of state authority. In such situations, legitimacy in the end depended on the ability to use military force. Control of the army is critical to success and even survival when civil authority breaks down. This made close ties between the commander and the army all the more crucial for the elite. The men who had served with the commander could form a following that could be relied upon for political support in legislative and electoral contests and to defend his interests when violence broke out. Equally, the Senate's inability to institute some program that would adequately compensate the demands of military service meant that veterans had to depend on their former commander's political support for their prospects after service of a distribution of land.

It was Rome's successful wars of conquest and imperial expansion that led to many of these consequences, and it was the failure of the Republican elite to solve the problems that this expansion had created that resulted in the importance of the army and veterans in the politics of the period.

The political value of the soldier's vote

168 CICERO, *ON BEHALF OF MURENA* 18.38

Elected as one of the consuls for 62, Lucius Licinius Murena was prosecuted for electoral bribery and corruption by one of his unsuccessful competitors. He was defended by Cicero and some of the most eminent advocates of the period. Cicero here stresses the importance of the military vote because of Murena's successful military career. He saw extensive service as a legate with Lucullus in the third war against Mithridates VI and then served as proconsul in Transalpine Gaul in 64. In 63, Lucullus celebrated his triumph for the war against Mithridates, and many of the soldiers who had participated in it must have been in Rome when Cicero made his defense of Murena. It is presumably to these soldiers that Cicero refers. It is striking that at this point Cicero can point to these veterans as a separate group within the citizen body. Their importance as a voting group is visible as early as the election of Marius to his first consulship in 107.

The elections for the consulship were held in the *Comitia Centuriata*. The first century to vote was chosen by lot.

> Do you think these things provide unimportant assistance and support in gaining the consulship? Is the goodwill of the soldiers, potent in numbers, influential because of their relatives, and possessed of great authority among the whole Roman people, unimportant in the election of a consul? Is the vote of the army of little importance? Generals, not interpreters of words, are chosen in consular elections. And so these are words of importance: "He revived me when I was wounded, he rewarded me with booty, we captured the enemy's camp under his leadership, we joined battle under his command, he never imposed greater labor on his soldiers than he did on himself, and he was as brave as he was lucky." How important do you think this in establishing a man's reputation and in creating goodwill? Indeed, if religious custom is of such weight to this point that the vote of the century chosen to vote first has prevailed, is it so remarkable that in this matter a reputation for enjoying good fortune and talk of this type has prevailed?

Sulla's march on Rome

169 APPIAN, *THE CIVIL WARS* 1.56–57

The year 88 was marked by a struggle led by one of the tribunes, P. Sulpicius, to solve the problem created by the spread of the granting of Roman citizenship to the Italians after the Social War. The new citizens had been confined to eight or ten of the thirty-five tribes to minimize their influence. Sulpicius proposed to distribute them throughout all of the tribes. Stymied in the gang warfare that signaled the increasing role of violence in Roman politics, he turned to Marius for help and in return for his support offered him the command against Mithridates, which had been given to Sulla, who was consul in this year. The rioting worsened and the other consul, Rufus, had to flee for his life, while Sulla after reaching an agreement with Marius left Rome for Nola, which was under siege by the army which had been assigned to the war against Mithridates.

His headquarters were probably at Capua, and Appian incorrectly locates the decisive events there.

It is striking that the army rank and file displayed so little hesitation about marching against Rome, since this was the first time that it was asked to intervene directly in politics. It has been suggested that in part this may have been due to the effects of the Social War, in which other Italian towns had been subjected to siege and capture. It may also be the case that many soldiers were not themselves Romans, but former Italian allies who would have had no particular love for the city. Difference in origin may explain the contrast between the army and Sulla's legates, most of whom refused to move against the city. The quaestor who supported him has been plausibly identified as Lucullus, who was a close associate of Sulla's. The acquiescence of the army may also have been made easier by a situation in which it was no longer clear who was the legitimate representative of state authority. Sulla's statement to envoys from the city that he was marching to free the city from tyranny illustrates the point. Although Sulla had had to flee Rome, he was still consul.

When Sulla arrived he lifted the suspension of business that had been in force and then pressed on to Capua to the army stationed there to bring it across to Asia for the war against Mithridates. He was not yet aware of any of the steps taken against him. After the resumption of public business and Sulla's departure, Sulpicius passed a law to make Marius, for whose sake it had been passed, commander in the war against Mithridates in place of Sulla.

After learning what had happened, Sulla decided to settle the matter by fighting. He called the army to an assembly. The soldiers were eager for war, as it would bring rich booty, and thought that Marius would select others in their place. Sulla spoke of the disgrace he had suffered from the actions of Sulpicius and Marius, making no clear allusion to anything else [for he did not risk mentioning the possibility of civil war]. He urged them to be prepared to obey orders. The men understood clearly what he meant and were afraid to miss the campaign. They spoke openly of what Sulla had in mind and called upon him to lead them with confidence to Rome. Sulla, delighted at this, led out the six legions immediately. But his superior officers apart from the quaestor fled to Rome because they could not tolerate the idea of leading an army against their own country.

170 APPIAN, *THE CIVIL WARS* 1.60

And so the civil struggle progressed from strife and rivalry to murder and from murder to open warfare. This was a citizen army moving to attack their homeland as if it were an enemy. From this point on, armies were decisive in internal struggles. There were frequent attacks on Rome and sieges and the rest of what war brings. From now on, neither shame nor law nor the constitution nor a sense of patriotism restrained the violence.

The late Republican army in battle

Pharsalus

171 CAESAR, *CIVIL WAR* 3.88–94

The outbreak of the civil war in January 49 was followed by Caesar's lightning conquest of Italy and Pompey's evacuation of his remaining forces to the East. Instead of pursuing Pompey immediately Caesar turned west to eliminate the seven Pompeian legions in Spain. Their removal would free him of the threat of an attack on Italy in his rear once he had begun to move his troops across the Adriatic to confront Pompey. Further, at this point the Spanish legions were the only large Pompeian force in the field and therefore an obvious object of attack. Within forty days Caesar had defeated the Republican forces through a war of maneuver without the need for a major battle.

Caesar's campaign in Spain had given Pompey time to gather his forces. Pompey with his headquarters at Dyrrachium on the Adriatic coast had raised a force of nine legions, including five from Italy and the remainder from the eastern provinces. In addition, he was awaiting the arrival of Metellus Scipio and his two legions from Syria. He could field 7,000 cavalry as well as numerous light-armed archers and slingers. Further, he had auxiliary forces from various eastern kings. His fleet controlled the seas and was stationed to prevent Caesar's crossing the Adriatic.

Caesar had twelve legions at Brundisium and cavalry, but insufficient shipping to transport them, and he was without a fleet that could contest the dominance of Pompey's. Despite these difficulties and lacking a suitable port, he was able initially to bring over a force of 15,000 infantry and 500 cavalry. These were followed after a lengthy interval by the arrival of Marc Antony with an additional four legions and 800 cavalry. The rather meager resources at Caesar's disposal were further diminished by his sending five cohorts to Aetolia under Calvisius Sabinus in an attempt to alleviate his supply problems and two legions dispatched to Macedonia under Domitius Calvinus to try to prevent a junction of Scipio and Pompey.

Caesar himself tried at first to outmaneuver Pompey as he had done to his lieutenants in Spain. Despite the disparity of forces Caesar began to construct extensive siege works to blockade Pompey, who was encamped near Dyrrachium. Pompey responded in kind. Since Pompey controlled Dyrrachium, which served as his port and was able to be supplied by sea, there was no possibility of reducing him by hunger. Caesar claims that in part the siege works were built to restrict the enemy's foraging and so diminish Pompey's immense advantage in cavalry. No doubt Caesar also hoped to affect the morale of Pompey's troops.

The prolongation of the siege created severe supply difficulties for Caesar, and a successful attack on the southern part of Caesar's fortifications led to a Pompeian victory in which Caesar's troops suffered heavy losses. These setbacks in combination with a severe grain shortage led to Caesar's abandoning of the siege and his moving southeast towards the richer area of Thessaly where provisions could be obtained and he could link up with Domitius and so prevent Scipio and Pompey from uniting their forces. Such a move would force Pompey to leave the coast and then Caesar might by restricting his supplies be able to compel him to offer battle on a field of Caesar's choosing.

With Pompey in pursuit, Caesar moved into Thessaly, which was friendly and had an abundant supply of grain. He was also able to affect a junction with Domitius and then decided to confine his operations to Thessaly. Meanwhile, Pompey had been joined by Scipio. Caesar now decided on battle and moved towards Pompey's forces. Pompey was encamped on a hill in the vicinity of Pharsalus. Later sources mention Pharsalus or Old Pharsalus. The latter site is of no help, since it has not been identified. Various locations have been suggested for Pompey's camp and the plain in which the battle was fought. Caesar does not name the location. The one feature definitely identified in Caesar's account is the Enipeus River, which flows to the north of Pharsalus. Other indications in Caesar's text favor a location for the battle north of the river, with Pompey's camp on one of the hills that ring the river on that side. Caesar encamped on lower ground to the east.

Caesar made a number of attempts to bring Pompey to battle; although Pompey did deploy for battle, he did so on the lower slopes of the hill on which his camp was situated, and Caesar correctly judged that the ground was unfavorable for an attack. Once again, lack of supplies and the possibility of maneuvering Pompey into a position where battle would be possible persuaded Caesar to move on August 9, 48.

What is far from clear is the reason for Pompey finally deciding to accept battle just as Caesar's forces were ready to march. Caesar gives no reason. At least one source claims that Pompey had decided on a strategy of attrition and was forced to give battle by his advisors. It has also been suggested that Pompey in his attempt to follow Caesar's forces had advanced too far from his camp when Caesar decided to turn and offer battle.

Pompey's plan was to protect his right flank by basing it on the Enipeus River, facing east with the sun at its back. His infantry was in the normal three-line formation, and he massed his cavalry on his left to overwhelm Caesar's cavalry and then to sweep around his flank and attack his rear. His order to his infantry to hold their ground and await Caesar's attack in formation indicates he was not confident of their ability to meet Caesar's legions on equal terms. Given the quality of his legions this was not unreasonable fear. Three of his legions were composed of raw recruits, while two others had served with Caesar. Pompey might well have had doubts about their loyalty. The Cilician legion had been assembled from two weakened legions which had formed the garrison of that province and had recently fought with the Parthians. Pompey's plan was unusual in assigning the decisive role to the cavalry, but given his preponderance in that arm and his doubts about his infantry it makes good tactical sense. If Caesar's account is accurate, his own cohorts were far below strength with about half of their regular complement. But most were battle hardened and had proven their loyalty under very harsh conditions.

Caesar's account makes clear that he foresaw the cavalry attack and deployed a fourth line of picked cohorts to meet the cavalry attack on his right flank. This makes the role of the third line normally used as a reserve a problem. Why was it not used to counter Pompey's cavalry? It is possible that he decided to employ them in the attack, since the cohorts of his first two lines were under strength.

Caesar's figures for the casualties on both sides should probably be accepted, although the disparity between the casualty figures for the winning and losing sides far exceeds the norm. He claims he lost 200 dead, including thirty centurions, while the Pompeians suffered 15,000 killed and 24,000 captured. The prolonged pursuit would have greatly increased the figure for the Pompeians, and the numbers given are in line with figures in Caesar's account of his battles in Gaul.

The characterization of the former *primipilus* Crastinus supplements Caesar's own speech. At a number of places Caesar mentions the bravery of centurions, which often serves to reflect their devotion to Caesar and his policies.

As Caesar approached Pompey's camp he saw that the latter had deployed his battle line in the following way: on his left were the two legions that Caesar had handed over in accordance with a senatorial decree at the beginning of their quarrel. These legions were the First and Third. Pompey has stationed himself in that part of the line. Scipio and the Syrian legions held the center. The Cilician legion, together with some Spanish cohorts which as I mentioned earlier had been brought over by Afranius, was on the right wing. Pompey had the most confidence in these units. He placed his remaining forces numbering 110 cohorts between his center and his wings. He had 45,000 men as well as about 2,000 veterans drawn from those who previously had held special duty assignments in his armies. Seven cohorts had been left behind to guard his camp and nearby outposts. These men were drawn from his whole force. His right wing was protected by a stream whose banks hampered movement.

Caesar deployed his battle line in accord with his previous practice. The Tenth Legion held the right wing and the Ninth the left, although it had been seriously weakened in the earlier battle at Dyrrachium. He had combined the Eighth Legion with it [the Ninth] to form a single legion from the two. He ordered each legion to protect the other. Caesar had eighty cohorts in his line, which totaled 22,000 men. Two cohorts were assigned to guard his camp. He placed Marcus Antonius in command of the left wing, Publius Sulla led the right wing, and Gnaeus Domitius held the center. Caesar took up his position opposite Pompey.

... Caesar was afraid that the large number of enemy cavalry would envelop his right wing so he drew cohorts from each legion and formed a fourth line. He stationed them opposite the enemy's cavalry and showed them what he wanted them to do, adding that the outcome of battle rested on their firmness and courage. He then issued an order to the third line and to the army as a whole that they should come to grips with the enemy without his command; he would give a signal with a flag at the appropriate time.

Caesar gave the customary speech to encourage the troops, listing their unfailing good services to him. In particular, he reminded them that they had witnessed the earnestness with which he had sought peace, how he had attempted to negotiate through Vatinius by personal meetings, how he had tried to hold discussions with Scipio through A. Clodius, and how at Oricum he had conferred with Libo about an exchange of envoys. He had never spilled his soldiers' blood without just cause nor deprived the state of the use of either army. After the speech, at the demand of his troops, who were burning with the desire for battle, he had the trumpet sounded as the signal for battle.

There was a veteran in Caesar's army, a man of unusual courage called Crastinus, who the year before had been the leading centurion in the Tenth Legion. After the signal for battle had been given, he called out to his men: "Follow me, men of my former unit, and serve your general as you promised. There is just this one battle left. When it is done our leader will regain his due standing and we our liberty." At the same time he looked at Caesar, saying: "Today, commander, I will act so that you will thank me whether I live or die. After his speech he was the first to run forward from the right wing, followed by 120 picked men, all volunteers from the same century.

There was only enough space between the two armies to allow them to meet. Pompey had instructed his men to receive Caesar's charge, to hold their position, and not to allow their line to become disorganized. It is said that he had done this on the advice of Gaius Triarius with the intention that, after breaking the force of the first rush, he would attack with his men in good order troops who had lost theirs. He also thought that the impact of the javelins would be less on soldiers who had kept their position than on those who were running as the javelins were thrown. He also thought that Caesar's men would be worn out by having to run twice as far as normal. My view is that Pompey was wrong about this. There is a certain keenness of spirit and a natural enthusiasm ignited by the desire for battle. Commanders ought to stimulate it, not suppress it. It is a useful custom from ancient times that both sides sounded the signal and that all raised their war cry. These things were thought to terrify the enemy and to encourage one's own side.

After the signal was given our men ran forward with their javelins leveled, but they noticed that the Pompeians were not charging, and because of their previous experience and training in earlier battles they spontaneously held their charge and stopped about halfway to the enemy line to avoid approaching them in an exhausted condition. They stopped for a while and then charged again, threw their javelins, and quickly drew their swords as Caesar had instructed. The Pompeians met the challenge. They stood up to the hail of missiles and the charge of the legions, keeping their ranks in order. They threw their own javelins and then used their swords.

At the same time the Pompeian cavalry on the left wing charged forward and all of the archers ran out. Our cavalry could not withstand this attack and retreated a little way. Their cavalry began to press more force-fully and to extend itself by squadrons and it began to surround our line from the rear on its open flank. When Caesar noticed this he gave the sig-nal to the fourth line, which he had formed from single cohorts. The cohorts quickly charged forward and attacked. They struck with such force at the Pompeian cavalry that it could not withstand them. All of them turned and not only gave ground but immediately fled in a headlong rush, making for the highest hills. Deprived of the protection of the cavalry, the archers and slingers were now defenseless and were cut down. With the same charge the cohorts surrounded the left wing of the Pompeian infantry, who until this point had kept position and had continued fighting, and attacked them from the rear.

At the same time, Caesar ordered his third line, which until this point had held its position and had not been involved in the fighting, to advance. The combination of fresh and uninjured troops replacing those worn out by com-bat and an attack from the rear was too much for the Pompeian infantry, and they all turned and fled. It did not escape Caesar that the reason for the vic-tory lay with the fourth line, which had been stationed to thwart the cavalry, as he stated while encouraging the troops. It was these cohorts who had thrown back the cavalry and these same units that had cut down the archers and slingers as well as surrounded the Pompeian left and had routed them.

Romans in battle against non-Romans: the battle of Carrhae

172 PLUTARCH, *LIFE OF CRASSUS* 24.1–37.2 (WITH OMISSIONS)

Despite strong senatorial opposition, the coalition of Pompey, Crassus, and Caesar known as the First Triumvirate was able to secure both consulships for 55. The two consuls, Pompey and Crassus, secured major commands to match Caesar's in Gaul. Pompey received the two Spains, while Crassus was given Syria. Both commands were for five years and each received a free hand to enroll as many troops as they thought necessary as well as the right to make peace and war at their own discretion. This last provision must have been especially attractive to Crassus. Both Pompey and Crassus had gained military glory and immense wealth in the course of their campaigns. In fact Pompey's wealth probably exceeded Crassus'. Crassus had last campaigned against Spartacus in 71 in an inglorious war and he must have felt the need to bolster his military reputation to equal his colleagues'. Syria was an attrac-tive prize. Pompey's widespread conquests in the East, with their easy victories and immense booty, must have made further war appealing. Victory would be easy and its financial rewards immense.

Little appears to have been known about the Parthians or their methods of fight-ing. The recent contest over the Parthian kingship was seen as an indication of inter-nal weakness. Crassus' immediate predecessor in the governorship had thought of intervening in Parthia before being distracted by affairs in Egypt.

Our main sources for the campaign and the battle of Carrhae are Plutarch and Cassius Dio. Plutarch's life of Crassus is the better source despite certain problems. It is clear that both authors try to lay the blame for the disaster on Crassus and portray him as greedy and incompetent, though Plutarch's portrait is a more nuanced treatment and contains some positive comments on Crassus' behavior.

Crassus crossed the Euphrates and entered Mesopotamia, which was Parthian territory, at Zeugma in southeastern Turkey, where he captured a string of Greek towns along the Balikh River, a tributary of the Euphrates which flows into it from the northeast. He assigned a garrison of 7,000 infantry and 1,000 cavalry to hold the towns. This must have been done to protect his line of communications back to Syria as he marched south along the Euphrates with the ultimate goal of reaching the Parthian capital of Ctesiphon on the Tigris. His initial advance met with little opposition, as the Parthians were unprepared for the invasion and the nature of the Parthian army made speedy mobilization very difficult.

Formally the Parthian army was under the king's control. There was probably a small standing army available for garrisons and other duties. For major campaigns the Parthian king relied on forces supplied by his nobles, who controlled huge estates. It was their tenants and slaves who supplied the bulk of the troops for major expeditions. It must have been very difficult to maneuver these armies on the battlefield, as there was little opportunity for training the entire force to operate as a single unit. These armies were difficult to hold together for long periods and presented problems of command because of the difficulty of disciplining important nobles.

The infantry was by far the weakest and least important part of the force, whose main strength lay in its cavalry. The heavy cavalry, called cataphracts or *clibanarii*, used a large thrusting spear as its main armament, with a sword as a secondary weapon, and were protected from head to foot by helmet and mail. Their horses were armored as well. As was the case with other types of cavalry, they could not mount a frontal charge on heavy infantry in close formation, but they were extremely effective against disorganized troops and enemy cavalry. The other major category of Parthian cavalry was formed of horse archers, who seem to have been lightly protected but had powerful and effective bows.

Crassus returned to spend the winter of 54–53 in Syria. The sources paint a picture of his unrestrained greed, but it is more likely that the time was spent in assembling the necessary finances to renew the campaign for the following year. More significantly, it appears that he did not use the time to train his men sufficiently. Considering that Crassus had been able to levy the men only with difficulty and they had had little time to develop group solidarity, this would turn out to be his most serious mistake. It appears that he did recognize the need for increased cavalry strength. His son, who had been serving as a legate with Caesar in Gaul, joined him in Syria with a force of 1,000 Gallic cavalry. He had also called on local client kings for further cavalry.

During his preparations for the opening of the campaign he was approached by Artavasdes, the Armenian king, with an offer of 6,000 cavalry and the promise of large numbers of additional troops. The force must have been substantial, although the numbers are probably exaggerated. However, the offer was contingent on Crassus invading by way of Armenia rather than moving straight into Mesopotamia. Armenia was a hilly and difficult country, as earlier Roman commanders had discovered, and supplies would have been a problem. It may be that Artavasdes' offer was made out of fear of a Parthian attack. The direct route into Mesopotamia offered a further advantage: Crassus would be able to relieve some of the garrisons he had established along the Balikh River which had come under attack. Crassus sensibly refused the offer.

In the spring of 53 Crassus once again crossed the Euphrates and marched to the Balikh valley. He probably had seven legions of reduced strength (about 28,000 men), 4,000 light infantry including archers, and 4,000 cavalry. He was met by his local allies and moved down the river until he reached Bambyce, later Hierapolis, in Syria, and then he struck east to the Balikh. Our sources portray the route to the Balikh as passing through a trackless desert and put much of the blame for the later disaster on the privations the army suffered in its journey, but in fact Crassus had taken an old caravan route dotted with oases and settlements, which would easily have supplied his army's needs. In early June he reached the Balikh.

The Parthian king had divided his army into two parts. He advanced on Armenia with one part to distract Artavasdes, while he left his chief commander, the Surena, to meet Crassus. His army was much smaller than Crassus', consisting of 10,000 cataphracts and horse archers. The Surena had also brought along a pack train of 1,000 camels to carry a reserve supply of arrows so that the horse archers could continually resupply themselves. Strangely, this innovation, so obvious for an army that depended so heavily on missile weapons, seems never to have been repeated by the Parthians. Crassus had begun to move east down the Balikh in the direction of Carrhae when the two armies encountered each other.

Neither force was well suited to face the other. The Roman infantry were well protected by their equipment and in close formation, and their line was impervious to the Parthian cavalry. In later encounters Parthians were rarely able to defeat Roman forces as long as they kept formation. Attacks that were successful were carried out against isolated detachments or lines of communication. The Romans were equally ill adapted to bring the enemy to battle and defeat him decisively because of the superior mobility of Parthian armies.

One of the greatest difficulties with Plutarch's account is his description of the formation Crassus adopted when the battle began. Plutarch claims that at first Crassus extended his formation to avoid being surrounded and then drew up his men in a square, alternating units of cavalry and legionary cohorts. But then without noting any changes he mentions that Crassus' son was in charge of one wing while his quaestor Gaius Cassius Longinus, the conspirator against Caesar, was in charge of the other. A hollow square has no wings, and the cavalry charge of Crassus' son later delivered would have disrupted the formation. It has been suggested that the formation was one described in ancient military manuals in which the troops are divided into two columns that march in parallel and can face in either direction.

The feigned retreat with the famous backward shot was a normal Parthian tactic. It was designed to destroy group cohesion by drawing off isolated detachments, and in this case it was successful in destroying over a quarter of the Roman cavalry and a substantial body of infantry during Crassus' son's attack. More critical for the final Roman defeat was the loss of morale caused by the prolonged arrow bombardment. Once morale was destroyed, the army's cohesion disintegrated, and isolated units were destroyed piecemeal during the Roman flight to Carrhae. The final disaster was exacerbated by the absence of a defensible base. The ancient sources claim that Crassus lost 30,000 and only 10,000 survived the retreat to Syria.

> The Romans were thrown into panic by the noise of the [Parthians] taking off the coverings on their armor. Their flashing helmets and breastplates of Margianian iron were brightly shining and their horses were armored with plates of bronze and iron....
>
> At first the Parthians had decided to charge and use their lances to push back and disorder the Roman front ranks. But when they saw the depth of the dense formation and the steadiness and self-possession of the men they moved back, giving the appearance of dispersing and breaking ranks. They encircled the Roman square without the latter realizing it. Crassus ordered his light-armed troops forward, but they did not advance far, as they were quickly overwhelmed by innumerable arrows, and ceasing their attack sought the shelter of the heavy infantry. This was the beginning of fear and disorder in the Roman ranks, as they saw the force and strength of these missiles which broke apart armor and ripped their way through soft or hardened protection.
>
> Now the Parthians stood separated by large intervals, and began to shoot their arrows from every direction simultaneously, not with accuracy [for with the compactness and density of the Roman formation it was impossible for an archer to miss his target] but their shots were made with force from bows that were large, powerful, and curved and which imparted great force to their arrows.
>
> The Roman situation was desperate. If they kept their formation they were wounded, or if they attempted to come to grips with the enemy they accomplished nothing and suffered equally, since the Parthians shot their arrows as they fled. They are together with the Scythians the most effective at this tactic.
>
> As long as the Romans had hope that the enemy would exhaust their supply of missiles and then would either stop fighting or come to close quarters, they maintained their confidence, but then they saw a number of camels loaded with arrows from which the Parthians who had first surrounded them took a fresh supply of arrows. Crassus, seeing no end to it, lost heart and sent messengers to his son to force an engagement with the enemy before they were surrounded. For the Parthians were pressing

Publius' wing especially hard, surrounding it and trying to get to the rear of the Roman line. Crassus' son took 1,300 cavalry, including the 1,000 who had come from Caesar, 500 archers, and eight cohorts of heavy infantry that were closest to him and charged. The Parthians who were enveloping him either because they encountered marshes or as some say arranging to attack him as far as possible from his father turned away and sped off.

Then Publius, shouting out that they did not stand their ground, charged on and with him Censorinus and Megabacchus. The cavalry followed him, and even the infantry kept pace, inspired by their hopes. They thought they had won and were pursuing a beaten enemy until they had advanced a long distance and became aware of the enemy's deception. The group of Parthians who had seemed to be fleeing wheeled around and were then joined by many others. The Romans halted, imagining that the enemy would close with them as they were few in number. But the Parthians deployed their cataphracts opposite them, and the rest of their cavalry rode around them in open formation, tearing up the plain, raising from its depths great heaps of sand, which fell in endless showers of dust so that the Romans' vision was obscured and they could not easily talk to one another. Herded into a confined space and falling on each other, the Romans were shot and died deaths that were neither easy nor quick.

Many were killed, and the survivors lacked the capacity to carry on the fight. Publius called on them to charge the cataphracts, but they showed him their hands riveted to their shields and their feet completely pinned to the ground so that they could neither flee nor defend themselves. Publius with the cavalry charged forward vigorously and came to grips with the enemy. The struggle was an unequal one both offensively and defensively, since the Romans' blows were delivered with short and ineffective spears against breastplates of rawhide and iron, while the enemy struck his blows with lances against the lightly protected or naked bodies of the Gauls upon whom Publius chiefly relied and with whom he had accomplished marvels. They grabbed the long Parthian spears and struggling with them unhorsed them although the weight of their armor made it difficult. Many of the Gauls dismounted and crawling under the enemy's horses stabbed them in the belly. These would rear up in their pain and trample their riders and attackers indiscriminately as they died. The Gauls were most affected by heat and thirst, since they were unused to them. They lost most of their horses, since these were driven on to the enemy's lances. Then they were forced back to the infantry, carrying with them Publius, who had been severely wounded. Seeing a small sandy hill nearby they all retreated to it and, after tying up their horses and placing them in the center their formation, locked their shields together facing outwards, thinking that they would in this way more easily hold off the barbarians. However, the opposite happened. For on level ground the rear ranks provide some relief to those standing in front, but here the unevenness of the ground which raised those in the rear exposed them to the enemy. There was no escape; all were equally struck by arrows, railing at their inglorious and useless deaths. The Parthians mounted the hill and speared the survivors who had continued the fight. It is said that they took no more than 500 prisoners and, cutting off Publius' head, they rode off quickly to attack Crassus.

His situation was the following. After he had ordered his son to attack the Parthians, he had received news that the enemy had suffered a defeat and was being strongly pursued. He saw that the enemy near him were no longer pressing his men with as much force [since most had moved to where Publius was] and was somewhat encouraged. Assembling his troops, he placed them for safety on sloping ground, expecting that his son would immediately return from the pursuit.

The first of the messengers dispatched by Publius when he fell into difficulties were intercepted by the barbarians and killed; those sent out later with some difficulty evaded the enemy and informed Crassus that he must come up to support Publius quickly in great strength, as otherwise he was lost. Now Crassus was prey to conflicting emotions. He stopped thinking rationally. Fear for the army as a whole kept him from bringing help to his son, while his feelings for Publius moved him in the opposite direction. Finally, he began to move the army forward.

Now the enemy came up with a great deal of noise, sounding their battle cry, and many of their drums started to sound around the Romans awaiting the start of the second phase of the battle. The enemy rode up with Publius' head impaled and displayed it, inquiring about his parents and family in an insulting manner. It was the sight of this more than any of the other horrors that unnerved and depressed the Romans. They were filled not with the desire for revenge, but with trembling and shaking.

Though he was speaking such words to encourage his troops, Crassus saw that they did not respond with any enthusiasm. When he ordered them to raise their battle-cry he saw their desperation; only a few responded, with a weak and ragged shout. In contrast, the barbarians' cry was clear and strong. Then their cavalry turned to their task, riding around the Roman flanks and shooting their arrows, while the cataphracts in front using their long spears herded the Romans into a smaller space, except for those who dared to charge the enemy to escape the arrows. Inflicting little damage, they died quickly from the great fatal wounds they received. The Parthians thrust their heavy iron spears into the horses, and they often had enough force for a single spear to pass through two men. The battle continued in this manner until nightfall, when the Parthians broke off contact.

Roman infantry in battle against cavalry: a different result

173 [CAESAR], *THE WAR IN AFRICA* 13–18

For the account of the African war included among Caesar's writings, see **93**. Despite being delayed in Italy by a mutiny and then political business at Rome, Caesar decided to confront the gathering Pompeian forces in Africa in a winter campaign. Under the leadership of Metellus Scipio and his legates Labienus, Petreius, and Afranius, the Republicans had assembled a force of ten legions, over 15,000 cavalry, and substantial numbers of light infantry and other troops supplied by King Juba of Numidia, who had joined with a large force of cavalry and additional light infantry.

Caesar assembled a force of six legions, all under strength, with about 2,000 men per legion. At least a third of the troops were new recruits and 2,000 cavalry. The army assembled at Lilybaeum in western Sicily. Despite the winter, Caesar with his usual unbounded confidence embarked his force in late December 47 and sailed for the African coast. He was faced with the problem that his opponents held the major ports. These difficulties were compounded by a storm that blew up during the crossing and scattered his forces. He landed near Hadrumentum with only 3,000 infantry and 150 cavalry, encamping by the town, even though the Pompeians had garrisoned it. Unable to take it, Caesar decided to move his camp farther down the coast to Ruspina, where he pitched camp on January 1, 46. Soon after setting up his headquarters at Ruspina he moved south, as he desperately needed a port for his dispersed forces and to assure the transport of his supplies. Leptis Minor on the coast went over to him, as did Sullecthum even further to the south, which provided him with the harbors he needed. By chance, the forces scattered by the storm during the crossing landed near Ruspina, and Caesar was able to affect a junction with them.

The arrival of the rest of his men increased Caesar's supply difficulties. Leaving the rest of his forces in camp, he set out to forage for grain with a force of thirty cohorts, 400 cavalry, and 150 archers. On his line of march, about three miles from his camp he encountered a combined force of cavalry and light-armed Numidian infantry under Labienus (see **151**).

The ensuing battle is reminiscent of Carrhae (see **172**). A force composed mainly of Roman heavy infantry was confronted by an overwhelmingly superior force of cavalry in open country, although Caesar gives no numbers for Labienus' troops. In essence, Labienus' tactics were the same as those of the Parthians: to pin the legions to the spot by encircling them with cavalry and then to wear them down by missile attacks until they lost cohesion. The difference in the result seems to have been due in part to several adjustments Caesar made in his formation in the course of the battle. He created a line that faced in both directions so that he could defend his rear as well as his front. More significant may have been his extension of his line, which must have thinned out the encircling cavalry force and probably assisted the breakthrough on the flanks by a combined force of cavalry and infantry. These maneuvers finally allowed his men to move to the safety of his own fortifications despite an attack that was launched after the arrival of additional Numidian troops under Afranius and Piso.

Despite Caesar's claim that the battle at Ruspina ended in his favor it is clear that he suffered a defeat. Nonetheless, it illustrates Caesar's ability to improvise in extreme circumstances. Numidian tactics so impressed him that later in the campaign he instituted a program of training for his men specifically designed to counter them (see **151**). The key difference between the disaster at Carrhae and Caesar's survival was the discipline his men showed in carrying out his commands. His order to his men not to advance farther than four feet from their lines must have been obeyed, and that allowed him to maintain the cohesiveness of his force. It was Crassus' failure to do so that was the major cause of his defeat.

For M. Petreius' earlier encounter with Caesar in Spain, see **132**. Little is known about the Pacideius brothers, who seem to have served as cavalry commanders under Labienus at Ruspina and in later campaigns in Africa. It is difficult to judge the truth of the conversation between Labienus and the veteran of the Tenth Legion. This legion was especially favored by Caesar and was in the center of the line at Ruspina. If nothing else, the legion's loyalty to Caesar contrasts strongly with Labienus' betrayal and is an effective piece of propaganda.

Meanwhile the enemy under the command of Labienus and the two Pacideius brothers arranged their battle line on a very broad front. Their line was made up for the most part of cavalry, and distributed among it were light-armed Numidians and foot archers. The cavalry was so densely arrayed that Caesar's infantry mistook them for infantry. In addition, the enemy's right and left wings had been reinforced by large numbers of cavalry.

Caesar, since he had only a small force, drew them up in a single line, placing his archers in front of it and his cavalry on his wings to oppose that of the enemy. He ordered his men to take care not to be surrounded by the multitude of the enemy cavalry. With his men in formation, Caesar thought that the battle would be an infantry contest.

While both sides waited expectantly for the coming battle, Caesar did not advance since he saw that, given the small number of his troops compared to the enemy's, the battle must be won more through cunning than by force. Suddenly the enemy's cavalry began to extend its line towards the flanks, encircling the hills with the aim of thinning out Caesar's cavalry and then surrounding it. They were only holding their ground with difficulty in the face of the enemy's numbers. Meanwhile, as the infantry were attempting to engage, suddenly light-armed Numidian foot along with cavalry charged forward from the densely massed cavalry squadrons. The Numidians hurled their javelins at the legions, and when Caesar's infantry charged them they fled back to their own cavalry formation. While their infantry kept up their resistance, their cavalry again came to their aid with a renewed charge.

Caesar saw that his men were being thrown into disorder by their pursuit of the enemy in this new style of warfare, and that his infantry was being wounded by the javelins of the Numidians nearest to them, since in advancing some distance from their standards in their pursuit of the enemy's cavalry they exposed their flanks, but the enemy cavalry easily evaded the soldiers' *pila* because of their speed. Caesar gave the order that no soldier was to advance more than four feet from the ranks. In the meanwhile, Labienus' cavalry, confident in their numbers, did not delay in surrounding Caesar's small force. Iulianus' cavalry, worn down by the multitude of the enemy and with their wounded horses, gave way a little as the enemy kept up his pressure. Within a short time the infantry were totally surrounded by the enemy's cavalry and, herded into a circular formation, were compelled to fight in a confined space.

Labienus, bare-headed, advanced to the front of his line, encouraging his troops and sometimes calling upon Caesar's troops in the following manner: "My fierce new recruit, what do you think you are doing? I pity you." The soldier answered: "Labienus, I am not a new recruit but a veteran of the Tenth Legion." Labienus replied: "I do not see the standard of the men of the Tenth." The soldier retorted: "I'll soon end your ignorance." At the same time as he removed his helmet so that he could be recognized, he threw his *pilum* with all his strength at Labienus so that it wounded his horse deeply in the chest, saying: "Labienus, learn that it is a soldier of the Tenth who attacks you." Despite this, all of Caesar's troops, especially the new recruits, were terrified and looked to Caesar, doing nothing more than avoiding the enemy's javelins.

Meanwhile, Caesar, recognizing the enemy's plan, ordered his line to extend itself sideways as much as possible and for alternate cohorts to face in opposite directions. In this way he broke open the enemy's encirclement of the middle of his line with his left and right wings. He attacked each section of the enemy with his cavalry and infantry, putting the enemy to flight by bombarding him with missiles. He did not press the pursuit very far because he feared an ambush and returned to his own lines. The same attack was also delivered by the rest of his cavalry and infantry. Once the attack was over and the enemy, wounded by missiles thrown from every direction, had been forced back a great distance, Caesar began to march his troops to their camp, maintaining the same formation.

While all of this was happening, M. Petreius and Cn. Piso with 1,600 select Numidian cavalry accompanied by a substantial body of Numidian infantry rode up to reinforce the enemy. The enemy recovered from his terror and with renewed spirits turned round his cavalry, and after receiving the reinforcements into his ranks began to attack the legionaries in the rearmost ranks and to impede their return to camp. Caesar, noticing this, ordered that the standards be reversed and for the battle to be joined once again in the open plain. With the enemy beginning to fight in the same way as before and refusing to come to close quarters, Caesar's cavalry found that their horses were slower in pursuit than before and were tiring quickly owing to their recent bout of seasickness, thirst, exhaustion, lack of numbers, and the wounds they had suffered. It was now late in the day; Caesar went round to all of the infantry cohorts and cavalry units and exhorted them to attack with one great effort and sustain it until they had driven the enemy beyond the farthest hills and had taken possession of them. When the enemy's barrage of missiles had slowed and had lost accuracy, the signal was given and he sent his cohorts and cavalry units against them. The enemy was driven from the field and pushed back behind the hills with little effort as Caesar's men gained control of them. He delayed there for a little while, and then his troops withdrew in formation at an easy pace to their own defenses. The enemy likewise made for his own fortifications after this setback.

Roman imperialism

All of the major ancient Mediterranean states were imperialistic. They sought either to conquer and annex new territory or to exert control indirectly through clients. Warfare was endemic among the major Hellenistic states and success in war remained the most important virtue of Hellenistic kings. The Romans conformed to this general pattern. Where they differed was in the intensity, duration, and success of their military effort. From the middle of the fourth century, almost every year new legions were levied, and the spring and summer were filled with military campaigns. It has been estimated that 15 percent of Roman males saw seven years of military service during the Republic. Even with the reduced campaigning that followed the Second Punic War the burden of warfare remained heavy.

The motivations that lay behind this unprecedented military effort have long been in dispute. One explanation for Rome's expansion was that it was a defensive reaction to external threats. It has been claimed that Rome waged war either in self-defense or to protect its allies. Some apparent justification for this view could be found in Roman religious practice. They employed a religious rite, the fetial procedure, which represented a declaration of war as a demand for reparations for unjust acts. In the first century, Cicero could claim that the Empire had been acquired by a series of just wars waged to defend the state or to protect its allies. However, fetial procedure was a formalistic ritual designed to win the favor of the gods and it in no way required that the demands made be reasonable. Its significance can be gauged from its sporadic use and its final disappearance after the 170s. The second-century Greek historian Polybius perceptively notes on more than one occasion the Roman concern to present their wars as just even when they clearly were not. Such a view was never tenable. The evidence clearly shows that in many cases there was no credible threat to Rome's security. Although the rhythm of its wars and the pace of its expansion varied over time, Rome remained an imperial and expansionist state as long as it survived. Given the nature of ancient politics it would have been exceptional if it had acted otherwise.

The drive for expansion was fostered and directed by a number of institutions and attitudes that affected various levels of Roman society. There was the intense competition for power and status among the nobility, especially after its enlargement in the mid-fourth century. Until the last century of the Republic such competition centered on office and military command. Success in war was the most important way for a noble to obtain *gloria* (glory) to enhance his reputation and standing. The importance of *gloria* obtained through war lay behind struggles over the choice of commander and over the right of successful generals to hold triumphs. The profits that war brought offered a way to memorialize that success through the erection of temples and later by triumphal arches. Starting in the third century, successful commanders began to dedicate temples along the triumphal route from the Campus Martius to commemorate their victories. The Roman system of military decorations (see pp. 213ff.), with the right to display them publicly, operated an incentive for the common soldier. Similarly, the holding and retention of military rank served as a spur to action best illustrated by the case of Spurius Ligustinus (see **87**) and the other former centurions during the levy for the war against Perseus.

Tangible incentives were of equal importance. A successful war, especially in the eastern Mediterranean, resulted in the capture of vast quantities of booty. The lion's share fell to the victorious commander and presented him with opportunities for self-enrichment that far surpassed any other source. It also gave him the means to create and strengthen relations with other men of his class by distributing large cash awards to his officers. Cash distributions to the troops after a triumph were a normal though not invariable custom that served to strengthen the ties between a commander and his troops that would continue even after military service. The increase in the amounts distributed in the course of the second century is noticeable and may reflect the increasing expense of public life. Successful warfare led to the capture of large numbers of slaves who could be profitably employed on the estates of the wealthy as well as earn substantial amounts for the captors when they were sold. It is hard to see any but an economic motive for the terror campaign carried out by Aemilius Paullus after the war against Perseus in 167 which resulted in the capture of 150,000 slaves.

Economic motives also operated lower down the social scale among the men serving in the legions. In addition to cash distributions there was the prospect of winning booty. Although the Romans developed a highly organized system which treated booty as belonging to the army as a whole, after a particularly difficult siege where there had been a heavy loss of life the commander might allow soldiers to seize booty for themselves. In addition, in the confusion that often followed engagements soldiers must have sequestered booty for themselves. Livy mentions the number of volunteers who came forward for the war against Perseus in 171 because earlier wars in the East against Philip V and Antiochus III had made soldiers rich. The levies in the second century for warfare in Spain suffered from a lack of volunteers and occasional riots against the levies. Granted that the wars in the

Iberian peninsula were more difficult, it was also the case that there was little prospect of profit for the legionaries serving there. Despite the enormous burden of warfare, opposition to declaring war in the assemblies was infrequent. Such opposition is recorded only twice, in 264 and 200. Both times resistance was the product of special circumstances.

The state also benefited from successful warfare. The profits from wars in the East enabled the state to abolish the *tributum* (see pp. 141f.) in 167. Booty was not the only advantage that warfare brought. During the wars of expansion in Italy large amounts of land were confiscated from the defeated and turned into public land. After wars overseas, Rome was often able to impose enormous indemnities on the losers. It has been pointed out that the vast amount of construction at Rome in the second century must have been financed by the profits from Rome's eastern wars.

The nature of Roman control in Italy also served to make war attractive. No tribute was demanded from defeated enemies in Italy. They were required to supply troops at Rome's request and support them while on campaign. This enormously increased the available manpower for military activity while at the same time reducing the burden on Roman citizens and presumably reducing opposition to military adventures. This meant that it was only in the context of war-making that Rome could publicize its power and control over its Italian allies. Such a system must have been a strong incentive to choose a military solution to foreign policy problems when there were other ways to settle disputes.

The conquest of territory and the exaction of tribute seem to have been less compelling motives in the Roman drive for empire. It appears that the Romans were less interested in directly controlling territory than in asserting dominance and removing any possible threats to their control. In the course of their expansion in Italy, the acquisition of land and the planting of colonies, which both relieved internal pressures and secured Roman control as well as increasing troop strength, were their main aims. Although they did interfere with local administration in Italy, their interference was never systematic.

Outside of Italy they pursued different policies in the East and the West. Their earliest directly administered provinces such as Sicily and Spain were areas where there were no political groupings that would have allowed the Romans to exercise indirect control. This situation is clearest in North Africa, where once the decision had been taken to destroy Carthage there was no state left through which the Romans could exercise authority. The formation of a province followed immediately after the war. In the eastern Mediterranean where such states did exist, the process of annexation proceeded far more slowly. After the Second Macedonian War the Macedonian monarchy was left intact. At the end of the third war in 167, Macedonian territory was divided into four self-governing republics which were forbidden to have relations with one another. By 146 the inability of these republics to deal with the revolt of Andriscus led to the creation of a province. Other examples of this approach can be found. After the defeat of Antiochus III forced the Seleucids out of Asia Minor beyond the Taurus Mountains, the Romans turned the territory over to Pergamum and Rhodes to administer. It was only when this solution failed that the Romans began to directly administer these areas.

Certain states were not annexed for prolonged periods of time. Cyrene, bequeathed to the Romans by Ptolemy VII, formally passed to Rome in 96 after the death of the last of his heirs. Despite the potentially rich revenues it could have provided it was not annexed until 74. It was the combination of internal disorder and the pirate menace that finally led to the creation of a province. Egypt was bequeathed to Rome by one of the Ptolemies in 88 or 87, but was not finally annexed until the end of the civil wars in 30 despite its unparalleled wealth. The reluctance to do so was the result of internal political struggles at Rome.

There seems never to have been a systematic policy of annexation. The decision to take over direct control was made on an individual basis. Two factors seem to have been predominant in such decisions: the need to guarantee Roman supremacy and the demands of Roman politics. The latter depended on the expansion of the administrative apparatus, the possible shifts in the importance and power of individuals in the oligarchy that would result from provincialization, and in the Greek East the importance attached to local opinion. Even after the Roman oligarchy discovered the possibilities for enrichment offered by provincial governorships, these factors constrained the creation of new provinces. Generating revenues for the state, although important, seems to have always been a less significant motive.

The disconnection between warfare and the creation of provinces is most apparent in the last century of the Republic. The pace of external wars slowed, but the rate of provincialization quickened. This seems mainly to have been the result of expansion into areas where there was no possibility for indirect control. On the eastern frontier of the Empire where there were such states, client kings were left in control as long as they were useful. Under the Empire, wars of conquest almost ceased, with few exceptions. When in 43 AD the Emperor Claudius began the conquest of Britain, a territory that some had regarded as financially unprofitable, that venture was set in motion by an emperor's need for military glory and not to remove a perceived threat.

174 VALERIUS MAXIMUS, *MEMORABLE SAYINGS AND DEEDS* 4.1.10

For Valerius Maximus, see **150**. The present passage relates to the censorship of P. Cornelius Scipio Aemilianus in 142. The authenticity of the incident has been questioned but it seems genuine. The *lustrum* was a ceremony of purification performed every five years by the censors. The *suovetaurilia* or *solitarilium* was a sacrifice of a boar, ram, and bull that formed part of the concluding ceremonies.

The meaning of the prayer and Scipio's addition to it are controversial. It has been interpreted as evidence for the systematic character of Roman imperialism or simply as a prayer for the health and well-being of the state. It is hard not to see Scipio's addition as referring to his destruction of Carthage and the other victories of 146. If this is so, he must have understood the original prayer as a request to the gods for success in war and for further conquests. This does not exclude a more general wish for the success of the state; rather, for the Romans, success in war and the benefits it brought were closely bound to each other.

Nor can we pass over the conduct of the younger Africanus in silence. When as censor he was completing the *lustrum* and was engaged in the sacrifice of the *solitarilium*, the scribe recited from the public tablets the prayer in which the immortal gods are asked to make the state of the people of Rome greater and larger. Scipio said that the state was great enough, and spoke the following words: "So I pray that the gods will preserve it forever." He ordered that these words were to be permanently added to the prayer. From this point on the censors have used this modest form of prayer when completing the *lustrum*.

175 POLYBIUS, *HISTORIES* 1.3.6

A constant theme in Polybius' history is the Romans' desire to expand their power and influence. He saw it as evident in their expansion in Italy. He claims that in the First Punic War the Senate was so delighted by the victory at Agrigentum in Sicily that they enlarged their original aim of aiding the Mamertini and thought they could increase their power by driving the Carthaginians entirely out of the island. As the following passage makes clear, the crucial event that opened the way to realizing their plan was the shattering defeat of their only serious rival for world power, Carthage, in the Second Punic War. He further supports his view by arguing in his discussion of the Roman constitution that it was particularly well adapted for offensive warfare.

Polybius' view was shared by other Greeks. In a speech by an Aetolian envoy in a conference held as early as 217 during the war against Hannibal, the claim is made that the Romans would not rest content with Italy and Sicily but would aim at the subjugation of Greece. In a vivid metaphor the envoy visualizes the Roman threat as the clouds that loom in the west.

However, the historical record that Polybius and other sources provide shows a far less consistent pattern. The Senate was far less unified in its view of foreign policy than Polybius implies. Roman expansion seems to have been hesitant and dictated far more by circumstances than Polybius allows. The conquests of the first century are a better illustration of Polybius' thesis.

After having defeated Carthage in the war against Hannibal and considering that they had accomplished the most crucial step in their plan for world domination, the Romans were first emboldened to reach out their hands for the rest and make their way with an army to Greece and to Asia.

176 LIVY, 36.17.13–16

This speech was delivered by the consul Manlius Acilius Glabrio on the eve of his victory over Antiochus III at Thermopylae in 191. Although it has clearly been reworked by Livy there is no reason not to assume that Livy found a speech of this type in his sources which may go back in part to the elder Cato, a contemporary. The use of "*imperium*" here as equivalent to "empire" is a product of the Late Republic first found in Cicero.

"You ought to keep in mind that you are not only fighting to liberate Greece, although it is a singular claim to distinction to free Greece first from Philip and now from the Aetolians and Antiochus. Not only will the treasure that now lies in the king's tent be yours, but also all of the equipment which is daily expected to arrive from Ephesus will fall to you. You will open Asia, Syria, and all of those wealthy lands as far as the rising of the sun to the Roman Empire. Then what will stop us from setting the boundaries of our empire from Gades [in the west] to the Indian Ocean, which holds the world in its embrace, or prevent the human race from venerating the Roman name second only to that of the gods? Make yourselves worthy of such rewards so that with the favoring help of the gods we can decide the matter in battle tomorrow."

Motives for conquest and expansion

Status and prestige

177 PLINY THE ELDER, *NATURAL HISTORY* 7.139

The Quintus Metellus who delivered this funeral eulogy of his father, who died in 221, was the consul of 206. His father had twice been consul in the First Punic War and had celebrated a triumph in 250. The list of accomplishments shows the importance of the nexus of military success, office-holding, and wealth that was vital to a Roman noble's status. It is important to note that in relation to military success the criteria for success include not only the holding of the most important military commands but also the possession of personal physical bravery. The demonstration by the general of that personal valor on the field was an important element in earning a reputation for manliness. Defeated generals often chose death on the battlefield as a way of validating of their manhood.

Quintus Metellus in the funeral eulogy which he spoke in honor of his father has written that his father had achieved those ten greatest things that wise men spend their life seeking. He had wished to be the best warrior, the foremost orator, the bravest general, to command the most significant military operations, to hold the highest offices, to possess the highest wisdom, to be considered the leading senator, to amass great wealth by honorable means, to leave behind many children, and to be the most eminent man in the state.

178 CICERO, *ON DUTIES* 1.74

Cicero's lack of military accomplishments was a political liability. When he was governor in Cilicia in 51–50 he tried to obtain a triumph from the Senate and he took his failure to do so to heart. It is no accident that the most important political figures among Cicero's contemporaries such as Pompey and Caesar were men who could boast of a string of military victories.

Despite the glory that military success still brought there is visible in the first century the development of alternative routes to political success. Fewer aristocrats held junior military posts such as military tribune which had once been required for further advancement (see p. 207). After 80 BC consuls cease to regularly campaign outside of Italy. This is probably connected to the changed nature of military command and the decline of military service among the most likely voters.

> Most people think that military achievements are more important than those of civilian life. This view needs to be corrected. Many men seek out battle because of their desire for glory, and that is especially true of men who are naturally highly courageous and possess great abilities, and this is even truer if they have military abilities and are warlike. Yet if we wish to be sound judges of these things, we can see that the achievements of peace are more important and bring greater fame than those of war.

179 POLYBIUS, *HISTORIES* 6.39.9–10

Polybius' remarks form part of a section devoted to various military decorations and punishments. He correctly sees it as a single system, which he approves of, designed to motivate legionaries to the fullest degree possible.

> Those who received these gifts [military decorations], apart from their high reputation with the army and their instant fame at home, also when they return home occupy a distinguished position in processions, since only those who have been decorated for valor are allowed to wear decorations on such occasions. These men place the booty they have won in the most conspicuous locations in their homes as a sign of and witness to their courage.

Tangible rewards

180 AULUS GELLIUS, *ATTIC NIGHTS* 6.3.7

This speech was part of a senatorial debate held in 167. The Rhodians, as Cato notes, had been faithful Roman allies and, after the war against Antiochus III, had received extensive tracts along the southern coasts of Asia Minor as a reward for their support. During the war against Perseus, the Rhodians, impressed by the initial Roman failure to defeat the king and with a faction favorable to Perseus in power, offered to act as mediators. The Romans viewed this as treasonous behavior and after their victory decided to punish Rhodes. Although war was not declared, Rhodes was stripped of its continental possessions, and a free port was established on the island of Delos which eventually destroyed Rhodes' commerce.

Only one Roman commander is directly accused of instigating a war for financial gain. Lucius Licinius Lucullus, consul in 151, who was active in Nearer Spain, was accused of attacking a Spanish tribe for the sake of booty. Economic motives do not seem to have been decisive in Roman decisions to go to war; rather, they seem to have predisposed the Romans to seek a military solution when more peaceful alternatives were available.

> After a part of the Senate complained about the behavior of the Rhodians, expressed their anger towards them, and finally gave their opinion that war ought to be declared against them, Marcus Cato rose and said that not a few of the leading senators were angry at men who had been their best and most faithful allies because they wished to seize and possess their wealth.

181 LIVY, 42.32.6

This levy took place in 171 for the campaign against Perseus. The soldiers were not wrong about the potential for amassing wealth for themselves. However, L. Aemilius Paullus, the victor over Perseus in 168, was to create much ill-feeling by denying his troops a cash award after this triumph.

Polybius notes the same motivations in his discussion of the preliminaries to the First Punic War. The desire for gain motivated not only the aristocracy but also those who filled the lower ranks. The pay they received was not much of an inducement, but the chance for booty and cash distributions by the commander in the wake of victory was a strong incentive.

> The lot assigned Publius Licinius to Macedonia and Gaius Cassius received Italy. The lots were drawn for the legions; the first and third legions were assigned to Macedonia while the second and fourth remained in Italy. The consuls conducted a more thorough levy than usual. Licinius enrolled veteran soldiers and centurions, with many submitting their names voluntarily because they had seen that those who had served in the earlier war in Macedonia or had fought Antiochus had become rich.

Justification of empire

This dialogue was composed by Cicero between 54 and 51. It is an attempt to define the best state. Cicero finds that state in an idealized Roman Republic.

Such a view inevitably raised the question of Rome's imperial expansion, and the passage cites two justifications for Roman rule. The first is that Rome's wars were fought either defending itself or to protect its allies. In part, Cicero may have been influenced by the fetial procedure, although the fetial procedure had long fallen into disuse by Cicero's period. It still shaped the way the Romans justified their decisions to go to war. This is particularly evident in the East, where the Romans were aware of the importance of public opinion. In other works Cicero adds other motives for imperial expansion, including the pursuit of glory and the natural right of the more powerful to subjugate those who are weaker.

The second major justification for conquest was made on the grounds that it was in the interests of the conquered. It assumed that certain nations and peoples did not have the capacity to govern themselves and therefore it was in their best interests to be subjected by a superior foreign power. This argument has had a long history that extends into the modern period. Its origin lies in justifications of slavery that appear in both Plato and Aristotle. It seems likely that its use at Rome began in the mid-second century and it developed as a result of the influence of Greek philosophy.

There was as well a religious component, best expressed in the poetry of Vergil, that saw Roman expansion as ordained by the gods. In the second Book of the *Aeneid*, Jupiter allots the Romans empire without end. The idea of a god-given empire is found throughout the imperial period.

The first explicit statement that Rome possesses an empire that is a unified whole rather than a collection of subject peoples appears at the beginning of the first century, although the lack of earlier evidence does not allow us to determine when the concept first emerged. The Romans' attitude to their empire was ambivalent. There was a recognition also expressed in Cicero that a claim to rule based on the benefits that Rome conferred was undermined by the greedy and exploitative behavior of Roman magistrates in the provinces. However, there is a deeper and more persistent vein of disquiet which has its roots in the view that the extension of empire removed the external checks that fear of a foreign enemy exerted on internal discord. This view first appears as well in the mid-second century and is fully developed in the works of Sallust in the late first century. In Sallust's view the growth of empire allowed the development of unchecked luxury that first weakened and then undermined Rome's moral fiber and led to the civil convulsions of his own time. Various dates are given by different authors for the start of this process, although they are unanimous in linking it with Rome's wars in the East.

182 CICERO, *DE RE PUBLICA* 3.35–37

Our people have gained dominion over the world by defending their allies....

And do we not see that dominion has been given to everything that is best for the greatest advantage of the weak? For what other reason does god rule men or the soul control the body, or rationality dominate desire, anger, and the other defective parts of the mind?

The destructive effects of empire

183 SALLUST, *THE WAR AGAINST CATALINE* 10.1–6

By the mid-second century we can trace the theme of Roman decline in various writers. Drawing on these sources, Livy associates it with the triumph of Manlius Vulso in 187, which inspired a taste for luxury that sapped Rome's moral fiber. Other Greek and Roman authors give various dates in the second century for the start of internal moral decline, which they ascribe to various factors.

Sallust's choice of 146 and the destruction of Carthage as the turning point probably depends upon a famous debate in 151 between Scipio Nasica and Cato on Carthage's fate. Nasica contended that the destruction of Carthage would sap Roman moral fiber as it would no longer have an external check to restrain moral and political deterioration. The choice of this date may have been influenced by the view that prolonged peace increased the development of luxury and a decline in morals.

When our republic had become powerful through its own efforts and because of its just dealings, after great kings had been conquered in war and fierce tribes and great nations subdued, and Carthage, the rival of the Roman Empire, had been totally destroyed, when land and sea lay open to us, then fortune began to grow cruel and throw everything into confusion. Wealth and leisure, desirable in other circumstances, brought misery and burdens to men who had found it easy to bear hardships, danger, anxiety, and difficulties. At first, the desire for wealth increased and then the longing for power; these are the soil from which all evils grow.

At first [these evils] grew gradually and were occasionally punished. Later, when they attacked the state like a plague, the city was transformed, and its empire, once the best and most just of its kind, became cruel and unbearable.

Siege warfare

Little is known about early Roman siege techniques. Livy describes a number of sieges in the fifth and fourth centuries. However, the factual basis of these descriptions is questionable. One striking feature of these siege accounts which may be true is the absence of the type of siege machinery commonly used in the contemporary eastern Mediterranean. The first recorded use of such machinery by the Romans occurred in the course of the First Punic War. In 258 they retook Camarina in Sicily, which had rebelled against them, with the help of rams which they had obtained from Syracuse. Artillery was also used during the war at Motya in western Sicily. These machines were also loaned by Syracuse. These borrowings point to an important difference between Hellenistic and Roman siege tactics. The Greeks relied on a wide range of siege machinery consisting of catapults, towers, and other devices to approach the enemy's walls, clear the defenders from them, and open a breach for their troops to storm a city. By the Second Punic War the Romans were using catapults and other machines borrowed from the Greeks, but their approach to siege warfare was fundamentally different.

The elements of this approach are already visible in the First Punic War at the siege of Agrigentum in 262. First, camps and forts were constructed at strategic locations to command the area surrounding the city walls and to serve as bases from which an assault could be launched. These strongpoints were connected to each other by trenches and ramparts to prevent the approach of a relieving force and to begin the process of wearing down the garrison by starvation. Agrigentum also provides the first evidence for the construction of a second wall beyond the first to defend against a relieving force. Caesar's siege of Alesia in 52, with its double walls and elaborate booby traps, represents the final development of this method.

The unsuccessful siege of Agrigentum is representative of the Roman approach to taking cities during the whole of the Republican period. If it was practical there was often an initial attempt to storm the city by escalade. If this failed, a contravallation of either a single or double wall was constructed. Artillery was used to clear defenders from the walls and to allow the construction of approach ramps and mining to force an entry into the city, although an assault over the city walls by means of ladders was attempted where possible.

Although a full range of devices, including stone- and dart-throwing catapults, siege towers, and rams, was used in sieges in the course of the third century, they were mainly employed to allow the construction of siege works. The less important role played by machinery in Roman sieges as compared to Greek ones may be the result of a difference in the nature of their armies. Hellenistic armies were professional forces with skilled corps of engineers who specialized in the construction of siege machinery. The annual levies of the Republican period were unsuited to the development of the required core of trained experts necessary in this, the most complicated form of land warfare. With the establishment of a professional army under the Empire, Roman armies regularly included a siege train and the experts required to build and maintain it.

Almost all of the reported sieges involving Roman forces were offensive operations, so there is little information about the methods the Romans used when defending cities or fortified positions. It was only during the period of the civil wars beginning in the 80s that Roman armies were forced on the defensive. For the most part, the sources provide little detail on these operations. The only extended description we have is Caesar's account of Pompey's defense of his base at Dyrrachium in the spring of 48. It was Pompey's decision to refuse battle and withdraw to his base on Dyrrachium that led to Caesar's decision to try to force a battle by besieging that base. As Caesar remarks, it was an unusual siege in that a smaller force, weaker in cavalry, was attacking an army superior in both. Caesar began building fortifications to restrict the area from which Pompey could draw supplies, especially for his cavalry, to hem them in so that they could not raid his own supply lines, and to goad Pompey to join battle by damaging his reputation.

Pompey's response was to build fortifications to secure as large an area as possible and to force Caesar to extend his own entrenchments and so make it difficult for him to garrison them. The situation was further complicated for Caesar by the fact that Pompey could be supplied from the sea and could use his fleet to land forces behind Caesar's fortifications and attack them from the rear. The siege was eventually broken after weeks of indecisive encounters by a massed attack on a gap in Caesar's defenses as they neared the coast. Although this was an unusual type of siege, it shows the use of entrenchments in defense as well as in offense.

Dyrrachium also highlights another difficulty faced by the attacker in siege warfare in the case of coastal sites. Cities or strongpoints situated on the coast had to be cut off from the sea to make a blockade effective. The prolonged siege of Lilybaeum, the main remaining Carthaginian base in Sicily during the First Punic War, failed because the Romans could not seal its harbor. In the absence of the necessary naval superiority the Romans blockaded harbors by the construction of moles, as they did at the siege of Carthage in 147–146.

In antiquity, sieges and urban warfare always remained difficult undertakings. Static warfare created supply problems and increased the chances of an epidemic in the besieging army. Betrayal or surrender was always a preferable alternative. Given the small chance of a successful assault, soldiers were exposed to protracted heavy labor and subject to higher casualties than in open warfare. Once the town was taken, a combination of revenge and greed usually led to at least a partial slaughter of the inhabitants, including women and children. Often males of military age were killed, and the women and children sold into slavery. At the fall of New Carthage in 209, Polybius records that Scipio ordered his troops in accordance with Roman custom to kill all of the citizens they encountered. Even cities that surrendered were not always safe from massacre. During the initial phases of the African campaign that ended the Second Punic War, Scipio besieged the large town of Locha. The siege was a difficult one and, just at the moment when the Romans were setting up their scaling ladders, the townsmen asked for a meeting and then a truce to allow them to evacuate the town. Scipio recalled his soldiers, but they failed to obey. They broke into the town and slaughtered the inhabitants, including women and children.

The siege of New Carthage

184 POLYBIUS, *HISTORIES* 10.12.1–15.3

Scipio arrived in northern Spain in the autumn of 210. The Carthaginians had inflicted two severe defeats on Roman forces, pushing them back into northern Spain. After assembling his troops, Scipio embarked on a prolonged training program designed to restore discipline and morale, which had been seriously damaged by the defeats. To challenge Carthaginian control of central and southern Spain, Scipio required a base south of the Ebro. The town of New Carthage was an obvious choice. It offered the only useful harbor on the east coast. By gaining control of it he could threaten other towns held by the Carthaginians along the coast and acquire the port he needed. In addition, the site had further advantages. New Carthage served as the major Carthaginian storehouse for treasure and war material. A number of hostages from the Spanish tribes had been collected there, and their seizure might allow Scipio to induce those tribes to change sides.

The military situation was also favorable. The city's garrison of 1,000 troops was too small to face assaults at multiple points. The Carthaginians had divided their forces into three armies, none of which was within ten days' march of the town, so no help could arrive in time. A surprise attack offered a reasonable chance of taking the town before any of the Carthaginian armies could march to its relief.

Early in 209 Scipio rendezvoused with his fleet and ordered it to sail to New Carthage. Keeping his destination secret, he rapidly advanced on the town with a force of 25,000 infantry and 2,500 cavalry.

New Carthage was situated at the end of a narrow peninsula that ran from east to west. To its north there was a shallow lagoon that Scipio had been told was fordable, especially in the evening when the water level in the lagoon dropped. It fronted on the sea to the south, and to the west there was a narrow canal between the lagoon and the sea that blocked the land approach to the town from the west. On his arrival Scipio set up camp to the east of the narrow neck of the isthmus. His camp was unusual in that it had defenses only facing to the east to guard against a relieving force. To the west the lines were left open to ease the problems of movement and perhaps to tempt the defenders to attack. Given the disparity of forces the Romans could afford casualties if the attack weakened the garrison.

Although Polybius' account of the siege and the Roman assault is relatively straightforward, it does raise some issues. The attack through the lagoon was delivered in the morning, while Polybius states that the water level fell in the evening and that Scipio was aware of it and had promised his men that Neptune would come to their aid as they made their assault across the lagoon. Sources ascribe this phenomenon either to the wind or to tidal action. The tides at New Carthage have little effect on water level, whereas wind significantly lowers the level of the lagoon. The timing of the attack and Scipio's remark about Neptune's aid remain a problem. It is perhaps best to take Scipio's remark to refer not to the lowering of the lagoon but rather to the fact, probably unknown to his soldiers, that it was fordable without any fall in its level. By chance the wind came up during the attack, which made the approach easier and added to the mystique that Scipio already enjoyed among his men. Livy's account of the siege assigns a greater role to the Roman fleet than Polybius' does, and this seems likely.

The siege of New Carthage was unusual in that the town was carried by assault rather than by a prolonged blockade. The crucial factor that made this possible was the small size of the garrison. Scipio must have been counting on this, as a blockade would have exposed him to attacks by the three Carthaginian armies, which might have rendered his position untenable.

The 2,000 troops that Polybius mentions must have been townsmen whom Mago armed.

The next day Scipio encircled the city from the seaward side with a fleet equipped with all types of missile weapons under the command of Laelius. On the landward side he sent forward 2,000 of his strongest troops together with ladder-bearers and began an assault at about the third hour. Mago, the garrison commander, divided his force of 1,000 men in two, stationing half in the citadel and the other half on the hill to the east of it. He selected 2,000 of the strongest of his remaining troops, armed them with weapons that he could find in the town, and stationed them at the gate that faced the isthmus and the enemy's camp. He used the rest to defend the entire circuit of the walls.

As soon as Scipio had given the trumpet signal to begin the assault, Mago sent the armed citizens through the gate, as he was convinced that this would startle the Romans and end the attack. They delivered a strong assault on the Romans, who had left their camp and were now deployed on the isthmus. A sharp encounter took place accompanied by a violent shouting match, with each side cheering their men on. The assistance each side received in the battle was unequal. The Carthaginians were rein-forced through a single gate and at a distance of a quarter-mile, while Roman reinforcements were close at hand and could reach the scene of the fighting by various routes. For this reason the contest was one-sided. Scipio had purposely deployed his men close to their camp in order to draw the enemy out farther, knowing that if he destroyed these troops who were the best of the city population they would lose heart and they would no longer dare to come out of the gate again. The struggle remained bal-anced for some time, as both sides used their best men. Finally, the Carthaginians were pushed back by the sheer weight of the Roman line and turned and fled. Many were killed in the course of the battle and the subsequent flight; the majority died when they trampled each other as they entered the gate. The inhabitants were so terrified by the battle that those defending the walls also fled. The Romans almost forced their way in with the fugitives and set up the scaling ladders unhindered.

When the first Romans advanced confidently to scale the ladders the height of the walls presented a greater danger than the defenders. The men on the wall were encouraged by the difficulties the assaulting troops encountered. Some of the ladders broke because of the weight of so many mounting them at the same time; at other points those who first mounted the ladders became dizzy because of the height and after slight resistance were thrown down. Also, whenever the defenders threw beams or other objects from the battlements, all the men on the ladders would be swept off and fall to the ground. Despite all this none of the measures they took could withstand the vehemence and eagerness of the Roman attack; while those first to mount were falling, others immediately took their places. However, since it was late in the day and the strain on the soldiers was intense, the general had the trumpet sounded to recall the attackers.

The garrison was overjoyed, thinking that they had warded off the danger. But Scipio was waiting for the tide to run out and readied 500 men with ladders on the shore of the lagoon and assembled fresh troops in front of the gate and at the isthmus. He addressed his men and then distributed more ladders than before so that the wall would be assaulted by greater numbers. At the signal for attack they brought their ladders to the wall and courageously mounted them at every point, causing confusion and loss of heart among the defenders. They had thought that they had been delivered from danger, but now saw it return. At the same time they were running short of missiles, and their heavy losses discouraged them. They defended against the assault with difficulty, but mounted a determined resistance. Just as the struggle around the ladders was reaching its peak, the tide began to ebb and the water recede from the edges of the lagoon gradually as a strong and deep current flowed through the mouth of the lagoon into the neighboring sea, so that those who had not been told of it in advance were amazed. Scipio had readied his guides and encouraged the troops who had been assigned to this attack. Obeying his orders, they hastened through shallow water. The whole army was astonished and took it for a divine act.... Encouraged by this, the men in large numbers made their way in close order to the gate and attempted to cut a way through the doors with axes and hatchets. Meanwhile, those crossing the lagoon reached the wall and finding it bare of defenders not only brought up their ladders without difficulty but gained control of the wall without a fight, since the defenders were fighting elsewhere, especially on the isthmus side and at the gate there. They had never thought that the enemy would reach the wall on the side of the lagoon, and most importantly they were able neither to hear nor to see anything of these crucial events because of the confused shouting and their being crowded together.

After gaining the wall, the Romans first made their way along it, slaughtering the enemy. In such an attack Roman weapons had great advantages. They then made their way to the gate. Some of them came down from the wall and began cutting their way through the bolts, while those outside started to force their way in. Those attacking on the ladders from the isthmus had overpowered the defenders and were now in control of the battlements. After having secured the walls they advanced on and occupied the hill to the east, routing its garrison.

The siege of Numantia

185 APPIAN, *THE SPANISH WARS* 15.90–96

The Celtiberians (see **156**) had put up a prolonged resistance to the Roman advance in Spain. Their most important center, the town of Numantia, with a population in 134 of about 4,000, had been subject to repeated and unsuccessful Roman attacks from the beginning of the Roman presence in Spain. As consul in 134, Scipio Aemilianus had been allocated the command against the Celtiberi. For his use of volunteers, see **156**. The capture of Numantia was crucial to the defeat of the Celtiberians. Scipio spent much of 134 in reducing the hinterland of the town, thereby isolating it. The town was situated on a high, steep hill that precluded direct assault, so a blockade was the only practical alternative.

The siege works constructed for the siege are a paradigm of Roman blockading methods. Starvation remained the ultimate means to compel surrender; although Appian's description of the privations, including cannibalism, endured by the inhabitants during the siege is a standard element in such narratives, in this case it may well be true.

> Scipio constructed seven forts surrounding the town and summoned forces from allied Spanish tribes. After their arrival he divided them into a number of sections and did the same with his own forces. He then appointed commanders for each section and ordered them to surround the city with a ditch and a stockade. The circumference of Numantia was about three miles, and the fortification was twice as large. Sections of it were assigned to each army section, with instructions to the effect that if they were harassed by the enemy they should raise a signal, either a red flag on a tall spear by day or a signal fire by night, so that either he or his legate could bring help. When the fortifications were completed and he could now repel any assault, he began to construct another ditch not far beyond the first and strengthened it with wooden stakes and also built a wall eight feet thick and ten feet high without counting the battlements. He built towers along the length of the wall at hundred-foot intervals. Since the wall could not be carried round the marsh, a ditch was dug there equal in width and height to the wall to serve as a substitute....
>
> The Durius [Douro] River, which flowed around the fortification, was of great use to the Numantines for the bringing in of provisions and the transport of men in and out of the city.... Since Scipio could not bridge it since it was broad and swift-flowing, in place of a bridge he erected towers on each bank and moored large logs with ropes to them, floating them in the river. Swords and spearheads were fixed in the logs, which were kept in constant motion by the force of the current. This prevented the enemy from swimming, diving, or sailing in the river. In this way Scipio achieved what he desired, which was that the inhabitants would have no contact with anyone; nor could anyone enter the city, and so it would be cut off from all knowledge of the outside world. In this way they would lack supplies and machines of every kind.
>
> After everything had been prepared and catapults, both missile and stone throwers, were mounted on the towers, their battlements were stocked with stones, darts, and javelins, and the forts were garrisoned with archers and slingers. Further, Scipio stationed runners along the full

length of the wall who, by passing information from one to the other, could keep him informed. He gave orders to the tower garrisons that at the first sign of trouble they should signal in turn in order that he could speedily learn of the trouble and then later receive a detailed report of it from the messengers.

His army now totaled 60,000 men with native troops. Half of them were detailed to guard the wall and when necessary move to where they were needed. A further 20,000 were assigned to fight from the battlements as needed, and 10,000 were to act as a reserve. The reserve also had positions assigned to them, which they could not leave without orders. At a signal, all were to take their assigned positions. Everything had now been carefully prepared by Scipio.

The Numantines made many attacks on the besiegers in different places. The swift actions of the besiegers created fear. Signals were raised and runners darted back and forth. Those who manned the walls sprang quickly to their assigned places, and trumpets sounded from all of the towers so that the entire circuit of the fortifications for six miles presented an alarming sight. Scipio inspected the entire position day and night. He thought that with the enemy entirely enclosed they would not be able to hold out for long.

Their hunger forced the Numantines to send five negotiators to Scipio to see if he would treat them with moderation if they surrendered....

When their provisions were exhausted and they had neither fruit nor animals or grass left they began, as happens under the harsh necessity of war, to lick boiled hides and when these failed they cooked and ate human flesh, first chopping up those who had died into small pieces for cooking; then nauseous at the flesh of the sick the stronger preyed upon the weaker. They were beset by every kind of misery, made savage by what they ate, and looked like wild beasts from the effects of hunger, plague, their long hair, and neglect. In such circumstances they surrendered to Scipio.

War at sea

Naval warfare was always of secondary importance to the Romans. When the situation demanded it they could and did mount tremendous ship-building efforts and were successful in naval encounters, but as soon as the need for sea power ended they allowed their fleets to decay and primarily depended on their Italian and foreign allies for warships and seaborne transport. It was not until the reign of Augustus that permanent fleets and naval bases were established in Italy.

This may in part be a reflection of a value system which idealized at least in theory the peasant soldier and his military qualities. Sparta provides a striking parallel of a society which also cultivated an idealized image of the hoplite and was equally uninterested in naval affairs until the necessity of defeating Athens in the Peloponnesian War forced it to build a naval force. The idealization of the peasant was accompanied by a devaluation of urban life. Since seafaring was closely connected to city life, this led to a corresponding under-appreciation of naval service. It is a consequence of this view that Rome drew the crews of its warships from naval allies and freedmen and its marines from the lowest census class eligible for military service. Even under the Empire the permanent imperial fleets were manned by crews drawn from freedmen and foreigners. On a more practical level, during the Republic Rome never developed a permanent system of financing for its war expenses, relying on the *tributum* (see p. 141), which was only levied to meet immediate military expenses. No navy could be maintained on such a basis. Finally, the successful conquest of Italy without the need of a significant naval force must have strengthened the tendency to ignore warfare at sea.

Rome's earliest attempts to deal with its naval needs reveal a persistent strand in its approach to the sea. Starting in the first half of the fifth century, Rome founded a series of small maritime colonies to provide coastal defense rather than establishing a naval force to police its shores. This development illustrates clearly the Roman approach of dominating the sea by gaining possession of the land. Given the limited range of ancient warships, this was an effective policy. This approach reappears throughout the Republican period. Naval fleets of any size were only constructed, as in the First Punic War, when there was no other solution to a military problem. As soon as success was achieved, these forces were allowed to wither and naval needs were met by drawing on allied vessels. In the First Mithridatic War, Sulla's quaestor L. Licinius Lucullus, who had been sent out in the winter of 87–86 BC to assemble naval forces, had to spend more than a year raising a small fleet among Rome's remaining allies in the East to face Mithridates' navy. It was Rome's success on land that made such indifference to naval requirements possible.

Until the First Punic War the sources mention only minor naval activity. In 311 two minor magistrates, the *duoviri navales*, were first appointed to command small squadrons of ten ships each whose primary duty seems to have been to prevent piracy. Their lack of importance is clear from the intermittent nature of their appointment. After 282 they cease to be appointed until 189–172, when they reappear on an irregular basis and then disappear forever. In 267 four *quaestores classici* were appointed whose major function seems to have been to superintend the new naval allies that Rome had acquired by its conquest of the Greek states of southern Italy. Rome's ability to call on them for experienced rowers and crews made possible its victory in the first war against Carthage.

Rome was particularly fortunate in that its first war against Carthage took place after major technological developments had changed the nature of war at sea. During the fifth century the major ship of the line had been the trireme with three banks of oars. It depended for its effectiveness on its speed and maneuverability, with the ram as its main offensive weapon. From about 400, perhaps as the result of developments in Sicily, the trireme was replaced by larger and heavier ships, the quadrireme and the quinquereme (fours and fives). There has been a great deal of controversy as to how these ships were rowed, but it seems likely that the name refers to the number of rowers per oar and not to the number of banks of oars. In the course of the third century we hear of much larger ships, but the quinquereme seems to have remained the standard ship of the line. The increased size of these ships led to a change in naval warfare. Instead of depending on ramming and maneuver to defeat the enemy these new vessels became floating platforms for artillery and marines, which overcame the enemy either by sinking him with a barrage of stones and catapult bolts or by boarding, although ramming still played a part. The new style of naval warfare favored Rome's superiority on land by turning naval battles into infantry assaults.

At the opening of the First Punic War in 264, Rome seems to have had no naval forces of its own and relied upon its naval allies to ferry its troops across to Sicily. It faced a first-rate naval power in Carthage, which had long dominated the western Mediterranean. Despite the fact that its standard naval vessel was the quinquereme, Carthage relied on the expertise of its crews to fight a war of maneuver by disabling and ramming enemy ships.

It was not until 261 when the Romans decided to expel Carthage completely from Sicily that they began to build a sizeable fleet to confront Carthage on the sea. The lack of Roman naval preparedness can be gauged from the story Polybius tells of the Romans using a captured Carthaginian quinquereme as a model, since their Italian allies used only smaller warships. Although the story has been doubted, it does not seem implausible and is paralleled by Rome's readiness to adopt foreign weaponry for land warfare. Such ships carried a crew of 300 naval personnel drawn from the naval allies and a normal complement of forty marines, which was increased to 120, with eighty select infantry drawn from the legions before a major battle. A fleet of one hundred quinqueremes and thirty smaller ships that probably belonged to Rome's allies was launched in 260 and defeated Carthaginian forces at Mylae in northeastern Sicily (see pp. 286ff.). In part, Rome's success was due to the development of a new boarding device, the *corvus* or raven. The exact form of the device has been endlessly debated, but essentially it was a pole-mounted boarding ladder with a spike or weight at its end which could be swung around and dropped on the decks of the opposing ship, locking the two vessels together and converting a sea battle into a land battle. Use of the *corvus* was discontinued later in the war, and it may have been due to the fact that it made ships less seaworthy. The highest number of Roman casualties resulted from losses to storms and not enemy action. Rome's success owed much to its vast manpower resources, which allowed it to man new fleets despite these severe losses.

Command was exercised by consuls or by proconsuls as part of their overall military responsibility, with one of the two consuls or a proconsul commanding the fleet while the other was in charge of the land forces. In the Second Punic War with its multiple theaters, praetors and propraetors also led independent naval forces. None of these commanders appear to have had any special expertise in naval warfare and must have relied on subordinates who had the special skills needed.

It seems likely that when the Second Punic War opened in 218 BC most of the ships at Rome's disposal dated to the First Punic War and so were at least three decades old. Given Carthage's naval weaknesses these ships were enough to assure naval superiority and to make Hannibal's task infinitely more difficult by denying him men and supplies that could have been sent by ship from Carthage rather than by the far more difficult land route from Spain.

In the course of the second century the Roman navy declined precipitously. In Rome's wars in the eastern Mediterranean it relied on allied fleets, primarily those of Pergamum and Rhodes.

The inability of these states to maintain their fleets, due in part to Roman polices, exposed the central and eastern Mediterranean to the depredations of pirate fleets, which in the absence of a strong naval power were able to assume unprecedented size and to develop an elaborate organization. It was not until Pompey's command in 67 that a large-scale police action was undertaken with a fleet of over 500 ships borrowed from friendly states that finally drove them from the seas.

The civil wars between 49 and 31 saw several major naval encounters, ending in the final naval battle at Actium and the defeat of Antony. Marcus Agrippa, the victor in that struggle, is credited with developing a catapult-launched grappling hook which repeated the success of the *corvus*. During the Republic and under the emperors, Rome continued to use the techniques of land warfare to assure its dominance on the sea.

The battle of Mylae and the corvus

After taking the major Carthaginian base at Acragas (see pp. 144f.) in southwestern Sicily, the Romans decided to expel the Carthaginians completely from the island. The only way to do so was to construct a fleet to defeat the Carthaginians at sea. Such a force would also allow the Romans to more effectively besiege those cities still allied to the enemy. It is not unlikely that Syracuse, which had joined the Romans in 263, supplied some of the technical expertise necessary, as neither the Romans nor their naval allies were familiar with the construction of large warships. One hundred quinqueremes and twenty triremes were built, according to a late source within sixty days. This seems incredible, but it is clear from Polybius that both sides were able to construct large numbers of ships in an incredibly short period. A sunken Carthaginian ship recovered off the west coast of Sicily provides evidence for mass production of such vessels, which would help explain the speed with which these fleets were constructed. The crews were supplied by the Italian naval allies, but they had to be trained, as quinqueremes required different rowing techniques than the smaller ships they were accustomed to. Along with existing allied ships, the Roman fleet may perhaps have numbered 140 ships.

The command in Sicily was divided between the consuls of 260, Gnaeus Duilius and Gnaeus Cornelius Scipio, who later received the cognomen Asina or she-ass as a result of his capture in the opening phase of this campaign. Duilius was assigned to the land forces, while Scipio was placed in command of the fleet. The new fleet sailed south along the Italian coast. However, perhaps deceived by information that the town of Lipara on the island of Lipari, an important Carthaginian base, would be betrayed to him, he sailed against it and was captured. Duilius immediately assumed command of the fleet.

The two fleets encountered each other off Mylae (modern Milazzo), located on a promontory in northeast Sicily not far from Lipari. Polybius' figure of 130 ships for the Carthaginian fleet has generally been accepted. However, he does not provide a total for the Roman force. It would have included the hundred quinqueremes and the twenty triremes that had been specially constructed. But it had suffered some losses and perhaps had added some captured Carthaginian ships. Probably the two fleets were roughly equal in size.

Polybius' description of the *corvus* is reasonably clear. There has been debate about whether the boarding ladder was hinged at the point at which it intersected with the pole. Polybius does not mention a hinge, and it is probable that the ladder's slot mentioned by Polybius served as the join between the pole and the ladder.

Polybius' description of the battle is lacking in detail, and nothing is known about how the fleets were formed up before battle. It seems hard to believe that the Carthaginians attacked in a disordered fashion, but Polybius expressly says so. A further difficulty is raised by his description of the fight with the second wave of Carthaginian ships. He implies that the *corvus* could be swung around to attack ships coming from any direction, but since it was mounted on the prow this seems impossible. The Roman ships must have been able to turn quickly enough to counter Carthaginian attacks from the side and rear.

Duilius was granted the first naval triumph after his return to Italy in 259. His triumph was commemorated by the erection of two columns decorated with the beaks of captured ships. The column's inscription is extant and, besides mentioning his successes on land in Sicily, stresses that he was the first Roman to win a naval victory.

186 POLYBIUS, *HISTORIES* 1.22.1–23.10

After the Romans neared the coast of Sicily and learned of what had happened to Scipio they immediately sent a message to summon Gaius Duilius, the commander of the land forces, and awaited his arrival. At the same time, finding that the Carthaginian fleet was not far off, they began to prepare for battle.

Since their ships were of indifferent quality and slow, someone suggested devices which would help them in battle, which they later called "ravens." These are constructed as follows: a round pole stood on the prow of the ship sixteen feet high and about one foot in diameter. It had a pulley on its top and around it was placed a boarding bridge made of crossed planks nailed together which was four feet wide and twenty-four long. There was an oblong hole in the bridge, which was placed around the pole twelve feet from its end. There was a knee-high railing on each side of the boarding bridge and at its end was fastened an iron object shaped like a pestle pointed at one end with a ring at the other end so that the whole apparatus looked like a device for grinding grain. A rope was attached to the ring by which, when the ship charged the enemy, they raised the ravens and let them down on the enemy's deck. At times they swung the raven around when ships collided broadside. When the ravens were fixed in the planks of the opposing ship's deck they locked the ships together if they had struck broadsides. If the ships' prows had collided, the troops charged over the boarding plank two abreast. The first two men protected the front of the column by raising their shields, while those behind protected its flanks by raising the outer rim of their shields over the railing. After preparing these devices the Romans awaited an opportunity for battle.

As soon as Duilius learned of the disaster that Scipio had suffered, he turned his army over to the military tribunes and made his way to the fleet. Hearing that the enemy was ravaging the territory of Mylae he sailed there with his entire fleet. On sighting him the Carthaginians were filled with delight and eagerly put to sea with 130 ships, since they despised the Romans for their lack of experience. The whole of the Carthaginian fleet sailed directly at the enemy, not considering it worthwhile to keep order, thinking that the enemy was there for the taking. They were led by Hannibal, the same man who had led his forces out of Acragas at night on a ship that had formerly belonged to Pyrrhus. As the Carthaginians approached, seeing the ravens being raised on each of the Roman prows, they were at a loss at the purpose of these devices. Nevertheless, as they thought the enemy's situation was hopeless their leading ships attacked with great daring. But when the opposing ships collided, they were always fastened to each other by the ravens. The Romans boarded the enemy ships by passing over the ravens, and this was followed by hand-to-hand fighting on the decks. Some of the Carthaginians were killed, while others surrendered, losing heart in the face of what had happened, as the struggle had turned into a land battle.

The Romans captured the first thirty-two ships that attacked them, with their crews, as well as the commander's ship, but Hannibal made an extraordinary and unexpected escape in a small boat. The rest of the Carthaginian fleet sailed up as if to attack but as they closed they saw what had happened to the leading ships and turned away, avoiding the attacks of the ravens. Trusting in their speed, they turned around, hoping to safely strike the enemy's sides or sterns. But when the ravens swung round, turning in all directions so that those who approached were held fast, they finally turned to flight, in fear at the novelty of what had happened, after losing fifty ships.

SUGGESTED READINGS

General

Adcock, F.E., *The Roman Art of War under the Republic* (Cambridge, MA, 1940).

Connolly, P., *Greece and Rome at War* (Englewood Cliffs, NJ, 1981).

Erdkamp, P., ed., *A Companion to the Roman Army* (Oxford, 2007).

Erdkamp, P., "Army and Society," in *A Companion to the Roman Republic*, ed. N. Rosenstein and R. Morstein-Marx (Oxford, 2006), pp. 278–96.

Garlan, Y., *War in the Ancient World: A Social History*, trans. J. Lloyd (London, 1975).

Gilliver, C.M., *The Roman Art of War* (Charleston, SC, 1999).

Goldsworthy, A.K., *Roman Warfare* (London, 2000).

Keppie, L., *The Making of the Roman Army* (London, 1984).

Potter, D., "The Roman Army and Navy," in *The Cambridge Companion to the Roman Republic*, ed. H.I. Flower (Cambridge, 2004), pp. 66–88.

Rich, J. and Shipley, G., eds., *War and Society in the Roman World* (London, 1993).

Rosenstein, N., "Republican Rome," in *War and Society in the Ancient and Medieval Worlds*, ed. K. Raaflaub and N. Rosenstein (Washington, DC, 1999), pp. 193–216.

Warry, J., *Warfare in the Classical World* (Norman, OK, 1995).

Reliability of the sources

Cornell, T.J., *The Beginnings of Rome: Italy and Rome from the Bronze Age to the Punic Wars (c.1000–264 BC)* (London, 1995).

Cornell, T.J., "The Value of the Literary Tradition concerning Archaic Rome," in *Social Struggles in Archaic Rome: New Perspectives on the Conflict of the Orders*, ed. K.A. Raaflaub, updated edn. (Oxford, 2005), pp. 52–76.

Gabba, E., *Dionysius and the History of Archaic Rome* (Berkeley, CA, 1991).

Horsfall, N.M., "Myth and Mythography at Rome," in *Roman Myth and Mythography*, ed. J.N. Bremmer and N.M. Horsfall, University of London, Institute of Classical Studies Bulletin Supplement 52 (1987), pp. 1–11.

Rawson, E., "The Literary Sources of the Pre-Marian Army," *PBSR* 39 (1971), pp. 13–31.

Wiseman, T.P., "The Credibility of the Roman Annalists," in *Roman Studies: Literary and Historical* (Liverpool, 1987), pp. 293–96.

1 Rome's earliest armies: the archaic and Servian period

The archaeology of early Rome and Latium

Forsythe, G., *A Critical History of Early Rome* (Berkeley, CA, 2005).
Holloway, R. Ross, *The Archaeology of Early Rome and Latium* (London, 1994).

Italy before the Romans

Meyer, J.C., *Pre-Republican Rome: An Analysis of Cultural and Chronological Relations* (Odense, 1983).
Pallottino, M., *A History of Earliest Italy*, trans. M. Rye and K. Soper (Ann Arbor, MI, 1991).
Scullard, H.H., *A History of the Roman World 753–146 BC* (London, 1961).
Smith, C.J., *Early Rome and Latium: Economy and Society c.1000–500 BC* (Oxford, 1996).

Early Etruria

Barker, G. and Rasmussen, T., *The Etruscans* (Oxford, 1998).
Cristofani, M., *The Etruscans: A New Investigation*, trans. B. Philips (London, 1979).
D'Agostino, B., "Image and Society in Archaic Etruria," *JRS* 79 (1989), pp. 1–10.
D'Agostino, B., "Military Organization and Social Structure in Archaic Etruria," in *The Greek City from Homer to Alexander*, ed. O. Murray and S. Price (Oxford, 1990), pp. 59–82.
Ogilvie, R.M., *Early Rome and the Etruscans* (London, 1976).
Scullard, H.H., *The Etruscan Cities and Rome* (London, 1967).

Early Roman political and social institutions

Astin, A.E., Walbank, F.W., Frederiksen, M.W., and Ogilvie, R.M., eds., *CAH*, 2nd edn., vol. VII, pt. 2, *The Rise of Rome to 220 BC* (Cambridge, 1989).
Cornell, T.J., *The Beginnings of Rome: Italy and Rome from the Bronze Age to the Punic Wars (c.1000–264 BC)* (London, 1995).
Forsythe, G., *A Critical History of Early Rome* (Berkeley, CA, 2005).
Heurgon, J., *The Rise of Rome to 264 BC*, trans. J. Willis (Berkeley, CA, 1973).

Rome's earliest military forces

Cornell, T.J., *The Beginnings of Rome: Italy and Rome from the Bronze Age to the Punic Wars (c.1000–264 BC)* (London, 1995).
Forsythe, G., *A Critical History of Early Rome* (Berkeley, CA, 2005).
Scullard, H.H., *A History of the Roman World, 753–146 BC*, 3rd edn. (London, 1961).

Clan and other non-state military forces

Drummond, A., "Early Roman Clients," in *Patronage in Ancient Society*, ed. A. Wallace-Hadrill (London, 1989), pp. 89–115.

Smith, C.J., *The Roman Clan* (Cambridge, 2006).
Versnel, H.S., "Historical Implications," in *Lapis Satricanus*, ed. C.M. Stibbe, G. Colonna, C. De Simone, and H.S. Versnel, *Scripta Minora* 5 (The Hague, 1980), pp. 97–150.

The Servian reforms

Last, H., "The Servian Reforms", *JRS* 35 (1945), pp. 30–48.
Nilsson, M.P., "The Introduction of Hoplite Tactics at Rome," *JRS* 19 (1929), pp. 1–11.
Ridley, R.T., "The Enigma of Servius Tullius," *Klio* 57 (1975), pp. 147–77.
Snodgrass, A.M., "The Hoplite Reform and History," *JRS* 85 (1965), pp. 110–22.
Sumner, G.V., "The Legion and the Centurionate Organization," *JRS* 60 (1970), pp. 67–78.
Thomsen, R., *King Servius Tullius: A Historical Synthesis* (Copenhagen, 1980).

Rome and the Latins

Alföldi, A., *Early Rome and the Latins* (Ann Arbor, MI, 1965).
Cornell, T.J., "Rome and Latium to 390 BC," in *CAH*, 2nd edn., vol. VII, pt. 2, ed. A.E. Astin, F.W. Walbank, M.W.Frederiksen, and R.M. Ogilvie (Cambridge, 1989), pp. 243–308.

Roman colonies

Salmon, E.T., *Roman Colonization under the Republic* (Ithaca, NY, 1970).
Sherwin-White, A.N., *The Roman Citizenship*, 2nd edn. (Oxford, 1973).

The political background of the early Republic

Brunt, P.A., *Social Conflicts in the Roman Republic* (London, 1971).
Drummond, A., "Rome in the Fifth Century I: The Citizen Community," in *CAH*, 2nd edn., vol. VII, pt. 2, ed. A.E. Astin, F.W. Walbank, M.W.Frederiksen, and R.M. Ogilvie (Cambridge, 1989), pp. 172–242.
Mitchell, R.E., *Patricians and Plebeians* (Ithaca, NY, 1992).
Raaflaub, K., ed., *Social Struggles in Ancient Rome: New Perspectives on the Conflict of the Orders* (Berkeley, CA, 1986).

Military tribunes with consular powers

Adcock, F.E, "Consular Tribunes and their Successors" *JRS* 47 (1957), pp. 9–14.
Boddington, A., "The Original Nature of the Consular Tribunate," *Historia* 8 (1959), pp. 356–64.
Ridley, R.T., "The Consular Tribunate: The Testimony of Livy," *Klio* 68 (1986), pp. 444–65.
Staveley, E.S., "The Significance of the Consular Tribunate," *JRS* 43 (1953), pp. 30–6.

2 The development of the manipular army

Rome's expansion in Italy

Cunliffe, B., *The Ancient Celts* (Oxford, 1997).
David, J.-M., *The Roman Conquest of Italy*, trans. A. Nevill (Oxford, 1996).
Harris, W.V., *Rome in Etruria and Umbria* (Oxford, 1971).
Keaveney, A., *Rome and the Unification of Italy* (London, 1987).
Oakley, S.P., "The Roman Conquest of Italy," in *War and Society in the Roman World*, ed. J. Rich and G. Shipley (London, 1993), pp. 9–37.
Rankin, H.D., *Celts and the Classical World* (London, 1987).
Salmon, E.T., *Samnium and the Samnites* (Cambridge, 1967).
Salmon, E.T., *The Making of Roman Italy* (London, 1982).
Schneider-Hermann, G., *The Samnites of the Fourth Century BC as Depicted on Campanian Vases and in Other Sources* (London, 1996).

The development of the manipular army

Connolly, P., "The Roman Fighting Technique Deduced from Armour and Weaponry," in *Roman Frontier Studies*, ed. V.A. Maxfield and M.J. Dobson (Exeter, 1991), pp. 358–63.
Harris, W.V., "Roman Warfare in the Economic and Social Context of the 4th Century BC," in *Staat und Staatlichkeit in der führen römischen Republik*, ed. W. Eder (Stuttgart, 1990), pp. 494–510.
Oakley, S.P., *A Commentary on Livy Books VI–X*, vol. II (Oxford, 1998).
Walbank, F.W., *A Historical Commentary on Polybius*, vol. I (Oxford, 1970).

The equipment of the manipular army

Bishop, M.C. and Coulston, J.C., *Roman Military Equipment* (Aylesbury, Bucks., 1989).
Burns, M.T., "The Homogenisation of Military Equipment under the Roman Republic," "Romanization"?, *Digressus* Supplement 1, pp. 60–85.
Feugère, M., *Weapons of the Romans*, trans. D.G. Smith (Charleston, SC, 2002).

Legionary cavalry

Connolly, P., "The Roman Saddle," in *Roman Military Equipment: The Accoutrements of War*, ed. M. Dawson, BAR International Series 336 (Oxford, 1985), pp. 7–27.
Hyland, A., *Equus: The Horse in the Roman World* (London, 1990).
McCall, J.B., *The Cavalry of the Roman Republic* (London, 2002).

Military command

Develin, R., *The Practice of Roman Politics 366–167 BC* (Brussels, 1985).
Eckstein, A.M., *Senate and General: Individual Decision Making and Roman Foreign Relations 264–194 BC* (Berkeley, CA, 1987).

Feig Vishnia, R., *State, Society and Popular Leaders in Mid-Republican Rome 241–167 BC* (London, 1996).

Höleskamp, K.-J., "Conquest, Competition and Consensus: Roman Expansion in Italy and the Rise of the Nobilitas," *Historia* 42 (1993), pp. 12–39.

Jashemski, W.F., *The Origins and History of the Proconsular Imperium to 27 BC* (Chicago, 1950).

Lintott, A., *The Constitution of the Roman Republic* (Oxford, 1999).

Rosenstein, N., *Imperatores Victi: Military Defeat and Aristocratic Competition in the Middle and Late Republic* (Berkeley, CA, 1990).

Suolahti, J., *The Junior Officers of the Roman Army in the Republican Period* (Helsinki, 1955).

Logistics

Erdkamp, P., *Hunger and the Sword: Warfare and Food Supply in Roman Republican Wars (264–30 BC)* (Amsterdam, 1998).

Roth, J., *The Logistics of the Roman Army at War* (Leiden, 1998).

Recruitment and the levy

Baronowski, D.W., "Roman Military Forces in 225 BC (Polybius 2.23–4)," *Historia* 42 (1993), pp. 181–202.

Brunt, P.A., *Italian Manpower 225 BC – AD 14*, 2nd edn. (Oxford, 1987).

Nicolet, C., *The World of the Citizen in Republican Rome*, trans. P.S. Falla (Berkeley, CA, 1980).

Military training

Campbell, B., "Teach Yourself How to Be a General," *JRS* 77 (1987), pp. 13–29.

Watson, G.R., *The Roman Soldier* (Ithaca, NY, 1969).

The Italian allies

Gabba, E., *Republican Rome, the Army and the Allies*, trans. P.J. Cuff (Berkeley, CA, 1976).

Harris, W.V., "The Italians and the Empire," in *The Imperialism of Mid-Republican Rome*, ed. W.V. Harris, Papers and Monographs of the American Academy in Rome 29 (1984), pp. 89–109.

McDonald, A.H., "Rome and the Italian Confederation (200–186 BC)", *JRS* 34 (1944), pp. 11–33.

Military pay

Crawford, M.H., *Roman Republican Coinage* (Cambridge, 1974).

Crawford, M.H., *Coinage and Money under the Roman Republic* (Berkeley, CA, 1985).

Watson, G.R., "The Pay of the Roman Army: The Republic," *Historia* 7 (1958), pp. 113–20.

The manipular army in battle

Lendon, J.E., *Soldiers and Ghosts: A History of Battle in Classical Antiquity* (New Haven, CT, 2005).

Lloyd, A.B., ed., *Battle in Antiquity* (London, 1996).

Sabin, P., "The Face of Roman Battle," *JRS* 90 (2000), pp. 1–17.

Smith, F.W, "The Fighting Unit: An Essay in Structural Military History," *AC* 59 (1990), pp. 149–65.

Zhmodikov, A., "Roman Republican Heavy Infantrymen in Battle," *Historia* 49 (2000), pp. 67–78.

The wars against Carthage

Astin, A.E., Walbank, F.W., and Frederiksen, M.W., eds., *CAH*, vol. VIII, *Rome and the Mediterranean to 133 BC* (Cambridge, 1989).

Cornell, T.J., Rankov, B., and Sabin, P., eds., *The Second Punic War: A Reappraisal* (London, 1996).

Goldsworthy, A.K., *The Punic Wars* (London, 2000).

Lazenby, J.F., *Hannibal's War: A Military History of the Second Punic War* (Warminster, 1978).

Lazenby, J.F., *The First Punic War* (London, 1996).

The battle of Cannae

Daly, G., *Cannae: The Experience of Battle in the Second Punic War* (London, 2002).

Sabin, P., "The Mechanics of Battle in the Second Punic War," in *The Second Punic War: A Reappraisal*, ed. T.J. Cornell, B. Rankov, and P. Sabin (London, 1996), pp. 59–79.

Shean, J.F., "Hannibal's Mules: The Logistical Limitations of Hannibal's Army and the Battle of Cannae, 216 BC," *Historia* 45 (1996), pp. 159–87.

The battle of Ilipa

Scullard, H.H., *Scipio Africanus: Soldier and Politician* (Bristol, 1970).

The battle of Cynoscephalae

Briscoe, J., *A Commentary on Livy, Books 31–32* (Oxford, 1972).

Walbank, F.W., *A Historical Commentary on Polybius*, vol. II (Oxford, 1967), pp. 572–85.

Walbank, F.W., *Philip V of Macedon* (Cambridge, 1967).

The battle of Magnesia

Bar Kochva, B., *The Seleucid Army* (Cambridge, 1976).

Grainger, J.D., *The Roman War of Antiochos the Great, Mnemosyne* Supplement 239 (Leiden, 2002).

The battle of Emporiae

Astin, A.E., *Cato the Censor* (Oxford, 1978).
Harris, W.V., "Spain," in *CAH*, vol. VIII, *Rome and the Mediterranean to 133 BC*, ed. A.E. Astin, F.W. Walbank, and M.W. Frederiksen (Cambridge, 1989), pp. 118–38.
Richardson. J.S., *Appian, Wars of the Romans in Iberia* (Warminster, 2000).

The battle of Pydna

Hammond, N.G.L., "The Battle of Pydna," *JHS* 104 (1984), pp. 31–47.

The aftermath of battle

Brunt, P.A., *Italian Manpower*, 2nd edn. (Oxford, 1985).

Changes in census requirements

Brunt, P.A., *Italian Manpower*, 2nd edn. (Oxford, 1985).
Gabba, E., *Republican Rome, the Army and the Allies*, trans. P.J. Cuff (Berkeley, CA, 1976).
Hopkins, K., *Conquerors and Slaves* (Cambridge, 1978).
Morley, N., "The Transformation of Italy, 225–28 BC," *JRS* 91 (2001), pp. 50–62.
Rathbone, D., "The Census Qualifications of the Assidui and the Prima Classis," in *De Agricultura, in Memoriam Pieter Willem de Neeve*, ed. H. Sancisi-Weerdenburg, R.J. van der Spek, H.C. Teitler, and H.T. Wallinga (Amsterdam, 1993), pp. 121–52.
Rosenstein, N., *Rome at War: Farms, Families and Death in the Middle Republic* (Chapel Hill, NC, 2004).

3 The army of the late Republic

The political background

Brunt, P.A., "The Fall of the Roman Republic," in *The Fall of the Roman Republic and Related Essays* (Oxford, 1988), pp. 1–92.
Crawford, M. and Beard, M., *Rome in the Late Republic*, 2nd edn. (London, 1999).
Gruen, E.S., *The Last Generation of the Roman Republic* (Berkeley, CA, 1974).
Lintott, A.W., *Violence in Republican Rome*, rev. edn. (Oxford, 1999).
Scullard, H.H., *From the Gracchi to Nero* (London, 1982).
Taylor, L.R., *Party Politics in the Age of Caesar* (Berkeley, CA, 1964).

The development of the cohort as a tactical unit

Bell, M.J.V., "Tactical Reform in the Roman Republican Army," *Historia* 14 (1965), pp. 404–22.
Kertész, I., "The Roman Cohort Tactics: Problems of Development," *Oikumene* 1 (1976), pp. 89–97.

Booty

Cheeseman, G.L., *The Auxilia of the Roman Imperial Army* (Oxford, 1914).
Churchill, B., "Ex qua quod vellent facerent: Roman Magistrates' Authority over *Praeda* and *Manubiae*," *TAPhA* 129 (1999), pp. 85–116.
McCall, J.B., *The Cavalry of the Roman Republic* (London, 2002).
Shatzmann, I., "The Roman General's Authority over the Distribution of Booty," *Historia* 21 (1972), pp. 17–28.

Spolia opima

Flower, H.I., "The Tradition of the *Spolia Opima*: M. Claudius Marcellus and Augustus," *ClAnt* 19 (2000), pp. 34–64.
Oakley, P., "Single Combat in the Roman Republic," *CQ* 35 (1985), pp. 392–410.

Military rewards and honors

Maxfield, V., *The Military Decorations of the Roman Army* (Berkeley, CA, 1981).

The triumph

Bonfante Warren, L., "Roman Triumphs and Etruscan Kings: The Changing Face of the Triumph," *JRS* 60 (1970), pp. 49–66.
Versnel, H.S., *Triumphus* (Leiden, 1970).

Military discipline

Brand, C.E., *Roman Military Law* (Austin, TX, 1968).
Lee, A.D., "Morale and the Roman Experience of Battle," in *Battle in Antiquity*, ed. A.B. Lloyd (London, 1996), pp. 199–217.

The burdens of service

Brunt, P.A., *Italian Manpower*, 2nd edn. (Oxford, 1987).
De Blois, L., "Army and Society in the Late Republic," in *Heer und Gesellschaft in der römischen Kaiserzeit*, ed. G. Alföldy, B. Dobson, and W. Eck (Stuttgart, 2000), pp. 11–31.
Evans, R.J., *Gaius Marius: A Political Biography* (Pretoria, 1994).
Hopkins, K., *Conquerors and Slaves* (Cambridge, 1978).
Keppie, L.J.F., "Army and Society in the Late Republic and Early Empire," in *War as a Cultural and Social Force: Essays on Warfare in Antiquity*, ed. T. Bekker-Nielsen and L. Hannestad (Copenhagen, 2001), pp. 130–6.
Patterson, J., "Military Organization and Social Change in the Later Roman Republic," in *War and Society in the Roman World*, ed. J.R. Rich and G. Shipley (London, 1993), pp. 92–112.
Rich. J.W., "The Supposed Roman Manpower Shortage of the Later Second Century BC," *Historia* 32 (1983), pp. 287–331.
Smith, R.E., *Service in the Post-Marian Army* (Manchester, 1958).

296

The Marian reforms

Astin, A.E., *Scipio Aemilianus* (Oxford, 1967).
Evans, R.J., *Gaius Marius: A Political Biography* (Pretoria, 1994).
Gabba, E., *Republican Rome, the Army and the Allies*, trans. P.J. Cuff (Berkeley, CA, 1976).
Parker, H.M.D., *The Roman Legions*, reprint (Cambridge, 1971).

After military service

Brunt, P.A., "The Army and the Land in the Roman Revolution", *JRS* 52 (1962), pp. 69–86.
Gruen, E.S., *The Last Generation of the Roman Republic* (Berkeley, CA, 1974).
Keppie, L., *Colonisation and Veteran Settlement in Italy* (London, 1983).
Salmon, E.T., *Roman Colonization under the Republic* (London, 1969).

The army in politics

De Blois, L., *The Roman Army and Politics in the First Century BC* (Amsterdam, 1987).
Keaveney, A., *Sulla: The Last Republican* (London, 1982).
Lintott, A.W., *Violence in Republican Rome*, rev. edn. (Oxford, 1999).
Sherwin-White, A.N., "Violence in Republican Politics," *JRS* 46 (1956), pp. 1–9.

The late Republican army in battle

Fuller, J.F.C., *Julius Caesar: Man, Soldier, and Tyrant* (New Brunswick, NJ, 1965).
Gelzer, M., *Caesar: Politician and Statesman* (Cambridge, MA, 1968).
Goldsworthy, A.K., *The Roman Army at War (100 BC – AD 200)* (Oxford, 1996).
Rice Holmes, T., *Caesar's Conquest of Gaul*, 2nd edn. (New York, 1971).
Seager, R., *Pompey* (Oxford, 2002).

Pharsalus

Fuller, J.F.C., *Julius Caesar: Man, Soldier, and Tyrant* (New Brunswick, NJ, 1965).
Gwatkin, W.E., Jr., "Some Reflections on the Battle of Pharsalus," *TAPhA* 87 (1956), pp. 109–24.
Pelling, C.B.R., " Pharsalus," *Historia* 22 (1973), pp. 249–59.

Carrhae

Colledge, M.A.R., *The Parthians* (London, 1967).
Marshall, B.A., *Crassus: A Political Biography* (Amsterdam, 1976).

Roman imperialism

Badian, E., *Roman Imperialism in the Late Republic* (Ithaca, NY, 1968).
Champion, C.B., *Roman Imperialism: Readings and Sources* (Oxford, 2004).

Harris, W.V., *War and Imperialism in Republican Rome 327–70 BC* (Oxford, 1985).

North, J.A., "The Development of Roman Imperialism," *JRS* 71 (1981), pp. 1–9.

Rich, J., "Fear, Greed and Glory: The Causes of Roman War-Making in the Republic," in *War and Society in the Roman World*, ed. J. Rich and G. Shipley (London, 1993), pp. 38–68.

Sidebottom, H., "Roman Imperialism: The Changed Outwards Trajectory of the Roman Empire," *Historia* 54 (2005), pp. 315–30.

Siege warfare

Campbell, D., *Besieged: Siege Warfare in the Ancient World* (Oxford, 2006).

Kern, P.B., *Ancient Siege Warfare* (Bloomington, IN, 1999).

Paul, G.M., "Urbs Capta: Sketch of an Ancient Literary Motif," *Phoenix* 36 (1982), pp. 144–55.

Ziolkowski, A., "*Urbs direpta* or How the Romans Sacked Cities," in *War and Society in the Roman World*, ed. J. Rich and G. Shipley (London, 1993), pp. 69–91.

Naval warfare

Casson, L., *Ships and Seamanship in the Ancient World* (Princeton, NJ, 1971).

Rodgers, W.L., *Greek and Roman Naval Warfare* (Annapolis, MD, 1937).

Thiel, J.H., *Studies on the History of Roman Sea Power in Republican Times* (Amsterdam, 1946).

INDEX